Pasinetti and the Classical Keynesians

Recent economic and financial crises have exposed mainstream economics to severe criticism, bringing present research and teaching styles into question. Building on a solid and vivid tradition of economic thought, this book challenges conventional thinking in the field of economics. The authors turn to the work of Luigi Pasinetti, who proposed a list of nine methodological and theoretical ideas that characterise the Classical Keynesian School. Drawing inspiration from both Keynes and Sraffa, this school has forged a long-standing and ambitious research programme often advocated as a competing paradigm to mainstream economics. Overall, the Classical Keynesian School provides a comprehensive analytical framework into which most non-mainstream schools of thought can be integrated. In this collection, a group of leading scholars critically assess the nine main ideas that, in Pasinetti's view, characterise the Classical Keynesian approach, evaluating their relevance for both the history of economics and for present economic research.

ENRICO BELLINO is Professor of Political Economy at Università Cattolica del Sacro Cuore.

SEBASTIANO NEROZZI is Professor of History of Economic Thought and Business History at Università Cattolica del Sacro Cuore.

Pasinetti and the Classical Keynesians

Nine Methodological Issues

Edited by

ENRICO BELLINO
Università Cattolica del Sacro Cuore

SEBASTIANO NEROZZI
Università Cattolica del Sacro Cuore

CAMBRIDGE
UNIVERSITY PRESS

CAMBRIDGE
UNIVERSITY PRESS

University Printing House, Cambridge CB2 8BS, United Kingdom

One Liberty Plaza, 20th Floor, New York, NY 10006, USA

477 Williamstown Road, Port Melbourne, VIC 3207, Australia

314–321, 3rd Floor, Plot 3, Splendor Forum, Jasola District Centre,
New Delhi – 110025, India

103 Penang Road, #05-06/07, Visioncrest Commercial, Singapore 238467

Cambridge University Press is part of the University of Cambridge.

It furthers the University's mission by disseminating knowledge in the pursuit of education, learning, and research at the highest international levels of excellence.

www.cambridge.org
Information on this title: www.cambridge.org/9781108831116
DOI: 10.1017/9781108923309

First published 2021

A catalogue record for this publication is available from the British Library.

ISBN 978-1-108-83111-6 Hardback

Contents

List of Contributors *page* vii

Foreword: The Political Economy of Luigi Pasinetti ix
Mauro Baranzini, Alberto Quadrio Curzio and Roberto Scazzieri

Introduction 1
Enrico Bellino and Sebastiano Nerozzi

1 Reality (and Not Simply Abstract Rationality) as the Starting Point of Economic Theory 13
Maria Cristina Marcuzzo

2 Economic Logic with Internal Consistency (and Not Only Formal Rigour): Realism and Internal Consistency in Piero Sraffa 30
Neri Salvadori and Rodolfo Signorino

3 Malthus and the Classics (Not Walras and the Marginalists) as the Major Inspiring Source in the History of Economic Thought: The Principle of Effective Demand and Classical Economics 50
Heinz D. Kurz

4 Non-ergodic (in Place of Stationary, Timeless) Economic Systems: Considerations Suggested by Joan Robinson's Distinction between Two 'Notions' of Time in Economic Theory 79
Ariel Dvoskin and Paolo Trabucchi

5 Causality vs. Interdependence: A Distinction That Conveys a World's View 112
Enrico Bellino and Sebastiano Nerozzi

6 Macroeconomics before Microeconomics: A Sceptic's Guide to Macroeconomics 157
Murray Milgate and John Eatwell

7 Disequilibrium and Instability (Not Equilibrium) as the Normal State of the Industrial Economies: A Methodological Standpoint on Structural Economic Dynamics 187
Ariel Luis Wirkierman

8 Necessity of Finding an Appropriate Analytical Framework for Dealing with Technical Change and Economic Growth: Technical Change, Structural Dynamics and Employment 214
Harald Hagemann

9 A Strong, Deeply Felt, Social Concern 233
Claudia Rotondi

10 Why the Classic-Keynesian Trend May Be of Interest to a Young Scholar Today 259
Nadia Garbellini

11 Pasinetti's Separation Theorem 290
Bertram Schefold

Author Index 317

Contributors

MAURO BARANZINI
Università della Svizzera Italiana

ENRICO BELLINO
Università Cattolica del Sacro Cuore

ARIEL DVOSKIN
Universidad Nacional de San Martin

JOHN EATWELL
Queens' College, University of Cambridge

NADIA GARBELLINI
Università degli Studi di Modena e Reggio Emilia

HARALD HAGEMANN
Universität Hohenheim

HEINZ D. KURZ
Universität Graz

MARIA CRISTINA MARCUZZO
Università di Roma La Sapienza

MURRAY MILGATE
Queens' College, University of Cambridge

SEBASTIANO NEROZZI
Università Cattolica del Sacro Cuore

ALBERTO QUADRIO CURZIO
Università Cattolica del Sacro Cuore

CLAUDIA ROTONDI
Università Cattolica del Sacro Cuore

NERI SALVADORI
Università di Pisa

ROBERTO SCAZZIERI
Università di Bologna

BERTRAM SCHEFOLD
Goethe-Universität, Frankfurt

RODOLFO SIGNORINO
Università degli Studi di Palermo

PAOLO TRABUCCHI
Università degl Studi Roma Tre

ARIEL LUIS WIRKIERMAN
Goldsmiths, University of London

Foreword
The Political Economy of Luigi Pasinetti

MAURO BARANZINI, ALBERTO QUADRIO CURZIO AND ROBERTO SCAZZIERI

Premise

We were pleased to accept the invitation from the editors of this volume, Enrico Bellino and Sebastiano Nerozzi, to write an introduction to this volume of essays, which is published in honor of Luigi Pasinetti's ninetieth birthday. For many decades, we have been closely associated with Pasinetti's research, though in different ways and in different capacities due to our belonging to different academic age cohorts. Through all those years, we have had many opportunities to discuss with him his contributions to economic theory, which we have always found greatly inspiring, even when following research tracks different from his. In a nutshell, we could say we all share with Pasinetti a deep commitment to the structural dynamics approach to economic theory and political economy. Our close personal and intellectual acquaintance with Pasinetti makes it difficult for us to write a standard comprehensive introduction, which would have to consider the manifold areas of our collaboration with him and involvement with his lines of research. On many occasions, we wrote essays dealing with specific features of his approach to economic theory. For this reason, we decided to focus our attention on what are, in our view, Pasinetti's key contributions to theory-building and to highlight the unifying train of thought flowing through all of them.

Between Classical Political Economy and Keynes

Pasinetti, whose work provides the running thread of the chapters in this volume, is undoubtedly one of the most distinguished, original and inspiring theoretical economists of our time. The roots of his approach to economic analysis are to be found in the works of the classical political economists and before them in the writings of those early scholars, such as the English political arithmeticians and the French physiocrats, who addressed the economic system as a set of relationships between 'funds of wealth' or productive sectors, giving rise to a structure that could be investigated independently of a direct attention to the decisions of individual or collective actors. The structural roots of Pasinetti's approach to economic theorising are explicit in all the domains of economic research to which he contributed in scholarly writings spanning over six decades. The criticism of unwarranted generalisations from individual decision makers to the economic system as a whole, without taking into account the structural interdependencies between components of the economic system (the economic system's *internal structure*), is a running thread of Pasinetti's contributions to economic analysis, from his early appraisal of measures of productivity change to his most recent writings on structural dynamics and the theory of value. Rejection of methodological individualism is a distinctive feature of Pasinetti's work, which, however, maintains a distance from traditional Keynesian approaches in its attention to the internal structure of production relationships and the constraints and opportunities facing a production economy evolving through time under the influence of technical progress and changing per capita consumption of physical goods and services. Pasinetti's contribution is firmly rooted in the reappraisal and analytical development of classical and pre-classical strands of production theory that have emerged since the first half of the twentieth century with the writings of economists such as Wassily Leontief, Piero Sraffa and John von Neumann (Quadrio Curzio, 1993; Scazzieri, 1993). Pasinetti has contributed to this line of thinking by systematically linking it to the theory of structural economic dynamics and the analysis of the institutional and policy changes that are needed if economic systems are to evolve dynamically while satisfying certain desirable properties such as full employment. The beginning of Pasinetti's intellectual path is at the crossroads between the Catholic University of Milan, where his initial academic training took place, and the University of Cambridge, where he spent most of his postgraduate training and where he started his academic career. This crossroads provides a cue to interpreting many of the intellectual routes taken by Pasinetti's work as an economic theorist (Baranzini and Harcourt, 1993; Baranzini and Mirante, 2016, 2018). The academic setting of post–World War II Italy was one in which a distinguished tradition rooted in general equilibrium theory à la Walras–Pareto coexisted with a robust interest in the prerequisites for the successful industrial transformation of an economic system along a growth trajectory. Economic theorising of the time at the University of Cambridge provided an ideal matching ground to Pasinetti's original Italian training, as pupils and followers of John Maynard Keynes were exploring a variety of ways in which Keynes's macroeconomic theory could be developed to address the conditions of dynamic economies subject to intense capital accumulation and structural change. Pasinetti's early theoretical work shows a strong influence of the Cambridge 'dynamic Keynesian' tradition combined with the classical and structural influence from Sraffa, Leontief, Richard Goodwin and Richard Stone. It is at this crossroads that we may trace the origins of the intellectual path of Pasinetti as a classical economist whose work is firmly rooted in the circular approach to 'the interdependence of means of production, production processes and produced goods' (Quadrio Curzio, 1986, p. 314) while at the same time being interested in the view of production as a *transformation apparatus* leading from labour and (produced) means of production to final goods and as a *structural apparatus* centred on the role of produced intermediate inputs in the reproduction and expansion of the economy (Quadrio Curzio, 1986, pp. 313–314).

Structural Interdependence, Savings and Capital Accumulation

Structural interdependence is a distinctive feature of Pasinetti's contributions to economic theory, both in his criticism of unwarranted generalisations from individual behaviour to systemic properties and in his criticism of macroeconomic theorising carried out without considering that changes in the composition of aggregate magnitudes are inevitable due to the very impulses driving the overall system's dynamics. Pasinetti's early work on the measurement of productivity changes was already a clear instance of this attitude, leading him to argue that productivity changes cannot be effectively measured unless the interdependence between productive sectors is fully accounted for; this insight resulted in highlighting the *reproducible* character of capital goods as means of production: 'There have been some attempts by economists ... to introduce capital into the picture, by making use of theoretical notions like the production function, but these attempts – in the writer's opinion – have neglected an important characteristic of capital – that it is reproducible and that its process of production is also subject to technical change' (Pasinetti, 1959, p. 270). In a complementary vein, Pasinetti's reformulation of the so-called Cambridge equation ($r^* = n/s_c$) emphasises the importance of entering the black box of macroaggregates (in this case, the aggregate propensity to save) to analyse the way in which changes in the composition of the income received by different social groups may be a trigger of macroeconomic dynamics. Pasinetti's reformulation of the Cambridge equation provides an *analytical benchmark* highlighting that, in a macroeconomy of pure profit receivers (called 'capitalists'), the rate of profits (r^*) compatible with full employment at a 'natural rate', determined by the rates of population growth and technical progress, is independent of the propensity to save of the other category of income receivers (labelled 'workers'), whose propensity to save (s_w) does not enter the equation. This analytical benchmark opens the analysis of the conditions for steady growth to the consideration of the differentiated saving and consumption behaviour of different groups in society (Baranzini, 1975, 1987, 1991, 1993). This provides a bridge between the dynamics of the macroeconomy and the long-term evolution of social and demographic structures, highlighting 'the link between the composition of income, the attitude towards the next generation, and the development, existence, and survival of different socio-economic groups or dynasties in the long-run equilibrium' (Baranzini, 1991, p. 220).

Towards a Theory of Structural Economic Dynamics

The search for the analytical linkages between systemic conditions and compositional changes of macroaggregates is also at the root of Pasinetti's decades-long investigation into the long-run evolution of an industrial economic system subject to the twin impulses of technical progress and of changes in per-capita consumption of physical goods and services. The challenge of *structural transformation* has been fundamental in stimulating the analysis of economic interdependencies among different sectors of the economy and their relationship with the overall dynamics of the wealth of nations since the beginning of systematic economic thinking (Quadrio Curzio, 1967, 1975, 1986; see also Hagemann, Landesmann and Scazzieri, 2003). Seventeenth- and eighteenth-century scholars, such as the political arithmeticians and the physiocrats, contributed insights into the *anatomy* of economic systems that economists such as James Steuart, Adam Smith, Thomas Robert Malthus and David Ricardo developed into a comprehensive assessment of the fundamental *dynamic impulses* leading to the transformation of economic structures. Later economists, such as Friedrich List, Werner Sombart, Joan Robinson, Nicholas Kaldor, Paolo Sylos Labini and John Hicks, followed suit when examining the long-run dynamics of structural change in economic systems subject to the discontinuities induced by technical change, mechanization and increasing competitive challenges at the international level (Quadrio Curzio and Pellizzari, 1999). Pasinetti's decades-long theoretical endeavour in the latter part of the twentieth century and up to the present has been pivotal in establishing the economics of structural change as a distinctive approach to the analysis of economic dynamics. Starting with the PhD dissertation he submitted to the Faculty of Economics and Politics of the University of Cambridge in September 1962 (Pasinetti, 1962), Pasinetti has identified structural change as the fundamental feature of the long-run dynamics of economic systems since the First Industrial Revolution and has consistently pursued the objective of a *theory of structural economic dynamics* as a means to understanding the constraints and opportunities facing any economic system following a trajectory of sustained long-run expansion. The gist of Pasinetti's contribution is to be found in the dual belief that (i) since the First Industrial Revolution, the evolution of industrial economies has been subject to producer learning in the shape of technical progress and to consumer learning in the shape of the Engel's law and that (ii) it is possible to identify analytical conditions turning the *uneven dynamics* generated by the two above dynamic factors into an *orderly process* in which non-proportional changes of productive sectors follow a path compatible with the maintenance over time of the full employment of the labour force and with the full utilisation of productive capacity (Pasinetti, 1965, 1981, 1993).

Vertical Integration in Economic Analysis: Measuring Technical Progress and Assessing the Economy's Dynamic Potential

The search for a conceptual framework suitable to the analysis of structural dynamics under full employment and full capacity utilisation led Pasinetti to outline central analytical contributions to the theories of production, growth, value and income and wealth distribution. These contributions are rooted in an original combination of classical and Keynesian lines of investigation, which are developed by also building on Sraffa's theory of a multisectoral production economy. Pasinetti's exploration of the notion of vertical integration in economic analysis (Pasinetti, 1973) is a central building-block in the construction of a theory of structural dynamics that, consistently with Pasinetti's early view of capital goods as reproducible means of production whose production process is subject to technical change (see Pasinetti, 1959), gives prominence to the need of measuring changes in the productive capacity of heterogeneous capital goods whose physical characteristics may change from one period to another. Vertical integration allows for addressing this problem by representing the production system as an apparatus for *transforming* a certain collection of production facilities (such as certain stocks of capital goods and certain quantities of labour) into a collection of final consumer or investment goods.[1] In particular, vertical integration leads to the construction of a particular unit of measurement, the *unit of vertically integrated productive capacity*, which 'continues to make sense, as a physical unit, whatever complications technical change may cause to its composition in terms of ordinary commodities' (Pasinetti, 1973, p. 24). The representation of a production economy in terms of vertically integrated productive capacity and vertically integrated labour coefficients has remarkable analytical implications for the measurement of technical progress: 'With technical progress, any relation in which capitals goods are expressed in ordinary physical units becomes useless for dynamic analysis. But relations expressed in physical units of productive capacity continue to hold through time, and actually acquire an autonomy of their own, quite independently of their changing composition' (Pasinetti, 1973, p. 28). What is also remarkable is that, in contrast to aggregate measures of the capital stock frequently used in economic literature, measuring the capital stock in terms of vertically integrated productive capacity does not conceal the physical identity of particular collections of capital goods at any given time: by running the vertical integration algorithm backwards, it is possible to return 'to the ordinary physical units any time that this is necessary, within each period', even if 'a different result will be obtained for each single period' (Pasinetti, 1973, p. 28). Building on his original vertical integration algorithm, Pasinetti subsequently introduced a new

[1] For a discussion of this feature of Pasinetti's theoretical framework and of its relationship with Smith's representation of the economy, see Quadrio Curzio and Scazzieri, 1984, 1990.

set of vertically integrated subsystems (the 'vertically hyper-integrated sectors'), which include 'not only the labour and the means of production for the reproduction of each subsystem, but also the labour and the means of production necessary to its expansion at its particular rate of growth $(g+r_i)$' (Pasinetti, 1988, pp. 126–127). Vertical integration and vertical hyper-integration provide building-blocks to the analysis of the fundamental properties of an economic system that expands over time along a structural change trajectory. This type of dynamic analysis is carried out in terms of what Pasinetti considers to be 'pure theory', which he identifies as a type of investigation in which it is necessary to achieve 'a clear distinction between givens and unknowns; and in which it should be possible (when necessary) to introduce *ad hoc* hypotheses in order to make manageable the transformation and simplification of systems that would otherwise be difficult to solve' (Pasinetti, 2013, p. 52). This approach should allow the economic theorist to move beyond the stage of static or stationary analysis and to fully engage with the complexities of dynamic systems subject to structural change:

I think that 'pure theory' can move beyond the 'photography'; in other words, that it could also 'film' a moving economic system. We know that the world, especially the industrial world, is continuously evolving, and the direction of some of its movements shows features of persistence that are typical of a first stage of economic analysis (the stage concerning fundamental relationships). Let us think of the progressive and inevitable changes of productivity, of the tendency towards the mechanization of production processes, and of the tendency implicit in Engel's law and conditioning consumer demand. (Pasinetti, 2013, p. 52)

Distinguishing between the Fundamental and the Contingent Properties of Economic Systems: 'Objective Efficiency' and the Theory of Value

The emphasis on the fundamental properties of the economic system, as distinct from the contingent and transitory features of it, is a constant element of Pasinetti's view of economic theorising which had already been clearly expressed in his inaugural lecture delivered at the Catholic University of Milan on 27 January 1965:

There are economic relationships that are so fundamental to an industrial society that they can be defined independently of the institutional-political-juridical set-up that a society has adopted. Think of the structural interdependence linking together the industrial sectors of an economic system, or else of the relationships among the increases of average productivity, of the level of wages, of investments, and of the general level of prices. These relationships can be stated in terms of objective efficiency, or as they have been called: in 'natural' terms. They remain the same in any institutional set-up, whether it is a market economy or a centrally planned economy. They are relationships which usually admit causal-type chains, even if they contain interdependent sub-systems. (Pasinetti, 1964–1965 [2019], p. 362)

Many years later, Pasinetti further refined this point of view when introducing what he called a 'separation theorem' for economic investigations:

This theorem states that we must make it possible to disengage those investigations that concern the foundational bases of economic relations – to be detected at a strictly essential level of basic economic analysis – from those investigations that must be carried out at the level of the actual economic institutions, which at any time any economic system is landed with, or has chosen to adopt, or is trying to achieve. (Pasinetti, 2007, p. 275)

The fundamental level of investigation provides the analytical context to Pasinetti's theory of structural economic dynamics. It is at this level of inquiry that Pasinetti carries out his search for the pattern of non-proportional changes compatible with a dynamic trajectory associated with full employment and full utilisation of productive capacity (Pasinetti, 1981). And at this level of inquiry, Pasinetti outlines the simplified framework of a pure labour economy allowing him to formulate what he has called a 'genuinely macroeconomic condition' (the condition $\sum c_i l_i = 1$), which represents 'a characteristic of the economic system as a whole, not of its sectoral features' (Pasinetti, 1993, p. 20). At the same time, the condition avoids the simplification of the aggregate approach by maintaining a focus on the pattern of connectivity that links together economic activities and makes them subject to a systemic constraint. The fundamental level of investigation is also the analytical context of Pasinetti's exploration into the theory of value, which Pasinetti develops by transforming Ricardo's search for an 'invariable measure of value' into the search for a 'dynamic standard commodity', which he defines as that composite commodity that 'always "commands" through time as many physical commodities as correspond to the quantity of (augmented) labour embodied into them' (Pasinetti, 1993, p. 74). The dynamic standard commodity meets the Ricardian requirement of an 'invariable standard of value' in the setting of a dynamic economy with technical progress. This ensures that changes in prices expressed in terms of this standard could be explained in terms of changes in the value of the commodity being measured rather than in terms of changes in the commodity used as standard of value. Under these conditions, the problem arises of how to ensure that the *structural requirement* of the proportionality of 'natural' relative prices to the corresponding physical quantities of labour, which is fundamental in a pure labour economy, is also satisfied in a dynamic economy under technical progress and inter-personal debt-credit relations. Pasinetti's way of addressing this problem has been to introduce a 'natural' rate of interest defined as 'that rate of interest that maintains through time the equality between labour embodied and labour commanded, i.e. that maintains unaltered through time all purchasing power relations in terms of labour' (Pasinetti, 1993, p. 92). The switch to the setting of a capital-using economy does not change the essence of the problem to be addressed. For, in this case, the economy has to face the reproducibility and expansion issue (the self-replacement and enlargement of the stocks of intermediate inputs needed in production processes), but it still has to ensure that relative prices meet the *structural coordination* requirements that proportionality with relative quantities of labour is intended to ensure in a pure labour economy (Quadrio Curzio, 1980). In this case, Pasinetti identifies the need for each vertically integrated sector to meet a profitability requirement that is normally different from one sector to another, thereby introducing the need for a 'natural' economic system to allow for a range of differentiated 'natural' rates of profits ensuring both the reintegration of the used-up productive capacity and the expansion of the stocks of intermediate commodities in each sector according to the 'own' rate of growth of that sector (Pasinetti, 1981, 1988).

Institutions and Institutional Change: From Natural Dynamics to Policy Assessment

The analysis of the 'natural' (i.e., structural) profitability conditions that a dynamic economy should meet on a structural change trajectory is one of the routes along which Pasinetti's theoretical work has opened up to the analysis of institutions and institutional change (Scazzieri, 1996, 2012a, 2012b). This field has been central in the most recent of Pasinetti's contributions, going back at least to his volume *Keynes and the Cambridge Keynesians* (Pasinetti, 2007). Here, Pasinetti's objective to explore the manifold implications of a theory of structural dynamics for the analysis of economic institutions and the design of economic policies becomes fully visible:

> The natural economic system, as I see it, does not come down to reality from heaven. It does not automatically come into being by itself. It has to be brought into actual existence – by us. But it is a moving framework (not a *stationary* one). This means that, within it, many profound tendencies are constantly at work, from its very foundations, which are continually making it evolve, i.e. *change* in its structure .... To bring the natural economic system into existence, to close its degrees of freedom and then to keep it going through time, a set of procedures, rules, regulations, administrative bodies is required, which for short I have called *institutions*. (Pasinetti, 2007, p. 306)

The consideration of the natural economic system becomes a *structural benchmark* in which specific assumptions give transparency to constraints conditioning individual actors or collective bodies, as well as to opportunities that individual actors or collective bodies *may or may not* take up along dynamic trajectories subject to tendencies continuously at work such as technical progress and Engel's law (Scazzieri, 2018; Cardinale and Scazzieri, 2019). Pasinetti's intellectual path comes full circle in his most recent explorations of monetary and debt-credit relationships. In this connection, Pasinetti highlights the dual character of money between means for transacting in the exchange sphere and means for governing deep relational and institutional structures in the social sphere (a conception partly derived from the work of Philip Grierson at Cambridge; see Grierson, 1977). This point of view has led Pasinetti to explore the relationship between rates of interest in the financial sphere and rates of profits in the production sphere and to highlight that, while the concept of 'rate of interest' emerges very early as regulator of interpersonal debt-credit relationships, the concept of 'rate of profits' has acquired prominence only at a much later stage due to the central position of productive capital since the First Industrial Revolution (Pasinetti, 2019). The institutional turn taken by Pasinetti's explorations into the long-term dynamics of industrial economies has reinforced his commitment to assessing institutions and policies from the point of view of the constraints and opportunities generated by fundamental interdependencies in the economic system as a production economy (Pasinetti, 2022).

A Summing Up

Pasinetti's contribution to economic scholarship has been invaluable. It has given new prominence and theoretical foundations to a research field of pressing relevance in the contemporary world. His distinctive style of economic theorising is characterised by a selective concentration of attention on aspects he considers to be indispensable to the understanding of a modern industrial economy (Pasinetti, 1986). At the same time, the analytical framework he has provided is open to a multiplicity of developments that may be inspired by the consideration of stylised facts that are different from those central in his framework (such as the relationship between technical progress and resource utilisation under structural or environmental scarcity or the relationship between accumulation behaviour and demographic dynamics) and yet may be conducive to further explorations into the links between the conditions for structural change on a 'natural' path and the actual institutions and policies that may get us closer or more distant from that path. This openness to further developments is a characteristic feature of Pasinetti's work in economic theory and will surely be a feature of its enduring influence in economic scholarship.

References

Baranzini M. (1975) 'The Pasinetti and Anti-Pasinetti Theorems: A Reconciliation', in *Oxford Economic Papers*, 27(3), pp. 470–473.

(1987) 'Distribution Theories: Keynesian', in Eatwell J. Milgate M. and Newman P. (eds.) *The New Palgrave Dictionary of Economics*, vol. 2, London, Macmillan, pp. 876–888.

(1991) *A Theory of Wealth, Distribution and Accumulation*, Oxford, Clarendon Press.

(1993) 'Distribution, Accumulation and Institutions', in Heertje A. (ed.) *The Makers of Modern Economics*, vol. II, Hants and Brookfield, Aldershot, pp. 1–28.

Baranzini M. and Harcourt G. C. (eds.) (1993) *The Dynamics of the Wealth of Nations: Growth, Distribution and Structural Change: Essays in Honour of Luigi Pasinetti*, Basingstoke, Macmillan; New York, St. Martin's Press.

Baranzini M. and Mirante A. (2016) *A Compendium of Italian Economists at Oxbridge: Contributions to the Evolution of Economic Thinking*, Cham, London and New York, Palgrave Macmillan.

(2018) *Luigi L. Pasinetti: An Intellectual Biography: Leading Scholar and System Builder of the Cambridge School of Economics*, Cham, London and New York, Palgrave Macmillan.

Cardinale I. and Scazzieri R. (2019) 'Explaining Structural Change: Actions and Transformations', in *Structural Change and Economic Dynamics*, 51 (December), pp. 393–404.

Grierson P. (1977) *The Origins of Money*, London, Athlone Press.

Hagemann H. Landesmann M. A. and Scazzieri R. (eds.) (2003) *The Economics of Structural Change*, vols. 1–3, Cheltenham and Northampton, Edward Elgar.

Pasinetti L. L. (1959) 'On Concepts and Measures of Changes in Productivity', in *The Review of Economics and Statistics*, 41(3), pp. 270–282.

(1962) 'A Multi-Sector Model of Economic Growth', PhD dissertation submitted to the Faculty of Economics and Politics of the University of Cambridge.

(1964–1965 [2019]) 'Causality and Interdependence in Econometric Analysis and in Economic Theory', in *Structural Change and Economic Dynamics*, 49(C), pp. 357–363. Italian original published in *Annuario dell'Università Cattolica del S. Cuore*, Milan, pp. 233–250.

(1965) 'A New Theoretical Approach to the Problems of Economic Growth', in *Econometric Approach to Development Planning*, Amsterdam and New York, North-Holland, pp. 571–696.

(1973) 'The Notion of Vertical Integration in Economic Analysis', in *Metroeconomica*, 25(1), pp. 1–29.

(1981) *Structural Change and Economic Growth: A Theoretical Essay on the Dynamics of the Wealth of Nations*, Cambridge, Cambridge University Press.

(1986) 'Theory of Value: A Source of Alternative Paradigms in Economic Analysis', in Baranzini M. and Scazzieri R. (eds.) *Foundations of Economics: Structures of Inquiry and Economic Theory*, Oxford and New York, Basil Blackwell, pp. 409–431.

(1988) 'Growing Sub-systems, Vertically Hyper-integrated Sectors and the Labour Theory of Value', in *Cambridge Journal of Economics*, 12(1), pp. 125–134.

(1993) *Structural Economic Dynamics: A Theory of the Economic Consequences of Human Learning*, Cambridge, Cambridge University Press.

(2007) *Keynes and the Cambridge Keynesians: A 'Revolution in Economics' to Be Accomplished*, Cambridge, Cambridge University Press.

(2013) 'Prospettive e limiti dell'economia quantitativa', in Nicola P. C. Zanella A. and Robbiati Bianchi A. (eds.) *L'economia quantitativa diventerà una tecnologia del futuro?* Milan, Istituto Lombardo Accademia di Scienze e Lettere, Incontro di studio, 51, pp. 43–55.

(2019) 'Closing Remarks', Fifth Thomas Guggenheim Conference in the History of Economic Thought: 'Financial Instability, Market Disruptions and Macroeconomics. Lessons from Economic History and the History of Economic Thought', Rome, Accademia Nazionale dei Lincei, 17–18 December.

(2022) *A Labour Theory of Value*, Cambridge, Cambridge University Press, forthcoming.

Quadrio Curzio A. (1967) *Rendita e distribuzione in un modello economico plurisettoriale*, Milan, Giuffrè.

(1975) *Accumulazione del capitale e rendita*, Bologna, Il Mulino.

(1980) 'Rent, Income Distribution and Orders of Efficiency and Rentability', in Pasinetti L. L. (ed.) *Essays on the Theory of Joint Production*, London, Macmillan, pp. 219–240.

(1986) 'Technological Scarcity: An Essay on Production and Structural Change', in Baranzini M. and Scazzieri R. (eds.) *Foundations of Economics: Structures of Inquiry and Economic Theory*, Oxford and New York, Basil Blackwell, pp. 311–338.

(1993) 'On Economic Science, Its Tools and Economic Reality', in Baranzini M. and Harcourt G. C. (eds.) *The Dynamics of the Wealth of Nations: Growth, Distribution and Structural Change: Essays in Honour of Luigi Pasinetti*, London, Macmillan; New York, St. Martin's Press, pp. 246–271.

Quadrio Curzio A. and Pellizzari F. (1999) *Rent, Resources, Technologies*, Berlin, Springer.

Quadrio Curzio A. and Scazzieri R. (1984) 'Sui momenti costitutivi dell'economia politica', in *Giornale degli economisti*, New Series, 43, pp. 37–76.

(1990) 'Profili di dinamica economica strutturale: Introduzione', in Quadrio Curzio A. and Scazzieri R. (eds.) *Dinamica economica strutturale*, Bologna, Il Mulino, Collana della Società Italiana degli Economisti, pp. 11–51.

Scazzieri R. (1993) *A Theory of Production: Tasks, Processes and Technical Practices*, Oxford, Clarendon Press.

(1996) 'Introduction to Pasinetti's Structural Economic Dynamics: A Symposium', in *Structural Change and Economic Dynamics*, 7(2), pp. 123–125.

(2012a) 'The Concept of "Natural Economic System": A Tool for Structural Economic Analysis and an Instrument for Policy Design', in Arena R. and Porta P. L. (eds.) *Structural Dynamics and Economic Growth*, Cambridge, Cambridge University Press, pp. 218–240.

(2012b) 'The Political Economy of Production of Commodities by Means of Commodities: A Comment on Pasinetti and Sraffa', in *Cambridge Journal of Economics*, 36(6), pp. 1315–1322.

(2018) 'Political Economy of Economic Theory', in Cardinale I. and Scazzieri R. (eds.) *The Palgrave Handbook of Political Economy*, London, Palgrave Macmillan, pp. 193–233.

Introduction

ENRICO BELLINO AND
SEBASTIANO NEROZZI

In 2005, Luigi Pasinetti was asked by his friend and colleague Pier Paolo Varri[1] how he would like his seventy-fifth birthday to be celebrated. Pasinetti immediately replied: 'let us discuss my new book!'. The book was, of course, *Keynes and the Cambridge Keynesians*, which was almost finished at that time. One of the most original and provocative parts was the 'Postlude: Fighting for Independence' of Book Two (The Cambridge School of Keynesian Economics), where he portrays what he considers the main features of the classical-Keynesian school, offering a list of nine theoretical and methodological characteristics, qualifying and unifying (to some extent, at least) the economists associated with it (Pasinetti, 2007, pp. 217–237). When, about a couple of years ago, John E. Woods (a student of Luigi Pasinetti at King's College in the late 1960s) and Philip Good (economics editor of Cambridge University Press) launched the idea of a collection of essays discussing Pasinetti's 'nine characteristics', we felt it certainly an appropriate, though a somewhat unconventional, way to celebrate Pasinetti's career as an economist.

Needless to say, we quickly and enthusiastically accepted their proposal to take over the project. However, our enthusiasm was to be short-lived. In a few days, a sense of anxiety took hold as we began to realise the size of the task before us. The exceptional personality of Pasinetti and his relentless and uncompromising eagerness to discuss and refine his ideas (and, even more, others' interpretations of them) caused us to question our original decision; possibly more frightening was the task of selecting just a few from among the many outstanding economists and scholars whose intellectual paths crossed with Pasinetti's, each of them certainly deserving of joining this collective endeavour and give her/his comments on one (or more) of his nine

[1] At the time, Varri was the director of the Institute of Economic Theory and Quantitative Methods at the Catholic University of Milan.

characteristics. It is thanks to Woods and Good's support that we became convinced not to abandon the project but to proceed with it.

Actually, the very reason that finally prompted us to persist in this endeavour and eventually led us to conceive this book as it now stands was not to celebrate Pasinetti's work and ideas (an effort that, though certainly well deserved, he probably would not appreciate much); rather, it was the awareness that such a book could be a valuable opportunity to put to the test and eventually develop Pasinetti's insights into the nature of the Cambridge Keynesian school and assess their ability to rescue present-day economics from its major flaws.

Indeed, Pasinetti has offered wide-ranging contributions to the development of a Keynesian theory of production, growth, and income distribution. On the one hand, his compelling critique of neoclassical theory and, on the other hand, his multi-sectoral framework for the analysis of structural dynamics can be counted among the most important achievements in the field of the classical and post-Keynesian theory. From his earliest publications, Pasinetti has consistently aimed to revive the methodology of classical political economy and integrate it with Keynesian economics to show how a classical-Keynesian approach, comprising the best of the two, would be better suited to explain the long-term dynamics of capitalist systems.

In his (2007) book, Pasinetti had discussed at length if a Cambridge school of 'political economy' exists. Drawing inspiration from both John Maynard Keynes and Piero Sraffa, though moulded in different ways, this school has been pursuing a long-standing and ambitious research programme that he sees as the main competing paradigm to mainstream economics, providing a comprehensive analytical framework into which most non-mainstream schools of thought can be inserted and give their specific contribution.

The nine building blocks presented by Pasinetti in order to define the main methodological *characteristic features* of the classical-Keynesian school are the following:

(1) Reality (and not simply abstract rationality) as the starting point of economic theory
(2) Economic logic with internal consistency (and not only formal rigour)

(3) Malthus and the Classics (not Walras and the Marginalists) as the major inspiring source in the history of economic thought
(4) Non-ergodic (in place of stationary, timeless) economic systems
(5) Causality vs. interdependence
(6) Macroeconomics before microeconomics
(7) Disequilibrium and instability (not equilibrium) as the normal state of the industrial economies
(8) Necessity of finding an appropriate analytical framework for dealing with technical change and economic growth
(9) A strong, deeply felt social concern

The more we meditate on them, the more we are convinced that these characteristics provide a broad methodological framework that deserves further attention from economists and historians of economic thought.

Actually, the history of the post-Keynesian approach at large (comprising both the so-called American and the European schools in that tradition) is more a story of divisions and discussions than one of agreement and research based on a common understanding. The post-Keynesian approach has often been animated by deep analytical and methodological quarrels and by growing distinctions between specific approaches, schools, and lines of research. This lack of unity, and sometimes even dialogue, is still an open question in the literature on the history of post-Keynesian economics and, together with other external factors, may help explain its failure to achieve a wider consensus among the economics profession. In the late 1960s and early 1970s, post-Keynesian economics was at its height. The cultural milieu of Cambridge and other research centres encouraged radical and unconventional thinking that seemed to fit perfectly with the vivid political atmosphere of the time; a wealth of different ideas and intuitions were opening new research fields whose development would require well-focused research groups and great commitment; the notable analytical successes that the school secured in theoretical battles against the marginalist approach and the Neoclassical Synthesis reinforced a sense of self-confidence; the expectation that the establishment of a new post-Keynesian paradigm was at hand boosted each school's efforts in pursuing their specific goals; and last, but not least, the bold characters of the most leading figures (Pasinetti included), each focused on the development of his own specific approach, diverted attention from research into the common ground between them.[2] All of this certainly played a role in enhancing internal competition and distancing the different stars (and their planetary systems) within the post-Keynesian galaxy. Unfortunately, this happened at a time when the whole and variegated Keynesian universe ('bastard' Keynesians first of all!) was put under the massive attack launched by Milton Friedman and completed by Robert Lucas. In a very few years, monetarism and new classical macroeconomics conquered most universities and research centres around the world. Keynesian economists (whatever school they felt to belong to) were gradually marginalised from most academic and economic policy circles. A twenty-year kingdom was established, so to speak, ruled by rational expectations, the efficient market hypothesis, and the policy ineffectiveness proposition: at the dawn of the new century, this eventually evolved into a New Consensus Macroeconomics, merging the new classical DSGE-type of models with some specific hypotheses on the working of actual markets and producing some 'Keynesian' results in the realm of economic policy.

Post-Keynesian macroeconomics never faded away: indeed, various centres and individual economists are still operating, pursuing original, relevant research and publishing in journals within the post-Keynesian tradition. Moreover, in the last decade, they have been able to achieve a broader audience, particularly among young researchers. Notably, since the 2008 crisis, there has been a growing dissatisfaction with New Consensus Macroeconomics, specifically with its inability to explain the working of actual capitalist economies, their interaction with financial markets, and their structural tendency to produce mass unemployment and income inequality. On the whole, the post-Keynesian tradition and its history have proved to be still alive and relevant to present-day debates.

Thus, Pasinetti's nine characteristics provide the opportunity to review the history of that tradition and try to discover – or, most likely,

[2] For example, on this purpose Pasinetti himself wrote: 'I have always wondered why in our relations with Pierangelo Garegnani – in our exchanges of letters, talks and discussions – we had never managed to be more constructive. I wondered, for example ... why in our writings Garegnani and I had always been so stingy with mutual quotations. Yet this aspect was just the opposite of what our common adversaries were doing. In part an explanation could be found in the fact that we were dealing mainly with different aspects of Sraffa's work .... Yet they were not in opposition, but were complementary' (Pasinetti, 2013, pp. 64–65, our translation).

to rediscover – some common ground between different approaches, which have individual merits on their own but could largely reinforce each other when evaluated within a more comprehensive framework.

Despite Pasinetti's firm commitment to the classical and post-Keynesian research programme, he has always been a reference point, in dialogue with a much wider group of economists. A cursory check on Scopus suffices to show that Pasinetti's works are constantly quoted by both heterodox and orthodox scholars. On the whole, we think that this critical and forward-looking assessment of Pasinetti's interpretation of the classical-Keynesian school will not only attract the attention of those economists already close to classical and post-Keynesian economics but will also offer key insights to the wider group of heterodox economists, who are looking for novel methodological perspectives in which their original, potentially path-breaking, research may find its place. Also, mainstream economists will find that this book provides clear terms of comparison with their own approaches, enabling them to have a richer understanding of the classical-Keynesian school.

Furthermore, Pasinetti's nine characteristics offer a broad basis for dialogue and discussion between open-minded economists who are willing to seriously take into consideration the heavy shocks and strains that financial crisis, technical change, and many urging problems such as rising unemployment, growing inequality, and climate change are posing to modern economic thought. We believe that these nine characteristics may show new ways of thinking about economics and become a source of inspiration to young scholars willing to attain a better understanding of present-day market economies and devise new approaches to economic policy. It is mainly in relation to their ability to open new frontiers of economic research or shed new light on current economic research that Pasinetti's nine characteristics should be valued.

Maria Cristina Marcuzzo (Chapter 1) deals with 'Reality (and Not Simply Abstract Rationality) as the starting point of economic theory' and points out that in Pasinetti's mind, the former principle is meant to discard one assumption in particular: the 'purely imaginary world of rationally behaving individuals'. Marcuzzo focuses especially on the notion of rational behaviour under conditions of uncertainty and imperfect knowledge as developed by Keynes and Richard Kahn. Contrary to Sraffa, who radically rejected the Marshallian approach,

Keynes and Kahn did not completely remove the idea of marginal calculation but retained and considerably developed Alfred Marshall's own ideas and insights into the importance of experience, customs, habits, and expectations in business decision-making. In this line of thought, business decisions are not the result of a perfectly rational ex-ante calculation of marginal costs and revenues, aimed at maximising profit and utility; rather, they emerge from a process of trial and error, where reasonableness rather than perfect rationality is the guiding principle. The author thus confutes the nihilistic and quasi-irrationalistic interpretation sometimes given to Keynes's animal spirits and points out how, in Kahn and Keynes, individuals make constrained choices being divided by 'best guesses' and uncertainty, first- and second-degree opinions, which, on balance, lead them to maintain their previous choices or change them in order to improve their position. Optimality and maximisation are thus ruled out from the realm of business decision making.

Neri Salvadori and Rodolfo Signorino, in their chapter 'Economic Logic with Internal Consistency, and Not Only Formal Rigour' (Chapter 2), highlight the interesting distinction between 'internal consistency' and 'formal rigour'. Without going into a definition of these terms here, we can immediately perceive the difference between them by a simple comparison of two books, both outstanding in economic theory: Gérard Debreu's *Theory of Value* and Sraffa's *Production of Commodities by Means of Commodities*. Beyond the different approaches and contents, these books speak two different languages. Debreu follows the language of 'formal rigour': starting from a set of axioms, the scientific nature of this analysis lies in the correctness with which the different propositions are progressively obtained. Sraffa follows a line of 'internal consistency'. The level of abstraction of his analysis is less marked: he starts from a numerical example of a primitive society and gradually extends his inquiry to a society where a surplus is realized and distributed between capitalists and workers, etc. Every 'proposition' is deduced following a logical procedure but according to a different method. The difference is not so much in the fact that Sraffa makes little use of mathematics. His method is well summarised in a key sentence found in Sraffa's papers and quoted by Salvadori and Signorino: 'But it is not enough that the conclusions of the theory are confirmed by observation: it is equally important that the path by which they are arrived at is the same both in theory and in reality' (D1/45, p. 4 recto, Sraffa's emphasis). The 'consistency' of the analytical process is thus 'internal' to the phenomena analysed, that is, strictly connected with the object of the inquiry.

Chapter 3, 'Malthus and the Classics (Not Walras and the Marginalists) as the Major Inspiring Source in the History of Economic Thought', is written by Heinz Kurz. The reference to the 'Classics' and the principle of effective demand are two elements considered fundamental for the Cambridge school by Pasinetti. Classical economists focused their attention on the phenomenon of production regarded as a circular process. The presence of the same set of commodities among both inputs and outputs allows them to ascertain the emergence of a social surplus, which must be divided between the social classes, according to forces that are regulated by a mix of technical and institutional elements. This was, in fact, the realm of classical political economy worked out by Adam Smith, David Ricardo, Karl Marx et al. Pasinetti complements these characteristics with the principle of effective demand, whose roots cannot be found in these authors. Keynes was the first to stress the importance of this principle for a 'monetary theory of production'. The Classics relied upon Jean Baptiste Say's law of markets, according to which every output generates its own demand. This was, for Pasinetti but even more so for Keynes, a limiting factor for classical analysis. The only exception was Thomas Robert Malthus, who is regarded as the forerunner of the principle of effective demand by Pasinetti. Kurz considers these aspects in his chapter. In particular, he focuses on one point, challenging the view that Malthus is actually the forerunner of the Keynesian principle of effective demand. Kurz shows how Malthus analyses the working of a pure exchange economy, where money is neutral. On the contrary, Keynes focuses on a monetary economy of production, where subjects taking savings decisions (households) are different from subjects taking investment decisions (entrepreneurs). Moreover, the lack of effective demand is originated by a high level of accumulation for Malthus but by a low level of investment for Keynes. On this basis, Kurz concludes that 'Malthus cannot be considered to have anticipated Keynes's Principle of Effective Demand'.

In Chapter 4, the preference for 'Non-ergodic (in Place of Stationary, Timeless) Economic Systems', that is, ones located in historical time, is discussed at length by Ariel Dvoskin and Paolo Trabucchi. The starting point of this chapter is the criticism that Joan Violet Robinson raised originally against the neoclassical description of a process of capital accumulation by means of a sequence of equilibria. The basic idea was that, for a system to be in equilibrium, a set of additional and tacit assumptions is required: that the system is in that position for, at least, a considerable period of time; that people expected the system would have been in equilibrium; and that people expect that it will remain in that equilibrium. In such conditions, no process of change can be represented by a sequence of changing equilibria because it clearly breaks the coincidence of expectations with the actual path of the economy. Such criticism was gradually extended by Robinson to the entire structure of the modern classical approach that was being built in the late sixties and the seventies. The criticism probably arose from the fact that classical economists characterised the theoretical positions of the economy with the assumption of a uniform rate of profit. This uniformity is clearly incompatible with what occurs in the process of change in actual economies. Classical economists, on their own, replied that this theoretical position was to be conceived as a centre around which actual economies tend to gravitate. A lively debate arose between Robinson and Garegnani on these points;[3] their positions could not be easily reconciled, and a deep split emerged between the two sides (the 'Sraffians' and some 'post-Keynesians'). Dealing with these issues in great depth, Dvoskin and Trabucchi aim to show why Robinson's critique does not apply to the modern classical approach. In particular, they argue that while Robinson's critique of the method based on a uniform rate of profit should be rejected, there is another aspect of that critique that has to do with the specific nature of the neoclassical theory, as this is based on the construction of supply and demand curves.

Enrico Bellino and Sebastiano Nerozzi, who consider the characteristic, 'Causality vs. interdependence' (Chapter 5), aim to show how many conceptual points of the classical-Keynesian analysis are based on a suitable interaction between causal and interdependent relationships. In a previous paper (Bellino and Nerozzi, 2017), they analysed Pasinetti's main contributions in the light of this distinction. The present chapter broadens their analysis to comprise the most prominent figures within the classical-Keynesian school. Following Herbert

[3] The exchange was originally published in Italian by Garegnani (Garegnani, 1979, pp. 119–143) and later reproduced in English (Feiwel, 1989, ch. 12).

Simon (1953), the terms 'causality' and 'interdependence' are interpreted, throughout the analysis, as analytical characteristics of the relations established in a specific theory rather than features of economic reality. A meticulous work of revisiting the analytical formulations of some essential foundations of both classical and Keynesian theories has been presented here to bring to the surface the sequential or the simultaneous nature of the relations between the main variables involved in the theories.

Murray Milgate and John Eatwell, in their chapter 'Macroeconomics before Microeconomics' (Chapter 6), paint a very effective picture of the birth and evolution of macroeconomics since Keynes. At that time, macroeconomics did not exist: there was no distinction between micro- and macroeconomics. Then, after Keynes's *General Theory*, this new field of economic research developed quite independently of the rest of economic theory. And it had to be this way, because Keynes's inquiry was a real *break* with the past. Probably Keynes, who focused on giving rapid answers to the burning issues created by the Great Depression, did not succeed in providing a comprehensive framework, alternative to neoclassical analysis. At the same time, the gradual incorporation of aspects of Keynes's analysis into the Walrasian framework of the neoclassical synthesis contributed to opening this divide between micro- and macroeconomics, micro being the realm of utility-maximising individuals and profit-maximising firms and of equilibrium between supply and demand functions *derived from the behaviour of these rational agents*. The aggregate relations considered by Keynes, gradually packaged as demand and supply *functions*, constituted what was called 'macroeconomics'. Yet, to regard them as demand and supply functions, it became necessary to consider one or more prices as *fixed*. In this wedge, the question about the 'rationale' of those fixed prices was inevitably raised: it became necessary to explain the convenience that rational agents had not to adjust their behaviour to market imbalances (for example, why unemployed workers did not accept a real wage cut in order to get a job?). These interpretations of Keynes's analysis led to the need for the 'micro-foundations' of the relationships between the main macroeconomic variables. It was *this* reading of Keynes's analysis that gave rise to the need to put micro before macro. Yet Keynes's analysis was free from this need: the relationships between macroeconomic variables outline the working of the entire system, which, for Keynes, is not merely the sum of the parts. It is for these reasons that macro comes before micro in classical and Keynesian analysis. In their chapter, Milgate and Eatwell show how the evolution of macroeconomics after Keynes has taken a route that at first diverges and then becomes even orthogonal to Keynes's programme[4].

Ariel Wirkierman, in dealing with 'Disequilibrium and Instability (Not Equilibrium) as the Normal State of Industrial Economies' (Chapter 7), performs an analytical reconstruction of the definition and interpretation of equilibrium and disequilibrium within the framework of structural economic dynamics, by connecting three aspects of Pasinetti's work. First, the author clarifies the importance of the distinction between pre-institutional and behavioural relations as a methodological standpoint for the analysis of industrial economies. Second, he explores Pasinetti's argument for a pre-institutional principle of effective demand, by contrasting two simple formal schemes each representing an industrial and pre-industrial society, respectively. Third, in order to extend the relevance of the principle of effective demand when productive capacity is also changing through time, the author connects some features of the contributions by Roy Harrod and Evsej Domar to Pasinetti's conceptualisation of dynamic equilibrium. Based on these building-blocks, the author finally develops and discusses some logical implications of Pasinetti's analytical scheme as regards to the (im)possibility of maintaining an equilibrium situation in industrial economies. Disequilibrium, characterised by effective demand being below productive capacity and structural dynamics leading to technological unemployment, seems to be the normal state of industrial economies.

The 'Necessity of Finding an Appropriate Analytical Framework for Dealing with Technical Change and Economic Growth' (Chapter 8) has been discussed by Harald Hagemann. The original (and still current) Ricardian dilemma about the effects of the introduction of 'machinery' on labour employment has been the backbone of much of Pasinetti's research, especially that on structural change. In fact, he examined a question that Keynes had, but which he did not have the

[4] The IS-LM model put Keynes's analysis in terms of (anomalous) demand and supply functions (a 'fix-price' model); with the AS-AD model the 'synthesis' is totally accomplished: economic policies have real effects only in the short run, because in the medium run the economy reaches its 'natural' equilibrium: thus, neo-Keynesian theory gets to conclusions very similar to monetarism.

opportunity to deal with systematically: the problem of technological unemployment and the conditions to keep full employment across time. The framework of structural change analysis allows us to study the effects of technical progress in their complexity: a more efficient way to produce commodities which means, at the same time, a *less labour-consuming* way to produce them; the introduction of new machines, new processes and new goods; an increase of real income. This manifold approach avoids the reduction of technical change to a supply-side phenomenon and addresses the need that all these effects have to be permanently managed by the 'institutions'. According to Hagemann, this view of technical change facilitates the link between the classical-Keynesians approach and Joseph Alois Schumpeter's analysis of innovation.

Claudia Rotondi deals with Pasinetti's final point: 'Strong, Deeply Felt Social Concern' (Chapter 9), describing how this principle represents a pillar in his scientific research programme. After having traced Pasinetti's manifold links with the Keynesian school, the author focuses on his contrasting evaluation of the 'pure exchange paradigm' and the 'pure production paradigm'. The author explains why Pasinetti regards the latter as the most fitted to describe the dynamics of modern industrial societies and illuminate some crucial social issues arising from them: the centrality of labour, the social function of capital, the role of institutions. In the end, Rotondi examines the connection between Pasinetti and the tradition of Italian economic thought, which has proven over the centuries particularly attentive to the complex linkages between ethics, economics, and institutions.

Nadia Garbellini, who has personally followed and supported Pasinetti's scientific work during the last fifteen years, offers her interpretation of his nine points and makes some proposals on how they can be developed in the field of economic research and policy. While some of her conclusions may appear quite provocative and partially disputable, Garbellini (Chapter 10) offers a bold and valuable testimony of how a young economist may draw inspiration from Pasinetti's lesson for grounding an original research programme open to multiple influences and methodological backgrounds.

Finally, an overall assessment of the nine contributions has been provided by Bertram Schefold (Chapter 11), assessing their relevance and opening new questions on the development of Pasinetti's insights into the nature of the classical-Keynesian tradition.

References

Bellino E. and Nerozzi S. (2017) 'Causality and Interdependence in Pasinetti's Works and in the Modern Classical Approach', in *Cambridge Journal of Economics*, 41(6), pp. 1653–1684.

Feiwel G. R. (ed.) (1989) *Joan Robinson and Modern Economic Theory*, Houndmills, Basingstoke, Hampshire and London, Macmillan.

Garegnani P. (1979) *Valore e domanda effettiva*, Torino, Einaudi.

Pasinetti L. L. (2007) *Keynes and the Cambridge Keynesians: A 'Revolution in Economics' to Be Accomplished*, Cambridge, Cambridge University Press.

(2013) 'Reminiscenze', in Fratini S. Levrero S. and Trabucchi P. (eds.) *In ricordo di Pierangelo Garegnani*, Università degli Studi Roma Tre, Facoltà di Economia 'Federico Caffè', Centro Ricerche e Documentazione 'Piero Sraffa', pp. 61–70.

Simon H. (1953) 'Causal Ordering and Identifiability', in Hood W. C. and Koopmans T. C. (eds.) *Studies in Econometric Method*, Cowles Commission, New York, John Wiley and Sons; London, Chapman and Hall, pp. 49–74.

1 *Reality (and Not Simply Abstract Rationality) as the Starting Point of Economic Theory*

MARIA CRISTINA MARCUZZO*

1.1 Introduction

The first item in Luigi Pasinetti's 'series of essential building blocks belonging to an alternative economic paradigm, with respect to the neoclassical one' is 'Reality (and not simply abstract rationality) as the starting point of economic theory' (Pasinetti, 2007, p. 219). He makes it clear that his attempt to single out the 'most important basic features of the "Cambridge Keynesian school"' is based on his own personal perception, so that 'the list [of the essential building blocks] need not be an exhaustive one; even less need it be one that would be found in the works of the members of the group (who neglected this aspect), or one that all of them would have endorsed at first sight' (Pasinetti, 2007, p. 219). With this in mind, let us see how Pasinetti explains what he means by *Reality*:

> The whole school always showed a strong aversion to a purely imaginary world of rationally behaving individuals, that, though fulfilling the rules of logic, does not show respect for facts. The conviction has always been that any theory needs to be based on factual evidence, to be evaluated right from the start and not only to be empirically tested at the end. (Pasinetti, 2007, p. 220)

Pasinetti's plea is for a theory which is 'firmly placed on an objective foundational framework' (Pasinetti, 2007, p. 219) rather than fictional reality.

This is clearly a rebuttal of the well-known approach advocated by Milton Friedman, according to which unrealistic assumptions do not matter, while predictive success is all that matters in assessing a theory;

* I am grateful to Enrico Bellino, Marco Dardi, Ghislain Deleplace, Sebastiano Nerozzi, Alessandro Roncaglia and Annalisa Rosselli for their comments. I have not always followed their suggestions, so they bear no responsibility for the views expressed here.

and, of course, it concerns an issue on which an ample literature has grown. In recent times, attention has turned to the notion of 'realism' in connection with general philosophical issues in general and philosophy of science and philosophy of economics in particular, such as ontological beliefs, modelling and mathematical rigour.[1]

For the purpose of this chapter, the scope of the discussion is much narrower. In fact, Pasinetti's plea is to discard not just the descriptive unrealism of assumptions in general but one assumption in particular: the 'purely imaginary world of rationally behaving individuals' (Pasinetti, 2007, p. 220). Truly, the assumption of rationally behaving individuals has been challenged in various strands of modern theory, notably experimental and behavioural economics, which have produced evidence that people often behave in ways that contradict the rationality principle. However, here Pasinetti is referring to something that he believes was typical of the 'Cambridge Keynesians',[2] namely, their placing at the centre of the analysis not abstract entities but flesh-and-blood economic agents acting in various specific markets.

The unrealism of the assumption of rationally behaving individuals lies not in its limited descriptive nature, which may be necessary for the sake of simplicity and supposed generality, but in the fabrication of an imaginary world rather than taking the world that we actually experience as the frame of reference. The fabrication of an imaginary world is often necessary to support a particular theory. This was an argument put forward by Piero Sraffa against Alfred Marshall's derivation of the equilibrium of the firm in competitive conditions in his 1925 and 1926 articles to show the unrealism of the assumptions behind it. As he famously concludes the 1930 symposium:

> I am trying to find what are the assumptions implicit in Marshall's theory; if Mr. Robertson regards them as extremely unreal, I sympathise with him. We seem to be agreed that the theory cannot be interpreted in a way which makes it logically self-consistent and, at the same time, reconciles it with the facts it sets out to explain. Mr. Robertson's remedy is to discard

[1] A useful review of several of these issues can be found in Mäki (2009). Lawson (1997) offers the most comprehensive discussion of the question of realism in economics.

[2] I have argued elsewhere that this is a misnomer, since Pasinetti includes Sraffa, who, although personally and intellectually close to John Maynard Keynes, can hardly be called a Keynesian (see Marcuzzo, 2014).

mathematics, and he suggests that my remedy is to discard the facts; perhaps I ought to have explained that, in the circumstances, I think it is Marshall's theory that should be discarded. (Sraffa, 1930, p. 93)

A similar argument was used by Keynes to say that the

classical theorists resemble Euclidean geometers in a non-Euclidean world who, discovering that in experience straight lines apparently parallel often meet, rebuke the lines for not keeping straight – as the only remedy for the unfortunate collisions which are occurring. Yet, in truth, there is no remedy except to throw over the axiom of parallels and to work out a non-Euclidean geometry. (*CWK*, VII, p. 16)

In this chapter, I will give a few examples of how rejection of 'abstract rationality' was put in practice by some authors in the Cambridge tradition. One is their interpretation of the maximisation rule of behaviour in a less precise and deterministic form. Although we find rejection of marginal calculation *in toto* only in the case of Sraffa, in Marshall and even more so in Keynes and Richard Kahn (the two other authors I will consider here as representative), maximisation is seen as the result of a 'trial and error' method and therefore hardly a comprehensive explanation of economic behaviour.

An example of rejection of abstract rationality is provided by Kahn in the case of investors' decisions in the money market. In his 1954 article on liquidity preference, Kahn argues that decisions are not optimising choices on the basis of identification of certain behavioural functions but rather constrained choices by individuals who are often divided by best guesses and uncertainty (Kahn, 1954). Here, of course, Kahn extends Keynes's vision of decision-making based on his notion of probability, but since it is perhaps a less known example of its application, it may merit closer consideration.

Finally, as another example, I take an interpretation of rationality by Keynes resulting from the awareness that the consequences of following individual self-interest are not always for the collective good. This applies equally to both the economic sphere (the fallacy of composition) and the political sphere, where reasonableness rather than rationality is the moral quality which addresses the collective good instead of individual benefit.

There are, of course, other examples of criticism of the assumptions in neoclassical theory that were raised by other protagonists of the Cambridge school. Prominent in this respect are Joan Robinson's repeated attacks on the notion of equilibrium, because it suggests imaginary movements in time and disregards movements which happen in history (see Marcuzzo, 2020). Also, Nicholas Kaldor's insistence on cumulative causation can be seen as an attempt to bring realistic assumptions into theoretical analysis. However, in this chapter, I narrow the focus to include fewer authors and examples; therefore, my presentation is neither to be taken as inclusive nor to be considered exhaustive.

1.2 From Marshall to Keynes: Profit Maximisation as a 'Trial and Error' Method

In Marshall, we find the entrepreneur described as possessing special qualities such as 'knowledge of things in his own trade', 'power of forecasting the broad movements of production and consumption' and the ability 'to judge cautiously and undertake risks boldly' (Marshall, 1920, p. 297). As far as his rule of behaviour is concerned, Marshall pointed out,

> Every business man ... estimates as best he can how much net product (i.e. net addition to the value of his total product) will be caused by a certain extra use of anyone agent .... He endeavours to employ each agent up to that margin at which its net product would no longer exceed the price he would have to pay for it. He works generally by trained instinct rather than formal calculation. (Marshall, 1920, p. 406)

When describing the entrepreneur's behaviour in the real world, the marginal rule becomes a matter of balancing the 'advantages' against 'disadvantages' of a change in a given situation or action. The equalisation of two exact magnitudes, such as marginal revenue ('net product' in Marshall's terminology) and marginal cost, is brought in only in determination of the equilibrium of the firm. However, Marshall looked to other factors to explain what guides business behaviour, attributing greater importance to the influence of habits and customs, to the institutional context and to business 'connections' (see, for example, Marshall, 1919, p. 196), meaning by this an extended knowledge of the market in which the businessman is operating, in all its technical and interpersonal aspects (see Becattini, 1962).

In the same vein, Kahn interpreted the profit maximisation rule not as a calculation actually and consciously undertaken by businessmen but as a 'trial and error' method. In his dissertation, 'The Economics of the Short Period', for instance, he wrote, 'instincts and intuitions will secure adherence to marginal principle in action when conscious apprehension is impossible. And, failing those, we may rely on the method of trial and error; experience, embodied in rule of thumb, will often indicate how profits may be maximised' (Kahn, 1989, p. 162).

Against the evidence that businessmen usually state that they consider average rather than marginal cost, he argued that 'it is the consequences of business men's individual acts, not of their general theories, with which we have to reckon' (Kahn, 1989, p. 159). Kahn's point is that proof that actual behaviour does in fact follow the marginal rule lies in 'success' in business, so profit maximisation as the only rule that is consistent with rationality is seen not as an assumption that describes how businesses behave but as the rule which, if followed, would guarantee maximum profit. Moreover, since firms do not know their individual demand curve, Kahn asked, how can it be supposed that it forms the basis for the search for the point of intersection with the marginal cost curve? Kahn claims that what matters is 'the business man's conception of his individual demand curve' arrived at by 'the method of trial and error'; thus, the only relevant assumptions are those 'that are in the mind of the business man when he maximizes his profit' (Kahn, 1989, p. 101).

In conclusion, Kahn always stressed the aspect of rationality which finds expression in the 'trial and error' method rather than in the optimising choice between possible and known alternatives. This 'rationality' pursued through trial and error works on the basis of the 'rewards' and 'punishments' of the competitive mechanism in more or less perfect markets.

This approach to the matter explains why Kahn was critical of mark-up pricing and remained faithful to the profit maximisation approach also in the cases of duopoly and a kinked demand curve, of which he was the inventor. He wrote: '[The kinked demand curve] is compatible with the traditional hypothesis of profit maximization ... all that the kinked demand curve explains is why the price remains where it is (for no other reason than that it happens to be there) until something happens to cause it to alter' (Kahn, 1952, p. 122).

In this view, profit maximisation is a rationalisation, not a description of actual behaviour. Kahn goes so far as to indicate that it is a false rationalisation, because the *marginal cost = marginal revenue* formula is followed by entrepreneurs by 'instinct rather than reasoning' (Kahn, 1952, p. 126), and it should be more generally interpreted as an ex post outcome which is attained by repeated attempts: 'Put in that more homely form, the concept [profit maximisation] does readily lend itself to the operation of the forces of trial and error, and to the display *of flair* – the success of which by no means depends upon the manner in which it is rationalized' (Kahn, 1952, p. 127).[3]

Now, turning to Keynes, it can readily be seen that he employed marginal language quite sparingly; reliance on the Marshallian apparatus – demand and supply curves – and acceptance of the 'classical' postulates are, in fact, limited in *General Theory*, probably also under the influence of Kahn, who remained persuaded of the validity of the Marshallian framework, which he saw no reason to discard. As I have argued elsewhere, Kahn might have had an influence on Keynes's choice 'to transform certain concepts into precise analytical tools [. . .] to obtain logically coherent results' (Marcuzzo, 2002, p. 445).

Even neglecting the influence that Kahn might have had on the matter, it is possible that the assumptions behind profit maximisation appeared to Keynes to be sufficiently explicit and general to make them acceptable, while other 'tacit assumptions are seldom or never satisfied, with the result that it cannot solve the economic problems of the actual world' (*CWK*, VII, p. 378).

Here we can measure the distance from Sraffa who, in the same years, was starting to attack marginal analysis at its foundations (Marcuzzo and Rosselli, 2016), evidently never managing fully to persuade Keynes of the need to discard it.

On the other hand, Keynes's path-breaking views on investment decisions and the determination of its prospective yields point to the influence of expectations and uncertainty in economic calculation and the role of speculation. In the *General Theory*, investment decisions, as opposed to determination of the level of individual output, are never made on 'a precise calculation of prospective profit': they are the outcome of a sort of probability calculation in which

> even after the event no one would know whether the average results in terms of the sums invested had exceeded, equalled or fallen short of the prevailing rate of interest . . . . If human nature felt no temptation to take a chance, no

3 For a more extended analysis of these points, see Marcuzzo and Sanfilippo (2006).

satisfaction (profit apart) in constructing a factory, a railway, a mine or a farm, there might not be much investment merely as a result of cold calculation. (*CWK*, VII, p. 150)

Another instance is the description of investment decision as guessing the prospective yields on the basis of a rational conjecture, taking into account the degree of ignorance of the causes influencing the results, through a procedure similar to trial and error. As Keynes wrote in a famous passage in the *General Theory*, 'our decisions to do something positive, the full consequences of which will be drawn out over many days to come [are not] the outcome of a weighted average of quantitative benefits multiplied by quantitative probabilities' (*CWK*, VII, p. 161).

This passage is clear evidence of Keynes's rejection of taking abstract rationality to represent what is behind entrepreneurs' actions; however, it is not a belief in the 'irrational' nature of the entrepreneur's decision process but a belief in a concept of constrained rationality, because of uncertainty and limited knowledge, which nevertheless is still an active factor in business choices.

As Roncaglia effectively puts it,

In Keynes's theory of probability, there is no objective rule to establish how the empirical evidence should affect the probability statement, or as to how additional evidence should change it. Thus, no bi-univocal correspondence can be established between evidence and a 'rational' probability statement. However, in Keynes's mind there clearly is the idea that the subject must somehow take the available evidence into account. In fact, together with internal consistency (no contradictions) in the system of beliefs, this is what distinguishes rational from irrational behaviour. (Roncaglia, 2012, pp. 448–449)

1.3 Sraffa's Alternative

A more radical stance against marginal calculation to describe business behaviour was taken by Sraffa, as evidenced in his unpublished papers. Sraffa often argued that in economics it is not possible to resort to infinitesimal calculus, because variations are highly unlikely to come about in a continuous manner but rather occur in discrete form and, more importantly, because change hardly ever takes the form of variations in magnitudes that leave the overall structure unchanged.

Economic changes in one variable affect the whole structure; this is one of the reasons why the marginal analysis is ill-founded: 'Where marginism goes astray is in (falsely) assuming ... that it has general applicability whereas in fact it only applies exceptionally (in cases where partial change is feasible, there is independence, the whole is not affected)' (D3/12/42.9).[4]

On various occasions over the years, Sraffa objected to Marshall's use of the case of an 'alert' railway manager who deals with the increasing number of passengers by altering the composition and size of carriages in a train, 'constantly weighing the net product in saving of time and of annoyance to passengers, that will accrue from the aid of a second guard on an important train and considering whether it will be worth its costs' (Marshall, 1920, p. 427).

This was an example to which Sraffa returned many times; as late as 1963 we find him arguing that

> his [the alert manager's] main task is to sack a porter here, add a coach to a train there, or shorten a platform elsewhere. The idea is that the process of change can be reduced to a continuous process, like shortening platforms: 'a penny is the basis of a million', and so a process of shortening, adding[,] sacking in detail is the route from one position to another. (D3/12/42.12)

In conclusion, even if supply and demand functions (for goods and factors) were continuous so that marginal calculus were applicable, there would still be one obstacle to adopting it as method in economic analysis, 'even if the external circumstances were the same, the result would be different because man learns from experience, or at any rate is changed by it, forms and transforms habits, etc.' (D3/12/42/11 recto).

There is no place for abstract rationality in *Production of Commodities* since there are no explicit behavioural assumptions in the book and prices and distribution are determined by none of them. Even the uniformity of the rate of profit is not described as the outcome of a process in time but is assumed to be prevailing, and what we are given is just a 'photograph' at one instant in time.[5] When working on

[4] References to the Sraffa Papers, which are kept at Trinity College Library, Cambridge, most of them available online, are given hereafter following the catalogue classification.

[5] This is a disputed issue in the literature, beyond my scope here. For a recent and controversial discussion of this point, see Sinha (2016).

his equations, Sraffa was troubled by the idea of introducing a subjective element in the mechanism of price determination, in the shape of 'inducement' for capitalists to move from lower to higher rate of profit industries. In a 1931 manuscript, we read: 'The assumption (in the 2nd equations) that the rate of interest (surplus) is equal in different industries is too much [*sic*] rationalistic: it assumes that the capitalists are "perfect economic men", who *move* their capital accordingly' (D3/12/9:9).

This is not to say that Sraffa's vision excludes subjective or purely mental forces at work in the real world (such as expectations, beliefs or motivations) but only that these 'magnitudes' are neither observable nor measurable and so cannot form the basis of scientific explanations according to Sraffa's own epistemology. Among the notes taken between May and July 1928, we read: 'the recognition of the fact that the opinions of the actors have an influence must not lead the economist to believe that they are all the real facts themselves, or much less their objective explanation, as Marshall does' (D3/12/9/32).

In conclusion, while Marshall, Kahn and Keynes held that subjective elements – albeit not in the form of abstract rationality – need to be part of the *explanans* of the decision-making mechanism that lies behind market outcomes, Sraffa did not deem them necessary as far as the price mechanism was concerned but left open the possibility that norms and customs, embodying non-observable entities, exercise their influence in other parts of the analysis.

1.4 The Real versus the Imaginary World in Which Decisions Are Taken

Kahn dropped the strict 'maximising rule' altogether when analysing entrepreneurs' behaviour and investment decisions in financial markets. The existence of uncertainty and various degrees of conviction with which opinions are formed and held by individuals makes the decision process similar not to an optimum solution but rather to a condition reached when sufficiently strong motives to do otherwise are lacking.

Kahn is depicting a 'world in which different persons hold different views and none of them hold any views with complete conviction . . . a world of doubt and disagreement and one in which different persons not only take different views which are influenced by different degrees of conviction, but are sensitive to risk in different ways' (Kahn, 1954, pp. 235–236). Kahn contrasts it with 'an *imaginary* world of expectations held with unanimous and complete conviction' (Kahn, 1954, pp. 235–236, my italics).

In financial markets, we encounter two kinds of investors: those who hold definite expectations for the future of interest rates and those 'who do not have a clue' whether the rate of interest is going to increase or decrease. The same division also exists in the mind of an individual investor, who can have contradictory preferences and decide to hold money and securities at the same time, with no definite choice between the two. It is as if each individual investor always had two opinions – as first degree (best guess) and second degree (conviction) – on buying, selling or keeping securities as an alternative to money. While the first-degree opinion – that is, whether to be bullish or bearish according to the kind of forecast of the future trend in security prices – may be taken to point to the path to follow, the second-degree opinion is the doubt that clouds the forecast.

Thus, Kahn argues that a finite elasticity of the demand for money relative to the rate of interest is associated not only with the heterogeneity of expectations held by the public divided between bulls and bears but also with the lack of conviction individuals show in their own conjectures. It is as if bullish and bearish sentiments 'operated inside each person's mind, one being responsible for his holding securities and one for his holding money' (Kahn, 1954, p. 247).

It follows that the guiding behaviour of an individual cannot be represented as in the case of complete preferences, since the individual is confronted with several feasible positions which could be equally preferred; it is the degree of conviction of one's expectations of the future course of events which may alter the order of preferences and therefore the choice between money and securities.

As Dardi explained:

> In Kahn's approach the chosen position, although – one may assume – maximal in the individual preferences, does not necessarily dominate all the non-maximal positions that are feasible in the circumstances ... the fact that individuals, from the position they are in, do not find other feasible positions interesting, does not mean that if they were in one of these positions they would want to move towards the position where they in fact are. What we may say is that they prefer to retain the asset composition they have, not that they have the asset composition they prefer. (Dardi, 1994, p. 96)

Rational behaviour becomes the 'best possible action' in the circumstances, characterised – in the real world – by doubts about the reliability of one's own expectations.

1.5 Reasonableness[6]

Just as utilitarian calculus may not be the best rule for action in individual decision-making on investments, Keynes contended that it may prove equally unsuitable in other situations where following the rationality implied by economic theory might lead to very unsatisfactory outcomes.

The rational pursuit of individual interest in economics, according to the utilitarian creed, does not guarantee the collective good, which Keynes identified with full employment. It is an assumption that leads to a false notion, which Keynes identifies as the fallacy of composition. For instance, attempts to reduce real wages or increase the saving of individuals on the basis of an individual rationale will not achieve the aim if undertaken by all, since the aggregate prevails over the individual effect. Another example is when the level of aggregate demand is kept drastically low within a country to satisfy the concerns of the victor or creditor, leading to a deflationary potential for all the economies. Thus, lack of reasonableness leads to consequences that are not only morally reprehensible but also economically disastrous for anyone who has sought guidance solely from the individual point of view.

Keynes rejected utilitarianism, both in ethics and in politics, nor did he endorse consequentialism in his ethical philosophy, but he accepted it in his political philosophy, the purpose of which, he believed, was to provide reasons for action. According to Keynes, the goal of an ethically rational society could be achieved by overcoming the economic and moral obstacles that encumbered contemporary society. Keynes's appeal to overcome self-interest as the sole guide to action was made in the context of both internal and external economic problems. As far as full-employment policy was concerned, he endeavoured to persuade his 'countrymen and the world at large to change their traditional doctrines and, by taking better thought, to remove the curse of unemployment' (*CWK*, XXVI, p.16). In the case of post–First and

[6] This section draws on Marcuzzo (2010), (2018).

Second World War scenarios, he fought to persuade governments that it was 'only by a more comprehensive settlement, which attempts to offer everyone what is reasonable, and so far as we can make it fair, that the financial consequences of the war can be liquidated' (*CWK*, XXIV, pp. 291–292).

Keynes systematically applied the term *reasonable*, often in contrast with the reasons of the victor or creditor, to a guideline *not* characterised by utilitarian calculation, which may prove only apparently to be in the individual interest. Thus, reasonable action is guided by judgement, taking into account contingent, mutable circumstances as far as our knowledge can encompass the facts and it conforms to goals that are attainable only by moving beyond individualistic motivation or utilitarian calculation.

The same term was used by John Rawls in defining the characteristics of a plural and *just* society. In his book *Political Liberalism* we find this definition: 'The reasonable is an element of the idea of society as a system of fair cooperation and that its fair terms be reasonable for all to accept is part of its idea of reciprocity' (Rawls, 1993, p. 58).

But how exactly are we to take the term *reasonable*? Jurgen Habermas interprets it as distinguishing between those who accept the principle of *fairness and cooperation* and those who act *rationally* on the basis of their *own* (i.e., individual) conception of what is *good and just*. Thus, being *reasonable* is a moral quality lacking in those who behave in a solely rational way. To quote Rawls again: 'What rational agents lack is the particular form of moral sensibility that underlies the desire to engage in fair cooperation as such, and to do so on terms that others as equals might reasonably be expected to endorse' (Rawls, 1993, p. 51). This is, also according to Habermas, the source of the distinction between moral and ethical questions (Habermas, 1995, p. 125).

Questions of justice or moral questions lead to justifiable answers – justifiable in the sense of rational acceptability – because they are concerned with what, from an ideally expanded perspective, is in the equal interest of all. Ethical questions, by contrast, do not lend themselves to such impartial treatment because they refer to what, from the first-person perspective, is in the long run good for me or for us – even if this is not equally good for all. The sense Keynes attributes to the term *reasonable* shows a strong analogy with the quality described by

Rawls and interpreted by Habermas as *moral*, but it is anchored on the structure of his economic theory.

1.6 Possible Objections[7]

Having offered some examples that, I believe, may bear out Pasinetti's claim that 'The whole [Cambridge] school always showed a strong aversion to a purely imaginary world of rationally behaving individuals' (Pasinetti, 2007, p. 220), perhaps we should also consider the objections that may be (and in some cases have in fact been) raised against this idea.

First of all, it may be argued that it is not the assumption of rationality or of optimisation *per se* that is to be rejected, but their application to unsuitable contexts, where uncertainty and limited information dominate; the approach taken by Kahn and Keynes to financial markets can be seen as an attempt to demonstrate the unsuitability of those assumptions to explain the behaviour of speculators and investors. Marshall's attention to other factors to explain what guides business behaviour might also be interpreted not as a rejection of the rationality principle but as indicative of its limited explicatory power.

An objection to the interpretation of the profit maximisation rule as a 'trial and error' method and as typical of the Cambridge approach is that a number of neoclassical economists also seldom interpret the optimising behaviour as actual, conscious calculation by economic agents. This point was made clear by Fritz Machlup (1946) in his famous article 'Marginal Analysis and Empirical Research', where he stressed that in neoclassical economics trial and error rather than a strict calculus is the assumed pricing method. He writes, 'The business man who equates marginal net revenue productivity and marginal factor cost when he decides how many to employ need not engage in higher mathematics, geometry, or clairvoyance ... he would simply rely on his sense or his 'feel' of the situation (Machlup 1946, p. 535).'

He emphasized that it is not with businessmen's rationalization of their actions but with their actual behaviour that marginal analysis is concerned: 'The technical terms used in the explanation of an action need not have any part in the thinking of the acting individual.' (Machlup, 1946, p. 537)

[7] I am grateful to Dardi for making me take these objections into consideration.

Nevertheless, it seems to me that the 'trial and error' message gets lost in the constructions of models for the purpose of empirical testing, which is the standard approach in neoclassical economics, since the theoretical underpinnings of those models and their application in practice boil down to the solution of a standard max profit exercise. So the caveats and the awareness that precise calculation is neither in the minds of the agents nor the realistic representation of their behaviour cannot be taken as an opening to less stringent assumptions, since they do not find their way into the working of these models.

Coming to the notion of Keynes's 'animal spirits' as an alternative explanation of the guiding principle of entrepreneurial action, I think it should not be applied as a general rule, since the prospective yields of an investment retain a role in decision-making. I believe that investment decisions cannot be anchored on vague, psychological inclinations; and, in fact, recent interpretations of Keynes's theory may be seriously misleading (see, e.g., Akerlof and Shiller [2009]).

Finally, to the argument that I have put forward in relation to Keynes's and Kahn's theory – that the existence of uncertainty and various degrees of conviction with which opinions are formed and held by individuals makes the decision process similar not to an optimum solution but rather to a condition reached when sufficiently strong motives to do otherwise are lacking – it may be retorted that it is not a confutation of the maximisation rule but only a specification of its form. When the ordering is not completed, choices may be maximal in the individual preferences, although they do not necessarily dominate all the non-maximal positions that are feasible in the circumstances. So uncertainty and conflicting expectations may not be the reasons to dismiss rationality as a principle guiding individual action, since they simply reveal its more restricted applicability.

However, I believe that the two notions of rationality (according to Keynes and according to standard theory) should be distinguished. It is not just a matter of the context to which it applies or the completeness of the set of preferences but the fact of the rationality principle being embedded in the utilitarian approach within the neoclassical approach, while in Keynes there is no such connection.

Finally, on the notion of reasonableness to be contrasted to the notion of rationality, it may be objected that this is not something very different from the classic case of the prisoner's dilemma, which demonstrates that when there is conflict between individual rationality and collective rationality it can be resolved only by moral commitments or social sanctions. I agree that by following the game theory approach we get the same results and implications; but in Keynes's case, there is a much clearer focus on the consequences of decisions guided by self-interest and the role that persuasion can have in preventing their occurrences is that of a protagonist.

1.7 Conclusions

The Marshallian approach to economic behaviour as guided by customs and habits setting limits to the crude maximisation through marginal analysis was inherited by Kahn and Keynes, who accepted it in its modified form, namely, not as exact calculation but as the outcome of a trial and error method. Although they did not endorse Sraffa's rejection of its validity for price determination and income distribution, they shared the common objective of placing reality, rather than abstract rationality, at the centre of their analysis as the principle guiding behaviour. In other words, what characterises the approach is a vision of individuals less stereotyped than mere maximising machines. This means that there is room for rationality in depicting political and economic decisions, as long as we interpret it as constrained by limited knowledge, uncertainty.

On the contrary, rationality and optimal behaviour are twin concepts which are at the core of neoclassical economics, the latter being the consequence of the former; both presuppose perfect knowledge and a complete set of preferences, so that inconsistencies in choices can be ruled out. This is what I believe Pasinetti means by 'abstract' rationality. Pasinetti explicitly refers to Keynes as exemplary of the approach to analysing economic behaviour, never imputing it to abstract economic agents but always to individuals who have specific functions and characteristics, where customs, conventions and habits play an important part. Moreover, consumers, entrepreneurs or speculators always make their decisions in the face of uncertainty and limited knowledge, so their behaviour cannot be fully described as guided by an optimising rationality. Economic choices require evaluation of the available information, which is often contradictory or ambiguous and almost always offers insufficient evidence to predict the future course of events. In each specific case, the evidence we collect bears a different 'weight' in the argument we use to make our choices, on the basis of our knowledge and experience.

However, decision-making in a context of uncertainty does not imply the impossibility of making decisions according to reason, although the reason involved here is not the rationality employed in orthodox economic theory where, for instance, consumers are said to pursue their individual maximising utility over an infinite time horizon and with full knowledge of possible outcomes and perfect foresight.

Once these and other similar assumptions are discarded – being seen as belonging to an imaginary world, not a real one – the concept of rationality may still be used to describe behaviour but in a much more circumscribed sense. It may give rise to trial and error methods, conditional guessing or reasonableness, following a tradition which – bypassing the neoclassical parables – goes back to Classical Political Economy. In fact, the possibility of coupling the Cambridge approach and Classical Political Economy in the construction of a paradigm alternative to neoclassical economy has been an article of faith for Pasinetti, pursued throughout a lifetime's work.

References

Akerlof G. A. and Shiller R. J. (2009) *Animal Spirits: How Human Psychology Drives the Economy, and Why It Matters for Global Capitalism*, Princeton, Princeton University Press.

Becattini G. (1962) *Il concetto di industria e la teoria del valore*, Torino, Boringhieri.

Dardi M. (1994) 'Kahn's Theory of Liquidity Preference and Monetary Policy', in *Cambridge Journal of Economics*, 18, pp. 91–106.

Habermas J. (1995) 'Reconciliation through the Public Use of Reason: Remarks on John Rawls's Political Liberalism', in *The Journal of Philosophy*, 92, pp. 109–131.

Kahn R. F. (1952) 'Oxford Studies in Price Mechanism', in *Economic Journal*, 62, pp. 119–130.

(1954) 'Some Notes on Liquidity Preference', in *Manchester School of Economic and Social Studies*, 22, pp. 229–257.

(1989) *The Economics of the Short Period*, London, Macmillan.

Keynes J. M. (1971–1989) *The Collected Writings of John Maynard Keynes (CWK)*, Johnson E. and Moggridge D. E. (eds.) London, Macmillan.

CWK, VII, *The General Theory of Employment, Interest, and Money*.

CWK, XXIV, *Activities 1944–1946: The Transition to Peace*.

CWK, XXVI, *Activities 1941–1946: Shaping the Post-War World: Bretton Woods and Reparations*.

Lawson T. (1997) *Economics and Reality*, London, Routledge.

Machlup F. A. (1946) 'Marginal Analysis and Empirical Research', in *American Economic Review*, 36, pp. 519–554.
Mäki U. (2009) 'Realistic Realism about Unrealistic Models', in Ross D. and Kincaid H. (eds.) *The Oxford Handbook of Philosophy of Economics*, Oxford, Oxford University Press.
Marcuzzo M. C. (2010) 'Reason and Reasonableness in Keynes: Rereading *The Economic Consequences of the Peace*', in Arnon A. Weinblatt J. and Young W. (eds.) *Perspectives on Keynesian Economics*, Heidelberg, Springer, pp. 35–52.
(2014) 'Luigi Pasinetti and the Cambridge Economists', in *History of Economics Review*, 60, pp. 15–29.
(2018) 'Following in Shionoya's Footsteps: Perfectionism and Consequentialism in Keynes's Political Philosophy', in *History of Economic Thought*, 59, pp. 168–180.
(2020) 'Joan Robinson e la critica all'equilibrio', in Parisi D. Orsi C. E. (eds.) *Economia al femminile. Donne, lavoro e impresa in una prospettiva storica*, Firenze, Edizioni Nerbini, pp. 199–217.
Marcuzzo M. C. and Rosselli A. (2011) 'Sraffa and His Arguments against Marginism', in *Cambridge Journal of Economics*, 35, pp. 219–231.
Marcuzzo M. C. and Sanfilippo E. (2007) 'Profit Maximization in the Cambridge Tradition of Economics', in Forstater M. Mongiovi G. and Pressman S. (eds.) *Post-Keynesian Macroeconomics Economics: Essays in Honour of Ingrid Rima*, London, Routledge, pp. 70–86.
Marshall A. (1919) *Industry and Trade*, London, Macmillan.
(1920) *Principles of Economics*, London, Macmillan.
Pasinetti L. L. (2007) *Keynes and the Cambridge Keynesians: A 'Revolution in Economics' to Be Accomplished*, Cambridge, Cambridge University Press.
Rawls J. (1993) *Political Liberalism: The John Dewey Essays in Philosophy*, vol. IV, New York, Columbia University Press.
Roncaglia A. (2009) 'Keynes and Probability: An Assessment', in *The European Journal of the History of Economic Thought*, 16, pp. 489–510.
Sinha A. (2016) *A Revolution in Economic Theory: The Economics of Piero Sraffa*, Basel, Springer.
Sraffa P. (1930) 'Increasing Returns and the Representative Firm: A Symposium. A criticism – a Rejoinder', in *Economic Journal*, 40, pp. 89–93.

2 Economic Logic with Internal Consistency (and Not Only Formal Rigour)

Realism and Internal Consistency in Piero Sraffa

NERI SALVADORI AND
RODOLFO SIGNORINO*

2.1 Introduction

Looking back at the state of the academic debate in economics in the two decades of the so-called Great Moderation (Bernanke, 2004) before the Great Financial Crisis (Mishkin, 2010), an impartial observer could safely claim that the anti-Keynesian counter-revolution led by Robert Lucas, Thomas Sargent and associates came to dominate the academic scene (De Vroey, 2016, ch. 9). By contrast, as noted by Luigi Pasinetti (2007), John Maynard Keynes's and the Cambridge Keynesians' revolution is a mission still to be accomplished more than seventy years after the publication of the *General Theory*. From a policy perspective, the three decades between WWII and the end of the Bretton Woods system witnessed a hegemony of Keynesian economics: 'We are all Keynesians now', as a reluctant Milton Friedman admitted in a famous letter to *Time* in 1966 (Claar and Forster, 2019, ch. 6). Nevertheless, from a pure theory perspective, it is highly dubious that Keynes's economics ever became the ruling paradigm. For many theoretically inclined economists living in those years, the hiatus between micro- and macroeconomics was a distressful issue (Snowdon and Vane, 2005, p. 21). With the benefit of hindsight, the IS-LM-Phillips curve model may be defined as a general equilibrium toy model with slippery microfoundations and a very limited role, if any, for agents' expectations and dynamics. The swift triumph of Lucas's approach over the academic citadel and the apparent incapacity of

* We wish to thank Saverio Maria Fratini, Heinz D. Kurz, Maria Cristina Marcuzzo, Andrea Salanti and Paolo Trabucchi for their comments on a previous draft of this chapter. Usual caveats apply.

the Keynesian paradigm to reach full maturity and the status of a fully-fledged alternative to mainstream invites reflection. For Pasinetti, plausible explanations are adverse external circumstances (Keynes's health was seriously impaired after he suffered a heart attack in 1937 and his time and mental energies were increasingly absorbed by his duties as a civil servant during the years of war and in the aftermath of the peace), unwise behaviour by the leading Cambridge Keynesians (unable to cooperate and develop a consistent and unified corpus of economic doctrines, unable to attract or keep the best young economists of their times and, most of all, unable to plan their succession after retirement) and over-emphasis of the *pars destruens* over the *pars costruens* of the Keynesian enterprise (Pasinetti, 2007, pp. 33ff. and pp. 199ff.).

In our view, this last issue is the most significant one: following the lead of Thomas Kuhn's investigation of normal science and scientific revolutions, Pasinetti argues that when facing empirical evidence defying explanation within the accepted paradigm most scientists decide to definitively abandon the paradigm they are working in only when an alternative paradigm is available. In short, it takes a new paradigm to beat a ruling paradigm: even a thoroughgoing critique won't do.

This is one of the main reasons why Pasinetti devotes a 'Postlude' (Pasinetti, 2007, pp. 217–237) to support his advocacy of an alternative economic paradigm. Pasinetti identifies a list of nine essential building-blocks which, in his view, are distinctively Keynesian. The list is the following:

(1) Reality (and not simply abstract rationality) as the starting point of economic theory.
(2) Economic logic with internal consistency (and not only formal rigour).
(3) Malthus and the Classics (not Walras and the Marginalists) as the major inspiring source in the history of economic thought.
(4) Non-ergodic (in place of stationary, timeless) economic systems.
(5) Causality vs. interdependence.
(6) Macroeconomics before microeconomics.
(7) Disequilibrium and instability (not equilibrium) as the normal state of the industrial economies.
(8) Necessity of finding an appropriate analytical framework for dealing with technical change and economic growth.
(9) A strong, deeply felt social concern.

Pasinetti is not the only scholar working outside the mainstream who has tried to identify the common features of an alternative approach to economic theorising. According to Marc Lavoie (2014, pp. 12–13), economic orthodoxy is characterised by (i) instrumentalism; (ii) hyper model-consistent rationality, optimising agents; (iii) individualism, atomicism; (iv) exchange, allocation, scarcity and (v) unfettered markets. By contrast, the various heterodox traditions in economics share the following common traits: (a) realism; (b) environment-consistent rationality, satisficing agent; (c) holism, organicism; (d) production, growth, abundance and (e) regulated markets.

The two lists exhibit some significant overlapping. Both authors give the issue of realism pride of place. The emphasis on realism may also explain why Pasinetti appears to hold that formal rigour and internal logical consistency are not one and same thing and he appears to rank internal consistency higher than formal rigour *per se*.

Of course, most contemporary economists are keen to present their work as internally consistent and formally rigorous. So, what is the difference between orthodoxy and heterodoxy that Pasinetti considered so important? According to Pasinetti, 'Keynes, Kahn and Joan Robinson always stressed that economics is an art, which requires qualitative judgements about what sometimes appears seemingly contradictory evidence; it requires intuition to organise a maze of ideas and phenomena into a coherent whole' (Pasinetti, 2007, p. 221).

What is an art in any science is the choice of the assumptions and not the achievement of the results. Another 'artistic' element within scientific work is the path followed from the 'abstract' to the 'concrete', that is, from a very simple and highly idealised model to more encompassing and less idealised ones. Léon Walras, for instance, in the *Éléments d'Économie Politique Pure*, started from a pure exchange economy; then he introduced production without produced means of production, that is, capital goods; finally, he analysed capital goods and their accumulation. By contrast, Piero Sraffa, in *Production of Commodities by Means of Commodities*, started from an economy in which all existing commodities are produced by means of themselves in a self-replacing state with no choice of technique and no joint production; then he considered the possibility of production with a surplus; then he identified the commodity inputs necessary to pay wages with wages themselves and introduced the fact that wages may include part of the surplus; then he introduced joint production, fixed capital and land; finally, he investigated the choice of technique issue. The analytical consequences deriving from these two different paths are paramount even if Walras ended up analysing an economy where production is carried out (also) by means of produced means of production, and Sraffa ended up analysing economies in which production is carried out (also) by means of scarce natural resources. Following Walras's path, scarcity is the driving force behind economic outcomes, whereas following Sraffa's path, reproducibility is. Hence, the choice of the assumptions and the choice of the path to follow for the process of de-idealisation, or successive concretisation,[1] are unquestionably among the cornerstone of a theory.

Sraffa's role in the Cambridge approach to economic theorising is key. Accordingly, we aim to contribute to the analysis of the themes of realism and internal consistency beyond formal rigour within the so-called Cambridge Tradition in economics (Harcourt, 2012) by focusing on Sraffa's thought on these issues.

As is well known, during his life Sraffa never published a work explicitly devoted to epistemological issues. This fact should not be interpreted as a sign of Sraffa's lack of interest in such concerns. From Sraffa's unpublished manuscripts – kept at the Wren Library of Trinity College, Cambridge, and from the books of his personal library – we see that Sraffa had a strong interest in questions of philosophy of science (Kurz and Salvadori, 2005). Therefore, a reconstruction of Sraffa's epistemological theory can only be conjectural and must not leave out of consideration his unpublished manuscripts. In a previous work (Salvadori and Signorino, 2007), we analysed a specific aspect of Sraffa's epistemology, the threefold relationship between 'economic reality', 'the economist' and 'economic theory', and we focused almost exclusively on the published material and used unpublished manuscripts only sparingly to show that our statements based on the published contributions were confirmed by, or at least consistent with, the unpublished material. In this chapter, we shift our attention to a

[1] According to Leszek Nowak, 'the structure of a scientific theory t is thus given by a sequence of models M^k, M^{k-i}, . . . , M^i, A^{mi}, where M^k is the most abstract model with k idealising conditions, and M^{k-i}, . . ., M^i are its successive concretisations. Lastly, A^{mi} is an approximation of the least abstract of these models, M^i, to empirical reality' (Nowak, 1994, p. 20). Yet, as noted by Francesco Coniglione, 'this stage of ultimate "concretization" is never reached in science, so recourse to procedures of approximation is always necessary' (Coniglione, 1994, p. 20).

somewhat related theme, the relevance of the realism of the premises in the assessment of a theory, and we make extensive use of unpublished manuscripts, while being aware of the necessary caution in using material that an author has not published. (Caution is even more significant in the case of an author such as Sraffa who is particularly careful with his choice of words and extremely reluctant to publish anything except after a long period of reflection.)

2.2 Sraffa's Strategy of Criticism

From an instrumentalist point of view, a scientific theory is just an instrument to systematise experience and to make accurate predictions. Accordingly, instrumentalism allows for agnosticism as it concerns the truth status of scientific propositions (Mäki, 1998). To paraphrase the famous dictum by Deng Xiaoping, it doesn't matter if a theory is true or false so long as it catches data (at least better than available alternatives).

According to our reconstruction of his epistemology, Sraffa, during his entire intellectual carrier, adopted a radically different philosophical standpoint. In our view, Sraffa's criticism of Alfred Marshall's theory of value (Sraffa, 1925 [1998], 1926, 1930), Hayek's theory of business cycle (Sraffa, 1932a, 1932b), up to his intervention at the Corfù Conference on the theory of capital (Lutz and Hague, 1961, pp. 305–306) are all based on a common epistemological foundation that may be summarised as follows: the explanatory value of a given theory depends on its ability to select among the various (potentially uncountable) economic forces and mechanisms in action in a given situation, that is, the one(s) that the theorist holds to be the most relevant and that provide a logically consistent description of the chosen mechanism(s).[2] No theoretical explanation of a given economic phenomenon may be considered acceptable if it is based on ill-defined theoretical notions such as the notions of variable returns in a Marshallian partial equilibrium competitive model, the notion of neutral money and individual saving decisions in the Hayekian model of business cycle and the notion of a given quantity of capital in the

[2] On Sraffa's views on the notion of causality in economics see Marcuzzo and Rosselli (2020).

neoclassical theory of income distribution. Ill-defined theoretical notions stand in the way of an exact theoretical measurement of the magnitudes under investigation and thus prevent the theory from being correctly applied to the phenomena it was designed to explain.

Accordingly, Sraffa appears to follow a two-stage strategy of critique: first, a rigorous logical reconstruction of the theory under scrutiny, with a particular focus on the identification of its explicit and implicit assumptions; second, accurate description of the theoretical domain of the theory, that is, the field of the empirical phenomena that the theory, once logically reconstructed, is able to explain.

The archetype of this modus operandi is Sraffa's 1925 essay. In sections 2, 3 and 4, he rigorously reconstructed Marshall's theory of increasing costs, decreasing costs and constant cost industries, respectively, and then, in section 5, he pointed out that, in order to avoid internal inconsistencies, Marshall's doctrine of variable returns industries *inevitably* requires some further assumptions, *not to be found in Marshall's original texts*. For Sraffa, the case of constant costs is the only empirical domain logically compatible with the explicit assumptions of Marshall's theory, partial equilibrium and perfect competition. In order to extend the empirical domain of Marshall's theory to the case of decreasing costs sectors, it is necessary to introduce a further assumption; that is, decreasing costs are generated only by economies external to the individual firms of a given sector but internal to the sector itself. Any other assumption concerning the genesis of decreasing costs is incompatible with the explicit assumptions of Marshallian theory: firm's internal economies are incompatible with perfect competition while economies external to the sector under scrutiny are incompatible with partial equilibrium. Likewise, in order to extend the empirical domain of Marshallian theory to the case of increasing costs sectors, it is necessary to introduce a further assumption; that is, increasing costs are generated solely by the fact that a given sector employs all of a given factor of production. Any other assumption concerning the genesis of increasing costs is incompatible with the explicit assumptions of Marshall's theory. In conclusion, for Sraffa, the empirical domain of the Marshallian theory, once all the sufficient and non-contradictory assumptions have been made explicit, is not compatible with the most empirically relevant cases of non-constant costs: firms' internal economies, scale economies external to the sector and factors of production employed in different sectors (Signorino, 2000, 2001; see also Freni and Salvadori, 2013).[3]

Accordingly, Sraffa's reconstruction of the Marshallian partial equilibrium model of competitive markets is targeted to carefully identify the boundaries of its theoretical domain, that is, the set of empirical situations that are logically feasible within the model. In other words, the question addressed by Sraffa was the following: Which potentially observable facts concerning the industrial sectors of a given economy may be consistently analysed by means of the Marshallian partial equilibrium competitive model, *once all the various assumptions necessary to make that model logically consistent have been explicitly stated and their implications carefully spelled out and assessed*? Hence, Sraffa demonstrated that Marshall's theoretical model, once reconstructed in a logically consistent way, is endowed with a theoretical domain that is much narrower than most Cambridge economists of the mid-1920s were inclined to think. That is *the* reason why, for Sraffa, the Marshallian boxes on returns to scale are empty, as reported by John Harold Clapham (1922).

This modus operandi is made explicit in Sraffa's contribution to the 1930 *Economic Journal* Symposium on Increasing Returns and the Representative Firm:

[3] Obviously, theorists who want to tackle the issue of firms' internal economies or of scale economies external to a given sector and factors of production employed in different sectors could choose to drop either the perfect competition assumption or the partial equilibrium method and develop a theory of imperfect competition or a general equilibrium model, respectively. Sraffa was fully aware of both alternatives. As is well known, he initially followed the first route but soon switched to the second. Apart from his contribution to the *Economic Journal* Symposium on increasing returns (Sraffa, 1930), Sraffa did not further participate in the debate on the Marshallian theory of value. He rather focused on an analysis of 'the process of diffusion of profits throughout the various stages of production and of the process of forming a normal level of profits throughout all the industries of a country . . . [a problem] beyond the scope of this article' (Sraffa, 1926, p. 550; see also Eatwell and Panico, 1987 and Kurz and Salvadori, 1995, pp. 415–416). Accordingly, Alessandro Roncaglia (1978, 1983, 1991, 1998), among others, maintains that imperfect competition was but an ephemeral detour from the mainstream of Sraffa's research program. For Roncaglia, the 1925 paper would rather constitute the prelude to a radical criticism of the neoclassical theoretical approach, a criticism fully developed only thirty-five years later in *Production of Commodities*. Gary Mongiovi (1996) contends that Sraffa genuinely saw imperfect competition as a way to rescue Marshallian theory from practical irrelevance even if, by late 1920s, he saw there was another way: to ditch Marshall and to go back to the Classical economists.

I am trying to find what are the assumptions implicit in Marshall's theory; if Mr. Robertson regards them as extremely unreal, I sympathise with him. We seem to be agreed that the theory cannot be interpreted in a way which makes it logically self-consistent and, at the same time, reconciles it with the facts it sets out to explain. Mr. Robertson's remedy is to discard mathematics, and he suggests that my remedy is to discard the facts; perhaps I ought to have explained that, in the circumstances, I think it is Marshall's theory that should be discarded. (Sraffa, 1930, p. 93)

In the same vein, two years later, in his reply to Frederick von Hayek, Sraffa focuses on the issue of realism as concerns assumptions and the issue of internal consistency as concerns the defective explanatory power of Hayek's monetary model of the business cycle:

Dr. Hayek will allow me not to take seriously his questions as to what I 'really believe'. Nobody could believe that anything that logically follows from such fantastic assumptions is true in reality. But I admit the abstract possibility that conclusions deduced from them by faulty reasoning may, by a lucky accident, prove quite plausible. (Sraffa, 1932b, p. 250)

Once more, Sraffa made explicit the implicit assumptions required to generate the conclusions of Hayek's theory and assessed the empirical domain of the logically reconstructed Hayekian theory. The term 'fantastic' used by Sraffa may sound ambiguous since several meanings may be attached to this word. Such semantic ambiguity may obscure the exact sense in which Sraffa rejected the conclusions of Hayekian theory, once logically reconstructed, as devoid of explanatory power. In Sraffa's unpublished manuscripts, however, the passage in question has a different wording:

H. in his reply slips into the belief that his assumptions represent reality: it is necessary to emphasize (+ I have been wrong in not doing it) that they are *extremely unreal* – whatever conclusions may be drawn they have no practical bearing. The argument can only vert on whether he has deduced consistently – which he has not done. By starting from far-fetched assumptions + arguing inconsistently he may have reached conclusions which may sound plausible or at least not impossible. This result he could not have reached if he had argued correctly from his ass.[umptions], or incorrectly from reality. Two errors may partly cancel one another. Thus when he asks me 'whether I believe etc.' he misses the point: I do not believe any of the conclusions I have drawn – I only believe they follow from his ass.[umptions]. (D3/9/122, emphasis added)

Thus, Sraffa rejected Hayek's theory because, in his view, it is based on 'extremely unreal' assumptions – note that it is the very same expression already used to evaluate Marshall's assumptions in the final passage of his 'Rejoinder' to Robertson – and its apparent fit with the facts it is designed to explain is only due to a lack of internal consistency (and a lucky accident!). Once more, Sraffa appears to assess the explanatory value of a given economic theory by checking the realism of all its assumptions, whether explicit or implicit, and its internal logical consistency.

2.3 Sraffa's Assessment of the Successive Approximation Strategy

Closely connected with the realism of the premises issue is the distinction between the 'whole truth' and 'nothing but the truth' and the role of isolating abstraction in economics (see Mäki, 1992, 2005). Paraphrasing the famous aphorism by George Box, 'all models are wrong, but some models are useful', we may say that a necessary condition for a model to be useful is that it is wrong, *rectius* violates the 'whole truth' requirement by isolating some of the mechanisms that allegedly are in action in the 'world out there'. As Karl Popper put it, 'any model, whether in physics or in the social sciences, must be an oversimplification. It must omit much, and it must overemphasize much' (Popper, 1982, p. 361, in Hoover, 2017, p. 187). Theorists deliberately choose to violate both 'truth' requirements when they propose a first-approximation model, that is, when they make use of heuristic assumptions (Musgrave, 1981) or first-step assumptions (Mäki, 2000). From this perspective, it is interesting to investigate how Sraffa reconciled a strategy of successive approximations with its realistic approach to theory assessment. In the 1926 *Economic Journal* paper we read:

> as a simple way of approaching the problem of competitive value, the old and now obsolete theory which makes it dependent on the cost of production alone appears to hold its ground as the best available. This first approximation, as far as it goes, is as important as it is useful: it emphasises the fundamental factor, namely, the predominant influence of cost of production in the determination of the normal value of commodities, while at the same time it does not lead us astray when we desire to study in greater detail the conditions under which exchange takes place in particular cases, for it does

not conceal from us the fact that we cannot find the elements required for this purpose within the limits of its assumptions. (Sraffa, 1926, p. 541)

From this passage we highlight the following items:

(1) Sraffa has no qualm against a strategy of successive approximations. Therefore, Marshall's symmetrical theory of value considered as a fist-step approximation model is not to be rejected *per se*. This does not imply, however, that it is also a useful first-approximation model, able to generate a second-step approximation. Put briefly, a strategy of successive approximations is a kind of investment on the future. It means investing scarce time and intellectual resources today in view of an expected return tomorrow in terms of a more general model than the one developed today. Hence, it is necessary to carefully evaluate today what is the likelihood that subsequent approximations will materialise in the foreseeable future.
(2) For Sraffa, the main task of a good model is the selection of the most relevant mechanism(s) that operate(s) in the situation under scrutiny (all the other potentially relevant mechanisms are provisionally frozen in a more or less well-specified *ceteris paribus* or *ceteris absentibus* clause: see Salanti, 2014). Hence, just by abstracting from what the theorist assumes to be the less relevant factors, a model is false since it violates the 'whole truth' requirement, at least. As concerns specifically the theory of long-run competitive equilibrium prices, while it is plainly false to claim that cost of production is the *only* factor determining it, yet, for Sraffa (1926), it is possible to claim that, as concerns first approximation models, the Classical one is still the best available.[4]

[4] In the 1925 paper, Sraffa claimed that 'it can be said that all classical writers accept implicitly, as an obvious fact, that cost is independent of quantity, and they do not bother to discuss the contrary hypothesis' (Sraffa, 1925 [1998], p. 325). Similarly, in an oft-quoted letter to Keynes dated 6 June 1926, Sraffa wrote that 'Ricardo's theory . . . implies universal constant returns' (D3/6, p. 2.f.2. recto). By contrast, in *Production of Commodities*, Sraffa interpreted the Classical theory of value in the light of his assumption of given quantities. Indeed, from an analysis of the unpublished manuscripts, it is possible to argue that while Sraffa never changed his mind on the explanatory value of the Classical theory of value, his interpretation of the analytical structure of the latter significantly changed between 1927 and 1928 (see, in particular, Garegnani, 2005; see also Kurz and Salvadori, 2005, and Fratini, 2018).

(3) It is of great importance to evaluate the empirical domain of a first-approximation theory. When theorists look for successive approximations concerning empirical situations that do not fall within the empirical domain of the first approximation theory, then they must decide whether to make use of a different set of assumptions.

In Sraffa's unpublished papers in the Wren Library of Trinity College, Cambridge, we find an undated folder 'Lectures notes on economic theory' (D2/1).[5] It consists of a few sheets of paper written in Italian. Sraffa may have drafted these papers in the 1920s or early 1930s when it was natural for him to think and write in his mother language. (Later on, he progressively slipped into English mixed sometimes with typical Italian expressions, especially when he was temporarily in Italy.) The first sheet bears the title: 'Teoria economica: che cos'è?' ('Economic theory: what is it?', our translation). It deserves to be quoted in full:

> Reality is extremely complicated: the reasons why society produces, consumes, attributes certain values to certain things, etc., are endless: if we wanted to examine them all, taking into account all the conditions that determine economic facts, we would have to go down to analyse the particular conditions of each individual agent, his tastes, needs, etc. (e.g. how are bus ticket prices determined? Why did I take the bus this morning? etc., etc. What is common among all bus users? This is the essential point) Not only that, but the price of each commodity is influenced by the prices of all the other commodities (if bread is more expensive the bus drivers must be paid more and then the ticket price is to be increased) and then our research would extend more and more, so that for every little question we would have to investigate the whole universe. To know the causes of the price of a commodity would take so much knowledge to fill 1000 volumes! This is evidently impossible, there would be no human mind capable of containing and coordinating all that news, and then we would fall back into the confusion, into the ignorance from which we started. (D2/1, p. 1 recto, our translation)
>
> The task of the theory is to reduce those 1000 vols. to 10 pages: not to save paper, but to be able to embrace them all with a single glance, to see all the relationships together, to be able to coordinate them. The theory consists in this: to summarise, to simplify, that is to generalise. But every generalisation

[5] Sraffa's unpublished manuscripts may be accessed freely online at https://janus.lib.cam.ac.uk/db/ node.xsp?id=EAD%2FGBR%2F0016%2FSRAFFA.

is a loss of exactitude, therefore a departure from reality. This explains the possibility of different theories to explain the same phenomenon; it is a different appreciation of the importance of the facts that must be considered, and of those that must be set aside: but each theory contains a part of truth and a part of error. It is a matter of choosing the least inexact one. Or in some cases the most useful one - the one that best serves for the study of a certain issue may not serve for the study of another (e.g. price variations 1° dependent on monetary causes 2° dependent on production conditions). Scepticism that is always necessary in considering economic theories should not be pushed to excess, however, to discard them all as useless – otherwise one falls into ignorance, into the impossibility of understanding what is happening. Theories are a help. Difference with the exact sciences: these can generalise by neglecting a few important things: economics, as soon as it generalises, neglects important things. This comes from the complexity of facts and the backward state of science. (D2/1, p. 2 recto, our translation)

To accomplish its task, a theory must necessarily be unrealistic in the sense of violating both the 'whole truth' and the 'nothing but the truth' requirements. The theory must not only summarise and simplify (and thus it is at best a partial truth), it must also generalise by isolating the elements common to a plurality of different empirical situations. Hence, the theory distorts reality because it emphasises a part of reality. Sraffa here comes close to the concept of 'isolation' by means of idealisation, omission, vertical and horizontal isolation (see Mäki, 1992). Moreover, for Sraffa, different epistemic goals generally require the theorist to select different theories (i.e., theories generated by different isolation processes). It should be noted that, given an empirical phenomenon to be studied, the criterion for which a more exact theory (more approximate to reality) is to be preferred to a less exact one is to admit, even if implicitly, the legitimacy of a successive approximation strategy. Finally, Sraffa hints at what is today called the underdetermination of theory by data, that is, the possibility that the same empirical phenomenon may be explained by more than one theory. In Section 2.4, we highlight the relevance of this fact for an assessment of Sraffa's realistic epistemology.

2.4 Sraffa's Realism

Once again, we start with a quotation. It is taken from folder D1/45, 'Probable form of demand curves and effort'. It is dated pre-1928.

The correspondence between the facts observed and the conclusions of the theory [which draws its inspiration from the fundamental symmetry of supply and demand forces and considers (based on the hypothesis) that the essential causes concerning the determination of the price of a commodity can be simplified and grouped in a way that they may be represented by a couple of intersecting collective supply and demand curves] is so satisfactory that it is easy to understand how the theory quickly gained the consensus of the majority of economists.

Of course, it is recognised that there are divergences between theory and reality, but this fact does not destroy its value, for it is in the very nature of any theory. A theory is acceptable when it highlights the essential characteristics and takes into account the dominant forces of equilibrium, even if it then neglects the minor complications and frictions that delay or slightly modify the effects of the major forces, without substantially changing them.

But it is not enough that the conclusions of the theory are confirmed by observation: it is equally important that the path by which they are arrived at is the same both in theory and in reality. (D1/45, p. 4 recto, Sraffa's emphasis, our translation)

Any economic theory involves a process of isolation of some well-defined mechanisms that are assumed to play a fundamental role in determining the equilibrium outcome. 'Minor complications and frictions that delay or slightly modify the effects of the major forces, without substantially changing them' are ignored thanks to suitably crafted 'negligibility assumptions' (Musgrave, 1981).[6] But, for Sraffa, the model must also be a credible surrogate system of the selected part of the world it is designed to explain (the 'target system' in the jargon of contemporary philosophy of science (see Mäki, 2009).

[6] The classical example of a negligibility assumption is that of air resistance when the phenomena under scrutiny is the fall of a cannon ball from the top of the Tower of Pisa. As Richard Musgrave (1981) perspectively noted, 'In any empirical situation there will be countless factors about which we *might* formulate negligibility assumptions but do not: Galileo Galilei did not explicitly state that the colour of the experimenter's eyes or the day of the week on which he performed the experiment would not affect its outcome. Negligibility assumptions are stated only for factors which might be *expected* to have some effect but which, we claim, will not. Galileo knew that air-resistance *does* affect objects falling through great distances or feathers falling through small ones: hence he stated explicitly that its effect on the motion of the objects in his experiments was negligible' (Musgrave, 1981, p. 378, fn. 2, Musgrave's emphasis).

Given his awareness of the principle of the underdetermination of theory by data highlighted above – that is, from the fact that a given set of data can be explained by several alternative theories – Sraffa is led to stress that comparing the conclusions of a theory with the observed data is not a sufficient test to decide about the explanatory power of a theory. As in Hayek's case, the correspondence between theory and empirical facts may be due to mere chance combined with logical errors (of which the author of the theory is unaware).

It is possible to spot the same line of reasoning in several other passages spread out over Sraffa's manuscripts. We focus on just two further passages in which, in our view, Sraffa's way of thinking emerges most clearly. The first passage is taken from folder D1/40, 'Notebook of miscellaneous items including "Produttività decrescente"' (decreasing productivity, our translation). It is dated pre-1928.

However, it may be objected, the distinction [between increasing and decreasing costs industries] finds a correspondence in reality in the fact that the increased production of some commodities is followed permanently, and not only as a transitory effect, by an increase in price, while in the case of other commodities it follows a decrease; and although these are only theoretical schemes which must serve not for practical applications, not even indirect, but simply to train the mind to consider the complex problems of reality, nevertheless the hypotheses on which they are based must be the least possible arbitrary. It is to be recognised that in some cases there are industries that have the characteristics of one or the other group of hypotheses, the theoretical causes and effects correspond to the real ones, and so much so that the conception that is here criticised is justified; but in most real cases the observed effect is due to reasons entirely different from the theoretical hypotheses, reasons that often have no relation with the conditions of production, but with those of demand and generally of the market. If there is a coincidence (D1/40, p. 20 recto, our translation) between theoretical and practical effects, but a profound divergence between the hypotheses or causes, the theory is not only useless, but dangerous, because it puts us on a false path when we search for explanations of the concrete facts.

In the last part of this paper, we try to show how the concrete fact of variations in normal values corresponding to variations in quantity can often find a more plausible (probable) explanation than that of industries with increasing or decreasing costs. (D1/40, p. 21 recto, our translation)

The second quotation is taken from the folder D1/32, 'Semi-monopoly'. It is dated pre-1928:

> It is a fact that despite the expansion of the monopoly, there remains a wide range of industries in which there is a multiplicity of independent producers. It is a fact that as the quantity produced in each industry varies, the cost and the price often varies with it. These facts are well represented by the Marshallian scheme of fundamental symmetry which is expressed in two collective curves of D[emand] and S[upply]. The identity (correspondence) between the conclusions of the theory and the facts is so evident (satisfactory) that it is easy to understand that the theory gains so wide a consensus. But there are differences between the theory and the reality: this was naturally taken into account, it was in the nature itself of the theory. The theory must consider only the dominant forces, the main tendencies that determine the equilibrium, it highlights the essential characteristics, in short it simplifies reality in such a way as to make it dominable by our mind: it then neglects the minor complications, the frictions that delay or slightly modify the effects of the major forces, without changing them substantially. Does the theory before us meet these requirements? No: the differences between it and reality are of a very different character (route). Because it is precisely in the way (and not only to the extent) in which the results are achieved that reality and theory differ. (D1/32, p. 21 f.1 recto, Sraffa's emphasis)

> Granted this, the theory not only becomes useless because it does not help us to see in a simplified form the unfolding of the real process, but it is positively harmful and dangerous because it puts us on the wrong path in our attempts to explain that unfolding. It is symptomatic This explains why theory has always remained so separate from the realistic study of the facts: this explains Clapham's complaints. The boxes are empty because they leak from all sides. (D1/32, p. 21 f.2 recto, our translation)

Sraffa states that the apparent concordance between the predictions of the Marshallian theory and empirical observations leads many economists to accept the former as the correct explanation of the observed phenomena. Specific problems in applying Marshallian theory (Clapham's empty boxes) are justified by asserting that the theory of value in general and the Marshallian theory in particular is not designed to be directly applied to specific case studies. Against this type of reasoning, Sraffa states that, in order to produce a valid explanation of the observed facts a theory, although not explicitly constructed to be directly applied to the study of concrete cases, it must be built on the least arbitrary possible starting assumptions. Sraffa does not believe that the mere concordance between predictions of a theory and observed facts is the only or the most significant test that a theory must pass in order to gain a place within accepted scientific knowledge.

In fact, continues Sraffa, there are concrete real-world cases in which the mechanism isolated from the Marshallian theory coincides with the mechanism that, in Sraffa's view, is the relevant one in real world markets. In such circumstances, Sraffa states that Marshallian theory can be validly used. But there are other cases (in Sraffa's opinion the great majority) such as all those cases in which the variation of the average cost is due to economies external to the sector and to non-specific factors of production. In these cases, the mechanism isolated from the Marshallian theory does not coincide with the mechanism that for Sraffa is the relevant one in real world markets (downward sloping demand curve of the goods in question, as Sraffa makes clear in the second part of the 1926 paper). Therefore, in these circumstances, the Marshallian theory cannot be validly used for the explanation of the observed phenomena and this is the case regardless of the more or less perfect concordance between the predictions of the theory and the empirical observations. Moreover, in these circumstances, Marshallian theory is not only inapplicable; it is positively harmful because it cannot constitute a valid basis on which to construct subsequent approximations of the theory.

2.5 Concluding Remarks

In this chapter we have shown that, for Sraffa, the search for internal logical consistency was not an end in itself but one of the steps involved by his theory assessment strategy. Our work may also be seen as a contribution to the debate concerning the relationship between rigour and relevance within Sraffian economics (see Blaug, 1999, 2002, 2011; Garegnani, 2002, 2011; Kurz and Salvadori, 2002, 2011; Signorino, 2003a, 2003b; Salanti, 2014; Salvadori and Signorino, 2015). Granted our interpretation of Sraffa's epistemology, we claim that Sraffa's philosophical position is antithetical to instrumentalism, at least to its naïve version according to which the *only* relevant test of a theory is the concordance between the predictions of the theory and the observed facts. Sraffa turns out to be a realist: the scientist's task is to explain the observed phenomena. Sraffa pragmatically accepts the notion of approximate truth. The opposition that we see is therefore among two positions that we attribute to Friedman (or at least what is the vulgate of his position) and to Sraffa. The paper by Friedman (1953) is *the* one methodological essay that has shaped the mainstream view of economic theorising. For most readers, the main takeaway is that 'Truly important and significant hypotheses will be found to have "assumptions" that are wildly inaccurate descriptive representations of reality, and, in general, the more significant the theory, the more unrealistic the assumptions (in this sense)' (Friedman, 1953, p. 14). To put it bluntly, what really matters is the empirical fit of the conclusions with the available evidence. For Sraffa, it is basically the opposite. While we have not compared, due to space constraint, Sraffa's epistemological view with those entertained by other leading figures of the Cambridge tradition (for a comprehensive assessment readers may refer to Pasinetti, 2007 and, more recently, Nuno Ornelas Martins, 2014), we hope that our work may be seen as a contribution to the clarification of the methodological underpinnings of the Cambridge tradition in economics.

References

Bernanke B. S. (2004) 'The Great Moderation', Remarks by Governor Ben S. Bernanke at the meetings of the Eastern Economic Association, Washington, DC; available at www.federalreserve.gov/boarddocs/speeches/2004/20040220/

Blaug M. (1999) 'Misunderstanding Classical Economics: The Sraffian Interpretation of the Surplus Approach', in *History of Political Economy*, 31(2), pp. 213–236.

(2002) 'Kurz and Salvadori on the Sraffian Interpretation of the Surplus Approach', in *History of Political Economy*, 34(1), pp. 237–240.

(2009) 'The Trade-Off between Rigor and Relevance: Sraffian Economics as a Case in Point', in *History of Political Economy*, 41(2), pp. 219–247.

Claar V. V. and Forster G. (2019) *The Keynesian Revolution and Our Empty Economy*, New York, Springer.

Clapham J. H. (1922) 'Of Empty Economic Boxes', in *The Economic Journal*, 32(127), pp. 305–314.

Coniglione F. (2004) 'Between Abstraction and Idealization: Scientific Practice and Philosophical Awareness', in *Poznan Studies in the Philosophy of the Sciences and the Humanities, Special Issue Idealization XI: Historical Studies on Abstraction and Idealization*, 82 (11), pp. 59–110.

De Vroey M. (2016) *A History of Macroeconomics from Keynes to Lucas and Beyond*, Cambridge, Cambridge University Press.

Eatwell J. L. and Panico C. (1987) 'Sraffa, Piero', in Eatwell J. Milgate M. and Newman P. (eds.) *The New Palgrave: A Dictionary of Economics*, vol. 4, London, Macmillan, pp. 445–452.

Fratini S. M. (2018) 'Theories of Value and Ultimate Standards in Sraffa's Notes of Summer 1927', in *Bulletin of Political Economy*, 12(1–2), pp. 35–53.

Freni G. and Salvadori N. (2013) 'The Construction of the Long-Run Market Supply Curves: Some Notes on Sraffa's Critique of Partial Equilibrium Analysis', in Levrero E. S. Palumbo A. and Stirati A. (eds.) *Sraffa and the Reconstruction of Economic Theory: Volume Three. Sraffa's Legacy: Interpretations and Historical Perspectivs*, Basingstoke and New York: Palgrave Macmillan, pp. 189–216.

Friedman M. (1953) 'The Methodology of Positive Economics', Part I of Friedman M., Essays in Positive Economics, Chicago: The University of Chicago Press, pp. 3–43, reprinted in Mäki U. (ed.) *The Methodology of Positive Economics: Reflections on the Milton Friedman Legacy*, Cambridge, Cambridge University Press, 2009, pp. 3–43.

Garegnani P. (2002) 'Misunderstanding Classical Economics? A Reply to Blaug', in *History of Political Economy*, 34(1), pp. 241–254.

(2005) 'On a Turning Point in Sraffa's Theoretical and Interpretative Position in Late 1920s', in *European Journal of the History of Economic Thought*, 12(3), pp. 453–459.

(2011) 'On Blaug Ten Years Later', in *History of Political Economy*, 43(3), pp. 591–605.

Harcourt G. C. (2012) 'Cambridge Economic Tradition', in King J. E. (ed.) *The Elgar Companion to Post Keynesian Economics*, 2nd ed., Cheltenham and Northampton, Edward Elgar, pp. 61–68.

Hoover K. D. (2017) 'Situational Analysis', in McIntyre L. and Rosenberg A. (eds.) *The Routledge Companion to Philosophy of Social Science*, London and New York, Routledge, pp. 182–190.

Kurz H. D. and Salvadori N. (1995) *Theory of Production: A Long-Period Analysis*, Cambridge, New York and Melbourne, Cambridge University Press.

(2002) 'Mark Blaug on the Sraffian Interpretation of the Surplus Approach', in *History of Political Economy*, 34(1), pp. 225–236.

(2005) 'Representing the Production and Circulation of Commodities in Material Terms: On Sraffa's Objectivism', in *Review of Political Economy*, 17(3), pp. 413–441.

(2011) 'In Favor of Rigor and Relevance: A Reply to Mark Blaug', in *History of Political Economy*, 43(3), pp. 607–616.

Lavoie M. (2014) *Post-Keynesian Economics: New Foundations*, Cheltenham and Northampton, Edward Elgar.

Lutz F. A. and Hague D. C. (1961) *The Theory of Capital: Proceedings of a Conference Held by the International Economic Association*, London, Macmillan.
Mäki U. (1992) 'On the Method of Isolation in Economics', in *Poznan Studies in the Philosophy of the Sciences and the Humanities*, 26, pp. 319–354.
(1998) 'Instrumentalism', in Davis J. B. Hands D. W. and Mäki U. (eds.) *The Handbook of Economic Methodology*, Cheltenham and Northampton, Edward Elgar, pp. 253–256.
(2000) 'Kinds of Assumptions and Their Truth: Shaking an Untwisted F-Twist', in *Kyklos*, 53(3), pp. 317–336.
(2005) 'Models Are Experiments, Experiments Are Models', in *Journal of Economic Methodology*, 12(2), pp. 303–315.
(2009) 'Missing the World: Models as Isolations and Credible Surrogate Systems', in *Erkenntnis*, 70(1), pp. 29–43.
Martins N. O. (2014) *The Cambridge Revival of Political Economy*, London, Routledge.
Mishkin F. S. (2011) 'Over the Cliff: From the Subprime to the Global Financial Crisis', in *Journal of Economic Perspectives*, 25(1), pp. 49–70.
Mongiovi G. (1996) 'Sraffa's Critique of Marshall: A Reassessment', in *Cambridge Journal of Economics*, 20(2), pp. 207–224.
Marcuzzo M. C. and Rosselli A. (2021) 'On Sraffa's Challenge to Causality in Economics', in Sinha A. (ed.) *A Reflection on Sraffa's Revolution in Economic Theory*, London, Palgrave Macmillan, pp. 91–109.
Musgrave A. (1981) 'Unreal Assumptions in Economic Theory: The F-Twist Untwisted', in *Kyklos*, 34(3), pp. 377–387.
Nowak L. (1994b) 'On Ontological Assumptions of Idealizational Theory', in *Theoria*, IX(1), pp. 19–28.
Pasinetti L. L. (2007) *Keynes and the Cambridge Keynesians: A 'Revolution in Economics' to Be Accomplished*, Cambridge, Cambridge University Press.
Pigou A. C. (1922) 'Empty Economic Boxes: A Reply', in *The Economic Journal*, 32(128), pp. 458–465.
Popper K. R. (1982) *Unended Quest*, Lasalle, Open Court.
Roncaglia A. (1978) *Sraffa and the Theory of Prices*, Chicheste, Wiley & Sons.
(1983) 'Piero Sraffa and the Reconstruction of Political Economy', in *Banca Nazionale del Lavoro Quarterly Review*, 36(147), pp. 337–350.
(1991) 'Sraffa's 1925 Article and Marshall's Theory', in *Quaderni di Storia dell'Economia Politica*, 9, pp. 373–397.
(1998) 'Sraffa, Piero as an Interpreter of the Classical Economists', in Kurz H. D. and Salvadori N. (eds.) *The Elgar Companion to Classical*

Economics, vol. II, Cheltenham and Northampton, Edward Elgar, pp. 399–404.
Salanti A. (2014) 'Rigor versus Relevance in Economic Theory: A Plea for a Different Methodological Perspective', in *History of Political Economy*, 46(1), pp. 149–166.
Salvadori N. and Signorino R. (2007) 'Piero Sraffa: Economic Reality, the Economist and Economic Theory: An Interpretation', in *Journal of Economic Methodology*, 14(2), pp. 187–209.
(2015) 'Review of Boumans M. and Klaes M. (eds.) (2013) Mark Blaug: Rebel with Many Causes, Cheltenham, UK and Northampton, MA, USA, Edward Elgar', in *Journal of the History of Economic Thought*, 37(4), pp. 615–623.
Signorino R. (2000) 'Method and Analysis in Piero Sraffa's 1925 Critique of Marshallian Economics', in *European Journal of the History of Economic Thought*, 7(4), pp. 569–594.
(2001) 'An Appraisal of Piero Sraffa's *The Laws of Returns under Competitive Conditions*', in *European Journal of the History of Economic Thought*, 8(2), pp. 230–250.
(2003a) 'Rational vs Historical Reconstructions: A Note on Blaug', in *The European Journal of the History of Economic Thought*, 10(2), pp. 329–338.
(2003b) 'A Rejoinder', in *The European Journal of the History of Economic Thought*, 10(4), pp. 609–610.
Snowdon B. and Vane H. R. (2005) *Modern Macroeconomics: Its Origins, Development and Current State*, Cheltenham and Northampton, Edward Elgar.
Sraffa P. (1925 [1998]). 'Sulle relazioni fra costo e quantità prodotta', in *Annali di Economia*, 2, pp. 277–328. English translation by Eatwell J. and Roncaglia A. 'On the Relations between Cost and Quantity Produced', in Pasinetti L. L. (ed.) *Italian Economic Papers*, vol. III, Bologna, Il Mulino and Oxford, Oxford University Press, pp. 323–363.
(1926) 'The Laws of Returns under Competitive Conditions', in *The Economic Journal*, 36(144), pp. 535–550.
(1930) '"A Criticism; Rejoinder", (Contributions to the Symposium on "Increasing Returns and the Representative Firm")', in *The Economic Journal*, 40(157), pp. 89–93.
(1932a) 'Dr. Hayek on Money and Capital', in *The Economic Journal*, 42 (165), pp. 42–53.
(1932b) 'A Rejoinder', in *The Economic Journal*, 42(166), pp. 249–251.

3 *Malthus and the Classics (Not Walras and the Marginalists) as the Major Inspiring Source in the History of Economic Thought*

The Principle of Effective Demand and Classical Economics

HEINZ D. KURZ*

3.1 Introduction

According to Luigi Pasinetti's list, the third 'characteristic feature' of the Cambridge Keynesian School is the following: '*Malthus and the Classics (not Walras and the Marginalists) as the major inspiring source in the history of economic thought*' (Pasinetti, 2007, p. 222, emphasis in the original). In explaining this feature, Pasinetti pointed out that the break with the prevailing marginalist (Walrasian) orthodoxy is not purely negatively connoted, because at the same time it involves a 'revival of classical economic thought (especially that of Smith, Malthus, Ricardo, Marx)' (Pasinetti, 2007, p. 222).

This characterisation of an alternative to the mainstream as taking off inter alia from Robert Thomas Malthus and David Ricardo is bound to come as a surprise, and Pasinetti is of course aware of it. As is well known, Malthus and Ricardo hardly agreed on any economic issue they discussed, and Ricardo repeatedly showed that Malthus did not reason correctly.[1] Is Pasinetti's assessment of

* In parts of this chapter, I draw freely on Kalmbach and Kurz (2009). I should like to thank Peter Kalmbach for a fertile cooperation over many years. Given his impact on my thinking on the matters under consideration he might consider himself as virtually co-authoring what is valuable in this chapter. The responsibility for what follows is nevertheless entirely mine. Harald Hagemann, Rajas Parchure and the editors of this volume kindly sent me useful comments on an earlier version of the chapter.

[1] There appears to be one exception: the law of population. However, this exception is more apparent than real. Careful scrutiny shows that Ricardo did not endorse Malthus's law of population as a generally valid principle but stressed its historical contingency. In his debate with Malthus about the problem of value

Malthus's contribution perhaps too favourable? It is also well known that John Maynard Keynes firmly sided with Malthus against Ricardo. In his *Essay in Biography* on the former, he stressed: 'If only Malthus, instead of Ricardo, had been the parent stem from which nineteenth-century economics proceeded, what a much wiser and richer place the world would be to-day!' (*CWK*, x, pp. 100–101).[2] And while in the *General Theory* Keynes interspersed the praise he ushered upon Malthus with some mild reproach, he still regretted that Ricardo and not Malthus had determined the course of economics for a long period of time: 'Malthus, indeed, had vehemently opposed Ricardo's doctrine that it was impossible for effective demand to be deficient; but vainly. For, since Malthus was unable to explain clearly ... how and why effective demand could be deficient or excessive, he failed to furnish an alternative construction.' He concluded with the famous phrase: 'Ricardo conquered England as completely as the Holy Inquisition conquered Spain' (*CWK*, VII, p. 32).

Put in a nutshell, the main differences between the doctrines of Malthus and Ricardo appear to be the following: First, while Ricardo entertained the classical version of Jean Baptiste Say's law of markets, Malthus seemed to reject it and instead advocated some version of the principle of effective demand. Secondly, while Ricardo saw prices as determined by cost of production and explained profits in terms of the social surplus product (net of rents) left after all physical real costs in terms of means of production and means of subsistence of workers have been deducted from gross output levels, Malthus saw both prices and the distributive variables, wages, profits and rents, as determined by supply and demand of commodities and factors of production.

and distribution, he variously adopted the law, because it fixed the real wage rate at some given (subsistence) level and thus allowed him to explain profits and rents in terms of his surplus approach to income distribution as residuals. There are numerous passages in Ricardo's works and correspondence in which he clearly distances himself from Malthus's respective doctrine (see, for example, Kurz and Salvadori, 2006, 2015; see also Kurz, 2010, p. 1195).

2 When Keynes wrote his essay in biography on Malthus, he asked Piero Sraffa, who at the time was working on the edition of the works and correspondence of Ricardo, whether he could make use of the material Sraffa had collected and which included Ricardo's exchange with Malthus. In his letter to Keynes of 23 December 1932, Sraffa most willingly granted Keynes permission to do so, but added: 'don't treat too ill my David!' He was aware that Keynes estimated Malthus a great deal higher than Ricardo, an estimation not shared by him.

Their views clashed in numerous controversies between the two authors and there is no indication that they felt that they could eventually, after long debates, converge or at least be reconciled with one another. Being diametrically opposed, one could follow Ricardo *or* Malthus but not both. This raises the question what to make of Pasinetti's proposition that an alternative approach in economics, alternative to the marginalist/Walrasian mainstream, should take off from a reconsideration and development of ideas found in Ricardo *and* Malthus. *Prima vista* the answer appears to be a resounding 'no', this is not possible. Could a *seconda vista* possibly lead to a different view and indicate the compatibility of some of their ideas or is this a hopeless enterprise? If the answer to the former part of the question happens to be in the affirmative, how is it substantiated? Since, as will be argued in the following, Malthus's analysis is beset by numerous flaws and exhibits several shortcomings, and Ricardo's analysis is also not without unsolved problems and loose ends, how could a reconciliation of the two doctrines, or elements of them, ever be accomplished? And how could the doctrines of the other authors mentioned – from Adam Smith via Karl Marx to Keynes – come in? Does Pasinetti's concern with synthesising these elements amount to a search for a will-o'-the-wisp? Will it turn out to involve a mission impossible?

In this chapter, we try to provide elements of an answer to these questions. We proceed in the following way. In Section 3.2, we summarise the debate between Ricardo and Malthus about the possibility of a 'general glut' of commodities, meaning failures of aggregate effective demand. Since both authors advocated a version of Say's law of markets, the question is how on this basis Malthus could ever entertain the view that the economic system was demand constrained. Section 3.3 expounds briefly Keynes's Principle of Effective Demand, which hinges crucially on a rejection of Say's law and focuses attention on the coordination of investment, shaped by long-run profitability expectations of firms, and savings via the activity level of the economy as a whole. Section 3.4 asks in what sense Keynes could see in Malthus a precursor of his Principle of Effective Demand. It is argued that in important respects the doctrines of the two authors are fundamentally different. These respects concern especially the role of money in the economic system and the treatment (or rather non-treatment in the case of Malthus) of decisions to save and decisions to invest and how the two are coordinated. Section 3.5 takes a closer look at Ricardo's surplus-based approach to the theory of value and distribution, which, if fully and coherently developed, turns out to undermine Say's law. Sraffa provided a coherent formulation of the classical theory of value and distribution. In the course of the Cambridge controversies of capital in the 1960s and 1970s, to which Pasinetti contributed in important ways, some of its implications were made explicit, including phenomena such as reverse capital deepening, re-switching of techniques and non-conventional price and real Knut Wicksell effects. These phenomena fly in the face of conventional marginalist theory, which relies on Say's law. Section 3.6 takes stock of the aforementioned with explicit regard to Pasinetti's suggestion concerning the authors and theories that ought to inspire the sought re-orientation of economics. Section 3.7 concludes.

3.2 Ricardo vs. Malthus on the Possibility of a 'General Glut' of Commodities

In his edition of *The Works and Correspondence of David Ricardo* (Ricardo, 1951–1973), Sraffa documented the controversies of the two economists who were in contact with one another since 1811. In addition to the letters they exchanged, they discussed economic matters on the occasion of several meetings they had. On basically each and every subject they were of different opinions. When, in 1817, Ricardo published his *Principles of Political Economy*, Malthus answered in 1820 with a book with the same main title, which, however, does not contain a systematic exposition of what the title suggests but in large parts rather consists of a critical disquisition on Ricardo's *Principles*. As Malthus stressed in the preface of his treatise:

> There is one modern work, in particular, of very high reputation, some of the fundamental principles of which have appeared to me, after the most mature deliberation, to be erroneous; and I should not have done justice to the ability with which it is written, to the high authority of the writer, and the interests of the science of which it treats, if it had not specifically engaged a considerable portion of my attention. I allude to Mr. Ricardo's work, '*On the Principles of Political Economy and Taxation*'. (Malthus, 1820 [1989], pp. 22–23)

In the course of carefully studying Malthus's book, Ricardo composed his *Notes on Malthus* (*Works*, II), which, however, he did not publish during his lifetime and showed only to a few close friends. In letters to Malthus and John Ramsay McCulloch, he pointed out which parts of the book he found most questionable. To the latter he wrote: 'The most objectionable chapter in Mr. Malthus' book is that perhaps on the bad effects from too great accumulation of capital, and the consequent want of demand for the goods produced' (*Works*, VIII, p. 181). The reference is to part 3 of chapter 7, 'Of Accumulation, or the Saving from Revenue to add to Capital, considered as a Stimulus to the Increase of Wealth'. And to Malthus he wrote: 'The part of your book to which I most object is the last. I can see no soundness in the reasons you give for the usefulness of demand, on the part of unproductive consumers. How their consuming, without reproducing, can be beneficial to a country, in any possible state of it, I confess I cannot discover' (*Works*, VIII, p. 301).[3]

The controversial points of view ought to be seen against the background of the end of the Napoleonic Wars and the economic problems that accompanied the transition of the United Kingdom from a war to a peace economy. The fundamental question was whether a general overproduction of commodities was possible. Ricardo's view in this regard was uncompromising:

> No man produces, but with a view to consume or sell, and he never sells, but with an intention to purchase some other commodity, which may be immediately useful to him, or which may contribute to future production. By producing, then, he necessarily becomes either the consumer of his own goods, or the purchaser and consumer of the goods of some other person. It is not to be supposed that he should, for any length of time, be ill-informed of the commodities which he can most advantageously produce, to attain the object which he has in view, namely, the possession of other goods; and, therefore, it is not probable that he will continually produce a commodity for which there is no demand. (Works, I, p. 290)

And shortly afterwards, Ricardo stressed: 'Too much of a particular commodity may be produced, of which there may be such a glut in the

[3] The controversy between Malthus and Ricardo is succinctly recapitulated in Pasinetti (1974, ch. II, part 1; see also the Italian version 1977a). While Pasinetti expresses his sympathy for Malthus's alert mind as regards actual facts concerning effective demand failures and unemployment, he makes it very clear that Malthus's argument was too weak and poor and could not establish convincingly the principle of effective demand, as Keynes somewhat misleadingly insinuated.

market, as not to repay the capital expended on it; *but this cannot be the case with respect to all commodities*' (*Works*, I, p. 292, emphasis added). Therefore, in his view a general glut of commodities was impossible.

Modern readers of these passages can be expected to interpret them as clear expressions of what became known as Say's law. However, the meaning of this 'law' is far from obvious as, for example, the contributions of Robert Clower and Axel Leijonhufvud (1973 [1981]) and William Baumol (1977) document. Here we are concerned with the view of the British classical political economists on the matter, which revolves around the problem of saving and investment. In the *Wealth of Nations*, Smith had emphasised: 'What is annually saved is as regularly consumed as what is annually spent, and nearly in the same time too; but it is consumed by a different set of people' (Smith 1776 [1976], II.iii.18). Upon acts of saving, which are seen to imply a reduction in effectual demand, follow quickly acts of investment of the same magnitude, which imply an increase in effectual demand. Ricardo entertained essentially the same view: there cannot be a general glut because any loss in effectual demand is swiftly compensated by an equivalent addition to effectual demand. When the classical economists speak of 'accumulation of capital' they mean *saving-cum-investment*. They did not discuss in any depth the problem of the coordination of decisions to save and decisions to invest but simply took it for granted that whatever was being saved would be invested, either by the same person or by someone else. From this they concluded that there could be no failure of effectual demand at the level of the economic system as a whole.

It is this conclusion that Malthus disputed. Already in the introduction to his *Principles* he wrote:

Adam Smith has stated, that capitals are increased by parsimony, that every frugal man is a public benefactor, and that the increase of wealth depends upon the balance of produce above consumption. That these propositions are true to a great extent is perfectly unquestionable. No considerable and continued increase of wealth could possibly take place without that degree of frugality which occasions, annually, the conversion of some revenue into capital, and creates a balance of produce above consumption; but it is quite obvious that they are not true to an indefinite extent, and that the principle of saving, pushed to excess, would destroy the motive to production. (Malthus, 1820 [1989], p. 8)

He added: 'if production be in a great excess above consumption, the motive to accumulate and produce must cease from the want of will to consume' (Malthus, 1820 [1989], p. 9).

How did Malthus substantiate his view? The problem one faces when trying to answer this question is that while Malthus disputed the above conclusion of Smith and Ricardo, he clung to the premise upon which it rested – the equality or rather identity between saving and investment. Accumulating capital, he argued fully in line with Smith and Ricardo, implied that consumption by unproductive workers employed by wealthy people as menial servants or in the production of luxury goods gave way to consumption by productive workers producing means of production and means of subsistence. As Malthus emphasised:

> It is undoubtedly possible by parsimony to devote at once a much larger share than usual of the produce of any country to the maintenance of productive labour; and it is quite true that the labourers so employed are consumers as well as unproductive labourers; and as far as the labourers are concerned, there would be no diminution of consumption or demand. (Malthus, 1820 [1989], p. 352)

Hence, a diminished consumption of unproductive workers is not the cause of a general glut, Malthus insisted, because it will be compensated by an increased consumption of productive workers. What then brings about an insufficient aggregate demand? What bothered him a great deal are the additional amounts of commodities that the additional productive workers will produce. Who is going to buy them, where are the additional customers to absorb them? The class of workers consume as much as they did prior to the increase in saving, and the propertied classes, consisting of capitalists and the landed gentry, together save more than before. So, where does the badly needed additional effectual demand come from? To Malthus, a yawning gap opened between production and consumption – the economic system suffered from a lack of effectual demand.

This is the gist of Malthus's reasoning. The argument put forward obviously applies to *any* increase in saving alias investment and not just to an increase 'pushed to excess'. It therefore remains unclear up to which point the conversion of a proportion of revenue into capital is favourable to an increase in wealth and beyond which the economy goes into a tailspin. Malthus failed to identify what may be called an optimal propensity to accumulate, where 'optimal' is defined in terms of whether a problem of effective demand occurs.

Malthus's argument suffers from a number of shortcomings. Several of these throw into doubt Keynes's view that Malthus may be considered a precursor of his own theory. Malthus argued as if the economy was a pure exchange economy or an economy in which money was neutral. Money was not seen as a potentially bottomless sink, as in the writings of John Stuart Mill and then Marx.[4] The redirection of workers from producing 'luxuries' to producing 'necessaries' (wage goods) and means of production was assumed to be smooth: reallocating means of subsistence from 'unproductive' to 'productive' workers, to use Smith's distinction (Smith, 1776 [1976], II.iii.1–2), appears to be all that was needed. That is to say, Malthus assumed implicitly that neither skill differentials between the different types of labour nor capital stock differentials between the different industries and employments cause trouble. This may be true for a menial servant, say a cook, who leaves the estate of his master and gets employed in the canteen of a cargo vessel. In general, things are quite different and require some reskilling and putting in place first the necessary plant and equipment and providing the appropriate raw materials for the new tasks. The modern industrial system, of which Malthus (and Ricardo) saw only the beginnings, is characterised by a remarkable flexibility due to the increasing fixed capital intensity of production. This allows for an adjustment of output to changes in its composition (and even its overall size) via changing levels of the utilisation of productive capacity in the different sectors of the economy in combination with changing levels of the intensity of labour. However, this elasticity of production plays no role in Malthus's reasoning.

It is therefore unclear how in Malthus a general glut of commodities may obtain. A gap between saving and investment for the economy as a whole is ruled out by assumption. If too much of a particular commodity has been produced, Ricardo stressed, then this is so because the producer 'has miscalculated' (*Works*, II, p. 305). But this cannot be the case for all commodities and producers at the same time. Ricardo insisted: 'it is at all times the bad adaptation of the

[4] Malthus elsewhere in his book talks about the role of money, but to the best of my knowledge nowhere puts forward a view that might be interpreted as foreshadowing the idea of money as an abode of value and wealth or as reflecting liquidity preference that could cause an effective demand problem.

commodities produced to the wants of mankind, which is the specific evil, and not the abundance of commodities. Demand is only limited by the will and power to purchase' (*Works*, II, p. 306).

Malthus feared that in certain circumstances the will to purchase might dwindle. He contemplated the case in which 'indolence' – leisure time – on the part of the rich strata of society increases and argued: 'The effect of a preference of indolence to luxuries would evidently be to occasion a want of demand for the returns of the increased powers of production supposed, and to throw labourers out of employment' (Malthus, 1820 [1989], pp. 358–359). Confronted with this statement, with which Malthus raised an entirely new issue, Ricardo commented drily, if people prefer leisure to luxury goods, luxury goods will not be produced – how can there be an excess supply of them? Malthus's entire reasoning was flawed and contradictory and could not bear the brunt of his main thesis. As a consequence, his economic policy conclusion was also mistaken according to which it was 'absolutely necessary that a country with great powers of production should possess a body of unproductive consumers' (Malthus, 1820 [1989], p. 463). The unproductive consumers Malthus had in mind were the landowners, because capitalists were innately inclined or systemically compelled by competition to accumulate capital, and workers could not come to the rescue because of the law of population. Ricardo was at a loss to understand Malthus's recommendation and scoffed: 'A body of unproductive labourers are just as necessary and as useful with a view to future production, as a fire, which should consume in the manufacturers warehouse the goods which those unproductive labourers would otherwise consume' (*Works*, II, p. 421).

To conclude, Malthus failed to substantiate convincingly his view that a general overproduction of commodities was possible. Many of his arguments are essentially short run in character and concern the problem of how the economy responds to a sudden change in the propensity to accumulate or any other change in economic behaviour. Such changes typically involve adjustment problems of various kinds and severity. But the core of Malthus's reasoning shows that his main concern was with the lasting implication of too large a rate of capital accumulation on the performance of the economic system: too large a rate, he contended, does not necessarily go together with swift economic expansion but may paradoxically suffocate growth by destroying the 'motive to production'. Hence, he was not so much concerned with an adjustment problem that might lead to an economic crisis as with a lasting economic stagnation. The genuinely long-period nature of the issue Malthus had raised had not escaped Ricardo's attention and so his criticism understandably focused on it rather than on short-run difficulties of adjusting to new circumstances. Some commentators, interested first and foremost in the short run, accused Ricardo of refusing to engage in discussing an important issue with his adversary. Keynes was one of them. He maintained that Ricardo 'was stone-deaf to what Malthus was saying' (*CWK*, VII, p. 364). However, this verdict is difficult to sustain. This follows from what has been said above and also from what will be said in Section 3.3, which takes a closer look at how Keynes refuted Jean Baptiste Say's law and established in its stead what he called the Principle of Effective Demand (see also Pasinetti, 1974, sections 2 and 4).[5]

Before doing so, I should like to comment briefly on two passages in Ricardo's *Notes on Malthus*, to which Rajas Parchure has drawn my attention in private correspondence. The first one reads: '*if*, of the two things necessary to demand, the will and the power to purchase the will be wanting, and consequently a general stagnation of trade has ensued, we cannot do better than follow the advice of Mr. Malthus and oblige the Government to supply the deficiency of the people' (*Works*, II, p. 307, emphasis added). Here is the second one: '*If* the people will not expend enough themselves, what can be more expedient than to call upon the state to spend for them?' (*Works*, II, p. 450, emphasis added). Do these passages not reflect Ricardo coming around to Malthus's point of view at least in extreme cases? The context of the two passages however makes it abundantly clear that this is not so. Ricardo introduced the first passage with the proviso: '*If* his [Malthus's] views on this question be correct – *if* commodities can be so multiplied that there is not disposition to purchase and consume them, then undoubtedly the cure which he hesitatingly recommends is a very proper one' (*Works*, II, p. 307, emphases added). But, as Ricardo made clear elsewhere, he strongly disputed that Malthus's views were correct – the land of plenty or Cockaigne is not of this world. Hence Malthus's conclusion, while stringent, followed from an

[5] In this context, Pierangelo Garegnani's important works also have to be mentioned; see, in particular, his early essay in two instalments (Garegnani, 1978, 1979), first published in Italian.

utterly false premise and therefore was of no use at all.[6] As regards the second passage, Ricardo's seeming approval of Malthus's point of view is again only apparent rather than real. Just one page earlier, he had recalled: 'Mr. Malthus never appears to remember that *to save is to spend*, as surely, as what he exclusively calls spending' (*Works*, II, p. 449, emphasis added). With Say's law like an iron ball and chain around one leg, how could Malthus ever gain ground in his debate with Ricardo?

A well-known characterisation of two other economists applies *cum grano salis* also in the present case: while Ricardo chiselled in stone, Malthus knitted in wool. Malthus intuitively sensed that Ricardo was unable to address a serious economic problem, because the said iron ball also hampered his moves. And Malthus failed to rid himself effectively of the fetter, in a strange way, much of his reasoning simply ignored it. Keynes was impressed by Malthus's unswerving insistence on the possibility of effective demand failures against all odds and therefore was inclined to consider him a precursor of his own view. But was he really?

3.3 Keynes and the Principle of Effective Demand

Is there a sense in which Malthus may be called a precursor of Keynes whose work anticipated or at least foreshadowed elements of the theory of effective demand? What the two authors clearly had in common is this: they both recognised, and were keen to address, a problem which even a casual observation of the facts suggested, namely, that the economy did not gravitate around an expansion path characterised by the full utilisation of its productive capacity or even full employment of labour.[7] The economy rather exhibited on average, over a succession of booms and slumps, smaller or larger margins of

[6] It is not often that Ricardo would praise Malthus's logic.

[7] Whilst the marginalist interpretation of Say's law subsumed the labour market under 'la loi des débouchés' and assumed a tendency towards the full employment of labour, in Ricardo, the law was taken to apply only to commodities whose production is motivated by the aim of making profits but not to labour (or rather labour power), which is not so produced. Ricardo stated that there cannot 'be accumulated in a country any amount of capital which cannot be employed productively, until wages rise so high ... and so little consequently remains for the profits of stock, that the motive for accumulation ceases' (*Works*, I, p. 290). In this interpretation, the law applies to the capital stock but not to labour. For an

underutilisation of its productive resources and thus did not fully exploit its growth potential.[8] How does Keynes's explanation of the facts in the early drafts of *The General Theory* and related works and then in the published version of the book compare with what Malthus had to say on the subject?

The first striking feature of Keynes's explanation is that it presupposes a 'monetary theory of production' (*CWK*, XIII, pp. 408–411). Different from Malthus's approach, in Keynes's, money assumes a central role in the economic system. A monetary economy, Keynes insists, differs fundamentally from a pure exchange economy, especially because in a monetary economy Say's law does not apply; there is no presumption that selling a commodity will automatically and swiftly lead to buying some other commodities.

Secondly, and also different from Malthus, Keynes distinguishes clearly between saving and investment and the different motives and determinants of these. In Keynes's view, savings are a residual that follows from the decisions of consumers of how much of their disposable incomes to spend on consumption goods. Whereas in marginalist economics savers rule the roost and decide the path the economy takes in terms of their intertemporal decisions; in Keynes, savers are no active players but respond essentially to what is going on in the economy as a whole, especially as regards national income and employment. The latter are determined first and foremost by investors, who are the active part in the system and who force others to adjust to and comply with their decisions. These decisions concern future states of the economic world and the profitable opportunities they offer (see *CWK*, VII, ch. 11). These states cannot, however, be known in advance but are fundamentally uncertain. Investment therefore depends on entrepreneurs' long-term expectations, which may swiftly get upset in response to sudden changes regarding the perception of the state of the world, present and future. Long-term profitability expectations and the confidence with which these are held are by far the most important determinant of the volume of investment in a given situation. There are

in-depth confrontation of the views of Ricardo and Say see Gehrke and Kurz (2001).

8 It deserves to be mentioned in this context that industrial cycles were observed only from around 1820 onwards, after the manufacturing sector had reached a certain size and importance for the economy as a whole and cycles spread from there across the entire system.

some other factors, including the money rate of interest, that shape investment behaviour, but compared to profitability expectations they are of minor importance.

Keynes's respective view differs markedly from the marginalist view. In the latter, investors are seen essentially as executors of the wishes of savers, that is, they are attributed a purely vicarious role. In Keynes, on the contrary, investors are the active part of the economy, whose investment and innovation activities shape economic development and by activating the economic system determine output as a whole and employment. The basic idea underlying Keynes's view of the world is the income multiplier, which, in its simplest form, reads: $Y = (1/s)\ I$, where Y is national income, s the propensity to save and I investment. According to it, investment propels income to a level at which the savings out of it (sY) equal investment (I). This level may, but typically will not, be equal to national income at full employment. It will typically be associated with smaller or larger margins of unemployment. According to the Principle of Effective Demand there is no presumption that aggregate effective demand can be expected to gravitate around the path of full employment growth, or, in other words, that investment will on average match full employment savings:

> It is an outstanding characteristic of the economic system in which we live that, whilst it is subject to severe fluctuations in respect of output and employment, it is not violently unstable. Indeed, it seems capable of remaining in a chronic condition of sub-normal activity for a considerable period without any marked tendency either towards recovery or towards complete collapse. (*CWK*, VII, p. 249)

Keynes also deplored the unequal distribution of income in capitalist economic systems, which is caused at least partly by unemployment that keeps the aspirations of workers at bay.

But why does the system not lead to full employment by its own devices? This brings us to the third striking feature of Keynes's analysis, which finds no equivalent in Malthus's theory. The monetary economy in which we live is characterised, as we have already heard, by a fundamental uncertainty regarding future states of the world and possibly quickly changing expectations in this regard. In such conditions, the holding of cash, which yields no interest, need not be foolish, as earlier authors were inclined to think, but may reflect a perfectly sound behaviour. This is the case, for example, when the annual interest paid on a bond is smaller than the expected fall in the price of the bond. In this case, holding cash is superior to holding or buying bonds.[9] A preference for liquidity therefore does not necessarily express an atavistic love of money but a rational decision in an uncertain world. Money is not only a unit of account and a means of exchange, as Malthus had thought, it is also a store of value. The money received upon the sale of a commodity need not be spent again but may be kept in cash for shorter or longer periods of time. Money may be withdrawn from the economic circuit and kept idle for some time. This disrupts the circuit; sales dwindle and via several backward and forward linkages the economy can end up in a tailspin.

While Mill, Marx and others had already understood the role of money as an abode of value and wealth, Keynes deserves the credit for having elaborated an argument that renders this role and its implications much clearer than in any previous author. This does not mean that his explanation of effective demand failures is not without (serious) shortcomings, but he manages to carry the argument a good deal forward. Keynes distinguishes between two kinds of equilibria in a monetary economy. First, there is a stock equilibrium between money supply and money demand. Secondly, there is a flow equilibrium between saving, which constitutes 'leakages' in aggregate demand, and investment, which constitutes 'injections'.[10] Keynes rejects the conventional marginalist view that the rate of interest is the 'price' in terms of which savings and investment get equilibrated: 'In any case, given the state of expectation of the public and the policy of the banks, the rate of interest is that rate at which the demand and supply of liquid resources are balanced. *Saving does not come into the picture at all*' (*CWK*, XIV, p. 222). On the same page, he summarises neatly his point of view in regard of the problem of investment and saving. Investment presupposes the availability of liquid means but not of savings: 'If there is no change in the liquidity position, the public can save *ex ante* and *ex post* and *ex* anything else until they are blue in the face, without alleviating the problem in the least'. He adds: 'the banks hold the key

[9] With a whole set of assets with different risks, yields and maturities, the problem of 'portfolio selection' is, of course, a great deal more complex than in Keynes's cash vs. bond case.

[10] This distinction has not always been strictly kept apart by some interpreters and has led to dire confusions in the literature. These need not concern us here. See, therefore, inter alia Keynes (*CWK*, XIV).

position in the transition from a lower to a higher scale of activity' and 'the investment market can become congested through shortage of cash. It can never become congested through shortage of saving' (*CWK*, XIV, p. 222).

While in Keynes's explanation of effective demand failures, money, credit and liquidity more generally assume centre stage, in Malthus's explanation, the specific features of a monetary economy compared to a barter economy play no significant role. In Keynes, investment is also not tied to an abstention of consumption, as marginalist authors contend, but generates additional savings via an expansion of employment and production due to an increase in aggregate effective demand. This is the multiplier process mentioned above.

3.4 Malthus – A Precursor of Keynes?

We may now take stock of what has been said with respect to whether Malthus can be seen as a precursor of Keynes. First, Keynes leaves no doubt that Malthus, while possessed of a fair sense of realism in regard to the issue at hand, was unable to establish his view analytically: his poor logic and economics were not up to the task under consideration. Ricardo's impeccable logic, on the other hand, spotted mercilessly the shortcomings and contradictions of his opponent's argument, which is accused of trying to escape from one detected error to the next one.[11] Keynes leaves no doubt that Malthus's cardinal error was to cling steadfastly to Say's law and the assumed adjustment of the volume of investment to the pre-determined volume of savings. He failed to provide a compelling analysis of the different motivations of savers and investors and of the process through which their activities are coordinated. This is partly understandable because when Malthus wrote, the people who saved were often, but not always, also those who invested, that is, saver and investor were one and the same person. What was only largely but not fully true then was no longer true when Keynes wrote. At his time, the two types of agents were very different people, with the property of firms and their control becoming increasingly separated and family owned businesses replaced by joint stock

[11] For some examples of what may be called Malthus's problem hopping, see Kalmbach and Kurz (2009, pp. 177–178).

companies. Without thoroughly analysing the decisions to save and the different decisions to invest, and their interplay, nothing could be said about coordination successes or failures. As a consequence of adopting Say's law, both Malthus and Ricardo deprived themselves of the possibility of elaborating such an analysis. Whilst Ricardo understood perfectly well the implications of this adoption and reasoned in a logically sound manner, Malthus refused to accept the implications, insisted on what the observation seemed to imply and was bound to entangle himself in numerous contradictions. Ricardo relied on logic and economics, Malthus on realism. In these circumstances, it does not come as a surprise that the debate between the two was tedious and bore little fruit.

Keynes succeeded in elevating the discussion of the problem on to a new level of sophistication by distinguishing clearly between decisions to save and decisions to invest and the very different motives behind them. However, two closely intertwined shortcomings of his contribution prevented it from providing a fully satisfactory solution to the problem at hand. First, by limiting the main part of his analysis to the short run, Keynes left the issue of what would happen in the medium and long run largely open.[12] Would not a lack of effective demand and involuntary unemployment trigger adjustment processes that lead the economy more or less quickly out of a slump? Main advocates of the conventional viewpoint, especially Keynes's Cambridge colleague Arthur Cecil Pigou (1933), had not denied the possibility and actuality of slumps but had insisted that the economic system was possessed of homeostatic properties that tended to reinstate market equilibria.[13]

[12] The limitation to the short run is particularly obvious with respect to Keynes's assumption of a given capital stock that does not change despite the fact that there is net investment. Evsey Domar and Roy F. Harrod shortly afterwards took into account in addition to the income effect of net investment also the capacity effect, which in Harrod's analysis gave rise to the famous 'Instability Principle'.

[13] The picture of Pigou that has come down to us is not faithful to him. He actually saw business cycles caused essentially by changing expectations of firms regarding future economic prospects, which translated into fluctuations in investment demand and involuntary unemployment. He was even prepared to advocate expansionist policies in exceptional circumstances and joined forces with Keynes against the orthodox marginalist approach vis-à-vis the Great Depression advocated by Lionel Robbins and his acolytes at the London School of Economics.

Hence, more was needed than just the demonstration that the system could face effective demand problems in the short run. How did Keynes explain the 'evidence ... that full, or even approximately full, employment is of rare and short-lived occurrence' (CWK, VII, p. 250)?

What made him think that the economic system is insufficiently capable of self-regulating and in normal conditions cannot be expected to realise a tendency towards the full utilisation of its productive resources. Keynes rejected the marginalist idea that in case of unemployment the competition of workers would bid down real wages, which would increase the demand for labour and decrease its supply. He objected that only money wages can be bid down. This would, however, have effects that thwart the assumed tendency towards full employment. First, lower money wages imply a lower demand for consumption goods and, in competitive conditions, falling prices. Hence, lower money wages do not ipso facto lead to lower real wages; in fact, real wages may remain largely the same. Secondly, falling prices can in turn be expected to destabilise expectations and increase the real burden of existing debts in the economy and lead to bankruptcies of firms and cause a crisis of social trust. With underutilised productive capacity in the consumer goods industries, there is no reason to expect firms to increase investment demand; on the contrary, they might reduce investment or stretch out the realisation of already decided investment projects. In short, the usual remedy recommended by orthodox economists for how to fight unemployment may lead to results that are opposite to those expected. The policy prescribed by marginalist economists is not only ineffective – it actually worsens the situation.

Is there another channel by means of which the economic system could, like Baron Munchausen, pull itself out of the misery by its own bootstraps? Keynes admits that there is one, at least in principle: since investment depends also on the money rate of interest, this rate would have to fall to a level compatible with a volume of investment equal to full employment savings. However, Keynes was highly skeptical that this would in fact happen other than in exceptional circumstances. We have already heard that compared with long-run profitability expectations he took the impact of the money rate of interest to be modest. This raised the question whether the level under consideration did actually exist and, if it did, how it could be attained. According to Keynes, there were compelling reasons not to rely on it because of a strong preference for liquidity and thus a high demand for cash, which prevented the money rate of interest from falling sufficiently to stimulate investment up to the desired level.

Keynes tried to substantiate a downward rigidity of the money rate of interest in chapter 17 of *The General Theory*, 'The Essential Properties of Interest and Money' (*CWK*, VII, pp. 222–244). In this chapter, he had recourse to a concept used by Sraffa in his criticism of Hayek (Sraffa, 1932) – the concept of 'commodity rate of interest'. Sraffa was clear that this was an adaptation of Irving Fisher's concept of own rate of interest. In comments on Keynes's chapter, which Sraffa apparently never showed to anybody, including Keynes, and which surfaced only after Sraffa had passed away, he pointed out that the use Keynes had made of it was confused and confusing and failed to support his point of view.[14]

We may summarise the differences between the doctrines of Keynes and Malthus in the following way. First, while Malthus saw 'too large' a rate of accumulation as the source of a general glut of commodities, Keynes insisted that too small an investment demand was responsible for it. According to Malthus, too high a rate of accumulation leads to falling commodity prices and, for given money wages, rising real wages. Malthus in fact saw a lack of aggregate effective demand and too high real wages as almost synonymous when describing the problem under consideration. Alas, he failed to provide convincing reasons why high real wages should be accompanied by an insufficient effective demand. In Keynes, a lack of effective demand may, but need not, lead to falling prices. If it does, real wages need not rise, as we have already heard, since money wages could fall *pari passu* with prices. At any rate, while in Malthus real wages of the employed tend to rise in a slump, in Keynes they tend to stay largely the same. Hence,

[14] For a summary account of Sraffa's objections to the way Keynes had attempted to establish a downward rigidity of the rate of interest, see Kurz (2000, 2015). Contemporary experiences might be considered to confirm Sraffa's point of view: high levels of liquidity preference need not prevent the money rate of interest from falling even to negative levels.

in his case, it is not a change of income distribution away from profits and towards wages that frustrates the propensity to accumulate.

Malthus does not base his explanation of a general glut of commodities upon the behaviour of agents who withdraw money from circulation. He endorses explicitly Smith's view that hoarding is irrational and that only few people engage in it, which is why it has a negligible impact on the economy. Money is not the source of the problem, because its store of value function plays hardly any role whatsoever. In Keynes, things are very different: an increase in holding cash because of a rising speculative motive to liquidity dampens economic dynamism. However, Keynes saw a large liquidity preference shape the economy not only in the short, but also in the long run. The reason he gave was that the money rate of interest tended to be often 'the *greatest* of the own-rates of interest' of all assets and that 'certain forces, which operate to reduce the own-rates of interest of other assets, do not operate in the case of money' (*CWK*, VII, pp. 223–224). In short, the money rate of interest is seen to be bounded from below at a level that is above the level at which the volume of investment would be equal to full employment savings. However, as Sraffa showed, Keynes's argument is beset by several difficulties and cannot be sustained. In a depression, for example, in which commodity prices tend to fall, the value of money tends to rise, that is, its 'spot' value is smaller than its 'forward' value. This means, however, that what Keynes called the 'own rate of money interest' is low and lower than the own rates of interest of capital goods, contrary to what Keynes had contended.

We may conclude by saying that what is common to Keynes and Malthus is little more than the perception that the different, but in important respects similar, capitalist economic systems in which they lived exhibit in normal conditions levels of activity that do not fully utilise their productive resources. Both authors see a lack of aggregate effective demand as causing this. In other words, they see, in Malthus's terminology, a 'regulating principle' at work that differs from the 'limiting principle', where the former reflects the impact of an insufficient effective demand on economic activity, from which the latter abstracts (see Kurz, 1998).

Since Malthus cannot be considered to have anticipated Keynes's Principle of Effective Demand and since Keynes explicitly distanced himself from Ricardo's theory, what can be made of Pasinetti's claim that Malthus, the Classics and Keynes ought to be the major inspiring sources in economics? Are the doctrines of these authors not contradicting each other in fundamental respects? Or is there a way to show that despite all apparent differences they have something in common that can be developed and that improves our understanding of the phenomena at hand? It hardly needs to be stressed that if the answer happens to be yes, it cannot include what may, for short, be called 'bad economics' at which Malthus at times was particularly good. More precisely, we will ask whether in Ricardo's contribution we encounter the seeds of ideas, of which Ricardo himself was not aware, which however, if developed, render support to a criticism of the conventional marginalist view that all markets can be expected to clear at all times and there is no problem of effective demand. As will become clear in the following, the answer is in the affirmative. However, in the answer given, Malthus plays no role anymore.

It was Piero Sraffa who in his 1960 book laid the foundation 'for a critique of [marginalist theory]' by reviving the 'standpoint ... of the old classical economists' (Sraffa, 1960, pp. v and vi). Pasinetti, in several publications and especially in his *Lectures on the Theory of Production* (Pasinetti, 1977b; see also Pasinetti, 1974, chs. v and vi), elaborated on Sraffa's interpretation and showed how a bridge could be built connecting Ricardo's surplus approach to the theory of value and distribution and a theory of economic growth subject to Keynes's Principle of Effective Demand.[15]

3.5 Surplus Approach and Effective Demand

The idea of crossbreeding elements of the theories of Ricardo and Keynes might look extravagant, if not bizarre, vis-à-vis Keynes's judgement that 'Ricardo was the abstract and *a priori* theorist', a man 'with

[15] Pasinetti also mentioned Marx as one of the inspiring sources of the alternative approach to economics he has in mind. Marx in fact combined (a version of) the classical surplus approach to the theory of value and distribution with a theory of effective demand, in which what he called the problem of the 'realisation' of the surplus played an important role. Dealing with Marx's contribution is, however, beyond the scope of this chapter.

his head in the clouds' (*CWK*, x, pp. 95 and 98). While Ricardo certainly was an abstract theorist, he was also a man with considerable practical sense, experience and financial success. He cared for facts not only in money and banking but was keen to keep abreast with the latest developments in agriculture, manufacturing, commerce and trade regarding technical and organisational innovations. His adherence to Say's law, however, prevented him from comprehending the role of effective demand for the performance of the economy. Yet there are elements in his approach to the theory of value and distribution that undermine Say's law. Let us see which.

Ricardo insisted that in conditions of free competition, 'necessary' or 'natural' prices, $\mathbf{p}$, depend not only on the cost-minimising methods of production actually used to produce the various commodities but also on income distribution, that is, the rate (or share) of wages, w, or the rate of profits, r, in short:[16]

$$\mathbf{p} = \mathbf{p}(w).$$

Ricardo also understood that for a given system of production the two distributive variables, r and w, are inversely related to each other, that is, there is a relationship

$$r = f(w), \text{where } \partial r / \partial w < 0.$$

The capitals employed in the different industries of an economy, which, as Ricardo stressed, 'are not the same in kind' (*Works*, IX, p. 360), can only be conceived of as *sums of value* (expressed in terms of some standard of value, or numéraire). A fortiori they also depend on income distribution and change with it. Ricardo therefore rejected the idea, which became especially prominent with marginalist authors, that the 'quantity of capital' in a firm, an industry or the economy as a whole can be taken as known independently of the rate of profits.

We owe Sraffa (1960) the elaboration of the Classical approach to the problem of value and distribution, including a treatment of fixed capital, scarce natural resources and pure joint production, which we put to one side in this chapter except for a few brief remarks on fixed capital and its utilisation below. He also discusses the problem of the

[16] The argument presupposes for simplicity single production, that is, the absence of fixed capital, land and pure joint production; see Sraffa (1960, part I); Pasinetti (1977b); Schefold (1989); Kurz and Salvadori (1995, chs. 4–6).

choice of technique, that is, which methods of production cost-minimising producers can be expected to choose when there are several methods available for each commodity. A thorough investigation of this problem that is firmly rooted in the Classical economists' and especially Ricardo's contribution and yields results that were the object of what became known as the Cambridge controversies in the theory of capital (see Kurz, 2020). These results contradict the marginalist view that the rate of profits is determined by the marginal productivity of capital and the marginalist principle of substitution, according to which a change in the wage rate relative to the rate of interest (or profits) prompts cost-minimising producers to employ relatively less (more) of the factor of production that has become relatively more (less) expensive. The conventional principle of substitution underlies the usual demand function of a factor service that is inversely elastic with regard to its price. Here it suffices to mention the possibility of reverse capital deepening, or capital reversing, in the economic system as a whole: the relationship between the overall capital-labour, K/L, or capital-output, K/Y, ratio, on the one hand, and the r/w ratio, on the other, may exhibit segments that are increasing rather than decreasing, as conventional marginalist theory maintains. The negative implication of capital reversing for the theory can be seen when we confront a 'demand curve' for capital with a 'supply curve' of it (see, for example, Kurz and Salvadori, 1998). If the two happen to intersect only once at a level of the rate of profits at which the demand curve cuts the supply curve from below, the equilibrium is unstable. With perfect competition and therefore perfectly flexible w and r, a deviation of r from the equilibrium value would imply that one of the two types of income, wages and profits would get eliminated. This throws into doubt the explanatory power of the theory.

A remark is fitting concerning the widespread opinion that Sraffa's analysis in his 1960 book does not allow for effective demand to play any role whatsoever. In my view, this cannot be sustained. Here it suffices to draw the attention to a remark of Sraffa that should serve to dispel this opinion. He concludes chapter XI, 'Land', with a passage that reads (leaving out the final sentence):

> Machines of an obsolete type which are still in use are similar to land in so far as they are employed as means of production, although not currently produced. The quasi-rent (if we may apply Marshall's term in a more restricted sense than he gave it) which is received for those fixed capital

items, which having been in active use in the past, have now been superseded but are worth employing for what they can get, is determined precisely in the same way as the rent of land. (Sraffa, 1960, p. 78)

Wicksell aptly called obsolete fixed capital items 'rent goods'. These will be employed partly or entirely depending on the briskness of effective demand and they will yield their proprietors smaller or larger quasi-rents.[17] Those items of durable capital goods that belong to the cost-minimising technique will instead be fully utilised. Macroeconomic models of a Kaleckian and post-Keynesian type, which operate with a single rate of capacity utilisation for the system as a whole, fail to notice the coexistence of fully utilised fixed capital items, on the one hand, and partly or not at all utilised obsolete items, on the other. It plays, however, an important role in the dynamics of the economic system and the interplay of effective demand, relative prices and income distribution – especially when the products under consideration happen to be basic products. Hence, things are invariably more complex than is often assumed.

3.6 Taking Stock

We may now briefly take stock of what has been said with specific regard to Pasinetti's third characteristic of the suggested re-orientation of economics, taking 'Malthus and the Classics (not Walras and the Marginalists) as the major inspiring source in the history of economic thought' (Pasinetti, 2007, p. 222). Pasinetti drew the attention especially to two aspects of the suggested re-orientation, namely:

(i) the relevance of the principle of effective demand in the classical-Keynesian theories and
(ii) the framing of classical-Keynesian theories 'in a "production" rather than in an "exchange" paradigm'.

Cross-breeding valuable and valid classical and Keynesian perspectives on the economy in a coherent framework and contributing to the development of its potentials is indeed a main goal of Pasinetti's

[17] For a discussion of the problem of the optimal pattern of utilisation of fixed capital items within a Sraffian framework of the analysis, see Kurz (1986). For the formalisation of the problem of obsolete machines, see Kurz and Salvadori (1995, pp. 348–351).

respective proposal that also informs the present collection of essays on *Pasinetti and the Classical-Keynesians*. In my view, the following inferences can be drawn from the above argument with regard to the two aspects mentioned.

First, the resumption of the classical approach to the problem of value and distribution by Sraffa and its further elaboration and extension by Pasinetti (see especially 1974, 1977b, 1980) imply that the rate of interest (rate of profits) cannot be considered the factor that equilibrates savings and investment. Hence, from a consistently developed classical standpoint, it turns out that Say's law cannot be sustained. This would in all probability have come as a surprise to Keynes, who was very critical of Ricardo and accused him of not understanding what the facts suggested, namely, that effective aggregate demand mattered and that there could be general gluts of commodities. While compared to Malthus, Ricardo was by far the superior economic theorist, Malthus may be said to have sensed a crucial deficiency of the received classical doctrine without, alas, being able to identify its source, that is, a lack of a thorough analysis of the coordination of decisions to invest and decisions to save.[18] It was most prominently Keynes (and also Michal Kalecki) who provided the missing link and was able to refute Say's law. Keynes's opposition to it now gets compelling support from modern classical analysis. Freed from the straitjacket of Say's law, the way is wide open to elaborate on the principle of effective demand and develop a theory of capital accumulation that does not start from the premise of a permanently fully utilised capital stock and a fully employed workforce.

As regards the second aspect, let me be clear what in my view 'production paradigm' and 'exchange paradigm' could mean and what they cannot mean. It would certainly be wrong to claim that the marginalist authors, in contrast to the classical authors, focused

[18] While Pasinetti, who holds Ricardo in very high esteem, was willing to give credit to Malthus for his realism in the regard under consideration, it is interesting to note that George Stigler, who also thought very highly of Ricardo, emphasised: 'The triumph of Ricardo over Malthus cannot be regretted by the modern economist: it is more important that good logic win over bad than that good insight win over poor.' (Stigler, 1953, p. 599) In my view, Pasinetti is to be applauded for not sharing such an extreme position. The explanatory power of economic theories is not decided exclusively in terms of logical consistency. Repeatedly, progress in economic analysis was triggered by the discovery of phenomena the received theories could not explain.

attention exclusively on the sphere of exchange and were not concerned with the sphere of production. As a matter of fact, even the most radical representatives of Austrian subjectivism, such as Ludwig von Mises, who attributed predominance to needy individuals and their inclination to enter into contracts with each other about the exchange of goods and services, and who therefore saw acts of production and of supply unequivocally rooted in utility considerations of agents, spoke about production and felt that they could deal with it in a satisfactory way. However, this is not the case, as Sraffa, Pasinetti, Garegnani and others had made clear. In fact, the marginalist idea to be able to construct the theory of production and supply in complete analogy to the theory of consumption and demand, with the concepts of substitution among factors of production and of marginal productivity replacing the concepts of substitution among goods and of marginal utility, is mistaken. Sraffa disputed that there is such a fundamental symmetry between the properties of human nature and the technical conditions of industry (see Marshall, 1920, p. 170n.). To him, the postulated uniformity of the relationships was dubious: 'Is it not very strange that two such heterogeneous things as human nature and industrial technology should bring about results so similar' (Sraffa, 1998, p. 332). The assumed 'fundamental symmetry ... between the forces of demand and those of supply does not exist' (Sraffa, 1926, p. 535). Therefore, it is futile seeking to elaborate a theory of competitive value by starting from the sphere of consumption and exchange and telescoping the principles taken to rule in it to the sphere of production. The two spheres are distinct and subject to very different principles and 'laws'. The production paradigm endorsed and developed by Pasinetti respects this difference and follows in the footsteps of the classical authors. Endorsing the production paradigm has many advantages, including its concern with putting the focus on studying the economic system as a whole and distrusting partial equilibrium analyses. In fact, as was stressed by authors from William Petty, the physiocrats and Robert Torrens to Marx, commodities were produced by means of commodities. Their values could only be determined by looking at the economic system in its entirety and by taking into account the whole process of the social metabolism. The demand and supply of single commodities cannot possibly capture the intertwined production relationships with regard to a multitude of commodities. Trying to construct the theory of production in the image of the theory of consumption put economic theory on the wrong track that led into a cul de sac. Time is overdue to go back to the juncture at which the wrong direction was taken and start anew from there by reviving and developing classical-cum-Keynesian economic thought.

3.7 Concluding Remarks

Pasinetti's proposal to take as the 'major inspiring source' in a reorientation of economics the Classics, Malthus and Keynes, may at first be received with amazement if not outright opposition by those who are cognizant of the continuous quarrels between Ricardo and Malthus concerning each and every subject in economics they touched upon, with Keynes siding strongly with Malthus. However, close scrutiny shows that after some corrections of and further elaborations on important building-blocks of the analyses of Ricardo and Keynes, these turn out to be perfectly compatible with one another. They may indeed be said to contain the germs of a new economic theory that sheds the weaknesses of the theories from which it derives and improves upon their strengths. In this new construction, it turns out that Malthus will be somewhat the odd man out, because apart from his occasional sense of realism he had relatively little to offer in terms of a sound explanation of the facts he observed.

It is the development of Ricardo's surplus approach to the theory of value and distribution by Sraffa and refined by authors including Garegnani, Pasinetti, Bertram Schefold and Ian Steedman that shows the way to the mentioned reconciliation of the standpoint of the classical economists and especially Ricardo and that of Keynes. This is so because it turns out that Say's law can no longer be sustained other than in exceedingly special and in fact uninteresting circumstances. Liberated from the straitjacket of Say's law, the way is open towards a reformulation of the Principle of Effective Demand within an otherwise classical framework of the analysis.[19] This is, of course, only a first step on the way towards a more convincing theory of capital accumulation and economic growth that has to combine (i) the effective demand or income effect of investment, (ii) its capacity effect and (iii) what may be called the innovation effect of investment,

[19] For a reformulation of the multiplier in such a framework, see Kurz (1985).

because gross investment is the vehicle by means of which the capital stock of the economy is modernised. Pasinetti and others deserve to be credited with having contributed important elements to such a theory and thus of having begun to translate an inspiration drawn from the sources mentioned into remarkable pieces of work.

References

Baumol W. (1977) 'Say's (at Least) Eight Laws, or What Say and James Mill May Really Have Meant', in *Economica, New Series*, 44(174), pp. 145–161.

Clower R. W. and Leijonhufvud A. (1973) 'Say's Principle, What It Means and Doesn't Mean', in *Intermountain Economics Review*, 4(2), pp. 1–16. Reprinted in Leijonhufvud A. (1981) *Information and Coordination*, New York and Oxford, Oxford University Press.

Garegnani P. (1978) 'Notes on Consumption, Investment and Effective Demand: I', in *Cambridge Journal of Economics*, 2, pp. 335–353.

(1979). 'Notes on Consumption, Investment and Effective Demand: II', in *Cambridge Journal of Economics*, 3, pp. 63–82.

Gehrke C. and Kurz H. D. (2001) 'Say and Ricardo on Value and Distribution', in *The European Journal of the History of Economic Thought*, 8(4), pp. 449–486.

Kalmbach P. and Kurz H. D. (2009) 'Malthus: Vorgänger von Keynes?', in Hagemann H., Horn G. and Krupp H. J. (eds.) *Aus gesamtwirtschaftlicher Sicht. Festschrift für Jürgen Kromphardt*, Marburg, Metropolis, pp. 163–182.

Keynes J. M. (1973 et seq.). *The Collected Writings of John Maynard Keynes*, Moggridge D. (ed.), London and Basingstoke, Macmillan (cited as *CWK*, volume number, page number).

Kurz H. D. (1985) 'Effective Demand in a "Classical" Model of Value and Distribution: The Multiplier in a Sraffian Framework', in *The Manchester School*, 53(2), pp. 121–137.

(1986) '"Normal" Positions and Capital Utilization', in *Political Economy. Studies in the Surplus Approach*, 2, pp. 37–54.

(1998) 'Limiting and Regulating Principles', in Kurz H. D. and Salvadori N. (eds.) *The Elgar Companion to Classical Economics*, vol. 2, Cheltenham and Northampton, Edward Elgar, pp. 45–50.

(2000) 'The Hayek-Keynes-Sraffa Controversy Reconsidered', in Kurz H. D. (ed.) *Critical Essays on Piero Sraffa's Legacy in Economics*, Cambridge, Cambridge University Press, pp. 257–301.

(2010) 'Technical Progress, Capital Accumulation and Income Distribution in Classical Economics: Adam Smith, David Ricardo and

Karl Marx', in *The European Journal of the History of Economic Thought*, 17 (5), pp. 1183–1222.
(2015) 'Capital Theory, Crises, and Business Cycles: The Triangular Debate between Hayek, Keynes and Sraffa', in *Journal of Reviews on Global Economics*, 4, pp. 186–191.
(2020) 'The Theory of Value and Distribution and the Problem of Capital', in *European Journal of Economics and Economic Policies: Intervention*, 17(2), pp. 241–264.
Kurz H. D. and Salvadori N. (1995) *Theory of Production: A Long-Period Analysis*, Cambridge, Cambridge University Press.
(1998) 'Reverse Capital Deepening and the Numeraire: A Note', in *Review of Political Economy*, 10(4), pp. 415–426.
(2006) 'Endogenous Growth in a Stylised "Classical" Model', in Stathakis G. and Vaggi G. (eds.) *Economic Development and Social Change*, London and New York, Routledge, pp. 106–124.
Malthus T. R. (1820 [1989]) *Principles of Political Economy*, Pullen J. (ed.), Variorum edition, 2 vols., Cambridge, Cambridge University Press.
Marshall A. (1890 [1920]) *Principles of Economics*, 8th ed., London, Macmillan.
Pasinetti L. L. (1974) *Growth and Income Distribution: Essays in Economic Theory*, Cambridge, Cambridge University Press.
(1977a) *Sviluppo economico e distribuzione del reddito*, Bologna, Il Mulino.
(1977b) *Lectures on the Theory of Production*, London, Macmillan.
(1980) *Essays on the Theory of Joint Production*, London and Basingstoke, Macmillan.
(2007) *Keynes and Cambridge Keynesians*, Cambridge, Cambridge University Press.
Pigou A. C. (1933) *The Theory of Unemployment*, London, Macmillan.
Ricardo D. (1951–1973) *The Works and Correspondence of David Ricardo*, Sraffa P. with the collaboration of Dobb M. H. (eds.), 11 vols., Cambridge, Cambridge University Press.
Schefold B. (1989) *Mr Sraffa on Joint Production and Other Essays*, London, Unwin Hyman.
Smith A. (1776 [1976]) *An Inquiry into the Nature and Causes of the Wealth of Nations*, The Glasgow Edition of the Works and Correspondence of Adam Smith, Campbell R. H. and Skinner A. S. (eds.), Oxford, Clarendon Press.
Sraffa P. (1925 [1998]) 'On the Relationship between Cost and Quantity Produced', in Pasinetti L. L. (ed.) *Italian Economic Papers*, vol. III, Bologna, Il Mulino; Oxford, Oxford University Press, pp. 323–363, English translation from the Italian original by Eatwell J. and Roncaglia A.

(1926) 'The Laws of Returns under Competitive Conditions', in *Economic Journal*, 36(144), pp. 535–550.
(1932) 'Dr. Hayek on Money and Capital', in *Economic Journal*, 42, pp. 42–53.
(1960) *Production of Commodities by Means of Commodities*, Cambridge, Cambridge University Press.
Stigler G. J. (1953) 'Sraffa's Ricardo', in *American Economic Review*, 43(3), pp. 586–599.

4 Non-ergodic (in Place of Stationary, Timeless) Economic Systems

Considerations Suggested by Joan Robinson's Distinction between Two 'Notions' of Time in Economic Theory

ARIEL DVOSKIN AND PAOLO TRABUCCHI

4.1 Introduction

In seeking our path among the complex of questions raised by the fourth characteristic ascribed by Luigi Pasinetti to the Cambridge School (notoriously, questions pertaining to the 'treatment of time' stem in all directions and are reflected in practically any part of an economic theory), we believe it is convenient to start from a point Pasinetti himself refers to in his discussion of that characteristic: namely, the 'sharp distinction made by Joan Robinson between logical time and historical time' (Pasinetti, 2007, p. 226).

The reason is the following. Originally, the distinction was proposed to give evidence to certain elements whereby the neoclassical theory would fail to give a satisfactory account of a process of capital accumulation. As we shall see, these are basically, though by no means exclusively, elements preventing a full recognition of the degree of irreversibility ('non-ergodicity') that would be the feature of certain economic processes, changes in 'logical' time being prevalently used by Robinson as a metaphor for perfectly reversible changes. The fact is, however, that at a certain point Robinson felt that the criticisms she had raised against the neoclassical theory should also be directed against the classical theory, at least in the version we find in Piero Sraffa's *Production of Commodities*: 'The specification of a self-reproducing ... system such as that of Sraffa ... is in logical time, not in history (Robinson, 1974 [1978], p. 128). This has understandably resulted in, or has possibly given expression to, a fundamental division within what Pasinetti calls the Cambridge School; and it is for this reason that, although the question has already been addressed a number of times and without being able to cover the vast literature that has accumulated on the subject, we feel that we should start our comment from this particular point.[1]

In Sections 4.2, 4.3 and 4.4, we shall thus argue that, in its fundamental aspect concerning the degree of irreversibility that should be ascribed to certain economic processes, Robinson's critique cannot be extended to the classical theory, where the possibility of irreversibilities in both production and consumption processes is openly admitted. This will require, however, to distinguish carefully within that critique between what belongs to the way in which the theoretical position of the economic system is determined and what belongs instead to the way in which a meaningful relationship is established between that position and the observable position of the system. Indeed, in this latter respect we shall argue that, at least if we consider the two theories in their traditional presentation, the classical and the neoclassical theory do share the same method; but that this method, based as it is on the determination of a uniform rate of profit, is not seriously called into question by Robinson's criticisms.

At this point, we shall have to choose between the two directions along which our comment could be developed and that roughly correspond to the two aspects we have distinguished in Robinson's critique. In general, it can in fact be said that questions that have a 'chronological' dimension, and that thus have a distinct bearing on Pasinetti's fourth characteristic, arise both when we study how the theoretical position of the economic system evolves through time and when we study the movement (if there is one) by which the actual position of the economic system 'adjusts' to its theoretical position. In a certain sense, we are always concerned with the first movement; but this happens under the more or less tacit assumption that a correspondence between the theoretical and the actual position of the economic system has been somehow established. The study of the second movement is in other terms a fundamental condition, not so much for the study of the first one, as for its significance. It is, moreover, on the nature of this second movement that the greatest number of misunderstandings seem to have accumulated even among those who are convinced of the need of an alternative to the neoclassical theory.

[1] In this we shall mainly follow Garegnani (1989); Bharadwaj (1991); Eatwell (1997).

These two reasons appeared to us sufficient to devote the following two sections to an attempt at clarifying some of these misunderstandings. In particular, our attention will be directed to those misunderstandings that can be traced back to the identification, proposed especially by Alessandro Roncaglia in a number of works and to which Pasinetti (2007, p. 226) himself refers in his discussion of his fourth characteristic, between the theoretical position of the economic system determined by Sraffa and a 'still picture' taken 'at a given moment of time'.[2] Section 4.5 will consequently be devoted to the question of the need of an adjustment process in the classical theory, while Section 4.6 will discuss the 'persistence' of the theoretical position of the economic system that is required by such a process.

There is, however, a third reason behind our choice that should also be mentioned. Discussing the fourth characteristic ascribed by Pasinetti to the Cambridge School, one cannot fail to notice that a distinction which at first sight is very similar to that proposed by Robinson, namely, the distinction between 'logical' time and 'real' time, figures today with a prominent position in the neo-Walrasian reformulation of the neoclassical theory and that this happens precisely in connection with the relationship that can be established in this theory between the theoretical and the actual position of the economic system. In this comment we shall not discuss this distinction in full. In Section 4.7, we shall try, however, on the one hand, to show the relevance that such a discussion may have for the question of the comparability between alternative theories that underlies the whole set of characteristics ascribed by Pasinetti to the Cambridge School and, on the other, to show along which lines such a discussion can in our opinion most fruitfully be attempted at present.

4.2 Expectations and Successive Positions of the Economic System

As Robinson herself put it at a certain stage in the discussion, the central issue in her distinction between 'logical' time and 'historical' time turns around the 'confusion', into which in her opinion economic

[2] For a recent presentation of this idea, see Roncaglia (2010). This 'photographic' interpretation of the classical theory (or at any rate of *Production of Commodities*) can be found also in Blankenburg, Arena and Wilkinson (2012).

theory would only too often fall, between 'comparisons of equilibrium positions and the history of a process of accumulation' (Robinson, 1974 [1978], p. 135).

As we shall see, there are two closely related, yet distinct, possible interpretations of this 'confusion' that can in turn be traced back to two equally distinct propositions stating what economic theory should *not* do. Naturally, if we want to understand the possible bearing of Robinson's criticism on the classical as well as the neoclassical theory, on both interpretations the 'equilibrium' position of the system must be taken to mean its *theoretical* position as this is determined by those two theories. For no determination of that position in terms of an equilibrium can be found in the classical theory. Given this, the two propositions to which the confusion pointed at by Robinson can be traced back are the following: (a) a process of change which is undergone by the economic system should not be studied by means of the comparison between two different and *successive* theoretical positions of the system; (b) a single theoretical position of the economic system should not be determined by comparing two (or more) *alternative* positions of the system, which should instead more properly be studied one after the other as the result of a process of change.

The first proposition is probably the one that in the interpretation of Robinson's critique presents itself more naturally; and it is certainly the one by which that critique has been generally received. It is indeed in support of this proposition that Robinson has claimed that no matter how the theoretical positions of the economic system that are being compared are determined, there would be no *tendency* for the actual position of the system to move towards, or around, such theoretical positions. And it is for this reason that, at least if we look at the traditional presentations of the two theories, this particular version of Robinson's critique can legitimately be directed both against the neoclassical and against the classical theory.

The fact is immediately evident if we look at Adam Smith's *Wealth of Nations*. What we find here is, in the first place, the marked distinction between the 'market price' and the 'natural price' of a commodity, that is, between, respectively, the price that can actually be observed at any moment on the market and the price that is determined by the theory. Indeed, as Smith observes, these two prices are equal only when the quantity of a commodity 'which is actually brought to market' is no more nor less than its 'effectual demand', that is, the 'demand of those who are willing to pay [its] natural price'; but, given the accidental nature of the circumstances that may continually exert an influence on the first magnitude, this is not a state of affairs that one can expect to observe at any given moment. A second aspect that we find in the *Wealth of Nations* is, however, the constant tendency of market prices to 'gravitate' around natural prices. This depends, on the one hand, on the way in which the sign of the divergence between market prices and natural prices is 'regulated' by the 'proportion' between the quantity brought to market and the effectual demand of commodities and, on the other hand, on the conditions under which natural prices are determined: namely, on the fact that the natural price of a commodity is equal (if for the sake of simplicity we assume that land is superabundant and hence no rent is paid) to the sum of wages and profits that must be paid in order to produce the commodity, when wages and profits are at their 'natural', that is, 'ordinary or average', level. It is for this reason that divergences between market prices and natural prices will induce 'labourers ... and ... their employers' to flow out of those sectors where market prices are below their natural level and to flow into those sectors where the opposite is true. But, through the competition among sellers, a market price below its natural level will be the result of the quantity of the commodity brought to market exceeding its effectual demand, while, through the competition among buyers, a market price above its natural price will be the result of the quantity brought to market falling short of effectual demand. Hence, the movement of productive capacity from one sector to the other, which is induced by the difference between market prices and natural prices, will push in each sector the quantity brought to market towards the effectual demand and, as a consequence, the market price toward the natural price (Smith, 1776 [1976], ch. VII, pp. 72–75).

As we would expect, fundamentally the same adjustment process can be found in David Ricardo's *Principles* where what 'prevent[s] the market price of commodities from continuing for any length of time either much above, or much below their natural price', is ascribed to 'the tendency to equalize the rate of profits' in all sectors that follows from the competition among capitalists or to 'the desire, which every capitalist has, of diverting his funds from a less to a more profitable employment' (*Works*, I, pp. 88–92). But, despite the different determination of theoretical prices, the same approach to the relationship between these prices and observable prices can also be found in the traditional presentations of the neoclassical theory, where indeed theoretical prices satisfy the condition of a uniform rate of profit. Nor is the case limited to economists like Alfred Marshall, whose desire of being perceived as the successor of a substantially unbroken tradition that would go from Smith to John Stuart Mill is well known. The fact is equally clear, for instance, in Léon Walras who, after noticing that the state of 'equilibrium in production' determined by his equations is 'an ideal and not a real state', presents those equations as a satisfactory explanation of the object he had set himself in his theory only because such a state can be considered as 'the normal state of the system', that is, that towards which 'things spontaneously tend under a régime of free competition' (Walras, 1874–1876 [1956], p. 224).[3]

Robinson appears, therefore, to be absolutely right in ascribing to both the neoclassical and the classical theory in their traditional presentations a method based on the tendency of the actual position of the economic system to move towards, or, as we have said, to 'adjust' to, its theoretical position. The point is that her arguments in this respect do not appear to be such as to call that method into question.

The argument that is more often adduced by Robinson against the tendency of the economic system to move in the direction of its theoretical position seems in fact to be entirely based on the mere existence, at any given moment, of wrong expectations: '*As soon as* the uncertainty of the expectations that guide economic behaviour is admitted, equilibrium drops out of the argument and history takes its place' (Robinson, 1974 [1978], p. 126, our italics). But, clearly, the existence of wrong expectations is implicit in the very fact that, at any given moment, the actual position of the economic system generally is not, nor is supposed to be, a position that is characterised by a uniform rate of profit. Indeed, if each single producer anticipated exactly and in good time, on the one hand, all the changes in effectual demand and in the technical conditions of production and, on the other, the quantity produced by the other producers, differences between the quantity brought to market and the effectual demand of commodities would be practically impossible. The existence at any given moment of wrong

[3] For a deeper analysis of the relationship between theoretical and observable prices in the classical and in the neoclassical theory in their traditional presentations, see Vianello (1989) and Ciccone (1999).

expectations is in other terms an integral part of the method criticised by Robinson. But, as such, it does not seem able to call into question the tendency of competition to induce such a *correction* in expectations as is sufficient to bring the economic system back *towards* its theoretical position whenever it finds itself in a different position.

Of course, the correction in expectations that would be necessary in order to *reach* the theoretical position of the economic system is quite a different matter. But, although Robinson often refers to the question of how an economic system can be *in* its theoretical position ('never talk about a system *getting into* equilibrium, for equilibrium has no meaning unless you are in it already. But think of a system *being* in equilibrium and having been there as far back towards Adam as you find it useful to go so that every *ex-ante* expectation about today ever held in the past is being fulfilled today', Robinson, 1953 [1978], p. 144), this is by no means an element of what we may call the *traditional* method. Indeed, since in this method the tendency of the actual position of the economic system to move towards its theoretical position is based on the competition among capitalists and since, as such, this can only operate ex post, such a coincidence between the theoretical and the observable position of the economic system, though in itself not impossible, is precisely what we *do not* expect to observe even when the competitive process has been able of exerting an appreciable effect on the economic system.

4.3 Alternative Simultaneous Positions of the Economic System

As we already mentioned, there is a second possible interpretation of the 'confusion' pointed at by Robinson, leading in this case to the proposition according to which a single theoretical position of the economic system should not be determined by comparing two (or more) *alternative* positions of the system.

Admittedly, this second proposition is not the one that emerges more often nor, possibly, more clearly in Robinson's critical contributions. It seems, however, to come rather close to the basic idea that, although somewhat implicitly, can be found in the original formulation of her critique. It is, moreover, the form in which Robinson's critique is directly connected to the question of the reversibility, or non-reversibility, of economic processes.

It was in 1953 that Robinson, in a short but deliberately provocative essay (Robinson, 1953 [1978]), claimed that the whole demand and supply apparatus used by the neoclassical theory is simply based on a methodological mistake. Demand and supply curves, Robinson noted, are used to determine the equilibrium position of the economic system; and, though the system may never find itself in such a position, this is its theoretical position in that, she argued, the system is continually supposed to move in its direction. But the curves themselves by which the equilibrium position is determined are given independently of that movement. Thus, Robinson concluded, while any movement of the economic system must necessarily be 'through time' (as she would later say, through 'historical' time), in the neoclassical theory such a movement ends up resembling a movement 'through space', in that the same route can be covered more than once and, above all, in both directions (what she would later refer to as movements in 'logical' time).

That, as is the case in proposition (b), the problem concerns here a single theoretical position of the economic system and not, as in proposition (a), the evolution of this theoretical position over time, cannot be doubted. What is less clear is in what sense it can be said that the problem arises from the fact that, in determining that theoretical position, several alternative positions of the economic system have been involved. We shall see in a moment how this is connected to the reason why here Robinson speaks *at the same time* of the determination of the theoretical position of the economic system and of the movement of the system towards such position. First, however, it will be convenient to give a look at one of the main, and certainly most discussed, *consequences* that Robinson felt she could derive from her critique, namely, the thesis concerning 'the unimportance of reswitching' (Robinson, 1975 [1976], 1989).

In order to understand this particular thesis, it must be remembered that a basic proposition in the neoclassical theory is the one establishing the existence of an inverse relationship between the remuneration of a 'factor of production' and its demand. Such a proposition is in turn based on the possibility of ordering different techniques independently of value and distribution according to the proportion in which these techniques use the same productive factors. Now, such ordering meets no strictly logical problem when the factors of production can be measured in their appropriate technical units, as is the case with land or labour. This, however, is no longer true when the use of produced means of production is taken into account. In fact, as has been shown by the discovery of the closely related phenomena of 'reswitching' (by which the same technique can be convenient at two distinct levels of the rate of interest and not convenient for all the intermediate levels) and 'reverse capital deepening' (by which a fall in the rate of interest may lead to the choice of a relatively less capital-intensive technique), the amount of capital required by the economic system may alternatively rise and fall with a decrease of the rate of interest.

This, in a nutshell, was the fundamental result achieved at the end of the discussions on capital theory originating from the theses presented in Sraffa's *Production of Commodities* and during which Robinson constantly sided with the critics of the neoclassical theory. From a certain point onwards, however, Robinson's position with regard to this result has increasingly been that of affirming that what would be *analytically* rejected by the phenomenon of reswitching, that is, the existence of an inverse relationship between the rate of interest and the demand for capital, would in any case be *methodologically* indefensible: for movements along the demand curve for 'capital', by implying changes in the methods of production, generally occur as a result of a process of capital accumulation and would at any rate involve too radical a change in the conditions prevailing in the economic system for different points on that curve to be referred to the same position of the economic system.

At first sight, the question raised here by Robinson is that of the plausibility of the assumption of a sufficiently broad set of alternative production methods from which the economic system can choose: 'In real life, different techniques do not co-exist in time in a ready-made book of blueprints; they are evolved as accumulation goes on' (Robinson, 1976 [1989], p. 361). Considering that what Robinson had here in mind was the traditional version of the neoclassical theory, this, however, can presumably be granted by referring the theoretical position of the economic system to that relatively long period of time which is the generally recognised time horizon of this theory. The question becomes then whether that set of techniques can be given independently of the way in which the system moves in search of the most profitable one. The question is, therefore, to a large extent that of the reversibility, or non-reversibility, that can be ascribed to a change in the productive methods that are being used in the economic system.

It is thus clear in what sense the particular formulation of Robinson's criticism that can be traced back to our second proposition refers to the distinction between 'logical' time and 'historical' time. As already mentioned, changes in 'logical' time (or 'movements in space') are simply used as a metaphor for perfectly reversible changes.

What should also be clear, and what from our point of view is more important, is that, whatever its merit, in this case Robinson's criticism can be directed against the neoclassical theory but *cannot* be directed against the classical theory. Indeed, if we look at the demand and supply *curves* that underlie the neoclassical theory, what we see is that, no matter how they are determined, both curves have the characteristic of making reference to a number of *mutually exclusive* states of the economic system. In fact, the economic system cannot exhibit at one and the same time, for example, a high price and a low demand, and a low price and a high demand, for the same commodity. Now, the use of these alternative states in the determination of a single position of the economic system would no doubt be rather easily admissible if all that had to be determined was a position that the system *could* or, according to some optimality criterion, *should* be in. But, if what has to be determined is the position that the economic system actually is in, or a position that has some specific relation with the position the economic system actually is in, then a number of conditions must be fulfilled.

Clearly, if those alternative states must play a role in determining a position of the economic system that has one or the other of the two characteristics just mentioned, they must *exert their influence* on the system; and, if this has to happen without those states representing in themselves theoretical positions that the economic system sequentially is in, they must do so *simultaneously*. This means in the first place that, since such simultaneous influence cannot happen in the same instant (for the states of the economic system are mutually exclusive), it must occur over the same period of time, to which the theoretical position of the economic system must be consequently referred. Secondly, this means that the determination of this theoretical position involves the actual *movement* of the system from one of these states to the other: for there is no other way in which a state of the system may be said to have a role in the determination of another state of the same system. Finally, this means that, over the period to which the theoretical position of the economic system is referred, these alternative states do not depend on the order in which the system itself may possibly move from one to the other: which is clearly possible only if, at least to a large extent, these are reversible movements.[4]

A rather high degree of reversibility of all the main processes of change in the relevant economic variables is in other terms a necessary condition for a theory using those changes in order to determine a single position of the economic system. Such a requirement is therefore inescapable for the neoclassical theory, in that such a determination of the theoretical position of the economic system is precisely what follows from the use, for that determination, of the notion of an equilibrium between demand and supply. For the same reason that requirement cannot, however, be found in the classical theory. And it is this aspect of this theory, which in Smith and Ricardo can only be seen through the absence of any role for demand and supply curves in the explanation of value and distribution, that emerges explicitly in the Preface to *Production of Commodities*, where Sraffa underlies that, while the neoclassical theory 'requires attention to be focused on change' (Sraffa, 1960, p. v), no such requirement arises in the classical theory.

4.4 Historical Circumstances in Classical and Neoclassical Theories

Naturally, what we have just said could not by itself exhaust the broader question that seems to underlie both Pasinetti's fourth feature of the Cambridge School and, at least in its second formulation, Robinson's distinction between two notions of time: namely, the different role that in the classical and in the neoclassical theory historical circumstances may have in explaining the relevant economic variables.

Now, in this regard it seems convenient to refer in the first place to what has been described as the different *logical structure* of the classical and of the neoclassical theory. As is well known, this emerges at a

[4] This aspect of Robinson's criticism is made particularly clear in Bharadwaj (1991, p. 93). This appears natural if one thinks of the fundamental work done by Bharadwaj, on the one hand, on the way Marshall gradually turned Mill's still partly classical categories into the foundations for an explanation of value and distribution in terms of demand and supply (Bharadwaj, 1978) and, on the other, on the doubts cautiously expressed in this regard by Marshall (with an eye, among other things, to the question of reversibility) both in Appendix H of his *Principles* and in handwritten notes (Bharadwaj, 1972).

formal level in the particular nature that characterises the data on which a relevant part of the classical theory is based: namely, in the fact that, in this theory, the produced quantities of the different commodities, the technical conditions of production and, usually, the real wage are taken as given while determining relative prices and the remaining distributive variables but are in turn susceptible of being studied in a different part of the theory. No such notion of 'intermediate data' (Garegnani, 1998), and hence no distinction into two logically separate parts, can in fact be found in the more compact structure of the neoclassical theory. It would seem therefore that, in order to evaluate Robinson's distinction between two notions of time as an instrument capable of bringing some light on the question of the role that historical circumstances may have in the determination of economic variables, what should be established is the role that such a distinction may have in providing a *substantial* basis for the difference between the logical structure of the classical and of the neoclassical theory we have just mentioned.

From this point of view, it should be noted that, as we have seen, that distinction is certainly a way of underlining how a considerable degree of reversibility in the economic processes under study is a *necessary condition* for a theory based on the equilibrium between demand and supply. But to say that a theory needs a considerable degree of reversibility does not mean that that theory is necessarily wrong. What has to be shown is that there are relevant economic processes whose irreversible nature cannot be neglected. And it is in this regard that what in our opinion is the limitation of Robinson's criticism in its second formulation should be noted. The limitation lies in the predominantly *aprioristic* nature of that criticism by which it would seem that, since every economic process is to some extent irreversible, any theory that does not take this into account should be considered as necessarily wrong. This general implication is certainly not what we find in the classical theory. And not because the scarcely reversible nature of certain economic processes is ignored as one of the reasons why that theory is divided into two separate parts according to the different degree of generality that can be ascribed to the relations between economic magnitudes. But precisely because in the classical theory that lack of reversibility is given an explanation. One may think, for example, of the relative irreversibility of the historically attained level of subsistence wages, with its basis in the social norms that regulate the reproduction of the economic system and in the conflict which continually takes place around the definition of such norms. Or one may think of the role that the conflict between social classes may have in directing technical progress, the results of which, of course, remain available for society even when the conditions of that conflict have changed.[5]

Summing up what we have seen so far, we can thus say not only that Robinson's criticism in its second formulation cannot be directed against the classical theory but also that, provided it is cleared of its aprioristic elements, it must be recognised as a useful element in the comparison between the classical and the neoclassical theory.[6]

What may perhaps be useful at this point is to show one of the negative consequences of what we have described as the aprioristic

[5] It may be useful at this point to mention a second argument sometimes adduced by Robinson to support what we have called the first formulation of her critique and that, though relevant in itself, falls somewhat out of the scope of this comment. This second argument appears to be directed only at the classical theory in that it claims that a process of capital accumulation should not be studied using the comparison between different theoretical positions of the economic system because a change in *one* of the givens starting from which the first position is determined would generally entail changes in *other* givens as well (see, for example, Robinson, 1974 [1978], p. 128). Since, however, no one would deny that, for example, a change in the composition of the social product might require a significant change in the technical conditions of production, rather than a critique of the classical theory this seems a way to point out the *specific* way in which, on account of its particular structure, this theory must deal with changes in its 'intermediate data'. What we refer to here is in the first place the analysis of changes in output in 'two distinct logical stages' (Garegnani, 1983, p. 312) or in 'several subsequent steps' (Schefold, 1985, p. 141). Reference should also be made, however, to the treatment of produced quantities that is at the basis of Pasinetti's (1981) *Structural Dynamics*. We do not refer here to what Pasinetti has more recently called a 'separation theorem' consisting in the distinction between a 'natural system' and the study of a historically determined institutional set-up, which has to do with the distinction between normative and positive analysis and should be judged on its own merits (Pasinetti, 2007, p. 275). What we refer to is the separation *within* the 'natural system' between the evolution of the composition of output, on the one hand, and the system of prices, on the other. On this point, see Bellino (2015).

[6] That, with respect to the problems we have dealt with in this and the previous section, Sraffa's position has been that of identifying the particularly restrictive methodological requirements that should be met by a supply-and-demand theory, together with the observation that these requirements are not met by the specific processes involved in the determination of the theoretical position of the economic system, is suggested in Rosselli and Trabucchi (2019) through the study of an important manuscript by Sraffa from the second half of the 1950s.

nature of Robinson's criticism and hence the need to remove this aspect of that criticism if it has to be taken as the basis for an alternative to the neoclassical theory. If we go back to the first formulation of that criticism, we shall see that the main argument put forward in this respect by Robinson (the existence of wrong expectations) does not seem to have much to do with the question of the reversibility of economic processes nor, as a consequence, with the distinction between 'logical' and 'historical' time. We are now, however, in a position to point out what is perhaps the underlying reason for Robinson's opposition to the idea of a tendency for the economic system to move towards its theoretical position. Clearly, if it is believed that even the slightest change in the economic system brings about a complete novelty – if it is believed, in other terms, that irreversibility is an all-pervasive feature of *any* aspect of an economic system – then it would be true that 'time [going] only one way' it would be impossible to 'correct misdirections'. It would thus be true not only that 'equilibrium cannot be achieved by a process of trial and error' (Robinson, 1978, p. 12) but, what is more, that the same should be said of any significant tendency towards a theoretical position of the economic system.

In this extreme case, the two propositions that we have distinguished within Robinson's critical contributions would then be reduced to a single proposition. But not only such a proposition would have completely 'nihilistic' implications on economic theory (Eatwell, 1997), in that it would demand of economic theory the ability to determine, or at least to approximate, the actual position of the economic system in every single instant without showing the means by which this could be done. Such a proposition would, moreover, be hardly reconcilable with that degree of order that, imperfect as it is, we do after all observe in reality: that degree of order, that is, that, as Ricardo put it, compels us to 'confess that the principle which apportions capital to each trade . . . is more active than is generally supposed' (*Works*, I, p. 90).[7]

[7] If what we have called the aprioristic nature of Robinson's criticism in its second formulation is what in our opinion separates this criticism from the classical theory, it cannot be denied that the main reason for the misunderstandings that have arisen in this regard has to be sought elsewhere: and precisely in the thesis, which as we have seen Robinson derived from that criticism, concerning the supposed superiority of the methodological criticism of the neoclassical principle of substitution over the analytical criticism of that principle (the '*unimportance* of

4.5 The 'Photographic' Interpretation of the Classical Theory and the Need for a Process of Price Adjustment

Both the example we have just mentioned and the examples we have mentioned in Section 4.2 from Smith and Ricardo must clearly be considered conclusive as to the existence, in the classical theory, of a method based on an adjustment process of the actual position of the economic system to its theoretical position. This does not mean, however, that the classical theory necessarily *needs* such a method. After all, we already have in Say's law a remarkable example of an element that can undoubtedly be found in Smith and Ricardo but that can be convincingly argued does not necessarily belong to the classical theory.[8] Nor does what we have said in Section 4.2 and at the end of Section 4.4 mean that, with regard to such an adjustment process, the classical theory cannot meet any other difficulty beyond those pointed at by Robinson. As we said at the beginning, it is to those aspects of these two issues that are more closely related to the identification of the position of the economic system determined by the classical theory with a 'picture' taken 'at a given moment' that this and Section 4.6 will, respectively, be devoted.

In order to address the first issue, what has to be clarified is in the first place in what sense it can be said that a given economic theory needs an adjustment process: for, in general, it seems possible to think of two quite different notions of adjustment which, from our point of view, must be kept carefully apart.

The distinction can be illustrated by looking at the question of price adjustment. The first notion presents itself then when, being in possession of a theory of value and distribution, this theory is repeatedly applied to different 'dates' and one inquires whether, as time passes, the prices determined by the theory tend to obey some specific law. What is asked in this case is, in particular, whether the prices that are

reswitching'). It may then be useful to note that, in actual fact, the thesis does not seem to derive from that criticism. Not only because it is clearly the responsibility of every critical theory to indicate an internal contradiction, if there is one, in the dominant theory. The fact is that, admitting only the methodological criticism, the neoclassical principle of substitution, though discarded in the determination of a single theoretical position of the economic system, could easily reappear over a sequence of such positions.

[8] On this point, see the essays in Eatwell and Milgate (1983).

determined by the theory tend to remain constant from a certain 'date' onwards or whether they tend to 'adjust', in some specified sense, to certain 'terminal' values.

Now, it is immediately clear that it is always possible to inquire into the existence of an adjustment process of this first kind. But it should also be clear that all that can be established in this way is the existence of a certain property of the theory; and this, taken by itself, can add nothing to the validity of the theory, just as nothing can be detracted from it by the mere absence of that property. The fact is that in this first notion of adjustment we never have to do with prices that are, so to speak, 'external' to the set of theoretically determined prices.[9]

This in turn tells us in which case a process of price adjustment becomes necessary for a theory. This simply happens when what has to be ascertained is whether certain prices *that can be observed but that the theory is unable to determine* tend to 'adjust' to the prices that are determined by the theory: for it is only in this case (which, considering the nature of the prices involved, we can call the 'external' adjustment, just as we can call the first notion the 'internal' adjustment) that the occurrence of the adjustment adds by itself something and, what is more, something of essential importance, to the validity of the theory.

The need that an economic theory may have of an adjustment process is thus one and the same thing with the inability of this theory to determine, or at least to approximate satisfactorily, the actual path followed by the economic system instant after instant. From the point of view of the prices that are dealt with in the theory, it is therefore nothing else than the presence in such a theory of a sharp distinction between theoretical and observable prices. But this means that, in the classical theory, the need for an adjustment process cannot be doubted: and this simply because the uniformity in the rate of profit that characterises the prices that are determined by this theory is not what can commonly be observed, nor (what in this case is perhaps even more

[9] This is not to deny that even in this case the existence or non-existence of the adjustment may be relevant to the validity of the theory when this property is confronted with the observed facts. In this case, however, the absence, and not the presence, of the adjustment may be what is really important. As an example, we can mention Ricardo's theory of value and distribution, the validity of which would be seriously called into question if it could not be shown that the secular tendency to a stationary state that Ricardo himself sometimes appears to derive from it, but which has found no confirmation in reality, does *not* derive from any essential component of the theory itself.

important) what one expects to observe, in a given instant. Yet doubts on this point have been raised. What has to be established is, then, how this may have occurred and, in particular, how this is connected with the 'photographic' interpretation of the classical theory we mentioned above.

In order to do so, it will be convenient if we first go back to what we have seen in Section 4.3 concerning the role that the movement of the economic system may have in the neoclassical theory in the determination of its theoretical position. More generally, we must see how the different logical structure of the classical and of the neoclassical theory, that so far we have taken into consideration with regard to the role that historical circumstances may have in the two theories, is reflected in the different possibility of establishing, in each single theory, a clear separation between the determination of the theoretical position of the economic system, on the one hand, and the operation of competition among capitalists, on the other.

As we have seen, competition among capitalists operates by moving productive capacity from one sector to the other in response to sectoral differences in profit rates. It thus operates by modifying the composition of the social product. But, as we know, in the determination of value and distribution that we find in the classical theory, the composition of the social product is taken as given. There must then be a sense in which such a determination is independent of the competition among capitalists. Since the position of the economic system that is determined by the classical theory is characterised by a uniform rate of profit, this, however, could not be a case of absolute independence. A marked degree of independence may however present itself with relation to the circumstances from which, together with the social product, the classical theory determines the position of the economic system. And, indeed, it does not seem impossible to say that the social norms that lie behind a certain level of the subsistence wage, just as the technical conditions of production connected to a certain level of capital accumulation, are given in a fundamentally independent way from the *operation* of competition among capitalists.

Things are different in the neoclassical theory. Also this theory, like the classical theory, determines a position of the economic system in which the composition of the social product is the same as that of the effectual demand. As we have seen, a uniform rate of profit thus prevails also in the position of the economic system determined by the neoclassical theory. But, in addition to this, the neoclassical theory determines that position in terms of the equilibrium between supply and demand. To do this, instead of taking the composition of the social product as given, for each commodity the neoclassical theory establishes the relationship that should exist, on the one hand, between price and effectual demand and, on the other, between price and produced quantity. But, as we have seen in connection with the second formulation of Robinson's criticism, this means that the neoclassical theory can only determine the theoretical position of the economic system by means of the process that leads the composition of the social product to be the same as that of the effectual demand. Since, moreover, this theory does not determine the actual path followed by the economic system under the pressure of competition, this seems in turn to imply that the determination of the theoretical position of the economic system by the neoclassical theory is performed by means of what this theory considers the *underlying forces* that make themselves felt *in the course* of the operation of competition among capitalists.[10]

[10] The difference between the classical and the neoclassical theory we have just seen is far from new. Usually it emerges, however, in connection with the question of the extent to which in those two theories one can speak of a role for supply and demand. Thus, for instance, Knut Wicksell claimed that 'a fault' in Ricardo's theory of value is that of 'choosing two quite different explanations for the prices of commodities in the market and the so-called natural prices', only the former being 'explained as dependent on "supply and demand"' (Wicksell, 1893 [1954], p. 40). Here Wicksell forgets, however, that in the classical theory there is no determination of market prices, the 'proportion' between 'the quantity brought to market' and the 'effectual demand' of commodities being able to determine the sign but not the extent of the deviations of market prices from their natural level. Moreover, what Wicksell does not see is that what is absent in the classical determination of natural prices is only the neoclassical notion of demand *curves*. On the other hand, in spite of the highly problematic attempts by Marshall with his notion of temporary equilibrium, a proper determination of market prices cannot be found in the neoclassical theory either. If we don't misinterpret him, the correct connection between the point we have made in the text and the question of the role of demand and supply can be found in Bertram Schefold when he states that '[t]he *strict* conceptual difference between market price and natural price encountered in Smith and his classical successors disappears' in the traditional neoclassical theory 'because the "forces" of demand and supply reign both in and out of equilibrium' (Schefold, 2019, p. 17, our italics). A different view is taken by John Eatwell, who derives from the nature of collections of 'loci of potential equilibria' that is shared by both supply and demand curves that the idea according to which those curves would contain a reference to a 'market process' ('moving along the curves toward equilibrium') would simply be 'false' (Eatwell, 2019, p. 3n).

We can thus come back to the identification between the position of the economic system determined by the classical theory and a 'picture' taken 'at a given moment'.

It is clear that the difference between the classical and the neoclassical theory we have just noticed has an undeniable bearing on the way in which the need for a process of price adjustment can be *ascertained* for each theory. Since in the neoclassical theory the determination of the theoretical position of the economic system cannot be fully separated from the adjustment process to such position, no strictly methodological consideration concerning the distinction between two notions of price is here required to recognise the need for such a process. But this is also the *only* difference that can be found in this respect between the two theories. For surely in the neoclassical theory, no less than in the classical theory, the distinction between theoretical and observable prices is by itself sufficient to determine the need for an adjustment process.

It should then be clear in what limited sense the identification between the position of the economic system determined by the classical theory and a 'picture' taken 'at a given moment' may be valid. As long as we fix our attention on the determination of the theoretical position of the economic system, the metaphor of a 'picture' may certainly underline that absence of a process of change as an integral part of that determination that, as we know, distinguishes the classical theory from the neoclassical theory. Here too, however, the image is only partly adequate. Indeed, if it is true that the position of the economic system that we find in the classical theory does not require a process of change in order to be determined, this position has still to embrace an entire production process; and clearly this would not be directly observable in a single 'picture'. We mention this fact because, confronted with the unquestionable fact that Sraffa, as in general the classical theory, determines a position of the economic system characterised by a uniform rate of profit, it is only a *literal* interpretation of the image of a 'picture' that seems to give at least an appearance of truth to the idea that such a theory would not need an adjustment process.

This happens in the following way. In order to perform its task, an adjustment process must clearly lead the observable position of the economic system *towards* its theoretical position. Prior to this, however, another condition must be met. Just like any other process, the adjustment process requires a certain period of time within which to operate. It is thus essential that the theoretical position of the economic system does not change appreciably *before* the adjustment process has operated to a sufficient extent. But this would clearly be impossible if the position of the economic system determined by the classical theory had no greater persistence than that of a 'picture' taken 'at a given moment'. What this means is then that, rather than proving that this theory does not need an adjustment process, what would be implied by the 'photographic' interpretation of the classical theory is that, in its attempt at finding such a process, this theory would have to face insurmountable difficulties. The existence of these difficulties is, however, quite a different matter from the one we are now discussing; and it seems safer not to address it by looking at the implications of a metaphor that, being aimed at representing the absence of a process of change *in the determination* of the theoretical position of the economic system, can tell us nothing as to the existence of other processes that may take place in the economic system.

4.6 Changes over Time in the Position of the Economic System

The 'chronological' problem we have met at the end of the Section 4.5 has clearly to do with the change over time in the data starting from which the classical theory determines the theoretical position of the economic system. More precisely, the problem can be traced back to the relationship existing between, on the one hand, the change in the data by which that theoretical position is determined and, on the other, the operation of the adjustment process that should lead the economic system towards such position.

In order to discuss the possible existence and the extent of this problem, we must therefore first of all distinguish between changes in data that may occur *during* the adjustment process for reasons that are fundamentally independent of the adjustment process itself and changes in data that may occur *as a consequence* of the adjustment process. We must further distinguish between those changes in data that are of a negligible magnitude and those that are not. For, contrary to what is sometimes argued, the very nature of the 'external' adjustment does not seem to require that the theoretical position of the economic system remains absolutely constant during the operation of the adjustment process.

Let us start then with those changes in data that may be endogenously produced by the adjustment process and that are not negligible. The case may be illustrated by a simple example. Let us suppose to take a real 'picture' of the economic system in a given instant. Among other things, this picture will give us a certain composition of the social product. Since, however, we will have caught the economic system in an arbitrary moment during the progress of the competitive process, this will not, in general, be equal to the composition of the effectual demand. Hence, our picture will give us, along with the composition of the social product, a set of prices that, in general, will not be characterised by a uniform rate of profit.

In fact, what we will have here is a set of 'market prices' and, as we know, these are not the prices that are determined by the classical theory. Quite apart from this fact, it is at any rate clear that either these prices can be determined by some economic theory, or this is not possible. In the first case, however, the need for an adjustment process would entirely disappear and so would the problem we are discussing: for the economic theory in question would no longer be based on the distinction between theoretical and observable prices.

Let us consider then the second case and let us suppose that, with the data we have derived from our 'picture', we determine a set of theoretical prices that, as such, are distinct from the observable prices revealed by our picture but that (as is inevitable given the accidental nature of the data used to determine them) are not characterised by a uniform rate of profit. What we will have to find is, then, an adjustment process that, starting from the instant immediately following that in which the picture was taken, will lead the prices that will gradually become observable towards these theoretical prices.

Let us assume that, for this purpose, we look at the competition among capitalists. As we know, this will operate by adapting the composition of the social product that is given by our 'picture' to the composition of the effectual demand. Hence, the competition among capitalists, which should serve as an adjustment process towards our theoretical prices, will operate by modifying the data starting from which we have determined those prices. It is thus clear that until the competition among capitalists has made its influence appreciably felt on market prices, the adjustment process to which we have referred will not have manifested itself to a sufficient extent and that, when at last the competition among capitalists will have made its influence appreciably felt, the theoretical position towards which the economic system should adjust will at the same time have changed considerably.

What should be noted is in other terms the *logical* nature of the error we would have been making in the previous example. This is not to deny that any adjustment process has a well-defined 'chronological' dimension. The fact is more simply that in our example the adjustment process can *never* work because, be it ever so fast, its speed is necessarily the *same* as that at which the theoretical position of the economic system changes.

This leads us to a first conclusion: namely, that the classical theory, by determining, on the one hand, a theoretical position characterised by a uniform rate of profit and by looking, on the other, at the competition among capitalists as the adjustment process that should lead the economic system towards such position, does not incur in this error. This can also be said by stating that, since there is no logical obstacle to conceiving a situation in which the competition among capitalists takes place in the absence of those changes in data that are fundamentally exogenous with respect to such a process, there is at least one case that is both conceivable in itself and in which the method on which the classical theory is based is fully applicable.[11]

This, however, means in turn that, having passed the test of internal consistency, the *scope of application* of this method is entirely dependent on what can be said about the exogenous change in data.

Now, the first thing that must be said in this regard is that, should the speed at which the exogenous change in data takes place be of the same order of magnitude, or of a higher order of magnitude, than the speed at which the competition among capitalists operates, no significant relationship could be established between the theoretical position of the economic system and its actual position by referring to such competition. Indeed, what we would have here is, though for entirely different reasons, basically the same situation we have already met in connection with the endogenous change in data.

Naturally, even in this case – which it may be noted, is in its most extreme form the case that is contemplated by the 'photographic' interpretation of the classical theory – the operation of competition among capitalists would remain as an essential component of a

[11] The logical nature of the error we have mentioned, and the fact that the classical theory does not incur in this error, is underlined in Ravagnani (2002).

capitalist system and so would the constant tendency to correct divergences in sectoral profit rates. However, no specific position of the system characterised by a uniform rate of profit, as is the one that is determined by the classical theory on the basis of a well-defined set of data, would have a privileged role over the others. Contrary to what is sometimes claimed (e.g., Roncaglia, 2010, p. 187), in this case it would thus appear impossible to argue that the prices determined by the classical theory account for a 'systematic' aspect of the economy under study.[12]

In substance, the method at the basis of the classical theory is instead fully applicable in the opposite case, when the speed at which the exogenous change in data takes place is of a lower order of magnitude than the speed at which the competition among capitalists operates.[13]

[12] To this a further consideration must be added. If the change in data were indeed as fast as we are assuming, the existence of this change (although, of course, not its direction) would at least partly be anticipated by economic agents. The mere difference in the profit rate realised in two different sectors could therefore tell us very little about the direction in which the competition among capitalists will shift productive capacity, if to this we do not add the knowledge of the *expectations* that economic agents have about the future evolution of the order of profitability of those two sectors. But, by ascribing a decisive role to the expectations of individuals, we would not only have abandoned the classical theory as this has historically been developed (and, as suggested in Ravagnani (2002), most likely as this theory can logically be developed). Given the relation that is necessarily established between experience and the revision of expectations, we would probably be abandoning more generally the possibility of separating the theoretical position from the actual position of the economic system, while maintaining at the same time a significant connection between those two positions.

[13] This is undoubtedly true when the change in data is rather slow, not only with respect to the competition among capitalists but also more generally with respect to the time horizon normally considered significant for social phenomena. The case where the first, but not the second condition is met is, however, also conceivable. The relevance of this possibility depends on the fact that it has been observed that a rather high rate of change in data may not constitute an obstacle to the operation of the method underlying the classical theory, in that the speed at which the competition among capitalists operates may, within certain limits, depend directly on the speed at which some of the data change (Ravagnani, 2002). The example that has been proposed in this regard concerns phases of intense accumulation, when the amount of new capital goods, that are clearly directed to the most profitable sectors, is relatively high. The case certainly deserves considerable attention, if only because it shows how the distinction between changes in data that are exogenous with respect to the competition among capitalists and changes that are endogenous, useful at a first level of analysis, should more generally be taken with some caution. As for its

What has to be seen, then, is what *factual* considerations can make one or the other of these two cases more plausible.

Now, it must be said that there is a phenomenon, which is almost constantly present in a capitalist system, which by its very nature is necessarily continuous and, apart from particular, though historically highly relevant, circumstances, *gradual*: namely, the accumulation of capital. Naturally, if we consider that, as we have said, what concerns us are only relevant changes in data, a gradual change can be treated as a discontinuous change at relatively long intervals. It follows then that, to the extent that capital accumulation can be ascribed a decisive role in the change in the data underlying the classical theory, we have here a strong argument in favour of a rather broad applicability of the method underlying this theory.

But that this is indeed the case can hardly be doubted. It is indeed certain that in the classical theory the accumulation of capital is seen as a necessary condition for the appearance of those changes in the technical conditions of production that are sufficiently relevant to be taken into account in determining the theoretical position of the economic system.[14] Such changes represent in turn the condition for those relevant changes in the division between 'necessary' and 'luxury' commodities that are at the centre of the classical analysis of consumption. The accumulation of capital is in other terms at the basis of those *structural changes* in the economic system, on which Pasinetti has long worked, and which define from time to time the limits within which society must, consciously or not, make a choice about its future.

Naturally, to say that there is a strong argument in favour of a broad applicability of the method underlying the classical theory does not mean that this method can be applied in any case. Changes in data that are not fundamentally related to capital accumulation cannot of course be excluded. In addition, gradual changes in capital accumulation may

significance for the applicability of the method underlying the classical theory, however, the case is doubtful. It must indeed be considered that, even if we can rely on a prompt response from competition among capitalists, in the case of a relatively rapid change in data, we could still be faced with that need to take into account the evolution of the theoretical position of the economy over time in the very determination of that position that, as we have seen in note 12 with regard to individuals' expectations, can raise doubts at a general level and certainly does so within the classical theory.

[14] For a discussion of some relevant passages by Smith and Marx, see Piccioni (2000).

have less gradual consequences on the changes in the data of the theory, with tension accumulating for long periods of relative stasis and then exploding in shorter, *but not necessarily negligible*, periods of intense change. It is indeed possible that this is a rather common case for a capitalist economy. But this, which in itself is more generally a limit to the applicability of what we have called the traditional method,[15] seems hardly a problem for the classical theory that, on account of its particular structure, is at any rate based on the union of deductive reasoning and historical reconstructions.

4.7 'Logical' Time and 'Real' Time in the Neo-Walrasian Theory

As mentioned at the beginning, what we want briefly to discuss in conclusion is that aspect of the neo-Walrasian theory that has an immediate bearing on the fourth characteristic ascribed by Pasinetti to the Cambridge School: namely, the distinction, that can be found in this theory, between 'logical' time and 'real' time.[16]

In order to do so, we must first of all be clear about the nature of the neo-Walrasian theory as a particular *reformulation* of the neoclassical theory. On the basis of what we have seen so far, this can be easily done by saying that while the neo-Walrasian theory maintains the explanation of value and distribution in terms of an equilibrium between demand and supply that distinguished the neoclassical from the classical theory, it abandons what kept those two theories together, namely, the determination of a theoretical position of the economic system characterised by a uniform rate of profit. What must be said in the second place is, then, that this aspect of the neo-Walrasian theory must ultimately be traced back to the particular treatment of capital that is at the basis of this theory. We refer here to the fact that, among the data of the neo-Walrasian theory, we no longer find that single 'quantity of capital' that, with the notable exception of Walras, could be found in the traditional expositions of the neoclassical theory. What

[15] Cf., in this regard, Wicksell's explicit warning that the application of this method should be excluded in 'periods of great industrial development' (Wicksell, 1910 [1936], p. 167).

[16] 'Logical' time is sometimes termed 'fictional' or 'virtual' time (e.g., Mas-Colell, Whinston and Green, 1995). For the distinction between these two notions of time without, however, a different name being given to each, see Arrow (1968).

we find here is instead, precisely as in Walras, a set of physically distinct 'capital goods' on which, as a rule, no uniform rate of profit can be determined.[17]

It is easy to see then that the neo-Walrasian theory finds itself in a situation that is in many respects similar to the one we have described in Section 4.6. This is certainly true for the capital goods that we find among the data of this theory, which correspond to the capital goods that would be revealed by a 'picture' of the economic system taken 'at a given moment'. Now, as we have seen, in order to determine a significant relationship between theoretical variables and observable magnitudes a theory finding itself in these conditions should fundamentally choose between two possible alternatives: namely, between the determination of the path that, over a certain period of time, is actually followed by the economic system instant after instant and the determination, over that same period, of a sequence of theoretical positions of the economic system. In this second case, however, this theory should also identify an adjustment process, both capable of bringing the actual position of the economic system towards such theoretical positions and *faster* than the one that is determined by the competition among capitalists that, by rapidly changing the capital goods existing in the economic system, should explain its movement from one theoretical position to the following one.

It is in this regard that the distinction between 'logical' time and 'real' time plays an absolutely particular role in the neo-Walrasian theory. If, as we have seen, the distinction between two notions of time was used by Robinson in order to *compare* alternative economic theories, and if the same aim clearly belongs to the whole set of characteristics ascribed by Pasinetti to the Cambridge School, in the neo-Walrasian theory that distinction has the effect, if not the purpose, of making a comparison between this theory and possible alternative theories extremely difficult.

This happens in the following way. 'Logical' time is introduced in the neo-Walrasian theory as the notion of time within which what must take place is *exclusively* the adjustment process. Indeed, during logical time only negotiations between different agents can take place, while exchanges, and consequently production and consumption

[17] For the contradiction in Walras's theory of capital, see Eatwell (1987); Garegnani (1990); Petri (2004).

processes, are not allowed. Logical time is in other words the time during which what is generally called 'tâtonnement stability' should be studied and is in fact sometimes simply called 'tâtonnement time' (McKenzie, 2005, p. 67).[18] Production and consumption activities take place in 'real' time. Since, however, these activities normally take place continuously in the economic system, one is forced to conclude that logical time consumes only a single instant of real time or, as is sometimes said, that the former notion of time is 'orthogonal' to the latter. The introduction in the neo-Walrasian theory of two distinct notions of time has then the effect of obscuring which of the two alternatives we have mentioned above, whether the one requiring an adjustment process or the one not requiring such a process, this theory intends to follow.

This, however, is only the first effect. It is indeed not difficult to find single statements by neo-Walrasian theorists claiming that the neo-Walrasian theory would be able to determine prices as these can be observed instant after instant. For instance, such a belief significantly pervades Frank Hahn's attack on the critics of the neo-Walrasian theory: 'Why is "the rate of profit" an interesting unknown? Ask the neo-Ricardians. *If we knew all relative prices from now to doomsday, could we ask for more?*' (Hahn, 1975, p. 361, our italics). From what we have seen in this comment, however, it should be equally easy to convince ourselves that, as was the case with Robinson's distinction between two notions of time, also in the neo-Walrasian theory the notion of logical time can only be a *metaphor* and that in this case the metaphor can only be aimed at representing the extremely higher speed with which the adjustment process that would be at the basis of this theory would operate compared to the competition among capitalists.

[18] As is well known, the idea of a tâtonnement, with its strict separation between the adjustment process and consumption and production activities, can already be found in Walras. Here, however, the idea was not meant to have a fundamental theoretical role. Indeed, the assumption of a 'periodic annual market' that Walras adopts in the first six sections of his *Elements* is removed in section seven, where, 'in order to come still more closely to reality', it is substituted by the idea of a 'continuous market' likened to 'a lake agitated by the wind, where the water is incessantly seeking its level without ever reaching it' (Walras, 1874–1876 [1954], p. 379). This, however, is not compatible with the inclusion among the givens of the theory of a set of heterogeneous capital goods and consequently cannot be found in the neo-Walrasian reformulation of the neoclassical theory.

But this means in turn that such a metaphor cannot be judged in itself but only by looking at the substantial reasons that may possibly require, on the one hand, and justify, on the other, its adoption.

And it is at this point that in the neo-Walrasian theory we come across what can only be described as the frank admission that such a justification cannot be provided, together with the reluctance to take into consideration, not so much the possibility that this state of affairs could constitute a serious problem, as the possibility that it may have its origin in some *specific* characteristic of the neo-Walrasian theory itself. Take as a single but certainly significant example Kenneth Arrow and Hahn who, though stating that it would be 'foolish', or even a 'vulgar mistake' (Arrow and Hahn, 1971, p. 325) to dismiss tâtonnement stability – that is, stability occurring through a process that takes place in 'logical' time – because it 'bears too little resemblance to the actual world' (Arrow and Hahn, 1971, p. 265), admit, without any further comment, that '[a]t the moment the main justification for [such an analysis] is that there are results to report on the tâtonnement while there are no results to report on what most economists would agree to be more realistic constructions' (Arrow and Hahn, 1971, pp. 321–322).

It is difficult to escape the impression that what lies at the bottom of such an attitude is a situation in which the whole neo-Walrasian approach, and hence both the neo-Walrasian theory and the method by which this theory should establish a significant relationship between theoretical variables and observable magnitudes, has to such an extent turned for most economists into a *second nature* that any difficulty that arises within this approach is immediately perceived as the price that must be paid in order to have a general, and at the same time rigorous, economic theory. And it is clear what a powerful obstacle such a situation can represent for the comparison between alternative theories.[19]

[19] This is precisely what seems to have happened with the criticism that has been raised against the neo-Walrasian theory from the point of view of the traditional method (Garegnani, 1976; see also Eatwell, 1983; Petri, 1991 and 2004; Ciccone, 1999). Contrary to what had happened to the criticism raised against the traditional version of the neoclassical theory on account of its treatment of capital, this second criticism has been practically ignored.

Nor can the obstacle be circumvented by claiming that the current *fragmented*[20] state of economic theory would prove that the neo-Walrasian theory is no longer dominant. And not only because, even if this were true, the neo-Walrasian theory would still be the last general theory to have dominated in order of time. The fact is that the belief that, in order to establish a significant relationship between theoretical variables and observable magnitudes, economic theory does not need the condition of a uniform rate of profit is certainly a point that the neo-Walrasian theory has passed on to the current economic theory. To which it should be added that the state of fragmentation in which economic theory finds itself at present is probably to a large extent to be explained (at least as far as causes internal to the development of economic thought are concerned) with the belief we have mentioned above, according to which, beyond the boundaries of the neo-Walrasian theory, a theory that is both rigorous and general would be impossible.

This does not mean, however, that there is no way out from this situation. What should be noted in this respect is, in the first place, that, although the abandonment of the condition of a uniform rate of profit by the neo-Walrasian theory must ultimately be traced back to the abandonment by this theory of the attempt at treating capital as a single magnitude, the neo-Walrasian theory had its origins, and was initially developed, between the 1930s and the 1950s: that is, when the difficulties in the treatment of capital as a single magnitude were already well known to neoclassical economists but the impossibility of solving them had not yet been demonstrated, as would happen only subsequently with the publication of Sraffa's *Production of Commodities*. The absence of a clear separation between the traditional and the neo-Walrasian versions of the neoclassical theory may thus have strongly contributed to induce the first neo-Walrasian authors not to enquire whether, with the condition of a uniform rate of profit, also other aspects of the traditional method had to be abandoned. A precise field of investigation is thus open for the history of economic analysis: namely, to establish whether such peculiarities in the method underlying the neo-Walrasian theory as the use of the notion of 'logical' time are the result of the fact that this method was gradually formed by the union of aspects of the traditional method and

[20] We borrow the term from Roncaglia (2019).

aspects required by the new theory that are, in fact, mutually incompatible.[21]

Even this, however, would hardly be enough. It must then be considered that, though a comparison with the neo-Walrasian approach is at present practically impossible on those methodological questions on which it is most urgently needed, this theory is still a deliberate reformulation of the neoclassical theory. If, in other terms, the way the relationship between theoretical variables and observable magnitudes is conceived *might* be different in the neo-Walrasian theory, the determination of theoretical variables is to a large extent the same in this and in the traditional version of the neoclassical theory. But it is a point that we have seen both in connection with what we have called the second formulation of Robinson's critique and in discussing the limits within which the image of a 'picture' can be used in order to characterise the theoretical position of the economic system determined by the classical theory, that the determination of such a position in terms of an equilibrium between demand and supply has well-defined methodological implications.

What we have seen is, in particular, that the determination of the theoretical position of the economic system in terms of an equilibrium between demand and supply appears to be inextricably linked to the existence of an 'external' adjustment process. It should therefore be possible (and we hope to make a contribution in this direction in a separate work) to find directly in the categories used by the neo-Walrasian theory the mark of the need for such a process, thus approaching the discussion without being entangled on the purely metaphorical plane of the distinction between two notions of time. Naturally, if in this way it will be possible to identify a contradiction in the neo-Walrasian approach, this will probably not present itself in the way we should expect judging from the point of view of the traditional method. If, indeed, as Eatwell (1982, p. 223) has suggested, with the abandonment of the condition of a uniform rate of profit and the maintenance of the notion of equilibrium, the neo-Walrasian theory has become an 'intellectual mutant', this can hardly fail to reveal itself also in the way in which the contradictions within this theory make themselves felt.

[21] On one aspect of the coexistence in the first neo-Walrasian economists of notions derived from the traditional method and notions that belong to the new theory, see Gehrke (2003).

References

Arrow K. (1968) 'Economic Equilibrium', in Sills D. (ed.) *International Encyclopedia of the Social Sciences*, New York, MacMillan, pp. 376–389.

Arrow K. and Hahn F. (1971) *General Competitive Analysis*, San Francisco, Holden-Day.

Bellino E. (2015) 'Sraffa's Price Equations in Light of Garegnani and Pasinetti – The 'Core' of Surplus Theories and the 'Natural' Relations of an Economic System', in *Cahiers d'économie politique*, 69(2), pp. 15–44.

Bharadwaj K. (1972) 'Marshall on Pigou's Wealth and Welfare', in *Economica*, 39, pp. 32–46.

(1978) *Classical Political Economy and Rise to Dominance of Supply and Demand Theories*, Calcutta, Orient Longman Co.

(1991) 'History versus Equilibrium', in Rima I. H. (ed.) *The Joan Robinson Legacy*, Armonk, Sharpe, pp. 80–104.

Blankenburg S. Arena R. and Wilkinson F. (2012) 'Piero Sraffa and "the True Object of Economics": The Role of the Unpublished Manuscripts', in *Cambridge Journal of Economics*, 36, pp. 1267–1290.

Ciccone R. (1999) 'Classical and Neoclassical Short-Run Prices: A Comparative Analysis of Their Intended Empirical Content', in Mongiovi G. and Petri F. (eds.) *Value, Distribution and Capital: Essays in Honour of Pierangelo Garegnani*, London and New York, Routledge, pp. 69–92.

Eatwell J. (1982) 'Competition', in Bradley I. and Howards M. (eds.) *Classical and Marxian Political Economy*, London and Basingstoke, Macmillan, pp. 203–228.

(1987) 'Walras's Theory of Capital', in Eatwell J. Milgate M. and Newman P. (eds.) *The New Palgrave: A Dictionary of Economics*, vol. 4. London: Macmillan, pp. 868–872.

(1997) 'History versus Equilibrium', in Arestis P. Palma G. and Sawyer M. (eds.) *Capital Controversy, Post-Keynesian Economics and the History of Economic Thought: Essays in Honour of Geoff Harcourt*, vol. I, London, Routledge, pp. 350–359.

(2019) 'Cost of Production and the Theory of the Rate of Profit', in *Contributions to Political Economy*, 38, pp. 1–11.

Eatwell J. and Milgate M. (eds.) (1983), *Keynes's Economics and the Theory of Value and Distribution*, London, Duckworth.

Garegnani P. (1976) 'On a Change in the Notion of Equilibrium in Recent Work on Value and Distribution', in Brown M. Sato K. Zarembka P. (eds.) *Essays in Modern Capital Theory*, Amsterdam, North-Holland, pp. 25–45.

(1983) 'The Classical Theory of Wages and the Role of Demand Schedules in the Determination of Relative Prices, in *American Economic Review*, 73(2), pp. 309–313.

(1989) 'Some Notes on Capital, Expectations and the Analysis of Changes', in Feiwel G. R. (ed.) *Joan Robinson and Modern Economic Theory*, London and Basingstoke, Macmillan, pp. 344–367.

(1990) 'Quantity of Capital', in Eatwell J. Milgate M. and Newman P. (eds.) *The New Palgrave: Capital Theory*, London, Macmillan.

(1998) 'Sraffa: The Theoretical World of the Old Classical Economists', in *Journal of the History of Economic Thought*, 5(3), pp. 415–429.

Gehrke C. (2003) 'On the Transition from Long-Period to Short-Period Equilibria, in *Review of Political Economy*, 15(1), pp. 85–105.

Hahn F. (1975) 'Revival of Political Economy: The Wrong Issues and the Wrong Argument', in *Economic Record*, 51, pp. 360–364.

Mas-Colell A. Whinston M. and Green J. (1995) *Microeconomic Theory*, Oxford, Oxford University Press.

McKenzie L. W. (2005) *Classical General Equilibrium Theory*, Cambridge, MA, MIT Press.

Pasinetti L. L. (1981) *Structural Change and Economic Growth*, Cambridge, Cambridge University Press.

(2007) *Keynes and the Cambridge Keynesians: A 'Revolution in Economics' to Be Accomplished*, Cambridge, Cambridge University Press.

Petri F. (1991) 'Hicks's Recantation of the Temporary Equilibrium Method, in *Review of Political Economy*, 3, pp. 268–288.

(2004) *General Equilibrium, Capital and Macroeconomics: A Key to Recent Controversies in Equilibrium Theory*, Cheltenham, Edward Elgar.

Piccioni M. (2000) 'Prodotti netti negativi, accumulazione di capitale e cambiamenti nelle condizioni tecniche di produzione', in Pivetti M. (ed.) *Piero Sraffa: Contributi per una biografia intellettuale*, Roma, Carocci, pp. 191–202.

Ravagnani F. (2002) 'Produced Quantities and Returns in Sraffa's Theory of Normal Prices: Textual Evidence and Analytical Issues', in Boehm S. Gehrke C. Kurz H. D. and Sturn R. (eds.) *Is There Progress in Economics?*, Cheltenham, Edward Elgar, pp. 371–382.

Ricardo D. (1951–1973) *Works and Correspondence*, Sraffa P. and Dobb M. (eds.) Cambridge, Cambridge University Press.

Robinson J. V. (1953) 'The Production Function and the Theory of Capital', in *The Review of Economic Studies*, 21(2), pp. 81–106.

(1953 [1978]) 'A Lecture Delivered at Oxford by a Cambridge Economist', in *On Re-reading Marx*, Cambridge, Cambridge Student's

Bookshop, pp. 10–18; reprinted in *Contributions to Modern Economics*, Oxford, Blackwell, pp. 137–145.

(1974 [1978]) 'History versus Equilibrium', in *Indian Economic Journal*, 21, pp. 202–213; reprinted in *Contributions to Modern Economics*, Oxford, Blackwell, pp. 126–136.

(1975) 'The Unimportance of Reswitching', in *Quarterly Journal of Economics*, 89(1), pp. 32–39.

(1976 [1989]) 'Commento all'articolo di Garegnani', in Garegnani P. (ed.) *Valore e Domanda Effettiva*, Torino, Einaudi, Appendix A. Published in English in Garegnani, P. 'Some Notes on Capital, Expectations and the Analysis of Changes', in Feiwel G. R. (ed.) *Joan Robinson and Modern Economic Theory*, London and Basingstoke, Macmillan, pp. 344–367.

(1978) 'Keynes and Ricardo', in *Journal of Post Keynesian Economics*, 1 (1), pp. 12–18.

Roncaglia A. (2010) 'Some Notes on the Notion of Production Prices', in Vint J. Metcalfe S. Kurz H. Salvadori N. and Samuelson P. (eds.) *Economic Theory and Economic Thought: Essays in Honour of Ian Steedman*, London, Routledge, pp. 174–188.

(2019) *The Age of Fragmentation: A History of Contemporary Economic Thought*, Cambridge, Cambridge University Press.

Rosselli A. and Trabucchi P. (2019) 'Sraffa, the "Marginal" Method and Change', in *Structural Change and Economic Dynamics*, 51, pp. 334–340.

Schefold B. (1985) '"On Changes in the Composition of Output", in Political Economy', *Studies in the Surplus Approach*, 1(2), pp. 105–142.

(2019) 'Continuity and Change in the Transition from the Classical to the Neoclassical Theory of Normal Prices', in Rosselli A. Naldi N. and Sanfilippo E. (eds.) *Money, Finance and Crises in Economic History: The Long-Term Impact of Economic Ideas. Essays in Honour of Maria Cristina Marcuzzo*, London, Routledge, pp. 11–26.

Smith A. (1776 [1976]) *An Inquiry into the Nature and Causes of the Wealth of Nations*, The Glasgow Edition of the Works and Correspondence of Adam Smith, Campbell R. H. and Skinner A. S. (eds.), Oxford, Clarendon Press.

Sraffa P. (1960) *Production of Commodities by Means of Commodities*, Cambridge, Cambridge University Press.

Vianello F. (1989) 'Natural (or Normal) Prices: Some Pointers', in *Political Economy: Studies in the Surplus Approach*, 5(2), pp. 89–105.

Walras L. (1874–1876 [1954]) *Elements of Pure Economics*, London, Allen & Unwin.

Wicksell K. (1893 [1954]) *Value, Capital and Rent*, London, Allen & Unwin.

(1910 [1936]) *Lectures on Political Economy*, London, Routledge.

5 *Causality vs. Interdependence*

A Distinction That Conveys a World's View

ENRICO BELLINO AND
SEBASTIANO NEROZZI

5.1 Introduction

On several occasions, Luigi Pasinetti has explicitly remarked that classical and Keynesian explanations of some crucial phenomena of modern industrial economies are better conveyed by causal relations rather than by a fully interdependent system (Pasinetti, 1965,[1] 1974, 1997 and 2007). Quoting from the most recent reference:

> There are relations, in economics, that are genuinely interdependent. But there are other important economic relations that are characteristically asymmetrical, as far as the chain of causality is concerned. They should not be artificially forced into a logical frame in which everything depends on everything else, which is tantamount to introducing an unjustified sharp distinction which considers any specific variable as either totally unimportant (and in this case to be neglected) or of some importance and in this case to be considered exactly on the same level as, and symmetrically to, any one of the other variables, no matter how important these latter variables may be relative to the former. (Pasinetti, 2007, p. 226)

Pasinetti's interest in the notion of causality dates back to his initial studies at the Catholic University of Milan under the tutorship of Francesco Vito and the young Siro Lombardini. The latter, in particular, introduced Pasinetti to the study of econometrics and encouraged him to devote his dissertation and first research papers to the study of consumption and investment functions in econometric models (Pasinetti, 1955, 1956, 1957). He had the opportunity to clarify his concept of causality in his inaugural lecture delivered in 1964 for the newly established Econometrics course at the Catholic University of

[1] The original essay was published in Italian; an English translation has been published in *Structural Change and Economic Dynamics* (in 2019); the references are to this edition.

Milan, significantly titled 'Causalità e interdipendenza nell'analisi econometrica e nella teoria economica', which has recently been translated into English (Pasinetti, 1965).

In Pasinetti's view, the discussions in the 1950s among econometricians about adopting recursive rather than interdependent models brought to light a deeper demarcation at the theoretical level between two alternative approaches to economic theory. For the first time, these two logical frameworks emerged in connection with a very practical purpose – that of quantifying, or estimating, the parameters of economic relationships.

The Walrasian general equilibrium model gave rise to structural economic models in which the relationships between the endogenous variables are fully interdependent and perfectly symmetrical. Comparative static analysis studies the system's reaction to different external shocks, so that causality runs only from exogenous to endogenous variables. Given the set of parameters, the final equilibrium is determined by the values assigned to exogenous variables. These features correspond to a precise vision of the economic system, in which social interaction in the marketplace occurs between myriad individuals, each of them endowed with a different set of resources and preferences, but not qualitatively different from each other and, in any case, never able to exert any conscious and relevant influence on the final outcome of the whole economic process. In contrast, Keynesian and classical models follow a different approach in model-building:

> [t]heir framework perceives no need to permanently determine variables simultaneously. In fact, the large part of the explanations are mono-directional .... It is not surprising, that on returning to some concepts of Classical economics – as has happened with Keynesian and post-Keynesian theories – causal chains have once again appeared in the new economic theories .... This approach reverses the Ricardian causal chain while maintaining a causal chain of the same type. (Pasinetti, 1965, p. 361)

In his 1964 lecture, Pasinetti presented his notion of causality by resorting to two alternative logical structures representing the relations among the economic variables. The first logical structure may be represented by a system of equations where, given a set of exogenous parameters, all the endogenous variables can be determined by simultaneously solving all the equations of the system. This type of structure, perfectly symmetric, is called by Pasinetti (following Herbert Simon) an 'interdependent' or 'indecomposable' system which, in linear terms, can be represented as follows:

$$\begin{cases} Ax + By = w \\ Cx + Dy = z, \end{cases}$$

where A, B, C, D, w and z are given parameters, and x and y are unknowns (alternatively, A, B, C, D can be thought as given matrices, w and z as given vectors, and x and y as unknown vectors). In this case, x and y are determined *simultaneously*. A second logical structure is represented by a decomposable system of equations where the endogenous variable must be determined before and independently of the remaining variables, so that a sequential order emerges in the solution of the system:

$$\begin{cases} Ax + By = w \\ \qquad\; Dy = z. \end{cases}$$

In this case, the second equation must be solved *before* the first one: $y = D^{-1}z =: y^*$; then, after substitution into the first one, it concurs to the determination of x: $x = A^{-1}(w - By^*)$.

Recalling the criticisms by logical positivists of the concept of causality, Pasinetti adopted the formal notion proposed by Simon (1953), according to which causality is intended as an analytical characterization of the relation between the variables within a system, rather than a feature of economic reality:

As is well known, British empiricists from the XVIII century (especially David Hume) have denied that one can speak of cause and effect among associations of events that can be observed in empirical reality. As a consequence, some modern positivists of our time have even suggested deleting the word 'cause' from the dictionary of philosophy, since the notion is considered a source of confusion. I will let our philosopher friends handle the task of researching on the one hand the justifications for the empiricist concerns and on the other to illustrate the ineffectiveness of such extreme positions. I wish to stress simply that these lengthy discussions become irrelevant here. The discourse carried out, at least up to this point, is without prejudice for any of the conceptions of the associations of any real events, because the discourse has not been carried out on an ontological basis, but it has been carried out on a logical basis. The two systems of interdependent and causal equations have been presented as two logical schemes. Furthermore, the definition provided of causal chain does not contain in itself any affirmation regarding empirical reality. It simply has the meaning of an asymmetrical relation among the variables of a logical scheme. (Pasinetti, 1965, p. 359)

Following Pasinetti, a link between two or more variables is considered 'causal' if they are determined *sequentially*; it is 'interdependent' if they are determined *simultaneously*. In a previous essay (Bellino and Nerozzi, 2017), we have considered how the specification of one or more relations in causal terms plays an essential role in Pasinetti's major works. In the present essay, we shall try to extend our analysis and show how the interplay of causal and interdependent relations permeates both classical and Keynesian literature. In doing so, we shall try to trace the various notions of causality which, more or less explicitly, underpin the analytical structure of the works of different authors, ranging from David Ricardo and Karl Marx, to John Maynard Keynes, Piero Sraffa and the many strands of post-Keynesian thinking. In order to bring out from these theories the interaction between causal and interdependent links and to appreciate their interpretative implications, it is necessary to retrace, in some cases down to detail, the analytical and logical path followed in them.

5.2 Classical Economists

In the opening paragraph of the Preface to *Production of Commodities*, Sraffa outlines the analytical framework for his analysis:

No changes in output and … no changes in the proportions in which different means of production are used by an industry are considered …. The investigation is concerned exclusively with such properties of an economic system as do not depend on changes in the scale of production or in the proportions of 'factors'.

This standpoint, which is that of the old classical economists from Adam Smith to Ricardo, has been submerged and forgotten since the advent of the 'marginal' method. (Sraffa, 1960, p. v)

This assumption, normally recalled as 'given quantities', has probably been the starting point on which Pierangelo Garegnani, and after him, a large number of scholars, have grounded their reconstruction of the logical framework of classical economists concerning income distribution and value. Garegnani maintains that classical surplus theories can be separated into two distinct logical stages. The 'core' of surplus theories, which concerns the determination of the shares other than wages as a residual, and the relative prices of commodities. In this stage, the social product and necessary consumption (essentially, subsistence wages) are taken as given physical aggregates. The determination of the rate of profit and relative prices can be expressed through 'necessary quantitative relationships' (Garegnani, 1984, p. 297). The second logical stage comprises the social product, the wage rate and technical conditions of production that are treated as exogenous variables or, in Garegnani's words, 'intermediate data'.[2] Their determination is better investigated 'outside the core', also on the basis of institutional and historical circumstances specific to each economic system. This asymmetry between variables, whereby some are considered as exogenous or independent, while other variables are endogenous or dependent, can be expressed as analytical characteristics of the equations which constitute the core of the theory, which allows us to identify *causal* and *interdependent* links between the variables. The reasons behind these characteristics may be theoretical/interpretative as well as purely analytical. In what follows, we will investigate the core of the classical theories of income distribution and value through this perspective.

5.2.1 Causality in Ricardo's Analysis of Distribution and Value

The explanation of the determinants of income distribution between rents, wages and profits is, for Ricardo, 'the principal problem in Political Economy' (Ricardo, 1817, p. 5). After the determination of rents, which Ricardo explains on the basis of the differential fertility of various plots of land, the division of the remaining product between workers and capitalists is governed by an asymmetric principle: wages are determined by workers' subsistence, that is, the set of commodities which allows their maintenance and thus the reproduction of labour force, according to a historically determined standard of living. The *residuum* of the social product (net of rents), go to capitalists, in the form of profits. We observe, thus, an initial *sequential* ordering in the determination of income distribution: wages are determined *prior* to profits. This asymmetry in the determination of wages and profits contains a substantial element of the theory. Wages are *a necessary*

[2] The term has been proposed by Garegnani (2007).

deduction from the social product: a level below which the system cannot go without jeopardising the reproducibility of the labour force. Profits, being the residual, are not equally necessary: they can be reduced, for example, by taxation, without compromising, within certain limits,[3] the repetition of production activity.

There is a second level where the possibility to argue in causal terms has played (or, better, would have played) a relevant role in Ricardo's analysis. It concerns the problem of determining profits and the rate of profit, which has always constituted a formidable logical problem for classical economists. There are three sets of heterogeneous goods: the commodities entering the gross social output, those used as means of production by the entire system and those constituting workers' subsistence. So, in order to ascertain profits and the rate of profit, a comparison must be made in value terms. The difficulty arises when we adopt a price definition which requires the knowledge of the profit rate, as in Smith's definition of natural prices (Smith, 1776 [1976], ch. VII). This is probably the main reason why Ricardo is so keen to defend the labour theory of value. By linking relative prices to labour quantities only, he could avoid any circularity in determining prices and the rate of profit. Although Ricardo did not use mathematics in presenting his theories, we can more easily follow his reasoning by a simple formalisation. The rate of profit ruling in the entire system, π, is the ratio between the social surplus, and the necessary consumption. The necessary consumption contains annual wages, W, plus the replacement of the means of production worn out in the production cycle, K; the social surplus, S, is the excess of the social product, Q, over the necessary consumption. Hence,

$$\pi = \frac{S}{K} = \frac{Q - (W + K)}{W + K}$$

(for the sake of simplicity, we abstract from rents). But even if we consider the quantities of commodities involved in the above expression as given, it is evident that magnitudes Q, W and K can be related only in *value* terms, as each aggregate contains the various commodities in different proportions (flukes aside). This determination is well established only if the prices of the various commodities can be known

[3] These limits depend on capitalists' attitude to invest and by the degree of openness of the capital market.

prior to the rate of profit. This is evidently the case if relative prices are determined according to the labour theory of value. An example with just two commodities clarifies the point. The rate of profit of the entire system

$$\pi = \frac{p_1 q_1 + p_2 q_2 - (p_1 d_1 + p_2 d_2 + p_1 k_1 + p_2 k_2)}{p_1 d_1 + p_2 d_2 + p_1 k_1 + p_2 k_2}, \tag{1}$$

where q_1 and q_2 denote the gross output of a given period, k_1 and k_2 denote the replacement of capital goods employed in the period, d_1 and d_2 denote physical workers' subsistence, and p_1 and p_2 denote the commodity prices. Magnitudes q_i, k_i and d_i are given; p_i and π are unknowns, $i = 1, 2$. Let us suppose that prices cover wages and guarantee a uniform rate of profit to capitalists, that is,

$$p_i = w\ell_i(1 + \pi), \qquad i = 1, 2,$$

where w is the wage rate and ℓ_i is the quantity of labour necessary to produce 1 unit of commodity i. The ℓ_i are given. Observe that, as in this case the labour theory of value holds,

$$\frac{p_1}{p_2} = \frac{\ell_1}{\ell_2}, \tag{2}$$

the rate of profit is

$$\pi = \frac{\frac{\ell_1}{\ell_2} q_1 + q_2 - \left(\frac{\ell_1}{\ell_2} d_1 + d_2 + \frac{\ell_1}{\ell_2} k_1 + k_2\right)}{\frac{\ell_1}{\ell_2} d_1 + d_2 + \frac{\ell_1}{\ell_2} k_1 + k_2} = \pi^*_{\mathrm{LTV}}. \tag{3}$$

The expression on the right side of (3) *involves only known magnitudes*. The *sequential* determination of labour values prior to the rate of profit ensures here the correctness of the reasoning and excludes the risk of arguing in a circle. If, on the contrary, we abandon the labour theory of value and we adopt the definition of natural prices given by Smith,[4] the sequentiality of the reasoning is interrupted and a logical circularity emerges immediately: the determination of the rate

[4] Smith says: '[w]hen the price of any commodity is neither more nor less than what is sufficient to pay the rent of the land, the wages of the labour, and the profits of the stock employed in raising, preparing, and bringing it to market, according to their natural rates, the commodity is then sold for what may be called its natural price' (Smith, 1776 [1976], ch. VII).

of profit requires the knowledge of price, and the determination of (natural) prices requires the knowledge of the rate of profit. Ricardo was perfectly aware of such a problem (probably Smith wasn't). It is enough to deviate even a little from the 'simple rule' (2), for example, by supposing explicitly that prices also include wages to pay the 'indirect' labour, that is, labour necessary to produce the means of production (the capital goods) employed to produce commodities, that the entire construction breaks down. In this case, in fact, the price of each commodity would be

$$p_i = w\ell_i(1+\pi) + w\ell'_i(1+\pi)^2, \qquad i = 1, 2,$$

where ℓ'_i is the indirect labour which, being provided one period before the production cycle of commodity *i* (that is, two periods before the output of the commodity), must be capitalised for two periods. In this case, relative prices do *not* express a labour theory of value:

$$\frac{p_1}{p_2} = \frac{\ell_1 + \ell'_1(1+\pi)}{\ell_2 + \ell'_2(1+\pi)} = \frac{p_1}{p_2}(\pi), \tag{4}$$

except in the very particular case of a uniform capital intensity, measured by ratio ℓ'_i/ℓ_i. In this case, in fact, as $\ell'_i/\ell_i = \kappa$, the expression on the right side of (4) reduces to in (2). But in general, the relative price expressed by (4) depends on the rate of profit: if we tried to calculate π by using (1) and (4) we would still be arguing in a circle.

The last resort tried by Ricardo, to consider the labour theory of value 'the nearest approximation to truth, as a rule for measuring relative value, of any I have ever heard',[5] still consists in a way to preserve a *sequential* structure in the determination of profits and the rate of profit. In fact, if we adopt the ratio $\frac{\ell_1}{\ell_2}$ to approximate $\frac{p_1}{p_2}$, we determine the rate of profit π^*_{LTV} (see formula [3]); this rate of profit can now be substituted into formula [4] to calculate the 'true' relative price, $\frac{p_1}{p_2}(\pi^*_{\text{LTV}})$. The degree of approximation can now be ascertained by comparing $\frac{\ell_1}{\ell_2}$ with $\frac{p_1}{p_2}(\pi^*_{\text{LTV}})$.[6]

[5] Letter to Malthus, October 1820, in *Works*, VIII, p. 279.

[6] The question of how much of this error should be attributed to the commodity considered and how much to the measuring standard opens the well-known problem of the invariable standard of value. We do not enter the problem here; for details, see Bellino (2004).

Finally, we recall that none of the above steps was stated in formal terms by Ricardo. Yet, it is precisely the *sequential nature* of deductions that allowed him (and his readers) to command the entire reasoning without using mathematical formulations. Unfortunately, all of Ricardo's attempts to determine the rate of profit according to a sequential reasoning are grounded on the labour theory of value, a theory that, as his critics maintained, could not be accepted in a capitalistic system. The Ricardian theory of distribution and value remained thus in an unsatisfactory state. As is well known, one century and a half later, Sraffa resumed the Ricardian analysis of value and income distribution, just by being able to disentangle among the mutual dependencies among these variables.

5.2.2 Causality in Marx's Analysis of Values, Distribution and Prices

A well-defined *sequential* chain can also be found in Marx's analysis of value, distribution and prices. It is known that Marx *defined* the value of each commodity as the quantity of labour which is 'socially necessary' to produce it. The value of each commodity, denoted by letter z, can be divided into three components: the quantity of labour necessary to reproduce the 'constant capital' (the capital goods), the quantity of labour necessary to reproduce the 'variable capital' (workers' subsistence) and the 'surplus value', that is, the quantity of labour provided by workers which exceeds their subsistence. To fix ideas, we can follow the usual analytic representation, where three sectors, or industries, produce the constant capital (c), the variable capital (v) and a luxury good (l). The values produced by each industry are

$$z_c = c_c + v_c + s_c,$$

$$z_v = c_v + v_v + s_v,$$

$$z_l = c_l + v_l + s_l,$$

where z_i denotes the value of commodity i, and c_i and v_i denote the quantity of constant capital and of variable capital employed in sector i, and s_i is the surplus value, that is, non-payed labour provided in sector i, $i = c, sv, l$. Magnitudes c_i, v_i and s_i are *given*; the z_is are the *unknowns*. Human labour has the characteristic to produce a quantity of commodities whose labour content (value) is *higher* than the labour content (value) of the commodities that are necessary to produce the means of subsistence (that is, that are necessary to reproduce the workforce of a worker). Subsistence is thus called 'variable capital' as it enables workers to provide a quantity of labour *higher than* the quantity of labour embodied in their subsistence. On the contrary, the labour embodied in capital goods is called 'constant capital' because it is not able to confer a higher value to commodities. Human labour is thus *the* origin of the surplus of the system, which is then appropriated by capitalists in the form of profits, as we will see shortly.

Marx then defines rates of surplus (or of exploitation) with the ratios

$$\sigma_i = s_i/v_i, \qquad i = c, v, l.$$

As the competition in labour market makes the duration of the working day and the wage rate uniform among industries, Marx maintains that the rates of surplus value tend to be uniform among industries, that is,

$$\sigma_i = \sigma, \quad \text{which entails} \quad s_i = \sigma v_i, \qquad i = c, v, l.$$

The surplus value is thus *proportional* to variable capital. In other terms, the surplus value is originated by the variable capital only (and not by constant capital). But as capitalists are interested in the rate of profit, $s_i/(c_i + v_i) = \sigma/(1 + c_i/v_i)$, and these rates are not uniform (unless in the special case of uniform ratios c_i/v_i, that is, uniform 'organic composition of capital'), the capitalistic system redistributes the surplus value in proportion to total capital in order to obtain a uniform rate of profit. This redistribution is carried out by establishing a set of relative prices different from values, called 'production prices'. Based on the data of the system, that is, c_i, v_i and s_i, the overall rate of profit is determined by:

$$\pi = \frac{\sum s_i}{\sum c_i + \sum v_i}.$$

Once the overall rate of profit has been determined in this way, it is inserted into the 'transformation' equations to determine production prices:

$$\begin{aligned} p_c &= (1 + \pi)(c_c + v_c), \\ p_v &= (1 + \pi)(c_v + v_v), \qquad (5) \\ p_l &= (1 + \pi)(c_l + v_l). \end{aligned}$$

Also in this theory we see a definite *sequential* order. This causality contains a twofold aspect.

(1) Its function is to show that profits derive from the exploitation of workers by capitalists. In fact, the definition of the profit rate *based on values only* conveys, for Marx, the idea that profits are a magnitude that logically *precedes* production prices, that is, a magnitude that emerges in the 'structure' of the economy, at the levels of values, not in the 'superstructure', that is, the capitalist system. In the value system, the surplus appears proportional to the *variable* capital; this makes transparent the true nature of surplus and, consequently, of profits: *non-paid labour*. By making profits proportional to *total* capital, production prices support the mystification that all capital is productive, which would justify the appropriation of the surplus by capitalists. On the contrary, defining the rate of profit by means of values only shows that profits are simply disguised surplus value.
(2) The sequential order followed by Marx put his reasoning away from the risk of arguing in a circle.

In fact, it is precisely on a question of unacknowledged interdependence that the transformation procedure proposed by Marx is wrong. As is known, it has been carried out partially, only when commodities are considered among the outputs, not when they appear among the inputs (in equalities [5] the left-hand side is expressed in terms of production prices, while the right-hand side is expressed in values). A complete transformation like, for example, that carried out by Ladislaus von Bortkiewicz (1907), requires that the magnitudes on *both sides* of the equalities are expressed in value terms. Let $C = c_c + c_v + c_l$, $V = v_c + v_v + v_l$, $L = s_c + s_v + s_l$ be the total value of constant capital, of labour capital and of luxury good produced, and let φ_i be the (unknown) coefficient which converts the total value of output of industry i into its price of production, that is,

$$p_c = C\varphi_c, \quad p_v = V\varphi_v, \quad \text{and} \quad p_l = L\varphi_l;$$

these transformation coefficients are determined in such a way as to ensure a uniform rate of profit among industries:

$$\begin{aligned} C\varphi_c &= (1+\pi)(c_c\varphi_c + v_c\varphi_v) \\ V\varphi_v &= (1+\pi)(c_v\varphi_c + v_v\varphi_v) \\ L\varphi_l &= (1+\pi)(c_l\varphi_c + v_l\varphi_v). \end{aligned}$$

In this system, coefficients φ_i (and thus production prices) and the rate of profit are determined *simultaneously*. This appears to be the *actual* nature of the link between prices and the rate of profit. This is the reason why Marx's (and Ricardo's) attempts to study income distribution relations prior to prices were all unsuccessful. As we will see later, interdependency will be the way that Sraffa (1960) will follow in his reappraisal of the classical analysis of distribution and value, although with some qualifications that will be analysed thoroughly afterward.

5.3 Sraffa's Production of Commodities

5.3.1 Sraffa on Causality: Some Methodological Handwritten Notes

In his published works, Sraffa has never explicitly dealt with the notion of causality and causation. However, some methodological remarks about the notions of causality and interdependence in economic analysis can be found among his unpublished papers (probably all from the early thirties). A first insight regards the use of the notion of causation in political economy and science at large. It is intended as a deviation from a 'normal state' in which the economy lies:

> Cause [is] required only when there is a deviation from what is normal, or uniform, or constant. That is to say that it is required only to explain change or difference. The habitual, 'normal', or 'natural' course of events does not require explanations; rather, it serves to explain 'why' individuals behave in the way they behave – 'everybody does it'. (Sraffa, D1/9 4)

According to Sergio Parrinello, 'Piero Sraffa ... stresses the fact that the contrast (difference or deviation) applied in causal explanation is to be found between the actual situation and what is normal, i.e. what reflects common sense or the idea of the "uncaused" state adopted in classical mechanics' (Parrinello, 2013, p. 11). However, this apparently 'conventional' view of normal state and, by implication, of causality is just the starting point of Sraffa's reflection.

In another (very schematic) note, Sraffa tackles the issue of causality by many different, though closely interconnected, perspectives, trying to make clear the epistemological foundations of any discourse upon causality.

What is a theory.

(1) Two series of quantities measured independently. Labour – value
(2) Equations – need for constants. Who determines them? Infinite series of causes, at least up to the point where const. of nat. are found. But Marshall believes to have found the final explanation with his scissors: the two piers of the arch. Fine, but who determines the form (parameters) of the curves? Is it immutable? and if it were, how do the values change through history?
Marshall's causal chain: contradiction with lies. (Sraffa, D1/9 3, our translation)

Thus, a theory must always be drawn in terms of a structure of equations that are deemed able to explain the relations between two (or more) series of quantities.

Provided that perfect knowledge does not exist, and there is always an array of circumstances and relations that, at any moment, may exert some influence upon the observed phenomenon by varying degrees, the scientist must take care of purifying his theory from all its ambiguities as much as possible, make it internally consistent and avoid burdening it with questions that the theory ultimately cannot answer:

It is not by finding out more fresh relations and connections that it can be answered; but by removing the contradictions existing between those already known, and thus perhaps by reducing their numbers. When these painful contradictions are removed the question as to the nature of force will not have been answered but our minds, no longer vexed, will cease to ask illegitimate questions. (Sraffa, D1/9 8)

Theoretical effort and empirical observation must be kept clearly distinguished for Sraffa and must not be intermingled. Once devised as a consistent and solid structure of 'causal relations', the theory must be tested by ascertaining if

that knowledge of the cause enables us to predict, or infer, the effect ... Economists who do not take this objective test as the standard of what is the cause of an event, are always driven back to trace the 'ultimate causes, causae causantes, etc.' to the wants, desires, aversions, decisions, volitions and intensions (or inducements and rewards) of individuals. (Sraffa, D1/9 6)

After having explicitly criticised the trivial way in which neoclassical theory deals with causality and interdependence (as shown by Alfred Marshall, Vilfredo Pareto and Arthur Cecil Pigou), Sraffa spells out what is to be considered as their major methodological fault, that is, their inability to distinguish between theory and reality and their confusion between an allegedly rational human agency and the alleged rationality of their models.

Not keeping distinct the theory (equations) from the facts which it represents, they alternate between substituting the solution of the equations for the real movement of things or conversely the actual happenings for the theory. Of the first distortion Marshall + Pareto are conspicuous: the actual course of events is represented as a crowd of consumers, producers, monopolists and competitors busily solving systems of equations in order to find out what their rational conduct should be – and then accordingly to the theory: but the theory has been posited and solved before they acted . . . facts happen by means of the solution of equations; equations are a tool which moves reality. (Sraffa, D1/9 6–7)

However fragmentary and incomplete, we can find in these brief notes the methodological premises (not yet the logical ones)[7] of Sraffa's general refutation of the neoclassical approach: the necessity to remove all 'painful contradictions' involved in a theory. These same elements are at the basis of the logical reconstruction of the classical approach to value and distribution, on which we now focus.

5.3.2 Interdependence between Prices and the Rate of Profit

Sraffa (1960) enters straight into the old classical problem of determination of the rate of profit. By introducing the price equations for a system with a surplus entirely perceived by capitalists he states:

[t]he difficulty cannot be overcome by allotting the surplus before the prices are determined, as is done with the replacement of raw-materials, subsistence, etc. This is because the surplus (or profit) must be distributed in proportion to the means of production (or capital) advanced in each industry; and such a proportion between two aggregates of heterogeneous goods (in other words, the rate of profits) cannot be determined before we know the prices of the goods. On the other hand, we cannot defer the allotment of the surplus till after the prices are known, for, as we shall see, the prices cannot be determined before knowing the rate of profits. The result is that the distribution of the surplus must be determined through the same mechanism and at the same time as are the prices of commodities. (Sraffa, 1960, §4)

[7] Beyond whatever Sraffa's ideological orientation was, it must be stressed that his refutation of the neoclassical theory is based on *logical* arguments only.

Hence, the rate of profit and prices are all unknowns of a *simultaneous* equation system:

$$\mathbf{p} = (1 + \pi)\mathbf{A}\mathbf{p}, \tag{6}$$

where $\mathbf{p}$ is the price vector and $\mathbf{A}$ is a square matrix whose generic *i*-th row contains the quantities of the various commodities employed as means of production in industry *i* (processes are represented on the rows). For each commodity, let us fix the total output produced by each industry as the unit of measure of the respective physical quantity. Gross product is thus represented by vector $\mathbf{u} = [1, 1, \ldots, 1]^T$, (^{T} is the transposition symbol). The net product is $\mathbf{y}^T = \mathbf{u}^T - \mathbf{u}^T\mathbf{A}$.

It is evident that in system (6) the rate of profit and prices are determined *simultaneously*: this is the true nature of the link among these variables that troubled Smith, Ricardo (and Marx) for so long! As seen, the perception of interdependency among these variables was already caught by von Bortkiewicz, as well as by all those authors that anticipated the notion of production prices.[8] Old classical authors missed this point, probably because they were less familiar with mathematical tools.[9]

[8] A review of these contributions is provided by Kurz and Salvadori (1995, ch. 13, §4); see also Seton (1957); Garegnani (1960, chs. IV and V).

[9] Walras himself did not give evidence to the interdependence among prices and the rate of profit or, in his own words, the 'rate of net income' (we owe this observation to Roberto Ciccone). We reproduce here a simplification of Walras's (1874) formalisation (we abstract from land, and disregard capital depreciation and insurance premiums). The supply prices of capital goods, $\mathbf{p}$, are the sum of the expenses of production, which depend on rental prices of capital goods, $\mathbf{v}$, and on wages, w,

$$\mathbf{A}\mathbf{v} + \mathbf{l}w = \mathbf{p}, \tag{*}$$

which corresponds to Walras's equations at p. 271 ($\mathbf{l}$ is the labour coefficients vector). The conditions for having a uniform rate of income over the supply prices of capital goods are

$$\mathbf{p} = \frac{1}{1+\pi}\mathbf{v}, \tag{**}$$

which correspond to Walras's equations at p. 272. The substitution of (**) into (*) close the circle,

$$(1 + \pi)\mathbf{A}\mathbf{p} + \mathbf{l}w = \mathbf{p},$$

establishing an interdependent link between prices and the rate of profit of the same nature of Sraffa's price system (the only actual difference being in the determination of income distributive variables).

Let us return to system (6). **A** is given; **p** and π are unknowns. By setting $1/(1+\pi) = \lambda$ it becomes $\mathbf{Ap} = \lambda\mathbf{p}$, that is, the right eigenvectors system of matrix **A**. Among the eigenvalues of matrix **A** we select the dominant one, λ^*, because Perron-Frobenius theorems guarantees that λ^* is associated to a semi-positive eigenvector, $\mathbf{p}^*$, determined up to a scale factor. The ensuing rate of profit is

$$\pi = \Pi = \frac{1-\lambda^*}{\lambda^*}, \tag{7}$$

which is positive if $\lambda^* < 1$. This is known as 'viability' condition; we will return to it later.

5.3.3 The Standard Commodity and the Recovery of Causality

The subsequent step taken by Sraffa is to study how the rate of profit and relative prices change when the workers receive a part of the social surplus (when the wage is above subsistence). A new addendum appears in the price system, the wage component, which is thus paired to the profit component in sharing the surplus. The price equations are thus modified as follows:

$$\mathbf{p} = (1+\pi)\mathbf{Ap} + \mathbf{l}w, \tag{8}$$

where w is the wage rate and **l** is the vector of direct labour coefficients. Let us choose as unit of measure of labour the total quantity of labour employed in the various industries, that is,

$$\mathbf{u}^T\mathbf{l} = 1. \tag{9}$$

The additional distributive variable w introduces a second degree of freedom into the price equations. The first degree of freedom is closed by choosing a numéraire; like Sraffa, we (provisionally) adopt the net product, that is, we set:

$$\mathbf{y}^T\mathbf{p} = \mathbf{u}^T(\mathbf{I}-\mathbf{A})\mathbf{p} = 1.$$

The second degree of freedom should be closed by fixing one of the distributive variables, π or w, from outside system (8). But Sraffa prefers to solve the system parametrically with respect to this distributive variable. In particular, he focuses on how the rate of profit and relative prices change in response to a change in wages. However, for any given level of wages, system (8) determine the rate of profit and prices *simultaneously*: there is still *full interdependence* among these variables.

5.3.4 Standard Commodity: A Tool to Separate Distribution from Value

To carry out his analysis, Sraffa made extensive use of the notion of Standard commodity, which is a composite commodity consisting in the net output of an imaginary economic system, characterised by an exact proportionality relationship between the vector of gross output, $\mathbf{q}^T$, and the vector of its means of production, $\mathbf{q}^T\mathbf{A}$ (and, therefore, the vector of net product, $\mathbf{y}^T = \mathbf{q}^T - \mathbf{q}^T\mathbf{A}$). Given matrix $\mathbf{A}$ and vector $\mathbf{l}$, vector $\mathbf{q}^T$ can be determined analytically by the system

$$\mathbf{q}^T = (1 + R)\mathbf{q}^T\mathbf{A}, \tag{10a}$$

$$\mathbf{q}^T\mathbf{l} = 1, \tag{10b}$$

where scalar R appears as a physical rate of surplus, which is *uniform* within such a peculiar system. In system (10), vector $\mathbf{q}$ and scalar R are unknowns. As we can see, the transition from the actual to the Standard system is just a 're-proportioning' of the industries that keeps constant the amount of labour force employed at the level of the actual system, as ensured by condition (10b).

If we set $1/(1 + R) = \eta$ system (10) becomes $\mathbf{q}^T\mathbf{A} = \eta\mathbf{q}^T$, that is the system of left eigenvectors of matrix $\mathbf{A}$. In order to exclude negative solutions, we can consider the left eigenvector, $\mathbf{q}^{*T}$, associated to the maximum eigenvalue, λ^*. Hence, $\eta = \lambda^*$, which entails $R = (1 - \lambda^*)/\lambda^*$, that is,

$$\Pi = R: \tag{11}$$

the uniform physical rate of surplus and the maximum rate of profit coincide. The reasons for this equality lie in the particular proportions which characterise the Standard system: in this configuration, the vector of net product and the vector of its means of production have the same physical composition:

$$\mathbf{y}^{*T} \equiv \mathbf{q}^{*T}(\mathbf{I} - \mathbf{A}) = R\mathbf{q}^{*T}\mathbf{A}. \tag{12}$$

Hence, when the entire net product is devoted to workers, the rate of profit is at its maximum level, and profits consist of the entire vector of net product, $\mathbf{y}^{*T}$. Hence:

vector of profits : $\mathbf{y}^{*T}$,

vector of the means of production : $\mathbf{q}^{*T}\mathbf{A}$.

Thanks to (12), the vector of profits comes to be proportional to the vector of the means of production:

vector of profits $= R \times$ vector of the means of production.

This explains why $\Pi = R$.

An analogous *physical* determination of the rate of profit is possible within the Standard system when the Standard net product is distributed among profits and wages at the condition that workers receive a fraction of the Standard net product, that is,

$$\text{vector of wages} : \omega \mathbf{y}^{*T}, \tag{13}$$

hence

$$\text{vector of profits} : (1-\omega)\mathbf{y}^{*T}.$$

Again, from (12), the vector of profits is proportional to the vector of the means of production:

vector of profits $= (1-\omega)R \times$ vector of the means of production,

and the ensuing rate of profit can still be ascertained physically:

$$\pi = R(1-\omega). \tag{14}$$

Moreover, if we express wages (and the prices of commodities) in terms of the Standard net product, that is, if we impose

$$\mathbf{y}^{*T}\mathbf{p} = 1, \tag{15}$$

the wage share coincides with wages (in fact, $\omega = w\mathbf{q}^{*T}\mathbf{l}/\mathbf{y}^{*T}\mathbf{p}$ but, from [10b] and [15], we have $\omega = w$) and (14) becomes

$$\pi = R(1-w). \tag{16}$$

Equation (16) describes the relation between wages and the rate of profit in the Standard system. Its remarkable property is that it is *independent of prices* (we have not calculated them yet). Given the level of wages (expressed as a fraction of the Standard net product) the rate of profit is determined *before knowing prices*. This is a direct consequence that in the Standard system, despite the presence of a plurality of commodities, gross product, net product, means of production, wage and profit are all constituted by *the same* (composite) commodity.

There are no reasons, however, to expect that the rates of surplus of the various commodities, $R_i = (q_i - \mathbf{q}^T\mathbf{a}_i)/\mathbf{q}^T\mathbf{a}_i$, are uniform among industries in the actual system so that $R_i = R$ as in (10a); the proportions of the actual system do not reflect those of the Standard system. Yet, Sraffa showed that relation (16) holds in the actual system too. In fact, as we saw, the transition from the actual to the Standard system is just a re-proportioning of the industries. But, as the wage and the rate of profit are *uniform* across industries, this transition cannot change these uniform levels of w and π. We must only remember that relation (16) was built under the assumption that wages were constituted by a fraction of the Standard net product (see condition [13] above). This is not the case in the actual system. Yet, nothing prevents expressing wages and prices of commodities produced in the actual system in terms of the Standard net product (this just amounts to using equation [15]). In conclusion, (16) expresses the relation between wages and the rate of profit in the actual system, the only condition being to express wages and the prices of commodities in terms of the Standard net product.

This result puts us in the position to know the levels of both distributive variables *before* knowing prices. Once one of these variables is taken as given ($w = \bar{w}$ or $\pi = \bar{\pi}$), relation (16) determines the other one:

$$\pi = R(1 - \bar{w}) = \bar{\pi} \text{ or } w = 1 - \bar{\pi}/R = \bar{w}.$$

Then, by inserting the given level of wages (of the rate of profit) and the ensuing level of the rate of profit (of wages) into equations (8) we can solve with respect to prices: $\mathbf{p} = (1 + \bar{\pi})\mathbf{A}\mathbf{p} + \mathbf{l}\bar{w}$, that is,

$$\mathbf{p} = \bar{w}[\mathbf{I} - (1 + \bar{\pi})\mathbf{A}]^{-1}\mathbf{l} = \bar{\mathbf{p}}.$$

5.3.5 A Deeper Assessment of These Achievements

We have returned to a *sequential* determination: income distribution first, then prices! This feature of the solution procedure brings us back to the issues discussed in Section 5.2. The Standard system construction allows us to restore a sequential link between income distribution and prices, a result that previously seemed hopeless! Unexpectedly, Sraffa gives no particular emphasis to this result in the book. The Standard commodity occupies a prominent place throughout the book, but its role seems mainly that of providing a tool to prove the existence and the uniqueness of an economically meaningful solution to the price equations: it is known that Sraffa avoided using the Perron-Frobenius theorems on non-negative matrices (on this point, see Eatwell, 1981, p. 73). Only at the end of the book, in Appendix D entitled 'References to the literature', there are some interesting hints on this point.

> A method devised by Ricardo (if the interpretation given in our Introduction to his *Principles* is accepted)[1] is that of singling out corn as the one product which is required both for its own production and for the production of every other commodity. As a result, the rate of profits of the grower of corn is determined independently of value, merely by comparing the physical quantity on the side of the means of production to that on the side of the product, both of which consist of the same commodity; and on this rests Ricardo's conclusion that 'it is the profits of the farmer that regulate the profits of all the other trades'. Another way of saying this, in the terms adopted here, is that com is the sole 'basic product' in the economy under consideration.
>
> (It should perhaps be stated that it was only when the Standard system and the distinction between basics and non-basics had emerged in the course of the present investigation that the above interpretation of Ricardo's theory suggested itself as a natural consequence.)
>
> Ricardo's view of the dominant role of the farmer's profits thus appears to have a point of contact with the Physiocratic doctrine of the 'produit net' in so far as the latter is based, as Marx has pointed out,[2] on the 'physical' nature of the surplus in agriculture which takes the form of an excess of food produced over the food advanced for production; whereas in manufacturing, where food and raw materials must be bought from agriculture, a surplus can only appear as a result of the sale of the product.
>
> [1] In Ricardo's *Works and Correspondence*, I, xxxi–xxxii.
>
> [2] *Theorien über den Mehrwert*, I. 36 and III, 134, note.

In some unpublished notes, Sraffa has been more explicit. For example, in a note dated August 1955 he wrote:

> We can sum up the results of using the q-system as follows:
>
> 1) it proves the uniqueness, in certain circumstances, of the solution of the price-equations;
> 2) it gives a tangible <proof> demonstration that the rate of profits is not <fundamentally essentially> a price phenomenon. <does not arise from an addition to the price of product over that of the raw mat. etc.> <does not arise outside the sphere of prod.>
>
>   [This refutes the widespread opinion that profit arises from adding something on to the price of the end-product. Malthus is perhaps the most explicit supporter of this view; but the picture of a linear <straight line> (as opposed to a circular) production process, which begins with 'factors of production'

and ends in 'consumption goods' provides ideal condition for a 'price' theory of profit.]

3) it provides, in the Standard Commodity, an 'invariable medium' which isolates the causes of fluctuation 'on the side of the commodity' eliminating those from 'the side of money'.
4) the Standard Commodity establishes the straight-line <linear> relation between wages and the rate of profit. (Sraffa, D3/12/68.20, 28.8.55 to 30.8.55)[10]

In a short note written in a page of a notebook, he wrote:

Slogans not used
The St. Syst provides tangible evidence of the rate of profits as a non-price phenomenon.
A Dividend could be declared before knowing what is the price of the company's product. (Sraffa, D 3/12/43 f.4, attributed date: post-1945)

Why were such important considerations left out of *Production of Commodities*? Evidently, the priority of determining income distribution with respect to determining relative prices made possible by the Standard system is a truly relevant point in the reappraisal of the surplus approach. If, given wages, the rate of profit is determined prior to prices, then profits appear as a *physical* surplus arising directly from the sphere of production, not that of exchange (see, for example, Eatwell, 1975, section II, or Garegnani, 1984, section VII and, in particular, § 24). In other words, profits do not arise 'from the acts of buying and selling commodities' (Ciccone, 1998, p. 441) but from the excess of the quantities of commodities produced with respect to the quantities employed. No competition among sellers can drag them to zero, redistributing thus the benefits to the entire society. Yet, none of these elements found a place in Sraffa's book. One possible explanation of these silences is that the separation of distribution from value can be observed when wages are expressed in terms of a composite commodity which has nothing to do (in principle) with the actual bundle of workers' consumption. This prevents relation (16) to give an actual description of how *real wages* (that is workers' purchasing power) change as the rate of profit changes.[11] An explicit statement by Sraffa on these points would certainly have been helpful!

[10] Words inside symbols <> denote additions to the main text.

[11] If we consider wages as given, like classical economists, we should start from the (average) bundle **b** of commodities constituting the subsistence. But the transformation of this bundle in a 'given' wage would require the knowledge of

5.4 Keynes

Like for Ricardo, Marx and partially Sraffa, Keynes's *General Theory* is based on sequential analysis, which conveys the existence of causal relations within the economic system.

In chapter 18 of his masterpiece, Keynes makes clear the peculiar perspective through which he looks at the economic system and closely relates his methodological choices to the particular question he wants to tackle (what determines the level of income and employment) and to the practical use that the answer must allow for (the possibility to control and to manage the process of income and employment creation):

The division of the determinants of the economic system into two groups of given factors and independent variables is, of course, quite arbitrary from any absolute standpoint. The division must be made entirely on the basis of experience, so as to correspond on the one hand to the factors in which the changes seem to be too slow or so little relevant as to have only a small and comparatively negligible short-term influence on our *quaesitum*; and on the other hand to those factors in which the changes are found in practice to exercise a dominant influence on our *quaesitum*. Our present object is to discover what determines at any time the national income of a given economic system and (which is almost the same thing) the amount of its employment; which means in a study so complex as economics, in which we cannot hope completely accurate generalisations, the factors whose changes *mainly* determine our *quaesitum*. Our final task might be to select those variables which can be deliberately controlled or managed by central authority in the kind of system in which we actually live. (Keynes, 1936, p. 247)

Keynes spells out a precise sequence, a chain of causal relationships that he deems capture the essential features of an industrial economy. It is perhaps better to mention them in reverse order, from the last to the first, answering Keynes's fundamental question: what determines the actual level of income and employment at any moment?

(1) Effective demand determines the volume of production and employment.

prices: we would have $w = \mathbf{b}^T\mathbf{p}$. If, on the contrary, we consider the rate of profit as given, as suggested by Sraffa, the ensuing wages are expressed in terms of the Standard net product; their conversion into *real* wages (that is, in terms of workers' bundle) would still require the previous knowledge of prices: $w/\mathbf{b}^T\mathbf{p}$.

(2) Investments determine savings and consumption through the multiplier.
(3) Money interest rates and expectations determine investments.
(4) Expectations, liquidity preference, and money supply determine interest rates.

Through this causal chain, Keynes can describe the functioning of the capitalist system as a whole in the short term, leaving the dynamics of the system in the long run to one side.

Keynes is aware of significant interdependencies within the economic system but thinks that some forces are stronger and quicker than others in producing their effects upon income and employment. This is the reason why he describes the functioning of the capitalist system mainly in terms of causal or sequential relationships. The latter are to be intended, as already explained, not in mechanistic terms but, rather, as the form of the theory the economist must employ, in order to express the essential features of a dynamic and complex reality that cannot be directly observed or described in all its details.

Most economists in the neoclassical synthesis tradition and in the new-Keynesian approach identify Keynes's revolution with his rejection of the price-adjustment mechanism and its replacement with a quantity-adjustment mechanism based on the multiplier. This is not entirely incorrect, provided that we do not read this statement through the lenses of neoclassical theory, where quantities and prices are simultaneously determined. In any case, we must avoid reducing Keynes's analysis to a particular case of a 'more general' model where quantities and prices vary simultaneously. Otherwise, it is straightforward to reach the (quite disappointing) conclusion that unemployment is mostly the result of downward price and wage stickiness, which, by preventing price and wage variations from adjusting firms' costs to revenues, allows exogenous shocks to impose a reduction in real output and employment, via the multiplier. According to Pasinetti and most post-Keynesians, this interpretation not only contradicts Keynes's explicit statements about the inefficacy of wage cuts in increasing employment (irrespective of what assumptions are made on their rigidity) but fails to catch the essential message of Keynes's *General Theory*: that is, the principle of effective demand (Pasinetti, 1997).

The former, as developed in chapter 3 and 8 of the *General Theory*, establishes a clear *logical* precedence of demand over supply:

autonomous demand (investments, exports and public expenditures) determines the level of employment and, given a certain technique, the amount of income and production.[12] In doing so, the principle of effective demand reverses Say's law according to which aggregate supply determines aggregate demand, always maintaining the two in equilibrium. In Keynes's view, the chain of causality runs the other way round so that employment and output are demand constrained up to the level of full employment.

Therefore, the multiplier cannot be regarded as just an analytical device able to convey the quantity-adjustment mechanism in the context of interdependent fixed price markets: at a much deeper level, it reveals an essential feature of modern capitalist economies, that is, the fundamental asymmetry between investments (and the other components of autonomous demand), on one side, and consumption and savings, on the other: while the latter must be drawn from already existing income, investments are not bounded by existing income; for example, they can be financed by debt and credit creation. Moreover, investment decisions are not *backward* but rather *forward* looking, since they aim at taking advantage of an uncertain future. These two basic features make investments (and the other components of autonomous demand) the *causa causans* able to set in motion the whole economic system. Then, the multiplier is the proper analytical device, able to explain *how* investment decisions are able to generate that precise flow of income and savings exactly required to make a given level of investment financially sustainable and logically consistent with macroeconomic equilibrium.

Thus, any attempt to encapsulate Keynes's *General Theory* in a Walrasian demand and supply framework, where all prices and quantities are simultaneously determined, and everything depends on everything else, strips out his vision of how modern industrial economies

[12] It is true that certain passages are doomed to create confusion on this point. Keynes was not so eager to be crystal clear on the methodological foundations of his analytical work. Thus, the definition of effective demand as laid down in chapter 3 of *General Theory*, with its reliance upon decreasing returns and expected revenues, may also be interpreted as assuming an interdependent relation between aggregate demand and supply. However, Keynes insists on the former as the active variable, subject to sudden changes as expectations change, while the latter is passive and stable at least in the short run.

work and how economics can get a clue on what drives economic growth and determines employment.

According to most interpreters, Keynes adopted a Marshallian partial equilibrium analysis rather than a Walrasian one.[13] Under-employment equilibrium is defined as the result of a limited set of relevant variables. He has no interest in equilibrium as such, rather he focuses on the forces which determine equilibrium (Keynes, 1936, p. vii). Causal relations are crucial not only for interpreting economic outcomes but also as a guide for economic policy in changing those outcomes: in particular, they suggest the instrumental variable which economic policy can try to control in order to attain an improvement in employment and general welfare.

This fundamental methodological choice does not prevent Keynes, in his attempt to take important aspects of real economies in consideration and also to entertain a positive dialogue with his neoclassical fellows, to admit the existence of feedback effects and interdependencies. He clearly acknowledges that a change in investments and in national income may induce a growing demand for money and, thus, exert some influence on the level of interest rates:

> [t]he position of equilibrium will be influenced by the repercussions; and there are other repercussions also. Moreover, there is not one of the above factors which is not liable to change without much warning, and sometimes substantially. Hence the extreme complexity of the actual course of events. Nevertheless, these seem to be the factors which it is useful and convenient to

[13] According to Joan Robinson, Keynes's harsh criticism was mainly directed to the most rigid versions of neoclassical theory and aimed at making clear that partial equilibrium analysis should be abandoned in order to build a general theory focusing on 'output as a whole'. Robinson also noticed that Marshall was generally careful in taking care of the dynamic processes occurring in historical time: Krishna Bharadwaj also underscores how Marshall (contrary to Stanley Jevons, Léon Walras or Vilfredo Pareto) tried to incorporate some important ideas stemming from classical political economy, such as the concept of 'normal costs'. On the whole, despite his criticism of 'classical' economics, Keynes was profoundly influenced by the Marshallian way of reasoning: the short-term/long-term distinction (with his typical *ceteris paribus* assumptions) is employed by Keynes as a renown and generally accepted device able to cast his new thinking in a familiar and hopefully uncontroversial language. Less helpful for understanding the central message of the *General Theory* was Keynes's reliance upon the concepts of decreasing returns, utility of consumption, and disutility of labour. Moreover, the very idea of 'under-employment equilibrium' as a short-term phenomenon posed an array of interpretative questions.

isolate. If we examine any actual problem along the lines of the above schematism, we shall find it more manageable; and our practical intuition (which can take account of a more detailed complex of facts than can be treated on general principles) will be offered a less intractable material upon which to work. (Keynes, 1936, p. 249)

Keynes's care for accuracy and dialogue may explain his initial uncertainty regarding the attempts undertaken by John Hicks, James Meade, and others to express his main ideas in the form of a system of simultaneous equations: it took some time before he came to reject these representations, arguing that the IS-LM type of reasoning hides more that it can unveil (Keynes, 1937 [1973]; see also Hicks, 1973).

The reasons underpinning Keynes's rejection of the IS-LM type of reasoning are well known: first of all, he strove to point out, against profound misunderstanding and criticism on this point, that the rate of interest is a monetary phenomenon, determined only by the interaction between demand and supply of money, with no relation with the supply of savings:

The fact that any increase in employment tends to increase the demand for liquid resources, and hence, if other factors are kept unchanged, raises the rate of interest, has always played an important part in my theory. If this effect is to be offset, there must be an increase in the quantity of money .... But there is nothing in that to rehabilitate the theory that the rate of interest is fixed by the interaction of the supply of saving with the demand for investment as determined by the marginal efficiency of capital. (Keynes, 1973, p. 231)

Secondly, he placed the rising demand for liquidity due to the 'finance motive' within the institutional structure of the economy, assuming that the banking system can adjust almost any change in income with a growing provision of bank credit. When the process of income creation, set out by new investment via the multiplier, is considered in its historical time dimension, the problem arises of how the increased flow of investment may be financed *before* the correspondent flow of saving has been set apart. Keynes's answer to this question is straightforward:

It is the role of the credit system to provide the liquid funds which are required first of all by the entrepreneur during the period before his actual expenditure, and then by the recipients of this expenditure during the period before they have decided how to employ it. We have been all brought up ... in deep confusion of mind between the supply and demand of money and supply of savings; and until we rid ourselves of it, we cannot think correctly. (*CWK*, xiv, p. 285)

Paul Davidson, Robinson, and other post-Keynesians emphasized a more fundamental reason that induced Keynes to avoid any resort to an IS-LM type of Walrasian equilibrium framework (see Robinson, 1980, p. xvii; Davidson, 1991, p. 115): this reason is uncertainty.[14] For Keynes, neoclassical equilibrium analysis was just a 'pretty, polite technique which tries to deal with the present by abstracting from the fact that we know very little about the future' (Keynes, 1973, p.114,), while 'a monetary economy ... is essentially one in which changing views about the future are capable of influencing the quantity of employment' (Keynes, 1936, p. vii).

Simultaneous determination of variables would imply the existence of stable relationships between supply and demand for money, goods, or investments, and their prices in terms of interest rates. In the IS-LM model, these complex relations are described by two distinct and well-defined curves, each independent from the other. Yet, since money, interest rates, and investments link the present to the future, expectations are crucial in establishing their reciprocal relations and make them largely unpredictable. Moreover, a change in expectations (or in investments, or in interest rates) would affect all the above relations so that the curves would be interdependent. The interplay between investments, interest rates, and the demand for money can be understood only in the context of a sequential analysis whose structure can change from time to time according to different circumstances. No comparative statics would be possible in this context and, if attempted, would be either misleading or irrelevant.

[14] For some purposes, Keynes did employ a concept of logical time, but such usage was confined to countering standard theory's arguments on its own terms or in establishing preliminary statements identifying various causal relations; this is of little interest in analysing his general theory, which is conducted in historical time (see Robinson, 1980). 'Keynes's position on money and uncertainty requires a theoretical stance on time, where economic *processes* occur in real time and within a distinct form of economic organisation that cannot be analysed on the basis of universal laws deduced from a reductionist (individual agent) foundation' (Henry, 2003, pp. 343–344).

Other interpreters emphasise that the basic question about Keynes's analysis is not which features macroeconomic equilibrium has but rather which forces make equilibrium be what it is: thus, equilibrium is not a generic intersection between fully drawn aggregate demand and aggregate supply *curves*; rather, it is the equality between *expected* costs and revenues, determined in the *point* of effective demand as described in chapter 3 of the *General Theory*, where historical time and uncertainty play a relevant role (see Kregel, 1976; see also Setterfield, 2003, p. 108).

The fact that Keynes considers under-employment equilibrium as a permanent condition of the economic system does not prevent his analysis being essentially of a Marshallian short-run character: technology, population, tastes, output composition, the propensity to save and consume, changes in the price level or in relative prices are confined to the realm of 'ceteris paribus'. How they could change in the long term, as a response to present changes in output and employment, is an issue omitted from Keynes's main focus, to be fully taken-up in the post-Keynesian literature.

Robinson has suggested that Keynes's departure from neoclassical analysis goes hand in hand with the choice of historical time analysis over logical time (Robinson, 1980, pp. xiv–xv). Only in historical time, when certain specific circumstances may be taken into account and weighted for their relevance, can a causal order emerge. It is our opinion that, while Keynes made use of both time frameworks in his writings and also in the *General Theory*, his most important arguments were actually drawn in logical time.[15] His basic concepts – the multiplier, the marginal efficiency of capital, and liquidity preference – do not need any time dimension to be employed. Yet, it would be equally misleading to understand them as instantaneous processes: Keynes is perfectly aware that time is required for them to unfold their effects. However, it is their logical structure that Keynes aims to highlight, not their time dimension.

On the whole, Keynes's way of presenting the *General Theory* was not only a rhetorical means to place the novelty of his analysis in a framework as close as possible to the one familiar to the majority of the profession: it was inherent in his own training as an economist, fully embedded in the shadowing light of Marshall; moreover, it responded

[15] For a deeper understanding, we make reference to Chapter 4 in this volume.

to the same practical purposes as Marshall's microeconomics, that is, to set out an agenda for economic policy. Posing his theory under the headings of short-term equilibrium analysis, Keynes certainly escaped the confusing symmetries of Walrasian general equilibrium and could unveil the 'forces which determine changes in the scale of output as a whole' (Keynes, 1936, p. vii). At the same time, as highlighted by Pasinetti and other post-Keynesians, Keynes's persistent adherence to the Marshallian framework prevented him from developing, at a more fundamental level of analysis, a more clear-cut and unequivocal breach with existing economic thought.

5.5 Cumulative Causation and Path Dependence in Post-Keynesian Literature

Most authors in the post-Keynesian tradition have developed Keynes's basic ideas in the long run, trying to apply the principle of effective demand in a dynamic framework, where many of the ceteris paribus conditions assumed by Keynes must be allowed to change. It is at this junction that two different (and partially diverging) lines of research emerge: the first tries to describe the complex interplay between the forces at work in real economic systems which may induce output and employment to rise or fall, as a result of changes in effective demand, capital accumulation, income distribution, and technology; the second tries to figure out the logical properties of a system which, adopting Roy Harrod's terminology, is assumed to grow at its *warranted* or even natural rate of growth, provided that any possible problem of effective demand has been successfully resolved by policy authorities.

While the first line of research comprises authors like Michael Kalecki, Nicholas Kaldor, Richard Goodwin and Richard Kahn (and later by many American post-Keynesians), the second one has been developed mainly by Pasinetti, though Robinson, Kaldor himself, and Garegnani have dealt with it to some extent.

In both of these contexts, the issue of causality comes to the fore, though with different meanings and roles. In the first context, causality is to be mainly intended as cumulative causality. According to Geoffrey Harcourt and Peter Kriesler:

> The theory of cumulative causation ... comes from Adam Smith, Allyn Young (1928), Veblen and then Kaldor and Myrdal in the post-war period.

> The theory rejects the traditional neoclassical approach to economic theory whereby the factors responsible for uniqueness of equilibrium are independent of those responsible for local and global stability. This implies that the factors responsible for the trend are independent of those responsible for the cycle. As this too is rejected, it is one reason why cumulative causation and cyclical growth theory are closely related. The most succinct statement of all this is by Michal Kalecki (1968, p. 434): 'The long-run trend [is] but a slowly changing component of a chain of short-period situations ... [not an] independent entity.' (Harcourt and Kriesler, 2016, pp. 24–25)

The concept of effective demand, independently discovered by Kalecki in 1935, clearly reverses the causality chain underpinning classical political economy: according to the Polish-born economist, capitalists' investment decisions are the *primum movens* in producing a certain amount of income, which, in turn, gives rise to a certain amount of profits.

> Since profits in a given short period are determined by capitalists' decisions as to their consumption and investment formed in the past, the factors determining the distribution of income will affect not real profits but the real wage bill, and consequently the national output .... However great the margin of profit on a unit of output, the capitalists cannot make more in total profits than they consume and invest. (Kalecki, 1942, p. 260)

So, the causal chain runs from investments to profit (via the multiplier-accelerator interaction) and not vice versa. Like Keynes, Kalecki held that an act of saving is not automatically an act of investment so that Say's law is not valid either in the short or in the long run.[16]

The logical sequence underpinning Kalecki's reasoning is grounded on the vision of how and by whom the crucial decisions are taken in a capitalist economy.

[16] According to Krielser, 'Davidson also attempts to impute a sort of Say's Law to Kalecki, with savings determining investments, when he argues that (Davidson, 2000, p. 8) "whatever proportion of earned profits entrepreneurs do not spend on consumption is saved, but these savings are necessarily spent on buying newly produced capital goods". However, this mistakes the causal link between capitalists' savings and investment. For Kalecki, savings do not automatically translate into an act of investment, as is implied in the above statement. Rather, since investment and capitalist consumption themselves determine capitalist income (profits), it is investment that determines saving, and not vice versa, exactly as it does for Keynes' (Krielser, 2016c, p. 212).

Now it is clear that capitalists can decide to consume and to invest more in a given period than in the preceding one, but they cannot decide to earn more. It is, therefore, their investment and consumption decisions which determine profits, and not vice-versa. (Kalecki, 1971, pp. 78–79)

The economy is asymmetrically structured and gives capitalists and entrepreneurs the power to spend more than they can earn (thanks to financial facilities offered by the banking system), thus increasing their own earnings as the economy grows. On the contrary, 'workers cannot decide to earn more, since this depends essentially on the employment they are being offered by entrepreneurs' (Lavoie, 2006, p. 86). Of course, consumer spending may be artificially fuelled by credit and allows workers to consume more than they earn for some while. Yet, this additional consumption does not entail a higher income tomorrow. The case of business investment is different: provided that business expectations are fulfilled, leverage is a powerful way for increasing return on equity.

The clear distinction of the different roles and powers of capitalist and workers in modern capitalist society led Kalecki to break any artificial interdependence between consumption, investments and savings and employ a sequential analysis of how income is generated and distributed out of a given stream of investments.

In Kalecki's view (as explained in his seminal 1942 article), in long-run analysis average profits ($\bar{P}$) are determined by the average habitual capitalist's consumption ($\bar{A}$) plus average net investment ($\bar{I}$), divided by 1 minus λ, where λ is the fraction of profits consumed by capitalists:

$$\bar{P} = \frac{\bar{A} + \bar{I}}{1 - \lambda}$$

Given certain simplifying assumptions, the average rate of profit is attained by dividing the former equation by the average volume of capital. The latter is determined as $\bar{K} = K_0 + \frac{n}{2}\,\bar{I}$ where K_0 is the initial volume of capital equipment, n is the number of years under consideration and $\bar{I}$ are average investments over the period. We thus obtain the average rate of profit:

$$p = \frac{1}{1 - \lambda} \frac{\bar{A} + \bar{I}}{K_0 + \frac{n}{2}\bar{I}}$$

Since $\bar{A}/K_0$ is fully determined before the period under consideration, after simple transformations, Kalecki concludes that 'The average rate of profit p is determined as a function ... of the ratio of average investments $\bar{I}$ to the initial value of capital K_0' (Kalecki, 1942, p. 264).

Kalecki's reasoning comprises both micro- and macroeconomic level of analyses. At the microeconomic level, neoclassical price theory assumes joint determination of prices and incomes, at the point where marginal revenues are equal to marginal costs; in Kalecki's view, the mark-up is exogenously determined by the degree of monopoly and thus prices depend on the mark-up over a constant cost curve whose level is exogenously given (Kriesler, 2016a, p. 146). Imperfect competition, investment-induced innovation, and increasing returns characterising modern industrial systems fuel processes of cumulative causation and give rise to persistent divergences rather than equilibrium dynamics.

While the ex ante rate of profit and the average profit per unit of output depend on institutional factors external to the macroeconomic system, such as the bargaining power in industrial relations and the degree of competition in the goods market, the ex post rate and level of profits depend 'on the aggregation of all microeconomic investment decisions, and accordingly are out of the hands of any individual business' (Webster, 2003, p. 297). To put it briefly, microanalysis determines the share of profits, macroanalysis the total value of profits and the combination of both the level of output (Kriesler, 2016b, p. 173).

It is worth noting that in Kalecki the long-run analysis does not imply long-run stationary equilibrium: apart from cyclical fluctuations as determined by the variations of investments, the whole trend of the economy is 'subject to a complex process of long-run development' (Kalecki, 1942, p. 261).

It is interesting to note that Kaleckian economists have been criticised by Ian Steedman for not utilising the simultaneous determination approach to pricing used by general equilibrium and neo-Ricardian economists. According to Kriesler, Kalecki's use of the partial equilibrium method in cost and price analysis does not derive from ignorance of relevant interdependences but on the willingness to attain a tractable model for understanding the major forces at work into the economic system:

Any economy is an extremely complex set of phenomena with an extremely large number of important inter-relations. This complexity is increased by an order of magnitude when open economy effects are acknowledged. Now, there are two basic ways in which economists attempt to deal with such complexity. General equilibrium analysis attempts to capture all the essential relationships impinging on any problem. However, the precision which the analysis captures is at the expense of being able to use it meaningfully for understanding any particular society, so that the greater level of generality demands a higher level of abstraction. When all the major relations are analysed simultaneously, it is difficult to say anything meaningful about causality. Partial equilibrium is an attempt to allow causal inferences to be made by isolating a section of the economy and focusing on that, assuming other relations remain unaffected. Clearly this method will never be capable of generating precise answers to general problems. Rather, it is an attempt to approximate, but by doing so to be able to draw causal inferences and hence address policy problems. As has been noted elsewhere: 'it is better to be approximately right than to be precisely wrong!' (Kriesler, 2016d, pp. 218–219)

A similar way of reasoning may be found in the works of Kaldor. Despite Kaldor's slight interest in building up a fully-fledged and comprehensive dynamic macroeconomic model, his seminal and wide-ranging contributions in many crucial areas of economic theory made him one of the most influential and original economists of his time. Harcourt (2006, p. 172) highlights Kaldor's ability to grasp ideas stemming from different traditions of thought and to combine them into new concepts and research fields: the notion of increasing returns from Allyn Young, the foreign trade multiplier from Harrod, the concept of cumulative causation from Karl Gunnar Myrdal, the principle of effective demand and the paradox of thrift from Keynes.[17]

Kaldor (1972) openly rejected the mainstream notion of equilibrium, regarding it as a static device unable to cope with real economic phenomena occurring in historical time (Dow, 2007, p. 41). Rather, he made extensive use, especially in his later works, of cumulative, circular causation, and path dependence with reference to the

[17] Actually, Kaldor rather than Kalecki is properly to be credited for having coined, with reference to the paradox of thrift, the famous aphorism: 'Capitalists earn what they spend, and workers spend what they earn' (Kaldor, 1955–1956, p. 96).

connection between investment and innovation, to the role of exports in activating industrial development and economic growth, and to the role of endogenous money supply in the economic system.

In Kaldor's view, the process of cumulative causation runs from investment to innovation to (dynamic) increasing returns to profits and feeds upon itself.[18] Investments often entail the introduction of new machinery and new techniques so that an increase in the volume of investments also induces a qualitative change that fosters productivity and shapes specialisation patterns. In this context, the concept of equilibrium is of little use.

In an open economy framework, developed by Kaldor in a series of essays written between 1966 and 1972, exports play a similar role, especially when foreign demand concerns the capital-goods sector: again, increasing returns, dynamic economies of scale, innovation, and learning by doing exert their effects on the economy in a cumulative causation process which patently escapes any static, reversible and timeless equilibrium framework. Here, feedback effects and interdependencies may again be taken into consideration and enrich the analysis: yet the main driving forces of economic changes are clearly depicted.

Harcourt points out that Kaldor's methodological views underwent considerable evolution over his career:

> Kaldor moved away from the unnecessarily restrictive constraint of requiring full employment . . .. He became more and more dissatisfied with equilibrium

[18] Jerry Courvisanos compares Kaldor's view with Kalecki's, claiming that 'The causal sequencing of innovation and investment is reversed in work done by Nicholas Kaldor and Joseph Schmookler, with the rate of investment determining the rate of innovation. Kalecki also recognizes this sequence, despite having identified the innovation-driven process. Kalecki places this investment-driven process clearly into an appropriate context by viewing the innovation process as "part and parcel of 'ordinary' investment"' (Kalecki 1954, p. 158), or endogenous innovation. Instead of unidirectional causality, the discussion above clearly implies a circular flow, where one innovation process feeds into the other. Kaldor's principle of cumulative causation is the 'self-reinforcing dynamic' in the circular process of investment demand leading to innovation that then stimulates further investment. The distinction between exogenous and endogenous innovation specifies how innovation enters this cumulative causation process. In this context, R&D expenditure is central to the endogenous innovation process, with large firms with strong profit results having the ability to undertake large R&D spending, while registration of patents from R&D efforts reflects the clustering of innovations' (Courvisanos, 2003, p. 193).

economics, the notion of balance of forces, the strong tendency of economies to return to former resting places following shocks, or to seek out new ones following changes in underlying conditions. In its place he put the notion that, once economies get a run on (or off), they keep it up rather than return to the pack. His 'fairly drastic' changes in theoretical ideas formed for many years the basis of lectures to undergraduates at Cambridge, although he himself was 'not ... able to present the results in the comprehensive form of a model' [Kaldor, 1960, p. xxv]. (Harcourt, 2006, p. 175)

King highlights that increasing returns, cumulative causation and path dependence led Kaldor to attach an endogenous nature not only to technical change but also to the supply of labour and capital. This vision was clearly at odds with Harrod's notion of a 'natural' rate of growth given by the supposedly exogenous growth rates of the labour force and of technical progress (King, 2007, p. 761). We may notice here the Smithian flavour of Kaldor's view on the potentiality of an expanding industrial economy, which seems to be unlimited by any scarcity, both in a natural or social domain.

The very notion of 'stylised fact' christened by Kaldor can be related to the issue of causality. Stylised facts, emerging from 'abduction', may help select the proper relations which catch the most relevant aspect of economic reality. Sheila Dow recalls how Kaldor's views were clarified and extended by Tony Lawson:

Given the open nature of the economic system, detailed facts reflect a variety of tendencies at work under particular circumstances. By abstracting from this detail, stylised facts can form the basis of hypotheses. Here we see a version of the interaction of the mind with observed experience as a way of addressing the problem of induction, in the Newtonian/Smithian tradition. The Department of Applied Economics was established at Cambridge in 1945 to provide the empirical material on which such abductive reasoning could build. (Dow, 2007, p. 41)

On the whole, Kaldor's path-breaking efforts in so many different fields proved able to establish different streams of research: although having little interest in developing a consistent methodological framework, he shared the same aversion to equilibrium reasoning and looked for relevant cumulative causation forces at work in the real economy.[19]

19 In his own attempt to offer a classification of the different streams of post-Keynesians economists, Marc Lavoie suggests the existence of a 'Kaldorian post-Keynesian strand ... mostly concerned with the constraints arising from open

A somewhat similar inspiration may be detected in Robinson's long journey through twentieth-century economics. Starting from a strict Marshallian observance of static short-term equilibrium analysis, Robinson became more and more interested in long-term dynamics; under the powerful influence of Kahn, Sraffa, Maurice Dobb and, of course, Keynes, she became convinced, after the publication of the *General Theory*, that economic theory should be reconstructed from its basement. Robinson's endeavour to 'generalize the General Theory' aimed at recasting 'the Keynesian arguments in terms of the more fundamental categories of capital accumulation, labour supply, technical progress and natural resources' (Pasinetti, 2007, p. 108).

Actually, she firmly rejected the neoclassical notion of equilibrium as a mechanistic, timeless, reversible and self-adjusting device and came also to reject her *The Economics of Imperfect Competition*, exactly for being fully constrained by the straitjacket of Marshallian static analysis (Robinson, 1933). Since 1933, when she became involved in the making of Keynes's *General Theory*, Robinson came to think that long-term equilibrium dynamics could not be simply the adaptation of supply to 'normal' demand but should be worked out assuming that techniques of production and capital endowments changed over time, as investments were carried on by entrepreneurs.

During the 1950s and early 1960s, her inquiry delved into the logical conditions for achieving a cumulative long-term steady growth. This 'golden age' dynamic was meant to highlight the relations between economic growth, income distribution, technical progress, and the evolution of labour supply when full employment growth is maintained through time and business expectations are fulfilled. This effort, as Robinson put it, was an attempt to 'treat the analysis of accumulation according to Keynes' prescriptions' (Robinson, 1979, p. xvii).

The golden age model served as a point of reference to understand and evaluate the actual trends in the economy and 'classify the conditions that prevent [the golden age] from being fulfilled' (Robinson, 1979, p. xxvii). In Robinson's view, there are

economy considerations, such as the balance of payments constraints or the fundamental identity that links private financial saving, public deficit and the current account balance. In the 1970s, this strand became known as the New Cambridge School' (Lavoie, 2015, p. 41).

two kinds of economic arguments, each of which is useful in analysis provided that it is not stultified by being confused with the other. [The first] proceeds by specifying a sufficient number of equations to determine its unknowns, and so finding values for them that are compatible with each other .... The other ... specifies a particular set of values obtaining at a moment in time, which are not ... in equilibrium with each other, and shows how their interactions may be expected to play themselves out. (Robinson, 1962, p. 23)

In Robinson's view, equilibrium analysis is devoid of any notion of causation, while historical time analysis properly is.

Equilibrium analysis cannot tell us what the value of any particular variable will be at any particular point in time. It tells us what the values of several variables must be if the economy, or perhaps some part of it, is to be in equilibrium. Strictly speaking there is no causation. A number of variables are determined simultaneously. It is not valid to say *a* causes *b*, all we can say is that, if it has such and such a value, then, given the values of *d*, *e* and *f*, *b* must have such and such a value if equilibrium is to be achieved. On the other hand, historical analysis does have causal chains; it makes sense to say *a* causes *b*, whether or not the economy, or the part being analysed, is in equilibrium. (Nevile, 2016, pp. 51–52)

For most of her career, Robinson believed that long-term equilibrium dynamic analysis should be a necessary reference point for evaluating actual economic outcomes. Golden age analysis was to be intended as a 'logical construction, not a hypothesis about the behaviour of capitalist economies ... a base line against which to describe the vicissitudes of a developing economy; I do not know that any better system for combining logical with historical has yet been devised' (Robinson, 1979, p. xxiv).

According to some interpreters, from the 1970s, Robinson came to think that only historical analysis had relevance and came to reject the notion of equilibrium as such, not only in its neoclassical version (Bharadwaj, 1991). Along similar lines to Kaldor's, she came to depict an 'Economics without equilibrium':

To make the argument applicable to actual situations we have to leave equilibrium analysis behind and approach the problem in terms of historical process, the system continually lurching from one out-of-equilibrium position to another. (Robinson, 1962, pp. 6–7)

In Bharadwaj's and Jan Kregel's view, this final turn in Robinson's intellectual journey would be grounded on the growing awareness that uncertainty is a crucial ingredient in economic dynamics: in a world where the past is irrevocable and the future unknown, equilibrium analysis would be devoid of any relevance.

Certainly, in the 1970s, Robinson came closer and closer to those American post-Keynesians like Davidson, who seemed to attach no value of any sort to equilibrium analysis and stressed uncertainty being the main feature of capitalism. Along the same lines, she came to criticise Sraffa and the neo-Ricardians for their focus on a 'purely logical structure – an elaborate thought-experiment [where] there is no causation and no change' (Marcuzzo, 2003, p. 14).[20] According to Kregel, when asked about her paper 'History Versus Equilibrium' (1974) Robinson replied 'emphatically declaring in favour of the former' (Kregel, 1991, p. 108). Historical time analysis was deemed to address the more interesting and relevant questions concerning causation processes occurring in real economies.

Robinson's attitude towards equilibrium may be open to different interpretations: while she certainly lose interest in the 'golden age' dynamics in favour of historical analysis, she never rejected the latter. The two strands of causal reasoning still abided in her mind.

5.6 Concluding Remarks

Any attempt to explain how social systems work inevitably reflects the social scientist's worldview. The same applies – possibly even more – to the realm of economic analysis. Economic theories and, more specifically, economic models outline certain links between economic magnitudes and, inevitably, hide others. In the real world, almost all these links have a somewhat interdependent character. But theories are simplified representations of reality; by their nature, they cannot avoid *selecting* some relations as the most direct and relevant and ignoring or minimising others.

In the dominant theory, for example, the exogenous data of the general equilibrium model are preferences, endowments, technology, and the distribution of property rights over firms. On the basis of these 'fundamentals', the prices of goods and the rental prices of factors are

[20] See also Robinson (1980, ch. 11) and the controversy between Garegnani and Robinson, originally published in Italian in Garegnani (1979, pp. 119–143) and later reproduced in English, in Feiwel (1989, ch. 12).

simultaneously determined together with their allocation among consumers and production activities. The choices about which variables are to be considered as exogenous and which ones are endogenous contain some drastic but inevitable simplifications. One could observe that the equilibrium levels of endogenous variables may affect the exogenous data (the 'fundamentals'): for example, relative prices may affect the evolution of individual preferences as well as of technology; at the same time, the fundamentals may affect one another: for example, individual preferences may affect endowments or technology. There are many reasons why neoclassical theorists have chosen to disregard these possible feedbacks. They probably considered them less important than the relations between the data and the endogenous variables or than those among the endogenous variables themselves; moreover, the directions of these feedbacks may be less univocal than the links explicitly embedded in the model. Anyway, what is peculiar to the neoclassical approach is that the links between the endogenous variables are of the interdependent kind: goods prices and factors rental prices *jointly determine* the allocations of goods and factors.[21] This simultaneity in the determination of the endogenous variables of the equilibrium models conveys a picture where the allocation of goods and factors, the prices of the goods, and the rental prices of factors are the outcome of spontaneous or 'natural' market forces, able to harmonise the interests of the various agents of the economic system and to attain, under certain circumstances, the maximum social welfare. Thus, any attempt to modify this outcomes, via a deliberate coordination or decision process, contrasts the 'natural' and spontaneous order stemming from self-adjusting market forces and individuals' free will.[22]

[21] This is true also for partial equilibrium analysis, though in a more restricted sense: each price is co-determined with the quantity exchanged. The links among the markets, although not made explicit, are however taken into consideration in partial equilibrium analysis: in Marshall's words: 'The demand for raw materials and other means of production is indirect and is derived from the direct demand for those directly serviceable products which they help to produce' (Marshall, 1890, bk. v, ch. vi, § 1).

[22] This quite sweetened view of the working of an economic system pertains to the basic core of the theory, that is, the general equilibrium model of *perfect* competition. It must be recognised that several neoclassical authors have considered many cases of market or coordination failures, to bring the model down to reality. This has been obtained by assuming various forms of '*im*perfections': bounded rationality, strategic interaction, externalities,

The logical structure of the classical and Keynesian theories differs deeply on this very point: a varying interplay of sequential and interdependent links appears between the endogenous variables, depending on the specific issue under analysis. For example, in Ricardo, Marx, and Sraffa, output levels and the subdivision of the surplus are taken as given when production prices and the residual distributive variable are determined or prices are taken as given when quantities supplied adjust to effectual demand. In particular, the interaction between prices and quantities has been deliberately discarded in the classical-Keynesian approach. These theories are worked out along different dimensions, complementary to each other. They often contain a truly *analytical* part, which relates those aspects that, for their nature, can easily be expressed by univocal quantitative relations. However, this analytical core does not exhaust the investigation. In some cases, economic models are not closed and do not provide a univocal solution: they leave some aspects open. Those magnitudes that are taken as given in the strictly analytical relations are then explained by another part of the theory, by another set of quantitative relations or in a stage of analysis that is logically separated from the previous one and must be examined in cooperation with other disciplines. For instance, within the analysis of production prices, wage levels are determined by the bargaining power of the social classes or, more generally, by social or institutional circumstances; output levels – the famous 'given quantities' of production prices frameworks – are determined by consumption customs, the accumulation of capital and the technical conditions of production; relative prices – when determining the general level of macroeconomic activity – are determined by the mark-up rates of the various industries, etc.

According to the classical-Keynesian approach, the outcomes of economic systems are less automatic and univocal; the social and institutional dimension interacts more evidently with the technical and economic dimension than in the neoclassical approach. Moreover, this analytical structure makes the identifications of the 'instruments' for economic policy interventions easier and less prone to the alleged and deterministically derived reactions by 'self-interested', utility optimising and insulated economic agents.

frictions, asymmetric information, etc. These are tortuous efforts to obtain imperfect outcomes from 'rational' behaviours. However, all these phenomena are embedded within a set of interdependent relationships.

References

Bellino E. (2004) 'On Sraffa's Standard Commodity', in *Cambridge Journal of Economics*, 28(1), pp. 121–132.

Bellino E. and Nerozzi S. (2017) 'Causality and Interdependence in Pasinetti's Works and in the Modern Classical Approach', in *Cambridge Journal of Economics*, 41(6), pp. 1653–1684.

Bharadwaj K. (1991) 'History versus Equilibrium', in Rima I. H. (ed.) *The Joan Robinson Legacy*, Armonk, M. E. Sharpe, pp. 80–104.

Ciccone R. (1998) 'Surplus', in Kurz H. D. and Salvadori N. (eds.) *The Elgar Companion to Classical Economics, (L–Z)*, Cheltenham and Northampton, Edward Elgar, pp. 440–445.

Cord R. (2007) (ed.) *The Palgrave Companion to Cambridge Economics*, London, Palgrave-MacMillan.

Courvisanos J. (2003) 'Innovation', in King J. E. (ed.) *The Elgar Companion to Post Keynesian Economics*, Cheltenham and Northampton, Edward Elgar, pp. 191–195.

Davidson P. (1991) *Controversies in Post Keynesian Economics*, Aldershot, Edward Elgar

(2000) 'There Are Differences between Kalecki's Theory of Employment and Keynes's General Theory of Employment, Interest and Money', in *Journal of Post Keynesian Economics*, 23(1), pp. 3–25.

Dow S. C. (2007) 'Cambridge's Contribution to Methodology in Economics', in Cord R. (ed.) *The Palgrave Companion to Cambridge Economics*, London, Palgrave Macmillan, pp. 27–50.

Eatwell J. (1975) 'Mr. Sraffa's Standard Commodity and the Rate of Exploitation', in *The Quarterly Journal of Economics*, 89(4), pp. 543–555.

(1981) '"Poscritto" to the Italian translation of Eatwell (1975)', in Panizza R. and Vicarelli S. (eds.) *Valori e prezzi nella teoria di Marx*, Torino, Einaudi, pp. 70–73.

Henry J. F. (2003) 'Time in Economic Theory', in King J. E. (ed.) *The Elgar Companion to Post Keynesian Economics*, Cheltenham and Northampton, Edward Elgar, pp. 341–346.

Feiwel G. R. (ed.) (1989), *Joan Robinson and Modern Economic, Theory*, Houndmills, Basingstoke, Hampshire and London, Macmillan.

Garegnani P. (1960) *Il capitale nelle teorie della distribuzione*, Milano, Giuffré.

(1984) 'Value and Distribution in the Classical Economists and in Marx', in *Oxford Economic Papers*, 36(2), pp. 291–325.

(1979) *Valore e domanda effettiva*, Torino, Einaudi.

(2007) 'Professor Samuelson on Sraffa and the Classical Economics', in *The European Journal of the History of Economic Thought*, 14(2), pp. 181–242.

Halevi J. Harcourt G. C. Kriesler P. and Nevile J. (eds.) (2016) *Post-Keynesians Essays from Down Under – Volume I: Essays on Keynes, Harrod and Kalecki*, London, Palgrave Macmillan.

Harcourt G. C. (2006) *The Structure of Post-Keynesian Economics, the Core Contributions of the Pioneers*, Cambridge, Cambridge University Press.

Harcourt G. C. and Kriesler P. (2016) 'The Enduring Importance of The General Theory', in Halevi J. Harcourt G. C. Kriesler P. and Nevile J. (eds.) *Post-Keynesians Essays from Down Under – Volume I: Essays on Keynes, Harrod and Kalecki*, London, Palgrave Macmillan, pp. 15–33.

Hicks J. R. (1973) 'Recollections and Documents', in *Economica, New Series*, 40(157), pp. 2–11.

Kaldor N. (1955–1956) 'Alternative Theories of Distribution', in *The Review of Economic Studies*, 23(2), pp. 83–100.

(1960) *Essays on Value and Distribution*, London, Duckworth.

(1972) 'The Irrelevance of Equilibrium Economics', in *Economic Journal*, 82(328), pp. 1237–1255.

Kalecki M. (1935) 'A Macro-Dynamic Theory of Business Cycles', in *Econometrica*, 3(1), pp. 327–344.

(1942) 'A Theory of Profits', in *Economic Journal*, 52(206/207), pp. 258–267.

(1954) *Theory of Economic Dynamics*, London, George Allen & Unwin.

(1968) 'Trend and Business Cycles Reconsidered', in *Economic Journal*, 78(310), pp. 263–276.

(1971) *Selected Essays on the Dynamics of the Capitalist Economy*, Cambridge, Cambridge University Press.

Keynes J. M. (1936) *The General Theory of Employment, Interest and Money*, London, Macmillan.

(1937) 'The General Theory of Employment', in *Quarterly Journal of Economics*, 51(2), pp. 209–223.

(1973) *The Collected Writings of John M. Keynes, Vol. XIV, The General Theory and After, Part. II, Defence and Development*, Moggridge D. (ed.) London and Basingstoke, Macmillan St. Martin's Press.

King J. E. (ed.) (2003) *The Elgar Companion to Post Keynesian Economics*, Cheltenham and Northampton, Edward Elgar.

(2007) 'Nicholas Kaldor (1908–1986)', in Cord R. (ed.) *The Palgrave Companion to Cambridge Economics*, London, Palgrave-MacMillan, pp. 747–766.

Kregel J. (1976) 'Economic Methodology in the Face of Uncertainty: The Modelling Methods of Keynes and the Post Keynesians', in *Economic Journal*, 86(342), pp. 209–225.

(1991) 'On the Generalization of the *General Theory*', in Rima I. H. (ed.) *The Joan Robinson Legacy*, Armonk, M. E. Sharpe, pp. 104–109.

Kriesler P. (2016a) 'Kalecki's Pricing Theory Revisited', in Halevi J. Harcourt G. C. Kriesler P. and Nevile J. (eds.) *Post-Keynesians Essays from Down Under – Volume I: Essays on Keynes, Harrod and Kalecki*, London, Palgrave Macmillan, pp. 141–160.

(2016b) 'Microfoundations: A Kaleckian Perspective', in Halevi J. Harcourt G. C. Kriesler P. and Nevile J. (eds.) *Post-Keynesians Essays from Down Under – Volume I: Essays on Keynes, Harrod and Kalecki*, London, Palgrave Macmillan, pp. 161–176.

(2016c) 'Was Kalecki an "Imperfectionist"? Davidson on Kalecky', in Halevi J. Harcourt G. C. Kriesler P. and Nevile J. (eds.) *Post-Keynesians Essays from Down Under – Volume I: Essays on Keynes, Harrod and Kalecki*, London, Palgrave Macmillan, pp. 209–215.

(2016d) 'Answers for Steedman', in Halevi J. Harcourt G. C. Kriesler P. and Nevile J. (eds.) *Post-Keynesians Essays from Down Under – Volume I: Essays on Keynes, Harrod and Kalecki*, London, Palgrave Macmillan, pp. 216–223.

Kurz H. D. and Salvadori N. (1995) *Theory of Production – A Long-Period Analysis*, Cambridge, Cambridge University Press.

Lavoie M. (2006) *Introduction to Post-Keynesian Economics*, Houndmills, Basingstoke, Hampshire and New York, Palgrave Macmillan.

(2015) *Post-Keynesian Economics: New Foundations*, Cheltenham and Northampton, Edward Elgar.

Marcuzzo M. C. (2003) 'Joan Robinson's Economics', in King J. E. (ed.) *The Elgar Companion to Post Keynesian Economics*, Cheltenham and Northampton, Edward Elgar, pp. 211–215.

Marshall A. (1890) *Principles of Economics*, 9th (variorum) ed., with annotations by Claude William Guillebaud, London, Macmillan.

Nevile J. W. (2016) 'What Keynes Would Have Thought of the Development of IS-LM', in Halevi J. Harcourt G. C. Kriesler P. and Nevile J. (eds.) *Post-Keynesians Essays from Down Under – Volume I: Essays on Keynes, Harrod and Kalecki*, London, Palgrave Macmillan, pp. 50–68.

Parrinello S. (2013), 'Causality and Normal States in Economics and Other Disciplines', in *The European Journal of the History of Economic Thought*, 23(1), pp. 1–24.

Pasinetti L. L. (1955) 'La funzione del consumo in alcuni modelli econometrici applicati ai cicli economici', in *Rivista Internazionale di Scienze Sociali*, 26(5), pp. 397–421.

(1956) 'La funzione degli investimenti in alcuni modelli econometrici applicati ai cicli economici', *Rivista Internazionale di Scienze Sociali*, 28(2), pp. 125–151.

(1957) 'Un nuovo modello econometrico per la rappresentazione del sistema economico statunitense', *Rivista Internazionale di Scienze Sociali*, 28(1), pp. 57–62.

(1965 [2019]) 'Causalità e interdipendenza nell'analisi econometrica e nella teoria economica', in *Annuario dell'Università Cattolica del Sacro Cuore, A.A. 1964–1965*, pp. 231–250; English translation: 'Causality and Interdependence in Econometric Analysis and in Economic Theory', in *Structural Change and Economic Dynamics*, 49, pp. 357–363.

(1974) *Growth and Income Distribution: Essays in Economic Theory*, Cambridge, Cambridge University Press.

(1997) 'The Marginal Efficiency of Investments', in Harcourt G. C. and Riach P. A. (eds.) *A 'Second Edition' of the General Theory*, vol. I, London, Routledge, pp. 198–218.

(2007) *Keynes and the Cambridge Keynesians: A Revolution in Economics to Be Accomplished*, Cambridge, Cambridge University Press.

Ricardo D. (1817) *On the Principles of Political Economy and Taxation*, London, John Murray; used edition: Sraffa P. (ed.), (1951–1973), vol. I.

Rima I. H. (1991) (ed.) *The Joan Robinson Legacy*, Armonk, M. E. Sharpe.

Robinson J. V. (1933) *The Economics of Imperfect Competition*, London, Macmillan.

(1962) *Essays in the Theory of Economic Growth*, London, Macmillan.

(1974 [1979]) 'History versus Equilibrium', Thames Papers in Political Economy, London, Thames Polytechnic. Rept., in *Collected Economic Papers*, vol. 5, Oxford, Blackwell, pp. 48–58.

(1979) *The Generalisation of the General Theory and Other Essays*, London and Basingstoke, Macmillan.

(1980) *What Are the Questions? And Other Essays*, Armonk, M. E. Sharpe.

Seton F. (1957) 'The "Transformation Problem"', in *The Review of Economic Studies*, 24(3), pp. 149–160.

Setterfield M. (2003), 'Effective Demand', in King J. E. (ed.) *The Elgar Companion to Post Keynesian Economics*, Cheltenham and Northampton, Edward Elgar, pp. 105–112.

Simon H. (1953) 'Causal Ordering and Identifiability', in Hood W. C. and Koopmans T. C. (eds.) *Studies in Econometric Method, Cowles Commission*, New York, John Wiley and Sons; London, Chapman and Hall, pp. 49–74.

Smith A. (1776 [1976]) *An Inquiry into the Nature and Causes of the Wealth of Nations*, The Glasgow edition of the Works and Correspondence of

Adam Smith, Campbell R. H. and Skinner A. S. (eds.) Oxford, Clarendon Press.
Sraffa P. (ed.) (1951–1973) *The Works and Correspondence of David Ricardo*, 11 vols., Cambridge, Cambridge University Press.
(1960) *Production of Commodities by Means of Commodities – Prelude to a Critique of Economic Theory*, Cambridge, Cambridge University Press.
von Bortkiewicz L. (1906–1907) 'Wertrechnung und Preisrechnung im Marxchen System', in *Archiv für Sozialwissenschaft und Sozialpolitik*, 23, pp. 1–50; 25, pp. 10–51 and 445–488.
Young A. (1928) 'Increasing Returns and Economic Progress', in *The Economic Journal*, 38(152), pp. 527–542.
Walras L. (1874 [1954)]) *Elements d'économie politique pure, ou théorie de la richesse*, Lausanne, L. Corbaz & Cie Éditeurs; English translation: Jaffé W. (ed.) *Elements of Pure Economics, or the Theory of Social Wealth*, Homewood, Richard D. Irvin.
Webster E. (2003) 'Profits', in King J. E. (ed.) *The Elgar Companion to Post Keynesian Economics*, Cheltenham and Northampton, Edward Elgar, pp. 294–298.

6 *Macroeconomics before Microeconomics*

A Sceptic's Guide to Macroeconomics

MURRAY MILGATE AND JOHN EATWELL

Economics is a science of thinking in terms of models joined to the art of choosing models which are relevant to the contemporary world. It is compelled to be this, because, unlike the typical natural science, the material to which it is applied is, in too many respects, not homogeneous through time. [. . .] Good economists are scarce because the gift for using 'vigilant observation' to choose good models, although it does not require a highly specialized intellectual technique, appears to be a very rare one.

(Keynes, 1938)

6.1 Introduction

Given the state of contemporary macroeconomics, a sceptic might well ask whether the division of economic analysis into branches labelled microeconomics and macroeconomics is really one of form rather than one of substance. A sceptic might further enquire whether this partition is really used to facilitate the modelling of economic phenomena at different levels of aggregation or whether it is simply a device to obscure some fundamental inconsistences in economic thinking.

When John Maynard Keynes wrote in the *General Theory* of there being a 'vital difference between the theory of the economic behaviour of the aggregate and the theory of the behaviour of the individual unit' (Keynes, 1936, ch. 7, § IV), he had posed a challenge to mainstream economic thinking. At the time, his assertion was somewhat shocking. After all, ever since the days of Stanley Jevons, Léon Walras and Alfred Marshall, economists had been taught that everything one needed to know about the workings of a market economy could be deduced from what Marshall had called 'a study of mankind in the ordinary business of life' (Marshall, 1890 [1961], p. 1). In mainstream economic thinking, there was no 'vital difference' at all.

The consternation caused by the *General Theory* provoked a legion of responses – ranging from the claim that Keynes was quite wrong, to the assertion that he was saying nothing new. Much of economic thinking has been struggling to come to terms with this conundrum ever since. It is its failure to come up with a convincing resolution of this theoretical issue that ultimately lies behind the current reputational crisis in macroeconomics.

6.2 'Macroeconomics' before Macroeconomics

Keynes's modern biographer, Robert Skidelsky, is fond of saying that Keynes invented macroeconomics. This is almost, but not quite, true. It is certainly true that the branch of economics actually called macroeconomics emerged from the tumult of the Keynesian Revolution in the 1930s. Yet what we would today call 'macroeconomic' analysis had been going on at least since the systematic study of the nature and causes of the wealth of nations began – it's just that it wasn't called macroeconomics. Long before the term 'macroeconomics' entered the lexicon of economists, all of the familiar themes that one would find in any of today's macroeconomics textbooks had been debated – at least since the days of Adam Smith, if not before.

The precise origin of the term 'macroeconomics' is somewhat obscure. It has become customary to attribute it to Ragnar Frisch (1933), but that is a little misleading. To begin with, as early as 1931, Maurice Dobb had spoken of 'macroscopic, as distinct from microscopic, issues' in his *Introduction to Economics* (p. 622); and, in the case of Frisch, it is well to remember that he had not spoken of macroeconomics as such but rather of 'macro-dynamics'. Michał Kalecki had used the Frisch terminology at about the same time (Kalecki, 1933 [1935]). Furthermore, Frisch seems to have been more concerned with drawing a contrast between the 'dynamic' content of his approach and the 'static' character of Walrasian thinking than he was with delineating a relationship between macroeconomics and microeconomics at it is understood today.

By the early 1940s, however, the term seems to have been in fairly common use. Gottfried Haberler had used it in his *Prosperity and Depression* in 1937. Both Erik Lindahl and Herbert Robinson used it in 1939 in *Studies in the Theory of Money and Capital* and *The Economics of Building* respectively. Martin Bronfenbrenner and

Lawrence Klein used it in articles in *Econometrica* in 1943 and 1945 respectively. Jacob Marschak also used it in the *American Economic Review* in 1945. Arthur Marget actually provided a brief terminological history of it in the second volume of his *Theory of Prices* in 1942; and by 1948, its currency was sufficiently widespread for Kenneth Boulding to have adopted it in the second edition of his undergraduate textbook, *Economic Analysis*. Interestingly enough, the terminology did not appear in the first edition of Paul Samuelson's *Economics* in 1948; nor is it in his *Foundations of Economic Analysis* where, however, the term 'macro-dynamics' does appear.

The classical economists, from Smith down to Thomas Robert Malthus, David Ricardo and Karl Marx, were predominantly concerned with what would today be identified as 'macroeconomic' issues. The subjects of capital accumulation, the effects of the introduction of new techniques of industrial production on output and employment, the relative merits of tax-financed versus debt-financed public expenditure, the causes of movements in the general level of prices and the effects of monetary shocks on the real economy – not to mention the economy-wide impact of free trade versus protection – were their stock-in-trade. Indeed, with the possible exception of the theory of value and distribution, there was scarcely anything going on in the classical period that a self-respecting economist of today would identify as *not* being 'macroeconomics'.

The classical writers developed an understanding of the workings of a market economy by separating their treatment of the determination of the relative prices of commodities from their treatment of the levels of output and employment and the effects of technological change. Issues which we would today describe as 'macroeconomics' were deemed separable from the theory of value (Garegnani, 1987).

The classical economists did not deny that all aspects of the market system – prices, distribution and output – acted and reacted upon one another. The argument was rather that the analysis of relative prices could be conducted with the size and composition of output taken as a datum (that is, without taking into account, at this stage, the implications of changes in output). Likewise, the analysis of output was conducted with prices and distribution being taken as given. Once the explanation of the determination of these variables had been accomplished, their interactions were then examined in a more complex narrative. But this additional investigation left the process of determination of the relevant variables unaltered.

However, when neoclassical theory was developed around the middle of the nineteenth century – when the first neoclassical writers set out upon the path that would eventually give us the Marginal Revolution – things changed. The wholesale re-direction of economic thinking towards the analysis of the constrained maximisation of utility (and profits) by individually rational economic agents in a competitive market had the effect of combining the analysis of price determination with the theory of output and employment.

If the characteristic feature of classical thinking was *separability* when it came to the study of economic growth and fluctuations, then the characteristic feature of the neoclassical thinking that replaced it was *reducibility*. All economic phenomena could be reduced to being the result of the constrained maximisation of utility by rational individuals. The unified theory of cost and price, whereby wages were the reward (at the margin) to individual workers for foregoing leisure, and profits were the reward (at the margin) to individual capitalists for foregoing consumption, allowed prices and quantities to be determined without reference to anything other than individual decision-making under constraint. The theory of output and employment was simply the theory of the clearing of the markets for factors of production (including labour). The overall level of output and employment would be, as Milton Friedman put it, be 'ground out by the Walrasian system of general equilibrium equations' (Friedman, 1968, p. 8).

Yet a feeling that the study of individual market behaviour needed somehow to be more fully integrated with the study of the behaviour of the economy as a whole had begun to take root prior to the appearance of the *General Theory* in 1936. Writers who turned their attention to the subject of booms and slumps had already begun to explore familiar 'macroeconomic' themes in the first couple of decades of the twentieth century.

In England in the 1920s, a number of economists in and around Cambridge were busily at work trying to fill the gaps in the legacy they had inherited from Marshall on the subject of industrial fluctuations. Here explorations into the economics of the short-period by Arthur Cecil Pigou, Walter Layton, Dennis Robertson, Frederick Lavington, Ralph Hawtrey – and the pre-*General Theory* Keynes himself – stand out.

In Sweden, a new generation of economists including Erik Lindahl, Dag Hammarskjold, Erik Lundberg, Gunnar Myrdal, Ingvar Svennilson and Johan Åkerman had begun working on the time-sequence analysis of cumulative processes, taking their lead from Knut Wicksell – someone who had delved more deeply into 'macroeconomic' themes than any of the other early pioneers of neoclassical thinking.

In America, a slightly different path was followed. Wesley Clare Mitchell and Henry Ludwell Moore were working on the study of business cycles well before the First World War. But they were using the techniques of descriptive statistics and statistical inference respectively, rather than theoretical argument. Essentially, they were involved in the tasks of classification and estimation of cyclical movements. Irving Fisher was perhaps the only prominent American writer of the day working on business cycles from a theoretical point of view. Fisher's view of economic crises, or debt deflation as it has become known, is interesting if only because of its theoretical articulation. Almost alone among the pre-Keynesian neoclassicals, Fisher explicitly started from the Walrasian general-equilibrium model in an intertemporal setting, rather than from either Marshall or Wicksell.

The efforts of other empirically minded writers interested in business cycles should not be overlooked. Clément Juglar was, of course, a forerunner in this arena. Its exponents customarily deferred to the effects of the weather or the climate for an explanation – to crop cycles, hog cycles, rainfall patterns and the like. As one of them, Joseph Kitchin, put it in the early 1920s, short swings were 'influenced by excess or deficiency in crops which fall out of tune with the normal cycle'. Even Jevons, when he had turned his mind to the possible causes of industrial fluctuations back in the 1870s, was led to suggest that sunspot activity was a plausible suspect.

So, if all this 'macroeconomic' analysis was going on before the *General Theory*, in what sense might Skidelsky have been right to attribute the birth of macroeconomics as a separate field of study to Keynes? The answer is that the *General Theory* posed an additional problem for economics.

To the task of explaining economy-wide movements in output, employment and prices around an equilibrium where market clearing prevailed for all commodities and factors of production – as had been the earlier focus – Keynes had added a new problem: namely, the problem of reconciling the observed persistence of involuntary unemployment with the core neoclassical proposition that full employment would tend to be secured by the normal operation of the price mechanism.

Keynes had set out his own answer to this problem in unequivocal terms as soon as he began writing the drafts of what would become the *General Theory*. Mainstream 'equilibrium theory', he observed, had assumed that there were 'natural forces' tending to bring the level of output back to its 'optimum level' whenever 'temporary forces' had led it to depart from that level. But in contrast to orthodox 'equilibrium theory', Keynes went on to claim, the 'equilibrium level' towards which output tends to return 'is not necessarily the optimum level' (Keynes, 1932, p. 406).

In the *General Theory* itself, Keynes would make his case just as forcefully. The 'outstanding features of our actual experience', he said, was that 'we oscillate' around 'an intermediate position' – a position 'determined by "natural" tendencies, namely, by those tendencies which are likely to persist' – which was 'appreciably below full employment' (Keynes, 1936, p. 254).

It was this problem, the Keynes problem, and the response to it in mainstream circles, that gave birth to macroeconomics as we know it today – and it is this problem that underlies the current state of disagreement within the ranks of macroeconomists. Simply stated, the problem was this: could Keynes's proposition about there being a less-than-full-employment position determined by 'natural tendencies' be reconciled with the theoretical apparatus of neoclassical theory that characterised the 'natural position' of the economy as market clearing – that is, a position characterised by full employment?

6.3 Macroeconomics and the Keynes Problem

The 'equilibrium theory' to which Keynes had alluded was, of course, the theory of Marshall and of Walras. Given the preferences of individual agents, the technologies they had available to them and the constraints imposed upon them by their initial endowments, it was argued that under perfectly competitive conditions market-clearing equilibrium (and hence full employment) would prevail. It was a theory that was finally completed and codified by Kenneth Arrow and Gérard Debreu just after the Second World War. The *locus classicus* of this approach was Debreu's *Theory of Value* which appeared in 1959.

The status of this equilibrium was summed up by Milton Friedman. Equilibrium was, he said, 'a logical construct that defines the norm or trend from which the actual world is always deviating but to which it is tending to return or about which it tends to fluctuate'. He went on to emphasise that 'the hypothesis that the logical construct does specify the norm or trend in this sense is entirely compatible with the existence of uncertainty, just as the hypothesis that $s=\frac{1}{2}gt^2$ specifies the law of falling bodies is entirely compatible with the existence of air' (Friedman, 1970, p. 150).

This idea – namely, that actual economic outcomes might differ from but were constantly tending towards a centre of gravitation under the influence of competition – an idea that dates back to Smith's definition of 'natural price' – was decisive in the creation of modern macroeconomics. By defining market-clearing equilibrium as the 'norm or trend' (Smith's 'centre of gravitation') the question then posed was why does the economy not gravitate to that 'norm or trend'.

The first steps in answering this question were taken almost simultaneously, and it seems largely independently, by John Hicks, Alvin Hansen, Roy Harrod, James Meade, Franco Modigliani and Oskar Lange in their efforts to come to terms with the Keynes Problem. The details of these individual stories need not detain us here. It is not their individual differences that matter but their shared response to the Keynes Problem. This was to argue that there must be some reason why resources were not flowing in the right direction to restore full-employment equilibrium. There must be some barriers in the *short run* that were preventing the economy from gravitating back to equilibrium in the *long run*. Samuelson would later call this the arena of 'auxiliary constraints' (Samuelson, 1947, pp. 30–39). We have called the authors of 'short-run macroeconomics' as 'The Imperfectionists' (Eatwell and Milgate, 1983, ch.1 and 2011, ch.8).

The multiplicity of imperfectionist models that were constructed after the *General Theory* is extraordinary. The catalogue of frictions and rigidities that were offered as reasons to explain the persistence of involuntary unemployment ran the gamut of possibilities, from monopolies and monopsonies of one sort or another, banking practices that distorted financial markets, misguided monetary policy, through to transaction costs and insufficient price and/or wage flexibility and on to 'uncertainty' that distorts the operation of the price mechanism. The number of imperfections seems to have been limited only by the imagination of their authors.

Yet, despite the obviously ad hoc character of much imperfectionist thinking, Samuelson famously managed to convince economists that all was in fact well (Samuelson, 1948, pp. 5–6 and 233). Macroeconomics was not riven by intractable disagreement; it was not rife with ideological biases; it was not being made up on the hoof. Instead, there was a coherent body of macroeconomic thought – a grand Neoclassical Synthesis – that was sufficiently robust to warrant admission into the discourse of 'modern economic science'. And so it was that eventually the closed-economy IS-LM model, the aggregate supply-aggregate demand model, the income-expenditure model, the Mundell-Fleming model and the Phillips Curve all became part of the toolbox of the professional macroeconomist.

To a whole new generation of economists, Samuelson had bequeathed a suite of models which, depending upon the shapes of the curves involved, could be either 'Classical' or 'Keynesian' as the case required. As Samuelson put it in the first edition of his textbook, the 'analysis here described is itself neutral: it can be used as well to defend private enterprise as to limit it, as well to attack as defend government fiscal intervention' (Samuelson, 1948, p. 233).[1]

As to what determines the shapes of the curves, just ask any school pupil. They will tell you that if the prices of some goods or services are not fully flexible, then the curves will have 'Keynesian' shapes. If prices are flexible and not 'distorted' in any way, then the old 'Classical' story is true. To this structure was added another ingredient that would inform the conduct of macroeconomic policy – another curve, one that could likewise take on different shapes.

This was the celebrated Phillips Curve – appropriated from Bill Phillips's empirical study of the relation between unemployment and money wage inflation in Britain between 1861 and 1957 (Phillips, 1958). His findings were translated into a well-defined functional trade-off between inflation and unemployment that could be derived

[1] To a few, however, especially those who had worked closely with Keynes on the *General Theory*, it seemed that at a stroke wine had been turned into water; gold had been transformed into base metal. This is what Joan Robinson used to call Bastard Keynesianism – strong language, to be sure, but a razor-sharp insight into what had happened.

from the aggregate supply-aggregate demand model in the presence of sticky wages. The Phillips Curve showed how governments could trade off lower unemployment against inflation in the short run to achieve macroeconomic policy objectives – despite the fact that Phillips's own curve captured not just long-run but also secular tendencies.

To macroeconomists of the day, the policy conclusions drawn from this suite of models began to seem almost self-evident. Deficit spending could revive a flagging economy without necessarily causing too much inflation, fine tuning could be used to iron out the fluctuations of the business cycle, automatic stabilisers could be put in place to keep the economy at or near full employment and flows of expenditure on aggregate consumption and aggregate investment could be managed through an active fiscal policy. High economic growth, full employment and price stability were all achievable with the aid of the government.

It has to be said that at the time the Neoclassical Synthesis seemed to be working well enough on both a theoretical and practical level. As long as its policies were working – and economies did enjoy a Golden Age of high growth, low inflation and low unemployment, without periodic balance of payments crises – the public could let the macroeconomics profession get on with its job. As long as the central pillars of its theoretical edifice were felt to be solid, there was no need for sceptics to ask difficult questions – and if they did, they could be quietly ignored. By the middle of the 1960s and into the early 1970s, however, this comfortable reality was beginning to look rather different – both at the level of theoretical discourse and at the level of actual macroeconomic experience. The good times could only last so long. Unsettling events began to disturb the scene. Stagflation called into question the imperfectionist consensus.

Imperfectionist macroeconomic models were also in something of a sorry state. Even their best-known architect, Hicks, declared in his Yrjö Jahnsson Lectures of 1973 that there were serious problems – and he published that assessment the very next year in a little book whose title said it all: *The Crisis in Keynesian Economics*. It seemed that macroeconomists had either to choose to work with one or other – or none – of the models listed in the ever-burgeoning pages of the Handbook of Imperfections or to adopt a position on the tricky methodological question of how long the short run was. Unfortunately, there existed no deep theoretical basis for making such choices.

Friedman, for example, decided that the short run was nothing but noise and that equilibrium forces would soon re-assert themselves. Accordingly, he rejected each and every model in the Handbook of Imperfections. James Tobin, on the other hand, opted for a sticky-adaptive-expectations approach to the modelling of the economy. He declared that the idea that long-run equilibrating forces were strongly at work was akin to believing in Never-Never Land (Tobin and Buiter, 1976, p. 273).

6.4 Macroeconomics and Microeconomics

Yet, beneath the surface of all this apparent turmoil and confusion, some new ideas about how to approach macroeconomic theory were quietly brewing. Although emanating from different sides of a deep doctrinal divide between fiscal activists, on the one hand, and monetary conservatives, on the other, the common theme was that macroeconomics needed to get back to basics: it needed to rediscover its microeconomic foundations.

On one side of this doctrinal divide, there was Don Patinkin, Robert Clower and (writing together) Robert Barro and Herschel Grossman. They were all engaged in exploring the implications of rational agents finding themselves quantity-constrained either in product markets (Patinkin) or labour markets (Clower) – or, in the case of Barro and Grossman, in both. Axel Leijonhufvud's book *Keynesian Economics and the Economics of Keynes* (1968) on co-ordination failures emerged momentarily into the limelight on the back of what was soon to be dubbed 'disequilibrium macroeconomics'. In Cambridge, Frank Hahn had been working along similar lines with his notions of false conjectures and conjectural equilibrium. In Paris, Jean-Michel Grandmont and Guy Laroque (working together) and Jean-Pascal Benassy were developing formal disequilibrium models which attempted to incorporate money into general-equilibrium theory in a meaningful way. Imperfectionism had finally met general-equilibrium theory.

On the other side of the doctrinal divide there was Edmund Phelps and Friedman. At the time, they were working independently on the trade-off between unemployment and inflation – the Phillips Curve.

Recognising that their microeconomics had taught them that in full general equilibrium there could be no trade-off between unemployment and inflation (the labour market always cleared) and introducing the natural-rate hypothesis as a putatively more realistic analogue of the full-employment condition of standard general-equilibrium theory, they had to find a way to reconcile this theoretical necessity with the fact that empirical evidence seemed to indicate that there was such a trade-off.

Their suggested solution to this dilemma would change mainstream macroeconomic thinking. There were, they said, two Phillips Curves, not one: a long-run vertical Phillips curve *and* a short-run elastic Phillips curve. The former was associated with full equilibrium where consumption and production plans were realised, while the latter was associated with situations where those plans went awry due to errors of perception and prediction. The expectations-augmented Phillips curve was born.

Thus it was that, whatever road back to microeconomics was followed by the profession, what had emerged on both sides of the doctrinal divide was the recognition that equilibrium was, as Phelps nicely put it, an 'expectational concept'.

Equilibrium involves the mutual compatibility of a multitude of individual plans to buy and to sell, to save and to invest, to consume and to produce. In equilibrium, expectations are fulfilled. When, in the short run, they do not come true, unpleasant things like involuntary unemployment occur.

Robert Lucas's critique represented the high-water mark of this particular transformation of the macroeconomic landscape. The introduction of the rational-expectations hypothesis rendered the short-run Phillips Curve irrelevant even in the case of imperfect information – since its relevance derived from systematic errors in expectations which rational expectations precluded. Only exogenous 'shocks' now mattered – and the Lucas Supply Curve yielded as its corollary the famous (or, depending on your point of view, infamous) policy-ineffectiveness proposition.

Perhaps more than any macroeconomist before him, Lucas unfailingly deferred to what he was wont to call the underlying 'optimal decision-rules of economic agents' to account for macroeconomic phenomena. This was especially evident in the demolition job he conducted on the reliability of those large-scale macroeconometric models that were so beloved of the research departments of central banks, and Treasury officials, in the late 1960s and early 1970s.

Looking back, it is hard to understand why no one had raised Lucas's objections to those systems-of-equations macroeconometric models much earlier. If one had an unshakeable belief, as Lucas did, that every macroeconomic phenomenon – every component of aggregate effective demand – was the product of individuals making rational decisions at the margin of constrained choice, then the parameters of every behavioural equation in those models would change when rational agents altered their decisions in the face of changes in government policy. Yet, in the typical macroeconometric model used to predict the consequences of policy measures, the values of such parameters were instead assumed not to change. It was then but a short step to the real business-cycle models of the early 1980s.

It was Finn Kydland and Edward Prescott who first decided that economy-wide fluctuations in output and employment – that is, business cycles – should be viewed as capturing the optimal intertemporal responses of individual economic agents to random exogenous shocks to the real economy. As long as an economy is vulnerable to random exogenous shocks – natural disasters, innovations, geopolitical crises that disrupt the supply of imported raw materials or the introduction of new regulatory régimes – then rational agents will adjust to such shocks by changing their optimal decisions.

To put all this in another way, whereas the trip back to microeconomics begun by Patinkin and Clower had led to disequilibrium models of business cycles, the trip back begun by Phelps and Friedman had led to equilibrium models of business cycles.

The whole class of business-cycle models stemming from Kydland and Prescott's original intervention – comprising a body of thought about macroeconomic theory and policy that quickly became known as New Classical Macroeconomics – was hugely influential. The fashion for constructing models based upon the twin pillars of a general-equilibrium framework and rational expectations with misperceptions, proved to be irresistible. Lucas and Thomas J. Sargent asserted that the empirical content of old imperfectionist Keynesian economics was 'wildly incorrect' and 'fundamentally flawed' because of 'simple matters of fact, involving no subtleties in economic theory' (Lucas and Sargent, 1978, p. 1).

However, a counter-revolution soon sprang up. A group of younger economists clustered around Harvard Square felt that the facts of the performance the macro-economy failed to tally with the New Classical version of events. They set out on a project that would see them resurrect a more Keynesian understanding of the world but in an entirely new framework. They were content to embrace the microeconomic foundations of New Classical Economics and even the rational expectations hypothesis. But they looked to factors like efficiency wages or insider-outsider problems – namely, the possibility of hidden actions and hidden information more generally – to build their re-engineered macroeconomic models. They were selling old wine but in new bottles. The label on the bottles read: New Keynesian Macroeconomics.

New Keynesian Macroeconomics shared with its imperfectionist ancestors the basic idea that economy-wide underperformance was due to the presence of obstacles preventing adjustment to full employment; but it added good microeconomic credentials. It has since added pages and pages to the Handbook of Imperfections: staggered contracts, menu costs, monopolistic competition, adverse selection, moral hazard, limited commitment, default risk, sticky inflation and sticky information, to name just a few. In mainstream circles, frictions and rigidities arising from market imperfections were once again seen as an effective way of capturing Keynesian themes without overturning the most basic of neoclassical premises.[2]

In the last two of decades of the twentieth century, these developments led not only to an efflorescence of mathematically sophisticated macroeconomic models but also to a growing assertiveness in mainstream macroeconomic circles. Gone, it was felt, was the reliance on the kind of ad hoc modelling that had characterised the old 'Keynesian' way of doing macroeconomics. It was felt that in its place was a more rigorous and scientific way of proceeding.

The new research programme revolved around the development of dynamic stochastic general-equilibrium models of the kind first deployed in Kydland and Prescott's work on real business cycles. The new self-confidence was evident in the opening chapter of the first edition of Greg Mankiw's now ubiquitous textbook, *Macroeconomics* (1991), which bears the subtitle 'The Science of Macroeconomics'. This opening chapter began not with an epigram

[2] It has to be said that the work of Patinkin and Clower, and that of Barro and Grossman, was largely submerged with the success of the Monetarist counter-revolution of the 1970s. It was only with the emergence of the New Keynesian Economics that dim recollections of these forgotten forebears were re-awakened.

from, say, Smith or even Keynes, but with a little quotation from Albert Einstein.

6.5 An Inherent Contradiction in General-Equilibrium Macroeconomics

At about the same time that macroeconomists were on their quest to find microeconomic foundations for their models, things did not stand still in general-equilibrium theory. The custodians of general-equilibrium knowledge were patiently working away on the properties of market excess-demand functions. They asked a simple question: what does general-equilibrium theory tell us about the form of the excess-demand curve for labour?

In a series of papers in the 1970s, Hugo Sonnenschein (1972), Rolf Mantel (1974) and Gérard Debreu (1974) were able to show definitively what until then had been thought of merely as a possibility – namely, that even under perfectly competitive conditions the *only* properties of individual excess-demand functions that would be carried over to market excess-demand functions were that they would be continuous, that the volume of excess demand would not change in the face of an equi-proportional change in relative prices (homogeneity of degree zero) and that the value of all excess demands would always sum to zero (Walras's Law).

Subject only to it satisfying these three conditions, 'any mathematical function could be a market excess-demand function in a closed-economy model of pure exchange if there were a sufficiently large number of consumers' (Chipman, 2006, p. 106) – thereby ruling out the possibility of uniqueness and stability of equilibrium. This result is known in general-equilibrium circles as the Sonnenschein-Mantel-Debreu Theorem.

The significance of this result was summed up by Arrow. 'In the aggregate', he wrote, 'the hypothesis of rational behavior has in general no implications; that is, for any set of aggregate excess demand functions, there is a choice of preference maps and initial endowments, one for each individual in the economy, whose maximization implies the given aggregate excess demand functions' (Arrow, 1986, p. 388).

Unsurprisingly, this result had far-reaching effects on the once unrivalled status of general-equilibrium theory – not least for its putative status as a benchmark or centre of gravitation of the system in the sense that Friedman had invoked it. Even its own champions were now having serious doubts about its utility. Alan Kirman declared that general-equilibrium theory was 'empty in the sense that one cannot expect it to house the elements of a scientific theory, one capable of producing empirically falsifiable propositions' (Kirman, 1989, p. 127). Christopher Bliss put it more bluntly: the 'near emptiness of general equilibrium theory', he said, 'is a theorem of the theory' (Bliss, 1993, p. 227).

The consequences of the Sonnenschein-Mantel-Debreu results for contemporary macroeconomic thinking are profound. On the basis of rigorous general-equilibrium theory, it cannot be said whether a fall in the relative price of a good or factor of production will be accompanied by a rise in demand, or a fall or no change at all. Nothing can be said about the direction in which quantities react to changes in prices.

Yet it is exactly the characteristics of market excess-demand functions that are vitally important for macroeconomics. They are relied upon to ensure that movements in relative prices will have well-defined effects on the level of aggregate demand. In particular, the derivative of market excess-demand functions is generally taken to be negative – that is, such functions are taken to be decreasing in price. Accordingly, much of what macroeconomics has to say about the labour market is based on the supposition that a rise in the wage will be accompanied by a decrease in excess demand in the labour market. To make the same point in another way, if there is an excess supply (negative excess demand) of labour (involuntary unemployment), a fall in the wage is supposed to be accompanied by a fall in that excess supply. Most arguments favouring increasing flexibility in the labour market as a means to improving employment are firmly grounded upon this supposition. Yet, even in the absence of all imperfections, this supposition has no foundation in general-equilibrium theory.

Similarly, it is widely held in mainstream macroeconomic circles that a fall in interest rates will be accompanied by a rise in the volume of investment. If that does not happen, the cause is put down to some kind of imperfection in capital markets (expectations again). The whole experience of central-bank efforts to stimulate the economy through quantitative easing during the prolonged recession that followed the global financial crisis, together with most critical assessments of its degree of success, was grounded upon such notions as these. Yet they too, even in the absence of all imperfections, have no basis in general-equilibrium theory.

It important to point out that the (falsely) presumed shape of excess-demand functions is as essential to models with imperfections as it is to models that work with no imperfections. The Handbook of Imperfections presupposes that very shape – the long list of consequential deviations from the perfectly competitive general equilibrium makes no sense without it.

A nice example of this 'anything goes' result is to be had in the evidence on the effects of the introduction of minimum wage regulations. The standard presupposition is that these regulations will be followed, perhaps through knock-on effects on all wages, by reductions in aggregate employment. Yet in a celebrated study of the impact on fast-food employment of the 1992 increase in the New Jersey minimum wage, as compared with neighbouring Pennsylvania, where the minimum wage was unchanged, David Card and Alan Krueger found 'no evidence that the rise in New Jersey's minimum wage reduced employment in fast-food restaurants in the state' (Card and Krueger, 1994, p. 792). Similar results have been found when examining the effects of the introduction of the National Minimum Wage in the United Kingdom in 1998. For example, a meta-analysis of a sample of twenty-five such investigations by Marco Hafner et al., found 'no overall "genuine" adverse employment effect, neither on employment and hours nor on employment retention probabilities' (Hafner et al., 2017, p. x).

The Sonnenschein, Mantel and Debreu results demonstrate that the findings of Card and Krueger, and of Hafner et al., are entirely compatible with general-equilibrium theory.

6.6 The Science of Macroeconomics

It is rather extraordinary that an optimism of sorts has swept through the macroeconomics profession, where there is still a strong feeling that a 'fundamental science of macroeconomics' has finally been built upon the solid rock of its newly rediscovered general-equilibrium foundations – despite the fact that the Sonnenschein-Mantel-Debreu results prove that such foundations do not actually exist. For sceptics seeking to understand how this could be possible, the answer turns out to be simple – it is achieved by assuming away the foundations of general-equilibrium theory.

The dynamic stochastic general-equilibrium approach to macroeconomics remains the starting point for a plethora of models describing movements in aggregate output, employment and the price level because it is based upon the supposition that the economy as a whole behaves just like a rational individual decision maker.

The issues identified by Sonnenschein, Mantel and Debreu derive from the market resolution of multiple individuals' reactions to price and income effects in the determination of the shape of excess demand functions. By eliminating the multiplicity of individuals and replacing them with a single representative agent, market resolution disappears. The excess demand function can then be derived from a single utility function.

In this way, economy-wide responses to, say, governmental fiscal policy changes may be analysed by examining how a single rational utility-maximising agent would behave in the face of such policies. The economy will then behave in the same way. The representative agent saved the day. The result is akin to the imposition of a dictator to solve the problem of constructing a social welfare function as identified in Arrow's impossibility theorem.

The paradox of all this is, of course, that the original insight of Keynes that the behaviour of the economy as a whole was different from the behaviour of individuals, that the whole was not just the sum of its parts, the claim that launched macroeconomics in the first place, is rendered irrelevant. The macro-economy and the representative individual are one and the same. Macroeconomic behaviour is embodied in the utility function of the representative agent, whether it be the trade-off between work and leisure, the intertemporal allocation of consumption and saving or the provision of bequests to their representative grandchild. Hence, it is argued that the behavioural parameters of macroeconomic relations are derived from underlying microeconomic behaviour. More accurately, they are one and the same thing.

At this point, an aside may be in order. This contemporary notion of the representative agent bears no resemblance whatsoever – except in its name and the artificiality of its construction – to the much older concept of the representative firm originated by Marshall. Marshall had invented the representative firm to deal with what, for him, seems to have been a dimly perceived possibility that his idea that firms faced U-shaped average cost curves might be incompatible with perfect competition. The representative firm was invoked in order to eliminate the problems associated with the construction of cost curves for individual firms operating under competitive conditions and hence as price-takers in factor markets. Just after Marshall's death in 1924, it was Piero Sraffa who demonstrated that these misgivings were well-founded (Sraffa, 1926). There is no logically sound argument for the existence of a U-shaped cost curve in a perfectly competitive market.

The representative agent of contemporary macroeconomic models, on the other hand, was not invented to avoid problems with the equilibrium of the competitive firm. All households and firms were assumed to be working with given, well-behaved, utility and production functions. Households are, of course, amalgamated into one representative household, and firms into the economy's overall production set. Instead, the modern representative agent was invented to ensure that there was no difference between the behaviour of the individual and the behaviour of the economy as a whole.

The genealogy of this modern sleight of hand is difficult to pin down. Something approaching it is certainly present in Frank Ramsey's famous articles for the *Economic Journal* on taxation (1927) and on saving (1928). But he did not use the terminology. However, explicitly deferring to Ramsey, Allyn Young used exactly the modern construct, although he used the term 'representative consumer' rather than representative agent, in his review of Pigou's *Study in Public Finance* for the March issue of the *Economic Journal* for 1929. This may well have been its first appearance. The term 'representative consumer' was in relatively common use in the 1950s, although not always with the modern meaning. Samuelson used it in its modern sense in his paper on the transfer problem for the June issue of the *Economic Journal* in 1954, Friedman used it in his *Essays in Positive Economics* and Wassily Leontief used it in his note on growth and stagnation for the November issue of the *American Economic Review* in 1958. That terminology persisted until the last quarter of the twentieth century, when representative agent became the preferred usage.

But how could one represent all the diverse preferences of very large numbers of heterogeneous individual agents, even if they all had well-behaved preferences, in the utility function of just one representative agent? How could prices be seen as the resolution of excess demands in competitive markets when there is only one agent? The difficulty is not just that representative-agent models do not capture each and every aspect of reality. No model does that. At best, a model can only claim to capture the essential features of the reality they seek to model. Instead, the representative-agent model was, so to speak, a model of a model. But it preserved none of the essential features of the underlying model which it was supposedly modelling – namely, the essential features of the neoclassical general-equilibrium model.

Over the years, microeconomists had managed to come up with a number of restrictions on the basic general-equilibrium model that would permit the construction of 'well-behaved' excess demand functions, but they are all rather distant from anything that might be called 'approximating reality'. For example, a list of some sufficient conditions for exact aggregation would include 'identical homothetic preferences' or 'homothetic preferences and proportional incomes' (Chipman, 2006, p. 115). Few would deny that assuming everyone has 'identical preferences' does not seem to be an especially reasonable assumption to act as the starting point for a general analysis of individual choice. 'Homothetic preferences', by which is meant that for every individual doubling or tripling the quantity of every commodity consumed gives double or triple the amount of satisfaction, seems similarly to be an exception rather than a suitably general rule. 'Proportional incomes', which means that the share of aggregate income (the value of the individual's endowment) held by every individual remains rigidly fixed even as prices change, seems equally unappealing.

In short, as a general rule exact aggregation seems to be a rather far-fetched basis upon which credibly to build meaningful models of market demand and supply. In his forensic deconstruction of the representative-agent model, Alan Kirman concluded that there was 'no plausible formal justification for the assumption that the aggregate of individuals, even maximizers, acts itself like an individual maximizer' and that the representative agent 'deserves a decent burial, as an approach to economic analysis that is not only primitive, but fundamentally erroneous' (Kirman, 1992, pp. 118–119).

Of course, despite these theoretical shortcomings, it might nevertheless be argued that dynamic stochastic general-equilibrium models are 'useful' in the sense that they are a 'reasonable approximation' of reality and so provide a 'sufficient' guide to policy. To put it another way, such models might be like the contents of Friedman's famous 'black box' about which we need not concern ourselves as long as its 'predictions' seem right. Quite apart from the methodological doubts one might have about this kind of thinking, it stumbles at its own first hurdle when it is confronted with 'predictions'.

The global financial crisis of 2007–2008 suggests that not only are these models theoretically vacuous but also that they are capable of misleading even the most talented practitioners. In 2003, Lucas assured the American Economic Association that 'for all practical purposes' the 'central problem of depression-prevention has been solved' – and that while there remained 'important gains in welfare' to be had 'from better fiscal policies', these were gains to be had 'from providing people with better incentives to work and to save' rather than from a 'better fine tuning of spending flows' (Lucas, 2003, p. 1). Just months before the collapse of Lehman Brothers, Olivier Blanchard declared that there had been 'enormous progress and substantial convergence' in macroeconomics and that 'the state of macro is good' (Blanchard, 2008, p. 2). His words of reassurance echoed those of Michael Woodford who claimed that there was 'less disagreement among macroeconomists about fundamental issues than there was in the past' (Woodford, 2009, p. 267).

The financial crisis of 2007–2008 suggests that confidence in 'the science of macroeconomics' was seriously misplaced. It is hard to forget the look of discomfort on the faces of the academic macroeconomists who were asked by Matt Damon – towards the end of the 2010 Academy-Award winning film *Inside Job* – whether the public had a right to expect something better from economists and economics. One can almost feel sympathy for the professors of the London School of Economics when they were asked by Her Majesty Queen Elizabeth II (during a visit in November 2008) why nobody had seen the crisis coming. It took them several months to answer. After thinking long and hard about the question, they composed a three-page letter to the Queen to explain themselves. The best they could come up with was that there had been 'a failure of the collective imagination of many bright people' and that a few 'financial wizards' had intensified systemic risk through their financial innovations. Apparently, they concluded that there were no problems with mainstream macroeconomics or its toolbox of models and theories, so the Monarch could rest easy (see Stewart, 2009).

6.7 The Present Position of Macroeconomics

With the Handbook of Imperfections now as voluminous as ever it was – with no clear criteria concerning which model from its many pages to select (other than by appeal to some vague intuitive feeling about its congruence with reality) – and with the general-equilibrium core of macroeconomic thinking incapable of bearing the load it was being asked to carry (hence, the resort to representative-agent models) – the state of macroeconomics is looking decidedly parlous. It is difficult not to conclude that we may be witnessing a disintegration of the subject not unlike that which occurred in the 1960s and 1970s before the so-called Monetarist Revolution took root. This loss of coherence is evident not only in the state of the theoretical landscape of macroeconomics today but also in the state of its quantitative landscape and its policy discourse.

Consider the theoretical landscape.Many still cling to the dream that eventually a model of individual behaviour will be found that is compatible with, and will explain, the behaviour of the economy as a whole. Some even think that this will turn out to involve behaviour of the old-fashioned kind: individuals seeking to maximise utility at the margin of constrained choice. Others take a different view and turn instead to models of bounded rationality, preference reversal, satisficing, prospect theory, hyperbolic discounting and the like as replacements for the assumption of maximising behaviour as postulated in the standard model. All of these responses retain a basic commitment to the neoclassical vision expressed by Marshall, whereby economics is about the study of individuals in the ordinary business of life. It's just that they suggest that individuals in the ordinary business of life may behave in ways that are not compatible with what Marshall thought was rational action.

The differences between members of these two camps are not about whether we should or should not abandon attempts to find microeconomic foundations for macroeconomics. Instead, they are about exactly what those microeconomic foundations should be. Joseph Stiglitz put it succinctly when he said that mainstream macroeconomists had opted for 'the wrong microfoundations' (Stiglitz, 2018, p. 75).

While it is easy enough to argue against the hypothesis that individual economic action generally takes the form of constrained maximisation of utility, it is not at all clear whether there is any other single mode of behaviour that provides a more plausible starting point. If all one has to go on is the evidence of experimental economics and cognitive psychology, then the number of contenders appears to be virtually unlimited. Rather like the Handbook of Imperfections, a Handbook of Behaviours is now being compiled without a means of determining which, if any, of those behaviours is to be selected to replace utility-maximisation as the preferred basis for a general analysis of economic decision-making.

Against this, of course, it is always possible to contend that no general analysis of behaviour is possible. But to concede that all behaviour is either personally, situationally or even neurologically, specific – something which seems highly likely – is not compatible with presuming that Smith was right when he said that individual actions operating under the compulsions of market competition do result in systematic relationships between economic parameters (prices and quantities) and that it was the task of the economists to discover those relationships. The economy is not a chaotic, stochastic phenomenon. Persistent and systematic forces do indeed appear to be at work. However, they are not captured by neoclassical models of market equilibrium.

This brings us to the quantitative landscape of macroeconomic thinking today – and to the argument that it might be better to work with the quantitative resources available to us rather than with the theoretical resources of either general-equilibrium microeconomics or behavioural economics.

A quite popular response to the kind of theoretical predicaments we have been reporting – one that is thought to avoid these and other difficulties – has been to advocate a return to the 'best fit' approach to macroeconomic modelling. Take the available data, specify some functional relationships between macroeconomic variables and run econometric tests to find out which story is 'selected' by the data as the 'best fit'. Unfortunately, this seemingly modest proposal is not without its problems, as is well illustrated by empirical work on the aggregate production function. The standard Cobb-Douglas function is a relationship that typically fits aggregate data algebraically. It is therefore little removed from 'fitting' an identity (Shaikh, 1987).

Some have suggested that a way to avoid this dilemma would be to use statistical techniques that do not involve testing stories that have been invented in advance but instead to let the data tell the story – so-called non-parametric methods. While there are all sorts of methodological debates surrounding this approach, the practical problem with it is the size and the reliability of the data sets available to macroeconomists. Almost invariably, the data sets are too small and too unreliable. Moreover, data sets represent the past, not the future. If behaviour changes, perhaps because of the creation of new products or new markets, then the continuities of the past may be seriously misleading guides to the future. The invention of credit derivatives in the mid-1990s is a good example of this.

Another way of applying non-parametric methods to the study of market demand is empirical revealed-preference theory. It originated in work by Sydney Afriat (1967) and was taken up later by Hal Varian (1982). It is becoming more and more popular as the fortunes of the microeconomic-foundations project have declined.

The basic procedure is simple enough, but the mathematical route to the results is anything but simple. Take a data set – say, of market prices and market demand – and use revealed-preference theory to 'recover' the underlying preferences that would have yielded that data. This 'recoverability' question 'focuses on identifying the set of preferences (or set of utility functions representing the preferences) that are consistent with a given data set' (Crawford and De Rock, 2014, p. 506).

It is easy to see the attraction of this approach to macroeconomics. It would not require beginning with some set of microeconomic foundations that fail to generate market excess-demand functions which exhibited the desirable properties. This approach would circumvent the Sonnenschein-Mantel-Debreu results. It would also render it possible to determine whether it was 'true' that the economy as a whole behaved like a representative agent – without ever having to construct that representative agent *de novo* by showing that it was feasible to aggregate the individual excess-demand functions of many heterogeneous individual agents.

In short, it would render it possible to argue that the market might have a 'rational' mind of its own, over and above the many 'irrationalities' of individuals. This seems to have been the kind of thing that Friedrich Hayek had in mind when he spoke of a 'market order' spontaneously emerging from the 'process of competition'. It also seems to have been the kind of thing that Gary Becker had in mind when he spoke about 'supporting rationality at the market level' despite the irrationalities of individuals (Becker, 1962, p. 2).

But before empirical revealed-preference research could yield such striking results, there are some quite substantial obstacles that it would need to overcome. Varian himself urged caution on a number of fronts. 'The tests involved', he said, 'may be computationally infeasible for large data sets'. Furthermore, he recognised that 'the techniques do not typically summarize the data in a useful way' and 'it may be rather difficult to incorporate stochastic considerations in a satisfactory manner' (Varian, 1983, p. 100). In recovering preferences from any set of data, it must be assumed that there has been no change in the underlying preferences one is seeking to recover over the time period the data covers. All longitudinal data and all time-series data will be subject to limitations on this score.

This difficulty arises as a consequence of the familiar assumption of constancy of preferences that is required if revealed-preference exercises are to make any sense at all. So, not only is it easy to imagine circumstances whereby 'stochastic considerations' would prove to be difficult to deal with, as Varian suggested, but it is also easy to imagine circumstances where even the simple passage of time would prove rather difficult to accommodate as well. If one adds to this the now-celebrated philosophical conundrum associated with revealed-preference theory – namely, the one raised by Amartya Sen (1973) when he not-so-innocently asked what if observed choice is not the same as preference – then the prospect of constructive developments seems, at best, problematic.

6.8 Summing-Up

We can return now to the question posed at the very beginning of this chapter and venture an answer. That question was whether the division between microeconomics and macroeconomics is used simply to facilitate the modelling of economic phenomena at different levels of aggregation or whether it is a device to obscure some fundamental inconsistences in mainstream economic thinking.

Our answer should by now be clear. We contend that the division is indeed a device to obscure deep inconsistences between mainstream macroeconomics and microeconomics. The unified theory of Walrasian general equilibrium provides no foundation for the relationships studied at the macroeconomic level. It is incapable of answering questions such as what happens to employment if there is a fall in the real wage or how interest-rate policy affects total output – let alone what the difference is between savings and finance. Yet these are precisely the questions that policymakers need to have answered. The great merit of the *General Theory* was that in it Keynes provided a powerful framework within which such questions might be answered.

This, however, is not to say that each and every element in that broad framework is either unassailable or definitive. For example, while that framework recast the relation between consumption, investment and effective demand, the behavioural model Keynes then offered for the determination of the level of investment – the marginal efficiency of capital – was borrowed from Irving Fisher. Keynes explicitly acknowledged that debt. 'Professor Fisher', he said, used 'his "rate of return over cost" in the same sense and for precisely the same purpose as I employ the marginal efficiency of capital' (Keynes, 1936, p. 140). But, unfortunately, the centrepiece of Fisher's analysis of investment – a function describing the rate of return over cost that rested upon substitution between current saving (the sacrifice of consumption) and other fixed factors – was erroneous. Fisher believed that it could be derived from the neoclassical general-equilibrium model – a belief that turned out to be unfounded.

What is needed, then, is a theory of investment that is not based on the general-equilibrium apparatus. Whatever that alternative theory of investment turns out to be – it may even display an inverse relationship between the level of investment and the rate of interest – it cannot be derived from some putatively smooth substitution between labour and capital as imagined in mainstream macroeconomic thinking.

Similar problems arise in the analysis of the labour market. The law of one price will hold, in that competition will ensure that labour of equivalent quality commands a common wage rate. But once again the relationship between the wage rate and the demand for labour cannot be derived from general-equilibrium foundations.

It is perhaps worth adding at this point that many of the pages in the Handbook of Imperfections are filled with empirical observations of considerable descriptive importance. They often capture empirical regularities common to a whole class of cases, and as such they should be part of any general theory of output and employment. A good example of this was Edmond Malinvaud's appeal to empirical studies of price determination to justify his conclusion that 'short-term quantitative adjustments are much more apparent and influential than short-term price adjustments' (Malinvaud, 1977, p. 10). This is a widely accepted empirical fact.

It will be apparent, therefore, that the weaknesses of imperfectionist macroeconomic models do not reside principally in their empirical content being inaccurate or misleading. Instead, they reside in the way in which that empirical content is then to be understood. For rather than taking such empirical regularities as being, so to speak, *sui generis* – and attempting to understand and model them as such – they are understood and modelled (or sometimes even ignored) as irregularities, paradoxes, exceptions or imperfections when measured against some supposedly 'more general' model of how the market mechanism 'really' works. This is why it is that imperfectionist macroeconomic models can only ever be as good as that putatively 'more general' core upon which they rely for their analytical coherence.

Nevertheless, the weaknesses of mainstream macroeconomic thinking to which this modelling practice has given rise should not be allowed to obscure the fact that there also exists a significant lacuna within the *General Theory* itself. Keynes's theory of effective demand is above all a monetary theory of output and employment. But it is the relative prices of goods and services that link monetary flows and real quantities, and there is no theory of relative prices in the *General Theory*. This chapter has argued that neoclassical general-equilibrium theory cannot provide that link.

Whether this means that one might return to the approach to the theory of value and distribution of the old classical economists to fill the gap – an approach in which the determination of relative prices is separable from the theory of output and employment – is another story. After all, the classical analysis of output was less a theory of output than an assertion – an assertion that what is saved is invested – and the classical version of Say's law did not provide any mechanism whereby savings and investment are brought into equality.

Quite clearly, for reasons already enumerated, the neoclassical story about saving and investment – whereby individual plans to save and individual plans to invest are rendered mutually compatible by variations in the rate of interest (and other associated prices) – does not provide a satisfactory alternative to the classical assertion. However, Keynes's *General Theory* did offer an alternative to both the classical and neoclassical analysis of output – one whereby desired savings and desired investment are brought into equality by variations in the level of income – and that theory could replace the classical assertion.

But such speculations reach well beyond the scope of this chapter. They do conform, however, to what has been our general premise throughout – namely, that macroeconomics does require firm foundations in a theory of price determination and that neoclassical microeconomics is not up to that task.

References

Afriat S. (1967) 'The Construction of a Utility Function from Expenditure Data', in *International Economic Review*, 8(1), pp. 67–77.

Arrow K. J. (1986) 'Rationality of Self and Others in an Economic System', in *Journal of Business*, 59(4), Part 2, pp. 385–399.

Becker G. S. (1962) 'Irrational Behavior and Economic Theory', in *Journal of Political Economy*, 70(1), pp. 1–13.

Blanchard O. J. (2008) 'The State of Macro', National Bureau of Economic Research, Working Paper 14259, August.

Bliss C. (1993) 'Oil Trade and General Equilibrium: A Review Article', in *Journal of International and Comparative Economics*, 2, pp. 227–242.

Boulding K. E. (1948) *Economic Analysis*, 2nd ed., New York, Harper and Row.

Bronfenbrenner M. (1943) 'The Role of Money in Equilibrium Capital Theory', in *Econometrica*, 11(1), pp. 35–60.

Card D. and Krueger A. (1994) 'Minimum Wages and Employment: A Case Study of the Fast-food Industry in New Jersey and Pennsylvania', in *American Economic Review*, 84(4), pp. 772–793.

Chipman J. S. (2006) 'Aggregation and Estimation in the Theory of Demand', in *History of Political Economy*, 38(1), pp. 106–129.

Crawford I. and De Rock B. (2014) 'Empirical Revealed Preference', in *Annual Review of Economics*, 6(1), pp. 503–524.

Debreu G. (1974) 'Excess Demand Functions', in *Journal of Mathematical Economics*, 1(1), pp. 15–21.

Dobb M. H. (1931) 'An Introduction to Economics', in Rose W. (ed.) *An Outline of Modern Knowledge*, London, Victor Gollancz Limited, pp. 592–622.

(1937) 'Concerning Frictions and Expectations: Certain Recent Tendencies in Economic Theory', in *Political Economy and Capitalism: Some Essays in Economic Tradition*, London, Routledge, pp. 185–221.

Eatwell J. and Milgate M. (1983) *Keynes's Economics and the Theory of Value and Distribution*, London, Duckworth and New York, Oxford University Press.

(2011) *The Fall and Rise of Keynesian Economics*, Oxford and New York, Oxford University Press.

Friedman M. (1953) *Essays in Positive Economics*, Chicago, University Chicago Press.

(1968) 'The Role of Monetary Policy', in *American Economic Review*, 58 (1), pp. 1–17.

(1970) 'Comments on the Critics', in Gordon R. J. (ed.) *Milton Friedman's Monetary Framework: A Debate with His Critics*, Chicago and London, University of Chicago Press, pp. 132–177.

Frisch R. (1933) 'Propagation Problems and Impulse Problems in Dynamic Economics', in *Economic Essays in Honour of Gustav Cassel*, London, Frank Cass & Company, pp. 171–206.

Garegnani P. (1987) 'Surplus Approach to Value and Distribution', in Eatwell J. Milgate M. and Newman P. (eds.) *The New Palgrave: A Dictionary of Economics*, vol. IV, London, Macmillan, pp. 560–574.

Haberler G. (1937) *Prosperity and Depression: A Theoretical Analysis of Cyclical Movements*, London, George Allen and Unwin.

Hafner M. Taylor J. Pankowska P. Stepanek M. Nataraj S. and van Stolk C. (2017) *The Impact of the National Minimum Wage on Employment: A Meta-analysis*, Santa Monica and Cambridge, The Rand Corporation.

Hicks J. R. (1974) *The Crisis in Keynesian Economics*, Oxford, Blackwell.

Jevons W. S. (1878) 'Commercial Crises and Sunspots', in *Nature*, 19, pp. 33–37.

Kalecki M. (1933 [1935]) '*A Macrodynamic Theory of Business Cycles*', in *Econometrica*, 3(3), pp. 327–344.

Keynes J. M. (1932). 'Historical Retrospect', in Moggridge D. (ed.) *The Collected Writings of John Maynard Keynes*, vol. XIII, London, Macmillan, pp. 406–407.

(1936). 'The General Theory of Employment, Interest and Money', in Moggridge D. (ed.) *The Collected Writings of John Maynard Keynes*, vol. VII, London, Macmillan.

(1938). 'Letter to Roy Harrod', in Moggridge D. (ed.) *The Collected Writings of John Maynard Keynes*, vol. XIV, London, Macmillan.

Kirman A. P. (1989) 'The Intrinsic Limits of Modern Economic Theory: The Emperor Has No Clothes', in *Economic Journal*, 99, pp. 126–139.

(1992) 'Whom or What Does the Representative Individual Represent?', in *Journal of Economic Perspectives*, 6(2), pp. 117–136.

Kitchin J. (1923) 'Cycles and Trends in Economic Factors', in *Review of Economics and Statistics*, 5(1), pp. 10–16.

Klein L. (1946) 'Macroeconomics and the Theory of Rational Behavior', in *Econometrica*, 14(2), pp. 93–108.

Krugman P. (2009) 'How Did Economists Get It So Wrong?, in *New York Times Magazine*, 9 September, pp. 1–12.

Leijonhufvud A. (1970) *On Keynesian Economics and the Economics of Keynes: A Study in Monetary Theory*, Oxford and New York, Oxford University Press.

Leontief W. (1958) 'Theoretical Note on Time-Preference, Productivity of Capital, Stagnation and Economic Growth', in *American Economic Review*, 48(1), pp. 105–111.

Lucas R. E. (2003) 'Macroeconomic Priorities', in *American Economic Review*, 93(1), pp. 1–14.

Lucas R. E. and Sargent T. J. (1978) 'After Keynesian Economics', in *Proceedings of the Federal Reserve Bank of Boston's 19th Economic Conference: After the Phillips Curve: Persistence of High Inflation and High Unemployment*, Boston, Federal Reserve Bank of Boston, n.p.

Mankiw N. G. (2006) 'The Macroeconomist as Scientist and Engineer, in *Journal of Economic Perspectives*, 20(4), pp. 29–46.

Mankiw N. G. and Reis R. (2018) 'Friedman's Presidential Address in the Evolution of Macroeconomic Thought', in *Journal of Economic Perspectives*, 32(1), pp. 81–96.

Mantel R. (1974) 'On the Characterization of Aggregate Excess-Demand', in *Journal of Economic Theory*, 7(3), pp. 348–353.

Marget A. W. (1942) *The Theory of Prices: A Re-examination of the Central Problems of Monetary Theory*, vol. II, New York, Prentice Hall.

Marshall A. (1890 [1961]) *Principles of Economics*, London, Macmillan. Used edition: Ninth (variorum) Edition, with annotations by Claude William Guillebaud.

Marschak J. (1945) 'A Cross-Section of Business Cycle Discussion, in *American Economic Review*, 35(3), pp. 368–381.

Mas-Colell A. Whinston M. and Green J. (1995) *Microeconomic Theory*, New York, Oxford University Press.

Milgate M. (1982) *Capital and Employment: A Study of Keynes's Economics*, New York and London, Academic Press.

Phillips A. W. H. (1958) 'The Relation between Unemployment and the Rate of Change of Money Wage Rates in the United Kingdom, 1861–1957, in *Economica*, New Series, 25(100), pp. 283–299.

Ricardo D. (1818) 'Letter to T. R. Malthus, 30th January', in Sraffa P. (ed.) *The Works and Correspondence of David Ricardo*, vol. VII, Cambridge, Cambridge University Press.

Rizvi Abu Turab S. (2006) 'The Sonnenschein-Mantel-Debreu Results after Thirty Years', in *History of Political Economy*, 38, Annual Supplement, pp. 228–245.

Robinson H. W. (1939) *The Economics of Building*, London, P. S. King & Son.

Samuelson P. A. (1948) *Economics: An Introductory Analysis*, New York, McGraw-Hill.

(1954) 'The Transfer Problem and Transport Costs, II: Analysis of Effects of Trade Impediments, in *Economic Journal*, 64(254), pp. 264–289.

Sen A. K. (1973) 'Behaviour and the Concept of Preference', in *Economica*, New Series, 40(159), pp. 241–259.

Shaikh A. (1974) 'Laws of Algebra and Laws of Production: The Humbug Production Function', in *Review of Economics and Statistics*, 56(1), pp. 115–120

Solow R. M. (2010) Building a Science of Economics for the Real World. A Prepared Statement to the House Committee on Science and Technology, Subcommittee on Investigations and Oversight, July.

Sonnenschein H. (1972) 'Market Excess-Demand Functions', in *Econometrica*, 40(3), pp. 549–563.

Stewart H. (2009) 'This is How We Let the Credit Crunch Happen, Ma'am', in *The Observer*, 26 July.

Stiglitz J. (2018) 'Where Modern Macroeconomics Went Wrong', in *Oxford Review of Economic Policy*, 34(1–2), pp. 70–106.

Tobin J. and Buiter W. (1976) 'Long-Run Effects of Fiscal and Monetary Policy, in Stein J. L. (ed.) *Monetarism*, Amsterdam, North-Holland, pp. 273–309.

Varian H. R. (1983) 'Non-parametric Tests of Consumer Behavior', in *Review of Economic Studies*, 50(1), pp. 99–110.

(2012) 'Revealed Preference and Its Applications', in *Economic Journal*, 122(560), pp. 332–338.

Woodford M. (2009) 'Convergence in Macroeconomics: Elements of the New Synthesis', in *American Economic Journal: Macroeconomics*, 1 (1), pp. 267–279.

Young A. A. (1929) 'Review of a Study in Public Finance, by A. C. Pigou', in *Economic Journal*, 39(153), pp. 78–83.

7 Disequilibrium and Instability (Not Equilibrium) as the Normal State of the Industrial Economies

A Methodological Standpoint on Structural Economic Dynamics

ARIEL LUIS WIRKIERMAN*

[M]any phenomena which are evolutionary at the microcosmic level are stationary at the macrocosmic level. The individual is born, lives, and dies. And yet it may be that the population is stationary.

(Frisch, 1929, p. 392)

We start by discarding the idea of equilibrium as a state of rest to which a stable system is expected to return. [...] Our economy never returns. Its equilibrium may be said to exist if its component parts in their process of growth retain some proper relationship to each other, such as output to capital, steel to coal, costs to prices.

(Domar, 1952, pp. 490–491)

7.1 Introduction

Equilibrium is an organising principle of economic thinking. However, it would be limiting to argue that there is a consensus as to the interpretation of such a label, especially when Keynesian analyses are considered.

For example, the Neoclassical interpretation of a Keynesian equilibrium as a *position of rest with involuntary unemployment* (e.g., Hahn, 1987), as against Luigi Pasinetti's (1981) notion of an equilibrium situation, that is, an *unstable position with full employment*. In the former case, the definition of an equilibrium state cannot be separated from the mechanisms that may (or may not) lead to it, whereas in the latter, the explicit separation between both layers is crucial. In the former case,

* I am grateful to Enrico Bellino and Andrew Trigg for discussions on the content and comments on an initial draft of the chapter, respectively. Remaining errors are mine.

efficiency is an atomised property, whilst in the latter, efficiency is defined at the structural, rather than individual, level (Pasinetti, 1987).

Such a contrasting use of the equilibrium concept goes beyond the mere distinction between statics or dynamics: as Ragnar Frisch (1929) early recognised, it is our method of analysis which is static or dynamic, economic phenomena being either stationary or evolutionary.

In fact, evolutionary phenomena are a pervasive feature of industrial economies. Within this context, Pasinetti identifies two types of instability-generating sources: the principle of effective demand and structural dynamics (Pasinetti, 2007, pp. 229–231). But he also recalls John Maynard Keynes's outstanding faults of those same economies: 'failure to provide for full employment and its arbitrary and inequitable distribution of wealth and incomes' (Keynes, 1936, p. 372).

These sources of instability and societal faults are not unrelated, quite the contrary: structural dynamics of quantities and prices imply compositional changes that make full employment ever-increasingly harder to achieve (with a resurgent fear of technological unemployment), whilst asymmetries in income distribution amplify the mismatch between the multiplication of abstract purchasing power and actual spending decisions, making the principle of effective demand ever-increasingly important in determining activity levels.

The present chapter explores how Pasinetti's (i) methodological standpoint, (ii) formulation of the principle of effective demand and (iii) conceptualisation of equilibrium cumulatively build up into a scheme of structural dynamics (Pasinetti, 1965a, 1981, 1993), in which disequilibrium and instability emerge as the pervasive state of *industrial* economies. Within that framework, building blocks (i)–(iii) are used to understand one of those societal faults singled out by Keynes: the increasing difficulty to achieve and maintain full employment.

7.2 Methodological Standpoint: Pre-institutional and Behavioural Relations

A pervasive feature across Pasinetti's analytical frameworks is the careful distinction between pre-institutional and behavioural relations (Pasinetti, 2007, pp. 36–37). This has been rendered explicit early on:

> The distinction is between those relations which in an economic system are so fundamental as to be independent of the institutional set-up that society has chosen to adopt and those relations which are specific to a particular institutional set-up. For example, Prof. Wassily Leontief's input-output

inter-industry system is *independent of institutions*; it is a kind of analysis which can be carried out for a socialist as well as for a capitalist country. On the other hand, for example, the *processes through which prices are actually reached* are specific to particular institutional set-ups: they are different according to whether we consider a socialist economy, a capitalist economy, or any mixed type of economy. (Pasinetti, 1965b, pp. 103–104, italics added)

As evinced and exemplified by the quote above, a pre-institutional concept or relation is not one specified in an institutional *vacuum* but one which 'remains *neutral* with respect to the institutional organisation of society' (Pasinetti, 1981, p. 25, italics added). It is meaningful *across* institutional set-ups, for example, a centrally planned, capitalist or mixed economy, but its realisation occurs *within* a well-specified set of rules, mechanisms and behaviours operating in an *industrial* society.

Instead, institutional concepts are articulated in '*behavioural* relations meant to represent and explain the *effective* working of *actual* economic systems, within a well-defined institutional set-up' (Pasinetti, 2007, p. 37, italics added). Thus, behavioural relations are the characterising element of the institutional layer of analysis.

Crucially, Pasinetti (1981, 1993) is interested in the pre-institutional features of an *industrial* society. Such a society is characterised by 'the productive consumption of circulating and fixed capital as the means of production, to be used together with labour, and which should be *necessarily* replaced and accumulated, *if* this circular flow is to be reproduced at an expanding scale' (Garbellini and Wirkierman, 2014, p. 235). That is, Pasinettian pre-institutional concepts or relations do *not* apply to *pre-industrial* societies, they are historically embedded within the 'phase of industry' (Pasinetti, 1981, p. 2), accelerating since the second half of the eighteenth century.

To give an example, while wages and operating surplus (usually labelled 'profits') are pre-institutional categories, workers and capitalists are deeply institutional ones. The former have a functional role in relation to the net output of the economy: wages financing private consumption and profits financing investment. That is, a truly *functional* distribution of income.

Workers and capitalists are, instead, distinguished by their (lack of) ownership of means of production within the specific institutional set-up of a capitalist economy. Given that in stylised descriptions of a capitalist system workers receive wages as their main source of income, whereas capitalists have a command over the use of profits, the distinction between pre-institutional and behavioural categories is unnecessarily blurred.[1] In fact, when comparing in 1970 the System of National Accounts (SNA) – used by capitalist economies at the time – with the Material Product System (MPS) – used by countries in the (former) Soviet Bloc – Richard Stone noted that the 'value added account' in both systems included 'wages' and 'operating surplus' as organising concepts (Stone, 1970, p. 207).

The example of Leontief's 'input-output inter-industry system' – provided by Pasinetti's quote at the beginning of this section – effectively illustrates a scheme of pre-institutional relations. The three different quadrants of an input-output table, (i) intermediate transactions, (ii) value added and (iii) final demand, each closely relates to the (i) production, (ii) income generation and (iii) use of income and capital accounts, respectively, of the (currently used) SNA (UN, 2009, pp. 23–33). However, the income distribution accounts of the SNA – dealing with the *institutional* allocation and (re)distribution of gross value added generated – are not part of the input-output scheme. While the input-output table is compiled on the basis of *productive establishments* (irrespective of their ownership structure), the sequence of accounts of the SNA is organised around *institutional sectors* of the economy.

There is a specific instance of the pre-institutional configuration of the economy which Pasinetti labels 'natural': '[t]he "natural" magnitudes possess a series of remarkable normative properties but are singled out in a way that is independent of *how* they may actually be achieved' (Pasinetti, 2002, p. 337).

For example, in Pasinetti's *natural* economic system, total wages equal total consumption and total profits equal total new investments (Pasinetti, 1981, pp. 146–147). This is a desirable normative property as it renders possible the smooth reproduction of the expanding circular flow representing the economy. However, the specification of the natural configuration will not describe how profits adjust to match investment or vice versa, which instead depends on the set of behavioural relations assumed.

Moreover, it is possible analyse the structural features of an economy within a logically consistent set of pre-institutional relations, *even*

[1] The distinction between the fractions of income saved out of wages and profits with respect the propensities to save of workers and capitalists was an essential feature in Pasinetti's formulation of the 'Cambridge equation' (Pasinetti, 1962).

if there is a mismatch between total profits and investment. Thus, while a natural configuration presupposes a pre-institutional layer of analysis, the reverse is not true. This is relevant, inasmuch as several pre-institutional categories in Pasinetti's frameworks – such as the 'standard' rate of productivity growth (Pasinetti, 1981, pp. 101–104) – are useful for representing and *measuring* aspects of *actual* economies, irrespective of whether the underlying magnitudes satisfy the desirable normative properties of their natural configuration.

Pasinetti's quote opening this section is also interesting as it postulates that 'the processes through which prices are actually reached' pertains to the institutional layer of analysis, whereas the conditions required for the economy to be in a *natural* configuration remain pre-institutional. This methodological standpoint bears striking resemblance, albeit with a different terminology, to that adopted by Piero Sraffa in the path leading to the formulation of his system of production (Sraffa, 1960). In fact, a set of *computable* prices could be conceived as the answer to the following problem, posed by Sraffa:

> The problem is that of *ascertaining the conditions of equilibrium of a system of prices and the rate of profits, independently of the study of the forces which may bring about such a state of equilibrium.* Since a solution of the second problem carries with it a solution of the first, that is the course usually adopted in modern theory. The first problem however is susceptible of a more general treatment, independent of the particular forces assumed for the second; and in view of the unsatisfactory character of the latter, there is advantage in maintaining its independence. (D3/12/15: 2, emphasis added in Kurz and Salvadori, 2005, p. 433)

Ascertaining the 'conditions of equilibrium' is at the basis of the specification of the natural configuration of a set of pre-institutional relations in Pasinetti (1981, 1993). But to better understand such conceptualisation of (dis)equilibrium, it is necessary to explore the role of effective demand in an industrial society.

7.3 The (Pre-institutional) Principle of Effective Demand

The *principle* of effective demand plays a foundational role in Keynesian analyses (Keynes, 1936, ch. 3). But its definition, characterisation and interpretation are far from unique. Pasinetti (1974, 1997) suggests to distinguish between 'the basic process of income generation *by* effective demand' (Pasinetti, 1974, p. 36, italics added) and finding the *determinants* of effective demand. The former can be dealt with at a pre-institutional level, whereas the latter usually leads to specifying a multiplier mechanism through the *propensity to consume*, which is a *behavioural* relation based on a 'fundamental psychological law' (Keynes, 1936, p. 96).

At the *pre-institutional* level, the principle of effective demand can be rendered clear by contrasting an *industrial* society with a primitive, *pre*-industrial one:

> In primitive (agricultural) societies, each farmer tries to produce as much as he can. He will then take whatever amount of his produce is in excess of his needs to the market. And there this produce will fetch the price the market makes. In an industrial society it is not so. At any given point in time, productive capacity is indeed what it is – it cannot be changed. But productive capacity does not mean production – it only means *potential* production. In order that there may be *actual* production, there must be *effective* demand. (Pasinetti, 1974, pp. 31–32)

The depth of this statement lies in distinguishing an *inverted causal link* between output and its uses as a characterising feature of industrial societies, with respect to pre-industrial ones. This can be illustrated by specifying and discussing two simple models which emphasise this distinction.

The pre-industrial economy may be characterised by the following relations amongst aggregate magnitudes:

$$\Pi \equiv Y - C \quad \text{(Surplus)} \tag{1}$$

$$C = a_c N \quad \text{(Consumption)} \tag{2}$$

$$Y = \frac{1}{a_l} N \quad \text{(Output)} \tag{3}$$

$$N = \overline{N} \quad \text{(Labour force)} \tag{4}$$

The surplus (Π) in (1) is the residual after consumption (C) has been deducted from output (Y). Necessary consumption in (2) is determined by the (per-capita) consumption needs (a_c) to reproduce the labour force (N). Output (Y) in (3) is obtained by employing the labour force (N) at the current level of productivity ($1/a_l$). Finally, in (4), it is assumed that the labour force employed in the system is given ($\overline{N}$).

By replacing (4) in (3), note that output is determined independently of demand conditions:

$$\overline{Y} = \frac{1}{a_l}\overline{N}, \tag{5}$$

that is, *every* unit of labour produces as much as possible, bounded by the available technique $(1/a_l)$.

From (2) and (3), the consumption requirements to reproduce the labour force depend on the level of output:

$$C = a_c a_l Y. \tag{6}$$

Note that $a_c a_l$ represents the consumption requirement of the labour content of a unit of output. It allows to express each unit of labour into its consumption content. Therefore, $a_c a_l Y$ summarises the consumption needs allowing for the reproduction of the labour force.

Introducing (6) into (1), for output $\overline{Y}$ determined in (5), we *residually* obtain the surplus of the system:

$$\Pi = (1 - a_c a_l)\overline{Y}. \tag{7}$$

The causal link goes *from* output *to* the surplus (taken to the market to fetch a price). The direction goes from resources to its possible uses. Consumption may be seen as a *cost*, that is, the productive consumption of labour, rather than as an activating source of demand.

Figure 7.1 graphically depicts this causal link. Panel (A) shows the *basic* principle at work: resources (output) generate uses (consumption and surplus). A point of output on the x-axis is mapped through the 45° diagonal to a point of consumption and surplus on the y-axis: once $Y = \overline{Y}$, $C + \Pi$ are determined.

Panel (B), instead, depicts how the *distribution* of output between consumption and surplus is determined. Besides the 45° diagonal, the consumption ray representing (6) specifies the consumption requirements of the labour force at a given output level. Once output $\overline{Y}$ has been fixed using (5), consumption (C) is given by the vertical intersection with the consumption ray, whereas the vertical distance between the consumption ray and the 45° diagonal, at output level $\overline{Y}$, residually determines the size of the surplus (Π), exhausting total output at point *e*.

In this society, for a given level of productivity $(1/a_l)$ and (per-capita) consumption needs (a_c), a higher size of the surplus can only be obtained by increasing the (given) labour force $(\overline{N})$, leading to an

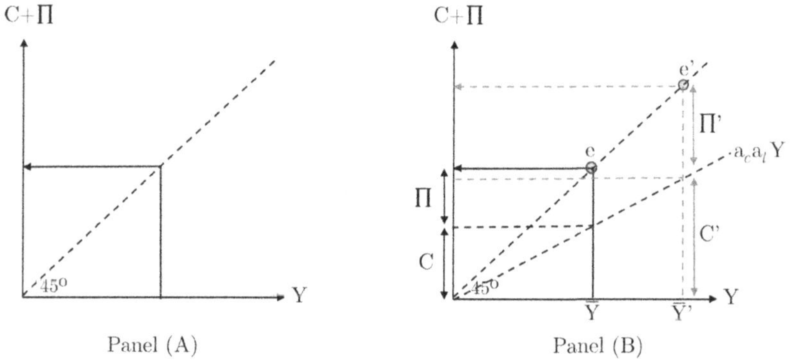

Figure 7.1 A pre-industrial society: From output (Y) to consumption and surplus ($C + \Pi$)

increase in output (from $\overline{Y}$ to $\overline{Y}'$ in Figure 7.1), which will then be distributed into consumption and surplus (C' and Π' in Figure 7.1, respectively), exhausting total output at point e'.

In contrast to this logic, the *principle* of effective demand operating in an *industrial* economy emerges from the following relations amongst aggregate magnitudes:

$$Y \equiv C + I \quad \text{(National income)} \tag{8}$$

$$C = a_c L \quad \text{(Consumption)} \tag{9}$$

$$I = \overline{I} \quad \text{(Investment)} \tag{10}$$

$$L = a_l Y \quad \text{(Employment)} \tag{11}$$

$$L \leq \overline{N} \quad \text{(Resource constraint)} \tag{12}$$

The components of national income (8) consist of consumption (C) and investment (I). In (9), aggregate consumption is determined by the (per-capita) demand (a_c) exerted by those employed (L). In (10), investment (I) is autonomous. Finally, expressions (11) and (12) imply that employment is determined by the labour requirements per unit of output (a_l) applied to the output scale (Y) of the system and that this level of labour demand is constrained by the (given) size of the labour force ($\overline{N}$).

By introducing (11) in (9), consumption is related to the level of income *through* employment:

$$C = a_l a_c Y. \tag{13}$$

Note that $a_l a_c$ represents the labour content of per-capita consumption demand, and it *numerically* coincides with $a_c a_l$ in (6), that is, the consumption content of a unit of output. Within the specific institutional set-up of a capitalist economy, the former may be interpreted as the 'value of labour power', whereas the latter as a 'propensity to consume' (Trigg, 2006, p. 19).

Substituting (13) for C as well as (10) for I in (8), and solving for output Y we obtain:

$$Y = \frac{1}{1 - a_l a_c} \cdot \bar{I}. \tag{14}$$

Comparing (14) with (7) renders apparent the contrast between an industrial and pre-industrial society, respectively. From (14), the causal link goes *from* investment demand *to* income. Consumption may be seen as an *activating* source of demand. But productive capacity, in this context given by the available labour force $\overline{N}$, does not necessarily translate into employment and output (as in the pre-industrial society). *Actual* production is only activated by *effective* demand, at least when $L \leq \overline{N}$.

Figure 7.2 graphically depicts this causal link. Panel (A) shows the *pre-institutional* principle of effective demand: uses $(C + I)$ generate resources (Y).[2] A point of aggregate consumption and investment on the y-axis is mapped through the 45° diagonal to a point of output on

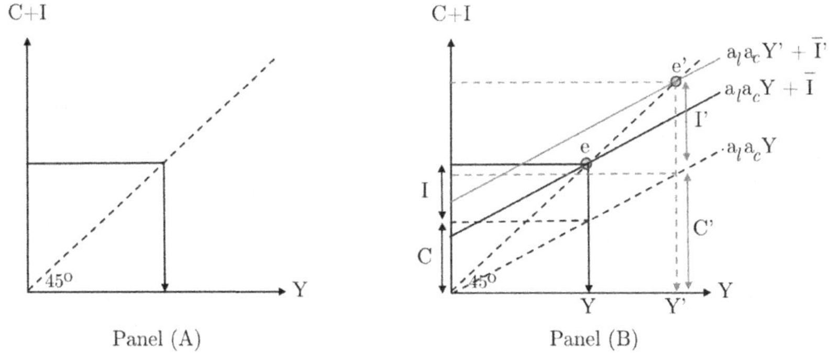

Figure 7.2 An industrial society: From consumption and investment $(C + I)$ to output (Y)

[2] The idea of graphically representing the principle of effect demand as in Panel (A) of Figure 7.2 may be found in Pasinetti (1974, p. 32).

the x-axis: this clockwise direction contrasts with the anti-clockwise direction found in Panel (A) of Figure 7.1. This is the deep asymmetry – highlighted by Pasinetti (1974) – between industrial and pre-industrial societies, as regards the role of demand in the determination of output (and employment).

Panel (B) of Figure 7.2 depicts how aggregate consumption and investment determine output and corresponds to the traditional textbook presentation of the 'Keynesian model of income determination' (Dornbusch and Fischer, 1993, p. 55). Besides the 45° diagonal, the consumption ray representing (13) specifies consumption demand per unit of output at *each* income level. A parallel upward shift of the consumption ray by the amount of autonomous investment gives the aggregate expenditure function ($a_l a_c Y + \bar{I}$). The point where aggregate expenditure crosses the 45° diagonal defines the output *actually* produced (point e in Figure 7.2). Consumption (C) is given by the vertical intersection with the consumption ray at that level of income, whereas autonomous investment is visualised as the vertical distance between point e and the point of consumption.

In this society, as long as $L < \overline{N}$, for a given level of productivity ($1/a_l$) and (per-capita) consumption demand (a_c), a higher level of output can only be obtained by increasing autonomous investment, as evinced by (14). The parallel upward shift of the aggregate expenditure function when $\bar{I}$ increases to $\bar{I}'$ makes current output (Y at point e) insufficient to satisfy aggregate demand ($C + I'$). Output will increase to reach point e' in Figure 7.2. In the *process of adapting* actual production to effective demand, higher levels of income induce higher aggregate consumption – along consumption ray (13) – until output reaches Y' and consumption becomes C'. But this adjustment process depends on behavioural relations about how the economy actually operates.[3] Therefore, the distinction between Panel (A) and Panel (B) in Figure 7.2 illustrates the difference between the pre-institutional and behavioural layers of analysis.

Within the context of the simple model specified by relations (8)–(12), it has been so far (implicitly) assumed that $L < \overline{N}$, that is, the

[3] For example, the 'multiplier' process which may be derived from expression (14) can be assumed to operate within the same accounting period ('instantaneously') or with a time lag (Pasinetti, 1974, p. 40).

labour force is not fully employed. Instead, when $L = \overline{N}$, the system (8)–(12) may be inconsistent if the level of investment is autonomous.

Indeed, from (11) when $L = \overline{N}$, output is constrained by the available productive capacity: $\overline{Y} = (1/a_l)\overline{N}$, so that consumption in (9) becomes $a_l a_c \overline{Y}$. Substituting this latter term for C in (8), and solving for I gives:

$$I = (1 - a_l a_c)\overline{Y}, \tag{15}$$

that is, investment is determined by full-employment output $\overline{Y}$.[4] Hence, if the autonomous level of investment in (10) is different from that implied by (15), the system becomes inconsistent.

Therefore, while the pre-institutional principle of effective demand remains a basic feature of an industrial economy, it becomes necessary to explore how it is related to the *growth* of productive capacity. Within that context, full utilisation of productive capacity and full employment need not coincide. The combination of the principle of effective demand with the '*derived demand* aspect of investment goods, due to their being used as means of production' (Pasinetti, 1981, p. 176) allows to single out the conditions for equilibrium growth, from a *pre-institutional* perspective.

7.4 Equilibrium, Full Employment and Stability

The conceptualisation of (dis)equilibrium and (in)stability in Pasinetti (1981, 1993) may be traced to the problem of determining the condition(s) which *must* be satisfied for the economy to expand at full employment and full capacity utilisation. Pasinetti's point of departure could be thought to be the contributions by Roy Harrod (1939) and Evsey Domar (1946).

However, it is not necessarily apparent how the notions of *warranted* and *natural* growth relate to Pasinetti's own framework. Setting up such a bridge, as well as discussing the dichotomy that Pasinetti identifies between pre-institutional and behavioural relations emerging from the Harrod-Domar model are the aims of this section. This conceptual discussion shall pave the way for the analysis of structural economic dynamics in *industrial* economies.

[4] Note the formal equivalence between investment in the industrial system and the surplus of the pre-industrial system determined in (7).

7.4.1 The Conditions for Equilibrium Growth

To keep things as simple as possible, reconsider aggregates at constant prices for a closed economy characterised by the same relations (8), (9), (11), (12) as above, but where investment I is no longer autonomous and the labour force N is allowed to vary:

$$Y \equiv C + I \qquad \text{(National income)} \qquad (16)$$

$$C = a_c L \qquad \text{(Consumption)} \qquad (17)$$

$$I = \kappa \Delta P \qquad \text{(Investment)} \qquad (18)$$

$$L = a_l Y \qquad \text{(Employment)} \qquad (19)$$

$$L \leq N \qquad \text{(Resource constraint)} \qquad (20)$$

Out of the two components of national income in (16), consumption (C) is defined as in (9). Instead, in (18), investment (I) is determined by the *acceleration principle*: κ represents the 'value of the capital goods *required for* the production of a unit increment of output' (Harrod, 1939, p. 16, italics added),[5] multiplying the *increase* in productive capacity (ΔP). Finally, employment is determined by the *given* labour input coefficient (a_l) applied to output (Y), that is, by labour demand requirements, and constrained by the size of the labour force N (which is now allowed to grow/decay).

In order to operate with relations (16)–(20), the starting point is to understand the task we are supposed to solve. Following Domar (1946): 'The economy will be said to be in equilibrium when its productive capacity P equals its national income Y. Our first task is to discover the *conditions under which this equilibrium can be maintained*, or more precisely, the *rate of growth* at which the economy *must* expand in order to remain in a continuous state of full employment' (Domar, 1946, p. 146, italics added).

Assume, first, that the economy is currently in an equilibrium. That is, income equals productive capacity ($Y = P$) and the labour force is fully employed ($L = N$). Therefore, (17) and (19) become, respectively:

[5] Assuming infinitely durable fixed capital, it represents a ratio between new investment and the increase in *capacity* output (Domar, 1946, p. 140). Moreover, it is implicitly assumed that 'all new capital goods are required for the sake of the increment of output of consumers' goods' (Harrod, 1939, p. 17).

$$C = a_c N \qquad \text{(Consumption)} \tag{21}$$

$$N = a_l Y \qquad \text{(Labour force)} \tag{22}$$

To find the growth rate at which the economy *must* expand to *maintain* this initial equilibrium, introduce (22) into (21) (obtaining $C = a_l a_c Y$), replace this expression for C in (16), and solve for Y:[6]

$$Y = \frac{1}{1 - a_l a_c} \cdot I. \tag{23}$$

Moreover, if coefficients a_c and a_l are fixed, then:

$$\Delta Y = \frac{1}{1 - a_l a_c} \cdot \Delta I. \tag{24}$$

Dividing each side of (24) by the corresponding side of (18), gives:

$$\frac{\Delta Y}{\Delta P} \cdot \frac{1}{\kappa} = \frac{1}{1 - a_l a_c} \cdot \frac{\Delta I}{I}$$

from where we see that the growth rate of new investment is given by:

$$\frac{\Delta I}{I} = \frac{\Delta Y}{\Delta P} \cdot \frac{1 - a_l a_c}{\kappa}. \tag{25}$$

Investment will grow in *equilibrium* when the change in productive capacity coincides with that of income, that is, when $\Delta Y = \Delta P$. Therefore, from (25), the equilibrium growth rate of investment will be g_w:

$$g_w = \frac{1 - a_l a_c}{\kappa} \tag{26}$$

which corresponds to the *warranted* growth rate in Harrod (1939, p. 17). Note that, from (23) and given that coefficients a_c and a_l are fixed, income and investment are tied by a constant proportionality relationship. Therefore, for equilibrium to be maintained, g_w is also the equilibrium growth rate of Y.

However, from (22) – as a_l is not changing – the expansion in income should coincide with that of the labour force:[7]

6 We assume that $a_l a_c < 1$, that is, the labour requirement to reproduce per-capita consumption is lower than 1, which means that the available labour in the economy is not entirely used up to reproduce aggregate consumption.

7 For a given a_l, we have: $\Delta N = a_l \Delta Y$, so that $\Delta N/N = a_l \Delta Y/N = \Delta Y/Y$.

$$\frac{\Delta Y}{Y} = \frac{\Delta N}{N} = g_n \tag{27}$$

which corresponds to the natural *growth* rate in Harrod (1939), when labour productivity $(1/a_l)$ is constant. It represents an upper bound, the 'maximum sustainable rate of growth that technical conditions make viable to the economic system as a whole' (Pasinetti, 1974, p. 96).

Therefore, if equilibrium is characterised by an expansion of productive capacity *pari passu* that of effective demand $(\Delta P = \Delta Y)$ – given by g_w – which also allows for a 'continuous state of full employment' – given by g_n – the consistency relation to be satisfied is:

$$g_n = \frac{1 - a_l a_c}{\kappa} \tag{28}$$

which solves the task we had set and corresponds to *a* 'Golden Age' dynamics (Cozzi, 1969, p. 12). It is important to emphasise that (28) is conceived as a relation between (given) magnitudes, rather than as a rule for determining *any* of the variables involved in the expression.

Interestingly, from (23) and (28), equilibrium investment must satisfy:

$$I = \kappa g_n Y \tag{29}$$

which can be inserted into (16) for I, together with (21) in the place of C, and solving for Y, we have:

$$Y = (1 - \kappa g_n)^{-1} a_c N. \tag{30}$$

Pre-multiplying both sides of (30) by the labour input coefficient a_l and considering (22):

$$N = a_l Y = a_l (1 - \kappa g_n)^{-1} a_c N. \tag{31}$$

The labour force N vanishes from both sides of (31), obtaining:

$$a_l (1 - \kappa g_n)^{-1} a_c = 1 \tag{32}$$

as a *necessary* condition for equilibrium growth. In (32), the coefficient:

$$\eta(g_n) = a_l (1 - \kappa g_n)^{-1} \tag{33}$$

represents the total – direct and (hyper-)indirect – labour requirements to reproduce a unit of output when the economy is expanding at the natural growth rate g_n (Pasinetti, 1977, p. 196).[8] Therefore, condition (32) may be compactly expressed as:

$$\eta(g_n)\cdot a_c = 1. \tag{35}$$

A condition analogous to (35), within the context of a multisectoral economy, represents a cornerstone of Pasinetti's approach to the concept of equilibrium (see, e.g., Pasinetti, 1981, pp. 46–48). When (35) holds, the economy is in an *equilibrium situation*: the expansion of productive capacity is matched by the growth of effective demand ($\Delta P = \Delta Y$) and the labour force is fully employed.

It is important to note the equivalence between conditions (28) and (35), especially when considering a *disequilibrium* situation. For example, if the actual growth rate of income is $\bar{g}$ such that $\eta(\bar{g})\cdot a_c < 1$, then:

$$\eta(\bar{g})\cdot a_c < 1 \quad \text{if and only if} \quad \bar{g} < \frac{1 - a_l a_c}{\kappa} = g_n, \tag{36}$$

that is, the economy is growing *below* the full-employment growth rate, while also $\Delta Y < \Delta P$, so that the increase in effective demand falls short of the *required* increase in productive capacity.[9] A similar analysis could be done for the case where $\eta(\bar{g})\cdot a_c > 1$.[10]

[8] This may be seen by developing the terms in the left-hand side of (33):

$$\begin{aligned} a_l\cdot(1-\kappa g_n)^{-1} &= a_l\cdot\left[1 + \kappa g_n + (\kappa g_n)^2 + \cdots\right] \\ &= a_l + a_l\cdot\kappa g_n + a_l(\kappa g_n)\cdot(\kappa g_n) + \cdots \end{aligned} \tag{34}$$

The first term of this infinite series, a_l, measures the direct labour required to produce a unit of output, the second term, $a_l\cdot\kappa g_n$ measures the labour required to produce the new investment goods that support the expansion of output, the third term measures the labour required to produce the new investment goods supporting the additional requirements of new investment, and so on for terms of higher order. From (28), $\kappa g_n = 1 - a_l a_c$, thus, given the assumption that $a_l a_c < 1$, the infinite series is convergent.

[9] The result in (36) can be obtained by noting that $\eta(\bar{g})\cdot a_c = a_l(1-\kappa\bar{g})^{-1}a_c < 1$ and, solving for $\bar{g}$ throughout the series of inequalities: $(1-\kappa\bar{g})^{-1} < (a_l a_c)^{-1}$ so that $\kappa\bar{g} < 1 - a_l a_c$, obtaining $\bar{g} < (1-a_l a_c)/\kappa = g_n$. Moreover, from (25), note that $\bar{g}/g_n = (\Delta I/I)/[(1-a_l a_c)/\kappa] = \Delta Y/\Delta P < 1$.

[10] Such a case would lead to inflationary pressures, as described in Pasinetti (1981, p. 48).

7.4.2 Pre-institutional and Behavioural Relations in Harrod and Domar

The derivation of the warranted growth rate – g_w in (26) – *formally* differs with respect to the routes taken by Harrod and Domar.

Consider Harrod first. His 'fundamental equation' (Harrod, 1939, p. 17), $G_w = s/C$ determines G_w based on the ratio between s, 'the fraction of income which individuals and corporate bodies *choose to save*' (Harrod, 1939, p. 16, italics added), and C, 'the amount of capital per unit increment of output required by technological *and other conditions* (including the state of confidence, the rate of interest, etc.)' (Harrod, 1939, p. 18, italics added).

For Harrod, 'the *sum of decisions* to produce [...] are on balance justified [when κ in (18) equals the] increment in the stock of capital divided by the increment in total output which *actually occurs*' (Harrod, 1939, p. 18, italics added). That is, warranted growth obtains when κ coincides with its ex post, realised counterpart $I/\Delta Y$.

The mechanism advanced by Harrod is deeply embedded in *behavioural* relations. The propensity to save s has been *chosen*, coefficient C reflects the technique in use but also the *state of confidence*. The matching between ex post investment and planned capacity expansion occurs for 'that addition to capital goods in any period, which producers *regard as ideally suited* to the output which they are undertaking in that period' (Harrod, 1939, p. 19, italics added). Thus, rather than *full* capacity utilisation, it is an expansion rate that fulfils effective demand *expectations*.

The case of Domar is different. While he relies on the 'multiplier theory' to determine changes in income, his methodological standpoint is closer to a pre-institutional layer of analysis. To begin with, Domar acknowledges 'the difficulties of determining productive capacity, both conceptually and statistically' (Domar, 1947, p. 37), that is, his framework was conceived in terms of magnitudes that should be *measurable*. Moreover, his interpretation of g_w in (26) is that it represents the (constant) compound rate at which investment is *required* to grow to *maintain* equilibrium (Domar, 1946, p. 141). In fact, Domar's analysis is carried out 'at a pure level of logical consistency' (Pasinetti, 1974, p. 95).

In contrast, Harrod aims to use the divergence between g_w in (26) and g_n in (27) to understand where the actual (average) growth rate $\overline{g}$ of a *capitalist* economy might be. This implies studying which *forces* or *adjustment mechanisms* are operating in the economy, capable of closing the divergence between g_w and g_n and making $\bar{g}$ approach this growth *norm*. The analysis of such adjustment mechanisms allows to define the *stability* properties of an equilibrium configuration, and it is inherently based on behavioural relations. For example, it depends on 'particular assumptions on how entrepreneurs react to divergence of reality from expectations' (Pasinetti, 1974, p. 97). Indeed, Harrod (1939) concluded on the 'inherent instability' of his warranted growth path.

While the Harrodian *warranted* growth rate is based on behavioural relations, his *natural* growth rate is pre-institutional: it is a *constraint* on the system, given by technological possibilities. In his framework of structural dynamics, Pasinetti (1981, 1993) followed Domar's approach but incorporated the Harrodian concept of *natural* growth to carry out a *pre-institutional* analysis of the (changing) compositional structure of industrial economies.

Based on this depiction, it might seem that the pre-institutional layer of analysis has little to say about (in)stability. However, while the study of actual adjustment mechanisms may provide a guidance to explain where the capitalist economy is going, a pre-institutional analysis may conclude on the practical impossibility of an equilibrium position being reached, making disequilibrium the *normal* state of industrial economies. Thus, rather than finding explanations as to why the economy is *not* returning to an equilibrium path, the focus might be defining a *normative* configuration towards which the system could be taken.

7.5 Structural Dynamics and Effective Demand in Industrial Economies

Pasinetti's framework of structural economic dynamics has been specified and discussed at length in Pasinetti (1965a, 1981, 1993) and further developed and generalised by Nadia Garbellini (2010). Thus, the aim of this section is to highlight some logical implications of Pasinetti's analytical scheme as regards the increasing difficulty to achieve and maintain full employment. These observations will be based on the building-blocks developed so far: the pre-institutional analysis of industrial economies, the principle of effective demand and the conceptualisation of (dis)equilibrium.

Pasinetti's framework provides a *multisectoral foundation* for the principle of effective demand, so the economy considered is characterised by $n-1$ commodities for final uses (each indexed by i), produced by means of capital goods and labour. The aim is to single out the conditions that *ought to* be satisfied *if* full capacity utilisation and full employment are to be maintained.

To keep the presentation as simple as possible, but at the same time be able to relate this scheme to relations (16)–(20) defined above, we assume an infinite lifespan for fixed capital goods, so that gross investment consists entirely of (capacity-generating) *new* investments. The *quantity side* of the system may be described by the following relations:

$$Y(t) \equiv \sum_{i=1}^{n-1} p_i(t)C_i(t) + p_{k_i}(t)J_i(t) \qquad \text{(National income)} \qquad (37)$$

$$C_i(t) = a_{in}(t)N(t), \quad \text{for } i = 1, \ldots, n-1 \qquad \text{(Consumption)} \qquad (38)$$

$$J_i(t) = \dot{C}_i(t), \quad \text{for } i = 1, \ldots, n-1 \qquad \text{(Investment)} \qquad (39)$$

$$N(t) = \sum_{i=1}^{n-1} a_{ni}(t)C_i(t) + a_{nk_i}(t)J_i(t) \qquad \text{(Labour force)} \qquad (40)$$

The components of (nominal) national income $Y(t)$ in (37) are the sum across sectors of nominal final consumption and nominal gross investment. As in (21), output for consumption of commodity i ($C_i(t)$) in (38) is given by the (per-capita) demand coefficient ($a_{in}(t)$) multiplying the size of the labour force ($N(t)$).

In (39), $J_i(t)$ represents the current output of capital goods used to produce final consumption good i, *measured* in units of productive capacity for that sector.[11] As in (18), equation (39) is based on an acceleration principle, but in this case the current output of capital goods is required to match the change in levels of *final consumption.*[12] It is crucial to note that the change in $C_i(t)$ also represents the *required* change in the *number* of units of productive capacity to support its

[11] See Pasinetti (1981, p. 36) for a discussion of the meaning of measuring capital goods in terms of (vertically integrated) productive capacity.

[12] For any variable X, we write: $\dot{X} = \frac{d}{dt}(X)$ to indicate the time derivative of X.

production. Therefore, equation (39) represents a necessary condition for full-capacity utilisation in sector i.

Finally, (40) states that the (aggregate) labour force $N(t)$ should match the sum across sectors of the labour content of output for consumption and investment: $a_{ni}(t)$ is the coefficient of labour requirements per unit of output for consumption in sector i, whereas $a_{nk_i}(t)$ is the coefficient of labour requirements per unit of output for investment in sector i.

To understand the relevance and implications of a *multisectoral* scheme with respect to an *aggregate* one, we first consider the case of uniform growth at natural rate g_n, already discussed in Section 7.4.

When the labour force – given at time $t = 0$ by $\overline{N}(0)$ – expands at steady rate g_n.[13]

$$N(t) = \overline{N}(0)e^{g_n t} \tag{41}$$

$$\dot{N}(t) = g_n N(t) \tag{42}$$

relations (38)–(40) become:

$$C_i(t) = a_{in}(t)\overline{N}(0)e^{g_n t}, \quad \text{for } i = 1, \ldots, n-1 \tag{43}$$

$$J_i(t) = \dot{C}_i(t), \quad \text{for } i = 1, \ldots, n-1 \tag{44}$$

$$\sum_{i=1}^{n-1} a_{ni}(t)C_i(t) + a_{nk_i}(t)J_i(t) = \overline{N}(0)e^{g_n t}. \tag{45}$$

As recognised by Terenzio Cozzi (1969, p. 28), for given technical ($a_{ni}(t)$, $a_{nk_i}(t)$) and (per-capita) consumption demand ($a_{in}(t)$) coefficients, equation system (43)–(45) is *overdetermined*: there are $2 \times (n-1)$ unknowns – $C_i(t), J_i(t)$ for $i = 1, \ldots, n-1$ – and $2 \times (n-1) + 1$ equations. Therefore, full utilisation of *sectoral* productive capacities (given by necessary conditions [44]) and full employment (implied by [45]) may only be mutually compatible by a *fluke*.

There are (at least) two equally valid ways out of this *impasse*.

[13] Note that (42) is obtained by taking the time derivative of expression (41):

$$\dot{N}(t) = \frac{d}{dt}\left(\overline{N}(0)e^{g_n t}\right) = g_n\overline{N}(0)e^{g_n t} = g_n N(t).$$

And this procedure may be applied to all variables changing at steady growth rates.

On the one hand, *if* full capacity utilisation and full employment are to be verified, then one of the determinants in (43)–(45) has to be *endogenously* determined, in order to make all equations mutually compatible. Amongst these determinants, it is plausible to think that *one* of the (per-capita) consumption coefficients, $a_{in}(t)$, may adjust so that (45) holds. For example, by choosing $a_{jn}(t)$, we would have:

$$a_{jn}^{*}(t) = \frac{\sum_{i=1, i \neq j}^{n-1} \left[a_{ni}(t) + g_n a_{nk_i}(t)\right] \cdot a_{in}(t)}{a_{nj}(t) + g_n a_{nk_j}(t)}, \tag{46}$$

that is, (per-capita) consumption coefficient $a_{jn}^{*}(t)$ is determined by all other *given* coefficients and ensures that all equations in (43)–(45) hold.

The intuition behind this solution may be seen clearly if – as in Pasinetti (1981, p. 38) – equation system (43)–(45) was articulated into a closed Input-Output model (Leontief, 1937). Even when one degree of freedom has been granted (by taking the labour force at any time t as given), the structural matrix of the system cannot be of full rank (n), so one of the columns (or rows) needs to be linearly dependent. This implies that (at least) one of the technical or consumption coefficients becomes endogenous, in order to obtain a non-trivial solution that complies with the full employment condition (45). As sharply observed by Leontief:

> Unless it is assumed that the values of all the coefficients are subject to some unknown law of prestabilized harmony, this requirement [equivalent to equation (45)] indicates that at least one of them is not a genuine independent datum but rather a variable which adjusts itself to the values of all the other parameters so as to satisfy the aforementioned consistency condition. [...] No economic system could possibly exist in which all the technical and consumption coefficients were independent of one another. (Leontief, 1951, p. 47)

Thus, from an economic perspective, when the technical conditions (represented by labour input coefficients $a_{ni}(t)$, $a_{nk_i}(t)$) are given, it must be the *structure* (and level) of (per-capita) consumption demand that adjusts to reach full employment.

On the other hand, *if* all technical and (per-capita) consumption coefficients *are* taken as *given*, due to the mathematical form of equation system (43)–(45), it is possible to obtain *meaningful* solutions for consumption in (38) and investment in (39), which do *not* comply with full employment condition (45) (Pasinetti, 1993, pp. 22–23).

Therefore, if an *equilibrium* situation is characterised by the simultaneous fulfilment of (43)–(45), whilst meaningful solutions may be obtained even when (45) does not hold, *disequilibrium* will be the normal state of *actual* industrial economies *when* all structural coefficients are taken as given.

However, the case of balanced growth considered so far conveys a notion of growth *without* development (Pasinetti, 1987, p. 993). In order to understand the deeper implications of the process of structural dynamics unfolding in an industrial economy, technical and (per-capita) consumption coefficients in each sector i are allowed to change at given, steady but *uneven* rates.[14]

$$a_{in}(t) = a_{in}(0)e^{r_i t} \qquad \text{(Consumption coefficient)} \tag{47}$$

$$a_{ni}(t) = a_{ni}(0)e^{-\rho_i t} \qquad \text{(Technical coefficient for consumption)} \tag{48}$$

$$a_{nk_i}(t) = a_{nk_i}(0)e^{-\rho_{k_i} t} \qquad \text{(Technical coefficient for investment)} \tag{49}$$

with time derivatives given by:

$$\dot{a}_{in}(t) = r_i a_{in}(t) \tag{50}$$

$$\dot{a}_{ni}(t) = -\rho_i a_{ni}(t) \tag{51}$$

$$\dot{a}_{nk_i}(t) = -\rho_{k_i} a_{nk_i}(t), \tag{52}$$

that is, r_i is the rate of change of (per-capita) consumption coefficient for commodity i, ρ_i is the rate of change of productivity in the production of final commodity i, and ρ_{k_i} is the rate of change of productivity in the production of productive capacity for consumption commodity i.

Assume we start from an equilibrium situation under uniform growth at rate g_n. How will equation system (43)–(45) change as we incorporate dynamic movements (47)–(49)?

Noting that $J_i(t) = \dot{C}_i(t) = \dot{a}_{in}(t)N(t) + a_{in}(t)\dot{N}(t)$, using (42) and (50), new investment in (44) becomes:

$$J_i(t) = \dot{C}_i(t) = (g_n + r_i)a_{in}(t)N(t). \tag{53}$$

[14] The assumption of steady rates of change is introduced here to simplify the presentation. See the detailed discussion in Pasinetti (1981, pp. 81–83).

Therefore, introducing (53) into (45), recalling (38) and (41) and rearranging terms, condition (45) becomes:

$$\sum_{i=1}^{n-1} \left[a_{ni}(t) + (g_n + r_i)a_{nk_i}(t)\right] \cdot a_{in}(t) = 1 \tag{54}$$

where the term in square brackets in (54):

$$\eta_i(t, g_n + r_i) = a_{ni}(t) + (g_n + r_i)a_{nk_i}(t) \tag{55}$$

captures the total – direct and (hyper-)indirect – labour required to reproduce a unit of commodity *i* and produce 'those means of production that are strictly necessary to expand such a circular process at a rate of growth $[(g_n + r_i)]$' (Pasinetti, 1988, p. 127). It is labelled 'vertically hyper- integrated labour coefficient' for commodity *i* (Pasinetti, 1981, p. 102), and is a (simplified) multisectoral counterpart to expression (33) in Section 7.4.[15]

Note that, even though $\eta_i(t, g_n + r_i)$ is a *technical* coefficient, it depends on the rate of change of final consumption commodity *i*, $(g_n + r_i)$ – via the investment relation (53). Thus, in an economy undergoing structural dynamics, $\eta_i(t, g_n + r_i)$ logically implies the impossibility to fully separate growth from (hyper-integrated) productivity (and its rate of change).[16]

Introducing (55) into (54) gives:

$$\sum_{i=1}^{n-1} \eta_i(t, g_n + r_i) \cdot a_{in}(t) = 1, \tag{56}$$

that is, a multisectoral counterpart to condition (35) in Section 7.4. Also in this case, (56) represents a *necessary* condition for the system to be in an *equilibrium situation*: a configuration of full capacity utilisation *and* full employment.

Condition (56) has been labelled the *effective demand* macroeconomic condition for equilibrium growth (Pasinetti, 1981, p. 86). It captures two key features of Pasinetti's framework.

First, it specifies the level *and* sectoral composition of (per-capita) consumption demand which should be achieved to maintain full

[15] The full generalisation of the concept of hyper-integrated labour requirements may be found in Pasinetti (1988, 1989).

[16] For a detailed discussion, see Garbellini (2010, pp. 105–108).

employment. As such, it represents an application of the (pre-institutional) principle of effective demand discussed in Section 7.3: in order to activate the full-employment level of outputs, there must be adequate *effective* final demand. In this sense, unless we *assume* an adjustment similar to (46), condition (56) will, most probably, *not* hold in actual industrial economies. Note also how the dependence of each sectoral (hyper-integrated) productivity coefficient (55) on the corresponding (commodity-specific) growth rate of consumption demand $(g_n + r_i)$ reinforces this conclusion.

Second, condition (56) states that the sum across sectors of the *shares* of labour force employed in each sector must add up to one. Each term $\eta_i(t)a_{in}(t)$ represents the comprehensive labour content of the units of (per-capita) consumption effectively produced in the system. As such, it allows to study the *structural* dynamics of employment, *even when* full employment is maintained at the aggregate level:

$$\frac{d}{dt}\left(\sum_{i=1}^{n-1} \eta_i(t)a_{in}(t)\right) = \frac{d}{dt}(1)$$

which amounts to obtaining:

$$\sum_{i=1}^{n-1} \dot{\eta}_i(t)a_{in}(t) + \eta_i(t)\dot{a}_{in}(t) = 0. \tag{57}$$

From (55), we have:

$$\dot{\eta}_i(t) = \dot{a}_{ni}(t) + (g_n + r_i)\dot{a}_{nk_i}(t). \tag{58}$$

Therefore, using (51) and (52), and dividing by $\eta_i(t)$, we obtain:

$$\frac{\dot{\eta}_i(t)}{\eta_i(t)} = -\rho_i \cdot \frac{a_{ni}(t)}{\eta_i(t)} + \left(-\rho_{k_i}\right) \cdot \frac{(g_n + r_i)a_{nk_i}(t)}{\eta_i(t)} = -\rho_i', \tag{59}$$

that is, the rate of hyper-integrated productivity change ρ_i' in (59) is a weighted average of the rates of productivity change for final consumption commodity i (ρ_i) and for supporting its capacity expansion (ρ_{k_i}).

Introducing (50) and $\dot{\eta}_i(t) = -\rho_i'\eta_i(t)$ – from (59) – into (57), we may rearrange terms to finally obtain:

$$\sum_{i=1}^{n-1} \left(r_i - \rho_i'\right) \cdot \eta_i(t)a_{in}(t) = 0, \tag{60}$$

that is, the share of employment in (hyper-integrated) sector i, $\eta_i(t)a_{in}(t)$ will increase (decrease) when per-capita consumption demand is expanding faster (slower) than productivity, so that $r_i - \rho_i' > 0$ ($r_i - \rho_i' < 0$). Thus: 'even if we start from the hypothesis that total full employment is in some way maintained over time [...] the maintenance of full employment at a global level requires a continuous process of re-proportioning of employment at the sectoral level' (Pasinetti, 1993, p. 51).

Therefore, the interplay between the structure of demand and productivity has far-reaching implications for *technological unemployment* in actual industrial economies: the fast pace of technological progress reflected in high values of ρ_i' needs to be counteracted by corresponding increases in r_i, if (56) is to be maintained.

But *can* (56) be maintained through time? In *exact* terms, it simply *cannot*. In fact, introducing (48) and (49) into (55), recalling (47), and using these expressions in (56), it is possible to obtain:

$$\sum_{i=1}^{n-1} a_{ni}(0)a_{in}(0)e^{(r_i-\rho_i)t} + (g_n + r_i)a_{nk_i}(0)a_{in}(0)e^{(r_i-\rho_{k_i})t} = 1. \qquad (61)$$

Formulation (61) for effective demand condition (56) implies that a sum of exponential functions (on the left-hand side) must be equal to a constant (on the right-hand side). As shown by Cozzi, this may only occur if (and only if) *all* exponents in each function are equal to zero (Cozzi, 1969, p. 45). That is, when $r_i = \rho_i = \rho_{k_i}$ for $i = 1, \ldots, n-1$. In economic terms, when there are *no* structural dynamics of employment. Thus, an *equilibrium* situation is impossible to be maintained over time in *exact* terms. And if achieved at some point, it will be highly *unstable*, given the pervasive structural dynamics of consumption and technology.

Thus, disequilibrium and instability, rather than equilibrium, is the *normal* state of *actual* industrial economies. However, this does not preclude the possibility of condition (56) being *approximately* satisfied in a dynamic context:

As a starting point, it is necessary to define what might be called a 'satisfactory' state of economic growth. It seems reasonable to consider as 'satisfactory' a state of economic growth in which the evolution of the economic system is taking place by maintaining both an *approximately* full employment of the labour force and an *approximately* full utilization of the productive capacities in the various branches of the economy. If this definition is accepted, then some *constraints* are immediately imposed on the growth of the economic system. (Pasinetti and Scazzieri, 1987, p. 527, italics added)

Therefore, rather than seeking explanations as to why the economy does not return to its equilibrium path, it may be more fruitful to empirically implement computable *norms* – such as (56) and (60) – in order to quantify how far (or close) actual economies are from them, providing a *compass* for policy.

References

Cozzi T. (1969) *Sviluppo e Stabilità nell'Economia*, Torino, Fondazione Luigi Einaudi.

Domar E. D. (1946) 'Capital Expansion, Rate of Growth, and Employment', in *Econometrica*, 14(2), pp. 137–147.

(1947) 'Expansion and Employment', in *The American Economic Review*, 37(1), pp. 34–55.

(1952) 'Economic Growth: An Econometric Approach', in *The American Economic Review*, 42(2), pp. 479–495.

Dornbusch R. and Fischer S. (1993) *Macroeconomics*, 6th Ed., New York, McGraw-Hill.

Frisch R. (1929 [1992]) 'Statics and Dynamics in Economic Theory' in *Structural Change and Economic Dynamics*, 3(2), pp. 391–401. Translated from the 1929 original Norwegian article which appeared in *Nationalokonomisk Tidsskrift*, 67, pp. 321–379.

Garbellini N. (2010) 'Essays on the Theory of Structural Economic Dynamics: Technical Progress, Growth, and Effective Demand', PhD Thesis, Università Cattolica del Sacro Cuore, Milano, XXIII cycle, A.Y. 2009/10.

Garbellini N. and Wirkierman A. L. (2014) 'Pasinetti's "Structural Change and Economic Growth": A Conceptual Excursus', in *Review of Political Economy*, 26(2), pp. 234–257.

Hahn F. H. (1987) 'On Involuntary Unemployment', in *The Economic Journal*, 97, (Supplement: Conference Papers), pp. 1–16.

Harrod R. F. (1939) 'An Essay in Dynamic Theory', in *The Economic Journal*, 49(193), pp. 14–33.

Keynes J. M. (1936) *The General Theory of Employment, Interest and Money*, New York, Harcourt, Brace and Company.

Kurz H. D. and Salvadori N. (2005) 'Representing the Production and Circulation of Commodities in Material Terms: On Sraffa's Objectivism', in *Review of Political Economy*, 17(3), pp. 413–441.

Leontief W. W. (1937) 'Interrelation of Prices, Output, Savings, and Investment' in *The Review of Economics and Statistics*, 19(3), pp. 109–132.

(1951) *The Structure of American Economy, 1919–1939: An Empirical Application of Equilibrium Analysis*, 2nd ed., enlarged, New York, Oxford University Press.

Pasinetti L. L. (1962) 'Rate of Profit and Income Distribution in Relation to the Rate of Economic Growth', in *Review of Economic Studies*, XXIX (4), pp. 267–279.

(1965a) 'A New Theoretical Approach to the Problem of Economic Growth', in *The Econometric Approach to Development Planning*, Vatican City, Pontificia Academia Scientiarvm, n.p.

(1965b) 'Discussion of "The Analysis of Economic Systems" by R. Stone', in *The Econometric Approach to Development Planning*, Vatican City, Pontificia Academia Scientiarvm, pp. 103–104.

(1974) *Growth and Income Distribution: Essays in Economic Theory*, Cambridge, Cambridge University Press.

(1977) *Lectures on the Theory of Production*, New York, Columbia University Press.

(1981) *Structural Change and Economic Growth: A Theoretical Essay on the Dynamics of the Wealth of Nations*, Cambridge, Cambridge University Press.

(1987) '"Satisfactory" versus "Optimal" Economic Growth', in *Rivista Internazionale di Scienze Economiche e Commerciali*, XXXIV(10), pp. 989–999.

(1988) 'Growing Subsystems, Vertically Hyper-integrated Sectors and the Labour Theory of Value', in *Cambridge Journal of Economics*, 12(1), pp. 125–134.

(1989) 'Growing Subsystems, Vertically Hyper-integrated Sectors: A Note of Clarification', in *Cambridge Journal of Economics*, 13(3), pp. 479–480.

(1993) *Structural Economic Dynamics: A Theory of the Economic Consequences of Human Learning*, Cambridge, Cambridge University Press.

(1997) 'The Principle of Effective Demand', in Harcourt G. C. and Riach P. A. (eds.) *A 'Second Edition' of The General Theory*, vol. I, London, Routledge, pp. 93–104.

(2002) 'Economic Theory and Institutions', in Nisticò S. and Tosato D. (eds.) *Competing Economic Theories: Essays in Memory of Giovanni Caravale*, London, Routledge, pp. 331–339.

(2007) *Keynes and the Cambridge Keynesians: A 'Revolution in Economics' to Be Accomplished*, Cambridge, Cambridge University Press.

Pasinetti L. L. and Scazzieri R. (1987) 'Structural Economic Dynamics', in Eatwell J. Milgate M. and Newman, P. (eds.) *The New Palgrave: A Dictionary of Economics*, London, Macmillan.
Sraffa P. (1960) *Production of Commodities by Means of Commodities*, Cambridge, Cambridge University Press.
Stone R. (1970) 'A Comparison of the SNA and the MPS', in Stone R. (ed.) *Mathematical Models of the Economy and other Essays*, London, Chapman and Hall, pp. 201–223
Trigg A. (2006) *Marxian Reproduction Schema: Money and Aggregate Demand in a Capitalist Economy*, London and New York, Routledge.
UN (2009) System of National Accounts 2008, ST/ESA/STAT/SER.F/2/ Rev.5. United Nations, New York.

8 Necessity of Finding an Appropriate Analytical Framework for Dealing with Technical Change and Economic Growth

Technical Change, Structural Dynamics and Employment

HARALD HAGEMANN

8.1 Introduction

Among the essential building-blocks of an alternative economic paradigm basically grounded on the phenomenon of production along a Keynesian-classical line according to Luigi Pasinetti is the 'necessity of finding an appropriate analytical framework for dealing with technical change and economic growth' (Pasinetti, 2007, p. 232). As is well known, the Cambridge Keynesians, including Nicholas Kaldor and Pasinetti, intensively analysed growth dynamics and the connection with income distribution. It is an outstanding peculiarity of Pasinetti's scientific life-work to emphasise that the development of capitalist economies since the Industrial Revolution is inherently associated with ongoing structural change. This stretches from his 1962 Cambridge PhD thesis 'A Multi-sector Model of Economic Growth', of which a summarised version has been published under the title *A New Theoretical Approach to the Problems of Economic Growth* (1965) in Vatican City to his pathbreaking *Structural Change and Economic Growth: A Theoretical Essay on the Dynamics of the Wealth of Nations* (1981) and the subsequent *Structural Economic Dynamics: A Theory of the Economic Consequences of Human Learning* (1993), to *Keynes and the Cambridge Keynesians: A Revolution to Be Accomplished* (2007).

'Pasinetti is possibly the last great system builder in the profession', Geoffrey Colin Harcourt writes on the front page of Mauro Baranzini and Amalia Mirante's (2018) intellectual biography of Pasinetti. It is an explicit and decisive aim of Pasinetti to accomplish the Keynesian revolution by developing an alternative economic paradigm which, in contrast to neoclassical economics with its emphasis on *exchange*, is fundamentally based on the phenomenon of *production*. This alternative analytical framework should be able to deal with capital accumulation and technical progress in a way that it comprises economic fluctuations and underutilised production factors which often characterise the development process of capitalist economies since the Industrial Revolution. In his lucid *Lectures on the Theory of Production*, Pasinetti (1977) has already presented the theory of production emerging from classical economic theory with clarity and logical rigour, thereby concentrating his analysis on the modern versions associated with Wassily Leontief's input-output system and Piero Sraffa's system of single-product industries and circulating capital. The book includes an introduction to dynamic production models. Chapter VII, in which Pasinetti sets out the model of a semi-stationary economy and derives the well-known duality relation between the wage-profit and the consumption-growth frontier, can be considered as a kind of bridge to his subsequent work on structural economic dynamics.

Empirical and historical analyses of growth processes, whether in advanced capitalist economies or in the catching-up phases of formerly underdeveloped countries, have clearly shown that ongoing *structural change* is one of the most important patterns of growth processes. Whereas this is a clear result of the significant contributions of such authors as Simon Kuznets, Leontief or in the literature on development economics by Paul Rosenstein-Rodan, Albert Hirschman, Paul Streeten, Walt Whitman Rostow and Hollis Chenery,[1] this fact has been completely neglected in all steady state models which dominated the post-war literature on growth economics for a long time. Pasinetti has rightly criticised the serious shortcomings of proportional dynamics in the analysis of capitalist growth processes time and again.[2] This proportional 'dynamics' represents nothing other than a stationary state on a 'higher level', that is, growth with constant structures. A main driver of modern economic growth associated with structural

[1] See Pasinetti (1993, pp. 9–11) and in much greater detail the contributions in vol. III of Hagemann, Landesmann and Scazzieri (2003). For a comparison of Pasinetti's with Kuznets's approach to the study of structural change and economic development, see Syrquin (2012). On empirical patterns of structural change, see also Syrquin (1988).

[2] See, for example, Pasinetti (1993, pp. 3–8).

change is technical progress. Pasinetti has often deplored the inadequacies of modern economic theory in the investigation of the role and consequences of technical change, as perhaps best elaborated in his lecture 'Economic Theory and Technical Progress' delivered at the 1999 Royal Economic Society conference in Nottingham. There he appreciates Roy Harrod for the effective 're-discovery of technical progress' in modern economic theory (Pasinetti, 1999, p. 14). In his attempt 'to keep high the torch of an alternative way of doing economics' (Pasinetti, 2007, p. xix) and to accomplish the Keynesian Revolution, Harrod's *Towards a Dynamic Economics* (1948),[3] which opened up 'new horizons towards that long-run analysis which Keynes had not faced' (Pasinetti, 2007, p. 34), has a particular role to play. According to Pasinetti, Harrod highlighted the relevance of the *rates of change*, with emphasis on the rate of population growth, the rate of capital accumulation and the rate of technical progress, that is, the growth of knowledge (Pasinetti, 2007, pp. 338–339).

The elaboration of an adequate theoretical framework for the analysis of structural economic dynamics imposed by technical progress and economic growth characterises Pasinetti's scientific life-work. Herein lies his most important and original contribution, in an area which transcends the works of the two great Cambridge economists who had the strongest influence on him: Piero Sraffa and John Maynard Keynes.[4] Technical progress was among the topics carefully avoided by Sraffa in his *Production of Commodities by Means of Commodities* (Sraffa, 1960). Among the most important achievements of Pasinetti's 'dynamic extension, along classical (Smithian/Ricardian) lines of the interindustry scheme conceived by Piero Sraffa' (Pasinetti, 2007, p. 304) is his construction of a *'dynamic' standard commodity*, that is, 'a particular composite commodity for which productivity is growing through time at the "average" growth of productivity of the economic system as a whole' (Pasinetti 1981, p. 105), thereby addressing David Ricardo's second problem of invariability of the standard of

[3] See also Harrod (1939).

[4] As Axel Leijonhufvud stated in his review essay at the time of Pasinetti's arrival: 'Cambridge was the one European center able to maintain genuine intellectual independence and to exert considerable worldwide influence against the growing dominance of American economics. The young Italian student became in time one of the foremost Cambridge economists of his generation' (Leijonhufvud, 2008, p. 529).

value (numéraire) with respect to improvements of technology. This is an ingenious addition to Sraffa's construction of a standard commodity as an invariable measure of value, that is, a composite commodity which is an invariable standard of value with regard to changes in income distribution.[5] No one has yet succeeded in solving both of Ricardo's problems simultaneously, that is, the elaboration of a standard of value which is invariable to changes in income distribution and technical progress. However, Pasinetti's dynamic standard commodity has the advantage to avoid a deflationary process which would be associated with labour as numéraire. By keeping the absolute price level constant in the case of productivity growth due to improvements in technology, the resulting 'natural' rate of interest would be positive and equal to the standard rate of productivity growth.

In his *General Theory* (1936), Keynes's focus undoubtedly is on the short run, which is illustrated by the fact that he does not only abstract from technical progress but also from the capacity effect of net investment. Whereas emphasis on the short run is fully understandable in times of a great depression, it has contributed to the widespread view that Keynes, in contrast to Karl Marx and Joseph Alois Schumpeter, had been disinterested in the long-run development of capitalist economies. Pasinetti rightly reflects that this view cannot stand a thorough and detailed examination and that 'Keynes contemplates both the short and the long run' (Pasinetti, 2007, p. 230). By the end of his life, Keynes was clearly worried by the problem of keeping full employment over time. He reflected on 'the long-term problem of full employment' and pointed out that '[e]mphasis should be placed primarily on measures to maintain a steady level of employment and thus to prevent fluctuations' (Keynes, 1943 [1980], p. 323).

It is a main concern of Pasinetti's analysis of structural economic dynamics (1981, 1993) to show how an economic system may maintain full employment through time when it is subject to dynamic impulses such as technical progress, a growing population (including changes in the ratio of active to total population or in the ratio of working hours to total time) and changes in consumers' preferences according to Engel's law.

[5] See Sraffa (1960, chs. IV–V).

An important element is a modern investigation of Ricardo's machinery problem. This allows an interesting view of the current debate of the future of employment as the consequence of the digitalisation of the economy. Furthermore, it is a good basis for a link with Keynes who, although not investigating deeper the causes and effects of technical progress in his *General Theory*, reflected on these issues in his important essay *Economic Possibilities for our Grandchildren*, published in October 1930 after the outbreak of the Great Depression but based on lectures he had already given since February 1928.[6] Here Keynes (1930) does not only analyse the long-run consequences of capital accumulation and technical change but also points out an important 'new disease', 'namely *technological unemployment.* This means unemployment due to our discovery of means of economizing the use of labour outrunning the pace at which we can find new uses for labour' (Keynes, 1930 [1971], p. 325). However, in contrast to Marx, Keynes did consider technological unemployment only as a *temporary* problem of maladjustment and not as a permanent problem. Pasinetti, on the other hand, regards the maintenance of full employment through time as a permanent task of economic policy in light of the ambivalent nature of technological change destroying old jobs, firms and even whole industries but at the same time creating new jobs, firms and industries. In Section 8.2, I will examine Pasinetti's analysis of the structural dynamics of employment as the outcome of both the structural dynamics of technology and demand more closely. In Section 8.3, some main characteristics of Pasinetti's approach are highlighted in contrast with other approaches for dealing with technical progress, economic growth and structural change, before some conclusions will be drawn in Section 8.4.

8.2 Vertically Integrated Sectors and the Structural Dynamics of Employment

It is one of the great merits of Pasinetti's analysis of structural change that he has shown clearly *the double-sided nature of technological change*, which so often is treated exclusively as a supply-side phenomenon.[7]

[6] See Hagemann (2019) and the contributions in Pecchi and Piga (2008) for greater details and a critical assessment.
[7] This section is based on Hagemann (2012, pp. 209–212).

Pasinetti has not only integrated the demand aspect of technological change into his theoretical framework but also the *interaction between the two sides*. The factor ultimately responsible for structural change is *technical progress as a result of learning*. Increases in productivity lead to increases in per capita income. Yet even with increases in real income, consumers do not expand their demand for each existing commodity proportionally. Moreover, new products emerge as a corollary of technical progress. This generalisation of Ernst Engel's empirical law, that is, the integration of the structural dynamics of demand, plays an important role in Pasinetti's analysis. Indeed, Pasinetti emphasises 'in the long run, it is the level of real income – not the price structure – that becomes the relevant and crucial variable' (Pasinetti, 1981, p. 73).[8]

It is a characteristic feature of Pasinetti's structural economic dynamics that only final commodities are considered. 'No intermediate stage, and thus no intermediate commodity, will be explicitly represented. All production processes will be considered as vertically integrated, in the sense that all their inputs are reduced to inputs of labour and to services from stocks of capital goods' (Pasinetti, 1981, p. 29).

As time goes by, the various vertically integrated sectors experience structural dynamics of both their production and their costs (and thus equilibrium prices), with important consequences for the development of the demand for labour, that is, it generates a certain *structural dynamics of employment*. If, with a constant labour supply, labour productivity in sector i grows with the rate ρ_i and demand for good i grows with the rate r_i, the sectoral demand for labour would only be constant in the special but unlikely case $\rho_i = r_i$. If r_i exceeds (is smaller than) ρ_i, sector i will expand (reduce) its demand for labour. With different rates of productivity growth and different sectoral rates of growth of demand, apart from the very special case in which demand grows in every single sector at exactly the same rate as labour productivity, reallocation of labour between the sectors will be necessary. Thus, a high level of employment can be maintained only with the necessary mobility of labour between sectors (and regions). Pasinetti's theoretical framework allows both expanding and declining industries to be observed in the process of structural change. When, in some

[8] Not surprisingly, the fact that relative prices and incentives play no part in Pasinetti's story is one of the few major points of critique in the otherwise favourable review essay by a highbrow neoclassical theorist (Malinvaud, 1995).

sectors, the introduction of new technologies causes high rates of productivity growth which cannot be matched by a proportional increase in demand because some level of saturation has been reached, then a decline in employment in these sectors cannot be avoided.

With a growing population, the economy must also enlarge its overall productive capacity continuously. Furthermore, a very definite relation between the rate of growth of sectoral demand and the amount of new investment has to be fulfilled in each sector. In order to maintain full employment over time, an effective demand condition and a capital accumulation condition must be satisfied. It is therefore very probable that, even if the economy starts from an equilibrium position with full employment of the labour force and full utilisation of productive capacities, the structural dynamics which cause that position to change will not result in the maintenance of full employment by the endogenous mechanisms of the market system.

If we take Pasinetti's economic system, in which production takes place by means of labour and capital goods needed to produce the final output,[9] then the *full-employment condition* amounts to

$$\underbrace{\sum a_{ni}\cdot a_{in}}_{1} + \underbrace{\sum (1/T_i)\cdot a_{nk_i}\cdot a_{in}}_{2} + \underbrace{\sum a_{nk_i}\cdot a_{k_in}}_{3} = 1 \tag{1}$$

Here a_{ni} and a_{nki} denote the labour-input coefficients per unit of consumption good i respectively the corresponding capital good k_i produced, a_{in} and a_{k_in} denote the demand coefficients per capita for consumption goods and the corresponding net investment, whereas a_{ki} indicate the replacement coefficients. The average lifetime of capital goods in the vertically integrated sector i $(i = 1, 2, \ldots, n-1)$ is $T_i = 1/a_{ki}$. Overall employment thus consists of the three components of

- demand for labour in the production of consumption goods (1),
- demand for labour in the production of replacement investment (2) and
- demand for labour in the production of net investment (3).

[9] See Pasinetti (1981, pp. 35–43). In this model, capital goods are produced from labour alone; whereas in the more complex model capital goods are also needed for the production of capital goods but still are specific for the corresponding consumption goods sector so that the various vertically integrated sectors are not interconnected, and no basic product in the sense of Sraffa exists.

The *capital accumulation conditions* for keeping full employment through time amount to

$$a_{k_i n}(t) = (g + r_i(t)) \cdot a_{in}(t) \quad i = 1, 2, \ldots, (n-1) \tag{2}$$

where g denotes the rate of population growth. They require the fulfilment of the Harrod-Domar equation in every sector of the economy. These are necessary but not sufficient conditions. The sectoral rate of change of employment is

$$\varepsilon_i = g + r_i - \rho_i \gtreqless 0 \tag{3}$$

Maintaining full employment over time also requires that the *effective demand condition*

$$\sum a_{ni}(0) \cdot a_{in}(0) \cdot e^{(r_i - \rho_i) \cdot t} + \sum (1/T_i + g + r_i(t)) \cdot a_{nk_i}(0) \cdot a_{in}(0) \cdot e^{(r_i - \rho_i) \cdot t} = \mu(t) \cdot \nu(t) \tag{4}$$

must be satisfied. Whereas μ represents the participation rate, that is, the ratio of active to total population, ν indicates the ratio of working hours performed to the total number of hours per period (year). The macroeconomic conditions depend both on technology and on the growth and composition of output.

Equation (4) is a generalisation of (1). In his 'more complete formulation of the effective demand condition' Pasinetti (1981, pp. 55–56) considers the participation rate and the average working time as important variables on the labour supply side. Whereas Marx's favourite example of a seventy-two-hour working week (six days of twelve hours) corresponds to the empirical reality of the most advanced British economy in his time, today we are roughly at about half of that working time (longer holidays included) in most advanced economies. This reduction was only possible due to technological progress, as sketched in Keynes's (1930) future scenario of a fifteen-hour working week for 2030. In most Western countries, the main change which took place in the participation rate in recent decades was a substantial increase in the participation rate of women.

From his analysis Pasinetti draws

> the important conclusion that the structural dynamics of the economic system inevitably tend to generate . . . *technological* unemployment. At the same time, the very same structural dynamics produce counter-balancing movements . . .

but not automatically. There is nothing in the structural evolution of technical coefficients on the one side and of per-capita demand on the other, as such, that will ensure ... the maintenance of full employment. Therefore, if full employment is to be kept through time, it will have to be actively pursued as an explicit aim of economic policy. (Pasinetti, 1981, p. 90)

In order to sustain full employment over time, society has to choose one of the following strategies or a combination of them:

(1) A Keynesian-type policy which will raise per capita demand for existing goods;
(2) the promotion of research and development of new goods. Since technological progress not only leads to an increase in productivity – but also to product innovations with high potential for an increase in demand, investment and employment – a more supply-side oriented policy of this Schumpeterian kind aims at strengthening the latter tendency in order to compensate for the former;
(3) a policy of shortening the working week or reducing the participation rate. Within certain boundaries, technological progress allows society to choose between producing more and/or better goods and enjoying more leisure time.

It is the main merit of Pasinetti's investigation to have shown so clearly that full employment will only be maintained if the economy is able to implement a continuous process of structural reallocation of labour between the sectors, in accordance with the twofold effects of technological progress on labour productivity and the evolution of demand. The structural dynamics of employment causes serious problems for firms and individuals, because it requires a very special pattern of investment behaviour and training as well as mobility between sectors (and regions) over time. However, Pasinetti bases his structural economic dynamics on a pure production model in which agents are absent. On this stage, there is therefore no room for incentives, motivations, expectations, price-responsiveness and behaviour.

The combined strategies of (1) and (2) might be called Keynes *cum* Schumpeter. Pasinetti rightly criticises the lack of integration of Richard Goodwin (1913–1996) in the Cambridge School of Keynesian economics.[10] As a consequence of the missed Keynes-Schumpeter connection 'the advantages that might have come from

[10] See Pasinetti (2007, pp. 205–216).

the presence of Goodwin, who was bringing with him the potential richness of his close acquaintance with Schumpeter' were squandered (Pasinetti, 2007, p. 234). Schumpeter's vision of the long-run development of capitalist economies could have added value to a substantially modified and enriched Keynesian vision of a permanently evolving economy. Whereas Pasinetti, not surprisingly, criticises Schumpeter for his praise of Léon Walras for his general equilibrium theory, he appreciates Schumpeter, on the other hand, as a brilliant economist for his awareness of the richness of institutions and the coining of appropriate terms such as 'creative destruction'. Pasinetti is consciously turning around Schumpeter's expression when he speaks of 'destructive creation' (Pasinetti, 2007, p. 316). By thus twisting the adjective and the substantive, Pasinetti's reformulation better expresses the core of Schumpeter's ideas that the process of creative destruction is not only the essential fact about capitalism but also that the net effect is a positive one contributing to a higher per capita income in the long run.[11]

8.3 The Appropriate Analytical Framework for Dealing with Technical Progress, Economic Growth and Structural Change

It has been a main aim of Pasinetti's elaboration of his structural economic dynamics to present a modern theoretical analysis of Ricardo's machinery problem. In the new chapter 31, 'On Machinery', in the third edition of his *Principles*, Ricardo retracted his previous view that the introduction of machinery benefits all classes in society and instead concluded '[t]hat the opinion entertained by the labouring class, that the employment of machinery is frequently detrimental to their interests, is not founded on prejudice and error, but is conformable to the correct principles of political economy' (Ricardo, 1821 [1951], p. 392). This chapter, which according to Sraffa marked 'the most revolutionary change' (Sraffa, 1951, p. lvii), had impressed both friends and foes and set the stage for later controversies on the displacement versus compensation effects of new technologies, which attracted many great and diverse economists, such as John Stuart Mill, Marx, Knut Wicksell or Paul Samuelson (1988, 1989). In his *History of Economic Analysis*, Schumpeter declared the controversy that went

[11] See Schumpeter (1942, ch. vii). For a modern analysis, see Dal Pont Legrand and Hagemann (2017).

on throughout the nineteenth century and beyond, mainly in the form of argument pro and con 'compensation' as 'dead and buried' (Schumpeter, 1954, p. 684). However, against the historical background of the microelectronic revolution and the introduction of industrial robots in modern industrial production processes since the late 1960s and increasing unemployment in the Western world since the first oil price shock of 1973/74, the spectre of technological unemployment came centre stage again.

Major studies on the macroeconomic consequences of technological change and of the necessary conditions for bringing an economy back to an equilibrium growth path, which started the investigation from Ricardo's analysis of the machinery problem, were done by John Hicks and Adolph Lowe. Whereas Hicks (1973) based his analysis in *Capital and Time* on a 'neo-Austrian' or *vertical* model of production processes in which a stream of labour inputs is transformed into a stream of consumption good outputs, Lowe (1976) is analysing the employment consequences of new technologies on the basis of a sectoral or *horizontal* model in his *The Path of Economic Growth*. The two alternative approaches thus represent the two alternative ways of disaggregating production processes. The two approaches have their comparative (dis)advantages. Whereas the horizontal model or circular view of production processes, as developed by Francois Quesnay, Marx, Leontief, Sraffa and John von Neumann, has its strength in the consideration of the sectoral interdependencies of production processes, the advantage of the Austrian approach lies in the consideration of the time aspect and its treatment of intertemporal complementarities.[12]

The pioneering traverse analyses of Hicks and Lowe have elucidated, within different types of models, that the ability of an economy to react to changes in the determinants of growth is limited by the quantity and structure of the existing capital stock.[13] Thus, in the case of an increasing growth rate of labour supply or, similarly, in the case of labour-saving technological change, the formation of additional real capital is

[12] For a more detailed comparison, see the contributions in Baranzini and Scazzieri (1990) and Landesmann and Scazzieri (1996).

[13] The explicit specification of the rigidities of a given stock of human capital, skill structures and the resource- and time-consuming process of transforming existing and evolving new skills, which may impose a different bottleneck on the transformation of an economic system, is neither in the focus of Hicks and Lowe nor of Pasinetti.

a precondition for the successful compensation of additional/displaced workers. In contrast to Hicks and Lowe, Pasinetti does not elaborate traverse analysis but concentrates on the restrictive conditions which have to be fulfilled in order for the economy to develop over time with full employment and full capacity utilisation, if it is subject to dynamic impulses such as technological change, a growing population (including changes in the ratio of active to total population or in the ratio of working hours to total time) and changes in consumers' preferences according to Engel's law. The equilibrium path over time is not a 'steady state' with constant structural proportions but one in which permanent changes in some basic magnitudes, such as the national product, total consumption, investment, overall employment and the sectoral allocation of labour, are associated with changes in these structural proportions. The dynamic movements of productivity, labour supply and structure of demand are typical features of any industrial system, independent of its institutional set-up.

Pasinetti develops his structural economic dynamics as a vertically integrated analysis. While conceding that Leontief's input-output model and Sraffa's 'production of commodities' system give more information on the structure of an economy *at any point in time*, Pasinetti points out that, because of the change of input-output coefficients and the 'breaking down' of the interindustry system *over time* (mainly due to technical progress) the vertically integrated model is superior for dynamic analysis (Pasinetti, 1981, pp. 109–117). Measuring capital goods in units of *vertically integrated productive capacity* of the final commodity 'has an unambiguous meaning through time, no matter which type of technical change, and how much of it, may occur' (Pasinetti, 1981, p. 178).

Pasinetti's analysis has demonstrated well how complex and difficult the keeping of full employment and full capacity utilisation becomes in an economy with structural change. 'But when technology and per-capita demand change as time goes on, then even if a perfect match between demand and productive capacity has been achieved at any given point in time, discrepancies are bound to emerge as time passes' (Pasinetti, 1993, p. 121). One of the great advantages is the focus on the double-sided nature of technological change which so often is treated only as a supply-side phenomenon. Pasinetti, on the other hand, integrates well also the demand side and the interaction between the two sides in his theoretical framework. In one of his early outstanding essays, Pasinetti (1960) has already criticised the complete neglect of the demand-side effect in all macroeconomic models. In reference to the work of the German statistician Engel on the evolution of demand over time, he has pointed out 'that when real *per capita* income increases the tendency of consumers *is not* to distribute the new income *proportionally* among the commodities previously bought, but, on the contrary, to direct the extra demand towards new goods' (Pasinetti, 1960, p. 232).

Now, even in a very complex model, it is impossible to endogenise all variables. Pasinetti has been criticised for assuming exogenously given growth rates ρ_i for labour productivity in sector i respectively for the growth rate of demand r_i. Thus, for Edmond Malinvaud the latter 'appears disputable. The endogenous changes in relative prices actually induce changes in the composition of consumption .... In order to explain the actual structural dynamics of final demand one must refer not only to new products and to income effects, but also to *price effects*' (Malinvaud, 1995, p. 62, my italics). Whereas Malinvaud's recommendation 'to borrow a little from "neo-classical" economics' has been resisted by Pasinetti, the critique, which was first raised by Bertram Schefold (1982, p. 549) in his review of Pasinetti's *Structural Change and Economic Growth* and later elaborated by Mark Lavoie (1997), that it is not legitimate to assume that the different rates of productivity growth in the various vertically integrated sectors are exogenously given, has caused more intensive discussions.[14]

Pasinetti and his critics agree that technical change is specific to the industry level and that changes taking place at the vertically integrated level are consequences of what happens on the industry level. For him, at any given point of time there exists a definite relation between a static input-output model and his dynamic vertically integrated analysis through a fully specifiable matrix of coefficients. The two are 'mutually complementary and completing each other. Inter-industry relations, referring to any particular point of time, represent a cross-section of the vertically integrated magnitudes, whose movements through time express the structural dynamics of the economic system' (Pasinetti, 1981, p. 117).

This implies that technical change, taking place at the industry level affects the changes in many (with irreducible matrices in all) vertically

[14] For greater details, see section 4 of Hagemann (2012).

integrated sectors which are all causally dependent on the same technical changes that take place at the industry level.[15] However, dependence does not run from one vertically integrated sector to another. Pasinetti's conception of vertically integrated sectors, as elaborated in his pathbreaking paper (Pasinetti, 1973) is based on Sraffa's conception of a *sub-system*, 'the net product of which consists of only one kind of commodity ... the whole of the labour employed can be regarded as directly or indirectly going to produce that commodity' (Sraffa, 1960, p. 89) and implicit in the theory of value of classical economists such as Ricardo. In 1988, Pasinetti extended the concept to *vertical hyper-integration* to generalise his 1973 analysis in which basic commodities exist but capital accumulation and growth are absent. 'This conceptualisation uses the notion of 'natural' (sectoral) rate of profit to transform all intermediate (capital) goods into labour, thus ending up with the pure labour scheme no longer as a simplification but as the most general scheme of a pure production economy' (Pasinetti, 2007, p. 303, n. 25). In Pasinetti's 'natural system', the economic relations are shaped in logical time, that is, they have a normative character. The rates of technical progress in all vertically (hyper-) integrated sectors are derived as an accounting magnitude from the sectors of production where investment decisions and technical progress take place. The vertically integrated sectors are hypothetical ex post constructions by the analyst. They differ completely from vertical models of the (neo-)Austrian type which do not include basic commodities and thereby cannot cover the fact that technical progress taking place in the production of basic goods indirectly affects productivity growth in all other sectors.

8.4 Concluding Remarks

In his attempt to construct an appropriate analytical framework for the investigation of technical progress, economic growth and structural change, Pasinetti puts emphasis on a *separation theorem* distinguishing between *natural* and *institutional* features.[16] In the first stage, the task is to develop a unified approach of the production (and learning)

[15] On causality and interdependence in Pasinetti's works and in the modern classical approach, see also Bellino and Nerozzi (2017).

[16] See, for example, Pasinetti (2007, pp. 275–279 and 323–331). See also Scazzieri (2012).

paradigm which focuses on certain fundamental properties and structural aspects which are valid for a wide range of institutional set-ups. In a second stage of investigation,[17] emphasis is on the analysis of behaviour relations etc. within a well-defined institutional set-up to explain what is going on in actual economies including the discussion of economic policy measures. The difference is particularly important in areas such as income and wealth (in)equality and social relations. The Industrial Revolution also had a deep long-run impact on the changes of institutions in modern societies. As Pasinetti (2007) discusses in greater detail in Book III, the differences between a Keynesian-Classical production paradigm and a neoclassical exchange paradigm are deeper with regard to the first than to the second stage of investigation. However, in the process of division of labour in this book, a more elaborate analysis of institutions and social concern, the ninth and final building-block of Pasinetti's alternative framework, is carried through by Claudia Rotondi.

Here, I only want to indicate an interesting parallel between Pasinetti and Lowe. In his instrumental analysis, Lowe (1965, 1976) distinguishes between *structural analysis* and *force analysis*. His structural analysis of changes in the major growth stimuli, such as labour supply or labour-displacing and capital-displacing process innovations, bears strong parallels with Pasinetti's natural analysis. Lowe got inspiration in the development of his three-sectoral model of production from Marx's schemes of expanded reproduction. In contrast to Russian and Indian planning models which also got inspiration from Marx's two-sectoral growth model, Lowe's analysis is not suffering from material determinism or a technocratic structural analysis which only emphasise the quantitative relations between the sectors which are required but neglect the motorial or behavioural features which are bound to prevail in any institutional set-up. The derivation of possible adjustment paths based on structural requirements is only a necessary first step in Lowe's instrumental approach to political economics, which is an attempt to formulate an economic policy designed to achieve the macro-goal of full employment in the mixed economy. Structural analysis has to be supplemented by what Lowe calls *force analysis*, that is, the study of micro-behaviour and motivations which induce suitable reactions on the side of the individual agents to set the

[17] See Pasinetti (1993, ch. VIII).

economy on a goal-adequate traverse. It is force analysis which has a special significance for the analysis of adjustment processes in market economies. Lowe's force analysis reveals the crucial role of expectations and the significance of a functioning price mechanism, thus raising economics above the level of a mere engineering science. That not only the structural analysis but also the force analysis of Lowe's political economics proves pertinent to discussions of economic reform is highlighted by Sukhamoy Chakravarty (1987) in his retrospective analysis of the Indian experience of development planning. Force analysis is particularly relevant for out-of-equilibrium processes, in theory as well as in the practice of the catching-up processes of formerly socialist economies after 1989.

It is a great strength of Pasinetti's analysis that he integrates structural change in economic growth analysis by considering the double-sided nature of technological change and the interaction between the supply side (growing productivity) and the demand side (increasing per-capita income) and the evolving structural dynamics of employment and consumption. This is also attested by Robert Solow, Pasinetti's long-time personal friend and opponent in several debates such as on capital theory, who as a 'friendly bastard Keynesian' emphasises that, because of evolving institutions and economic behaviour in modern societies, the Keynesian Revolution will never be accomplished but at the same time also points out:

> I think that Professor Pasinetti's own work on what he calls structural dynamics, on essentially how to extend the study of macroeconomic dynamics to incorporate the structural changes – some endogenous, perhaps most endogenous, but at least some still exogenous – in an analytical framework that is capable of looking at the evolution of capitalist economies. I am wholeheartedly in favour of that. (Solow, 2012, p. 271)

References

Arena R. and Porta P. L. (eds.) (2012) *Structural Dynamics and Economic Growth*, Cambridge, Cambridge University Press.

Baranzini M. and Scazzieri R. (eds.) (1990) *The Economic Theory of Structure and Change*, Cambridge, Cambridge University Press.

Baranzini M. L. and Mirante A. (2018) *Luigi L. Pasinetti: An Intellectual Biography. Leading Scholar and System Builder of the Cambridge School of Economics*, London, Palgrave Macmillan.

Bellino E. and Nerozzi S. (2017) 'Causality and Interdependence in Pasinetti's Works and in the Modern Classical Approach', in *Cambridge Journal of Economics*, 41, pp. 1653–1684.

Chakravarty S. (1987) *Development Planning: The Indian Experience*, Oxford, Clarendon Press.

Dal Pont Legrand M. and Hagemann H. (2017) 'Do Productive Recessions Show the Recuperative Powers of Capitalism? Schumpeter's Analysis of the Cleansing Effect', in *Journal of Economic Perspectives*, 31(1), pp. 245–256.

Hagemann H. (2012) 'Luigi Pasinetti's Structural Economic Dynamics and the Employment Consequences of New Technologies', in Arena R. and. Porta P. L. (eds.) *Structural Dynamics and Economic Growth*, Cambridge, Cambridge University Press, pp. 204–217.

(2019) 'Economic Possibilities for our Grandchildren', in Dimand R. W. and Hagemann H. (eds.) *The Elgar Companion to John Maynard Keynes*, Cheltenham and Northampton, Edward Elgar, pp. 162–167.

Hagemann H. Landesmann M. A. and Scazzieri R. (eds.) (2003), *The Economics of Structural Change*, 3 vols., Cheltenham and Northampton, Edward Elgar.

Harrod R. F. (1939) 'An Essay in Dynamic Theory', in *The Economic Journal*, 49, pp. 14–33.

(1948) *Towards a Dynamic Economics*, London, Macmillan.

Hicks J. (1973) *Capital and Time: A Neo-Austrian Theory*, Oxford, Clarendon Press.

Keynes J. M. (1930 [1971]) 'Economic Possibilities for Our Grandchildren', in Moggridge D. E. (ed.) *The Collected Writings of John Maynard Keynes*, vol. XI, *Essays in Persuasion*, London, Macmillan, pp. 321–332.

(1936 [1973]) *The General Theory of Employment, Interest, and Money*, in Moggridge D. E. (ed.) *The Collected Writings of John Maynard Keynes*, vol. VII, London, Macmillan.

(1943 [1983]) 'The Long-Term Problem of Full Employment', in Moggridge D. E. (ed.) *The Collected Writings of John Maynard Keynes*, vol. XXVII, *Activities 1940–1946: Shaping the Post-War World, Employment and Commodities*, London, Macmillan, pp. 320–325.

Landesmann M. A. and Scazzieri R. (eds.) (1996) *Production and Economic Dynamics*, Cambridge, Cambridge University Press.

Lavoie M. (1997) 'Pasinetti´s Vertically Hyper-integrated Sectors and Natural Prices', in *Cambridge Journal of Economics*, 21, pp. 453–467.

Leijonhufvud A. (2008) 'Between Keynes and Sraffa: Pasinetti and the Cambridge School', in *European Journal of the History of Economic Thought*, 15, pp. 529–538.

Lowe A. (1965) *On Economic Knowledge: Toward a Science of Political Economics*, 2nd enlarged ed., White Plains 1977, M. E. Sharpe.

(1976) *The Path of Economic Growth*, Cambridge, Cambridge University Press.

Malinvaud E. (1995) 'Luigi Pasinetti's *Structural Economic Dynamics:* A Review Essay', in *Journal of Evolutionary Economics*, 5(1), 59–69.

Pasinetti L. L. (1960) 'Cyclical Fluctuations and Economic Growth', in *Oxford Economic Papers*, New Series, 12(2), pp. 215–241.

(1965) 'A New Theoretical Approach to the Problems of Economic Growth', in *Pontificiae Academiae Scientiarum Scripta Varia, Vatican City*, 28, pp. 571–696.

(1973) 'The Notion of Vertical Integration in Economics Analysis', in *Metroeconomica*, 25, pp. 1–29.

(1977) *Lectures on the Theory of Production*, London and Basingstoke, Macmillan.

(1981) *Structural Change and Economic Growth: A Theoretical Essay on the Dynamics of the Wealth of Nations*, Cambridge, Cambridge University Press.

(1988) 'Growing Subsystems, Vertically Hyper-Integrated Sectors and the Concept of Vertical Integration', in *Cambridge Journal of Economics*, 12, pp. 125–134.

(1993) *Structural Economic Dynamics: A Theory of the Economic Consequences of Human Learning*, Cambridge, Cambridge University Press.

(1999) 'Economic Theory and Technical Progress', in *Economic Issues*, 4 (2), pp. 1–18.

(2007) *Keynes and the Cambridge Keynesians: A 'Revolution in Economics' to be Accomplished*, Cambridge, Cambridge University Press.

Pecchi L. and Piga G. (eds.) (2008) *Revisiting Keynes: Economic Possibilities for Our Grandchildren*, Cambridge, MA, MIT Press.

Ricardo D. (1817 [1951]) *On the Principles of Political Economy and Taxation* (1st ed. 1817; 3rd ed. 1821), vol. I of *Works and Correspondence of David Ricardo*, (ed.) Sraffa P. with the collaboration of M. Dobb, Cambridge, Cambridge University Press.

Samuelson P. A. (1988) 'Mathematical Vindication of Ricardo on Machinery', in *Journal of Political Economy*, 96, pp. 274–282.

(1989), 'Ricardo Was Right!', in *Scandinavian Journal of Economics*, 91, 47–62.

Scazzieri R. (2012) 'The Concept of "Natural Economic System": A Tool for Structural Analysis and an Instrument for Policy Design', in Arena R. and Porta P. L. (eds.) *Structural Dynamics and Economic Growth*, Cambridge, Cambridge University Press, pp. 218–240.

Schefold B. (1982) 'Review of Pasinetti (1981)', in *Kyklos*, 35, pp. 548–550.

Schumpeter J. A. (1911 [1926]) *Theorie der wirtschaftlichen Entwicklung*, Munich and Leipzig, Duncker & Humblot; English translation: *The Theory of Economic Development: An Inquiry into Profits, Capital, Credit, Interest, and the Business Cycle*, Cambridge, MA, Harvard University Press.

(1942) *Capitalism, Socialism and Democracy*, New York and London, Harper & Brothers.

(1954) *History of Economic Analysis*, London, Allen & Unwin.

Solow R. M. (2012), 'On Pasinetti and the Unfinished Keynesian Revolution', in Arena R. and Porta P. L. (eds.) *Structural Dynamics and Economic Growth*, Cambridge, Cambridge University Press, pp. 267–273.

Sraffa P. (1951) 'Introduction' to *The Works and Correspondence of David Ricardo*, vol. I, Cambridge, Cambridge University Press, pp. xiii–lxii.

(1960) *Production of Commodities by Means of Commodities: Prelude to a Critique of Economic Theory*, Cambridge, Cambridge University Press.

Syrquin M. (1988) 'Patterns of Structural Change', in Chenery H. B. and Srinivasan T. N. (eds.) *Handbook of Development Economics*, vol. I, Amsterdam, North-Holland.

(2012) 'Two Approaches to the Study of Structural Change and Economic Development: Kuznets and Pasinetti', in Arena R. and Porta P. L. (eds.) *Structural Dynamics and Economic Growth*, Cambridge, Cambridge University Press, pp. 69–87.

9 A Strong, Deeply Felt, Social Concern

CLAUDIA ROTONDI

Questions must be asked before answers can be obtained and, in order to make sense, the questions must be part of a logically co-ordinated attempt to understand social reality as a whole. A non-theoretical approach is, in strict logic, unthinkable.

(Myrdal, 1958 [1998], p. 233)

9.1 Foreword: An Unorthodox Economist

Luigi Pasinetti, in his 'Postlude: Fighting for Independence' (Pasinetti, 2007, pp. 217–237), states that a 'strong, deeply felt social concern' (Pasinetti, 2007, p. 234) is a characteristic feature drawn from John Maynard Keynes and useful to build a new and alternative economic paradigm.

The aspiration to develop an alternative paradigm places Pasinetti entirely among the 'heterodox' economists.[1] And from heterodox economists there is much to learn, as historians of economic thought know well.

A focus on methodology and on the history of ideas and facts are key categories often excluded from traditional economics courses (Hodgson, 2001), while in a heterodox approach, history is fundamental to the teaching of economics, starting from the belief that theories may only be understood within a specific social historical context.

We are here faced with the *vexata quaestio* of the choice between cumulative versus competitive conception of the progress of science in general and of economic science in particular.

[1] Economics in its classifications considers heterodox everything that remains outside of the mainstream, as identified by the dominant neoclassical economic theory since the Marginalist revolution of 1870. This definition is both inaccurate and too broad since it includes multiple approaches and schools, as the JEL B classification shows well.

Those who adopt a competitive conception of the development of economic thought are induced to focus especially on the genesis of the debates between the various schools of thought, to bring to light the assumptions on which they are based and the underlying conceptions of the world, in order to understand what has led to the prevailing, or the decay, of the different approaches.

Even in a view that simplistically considers heterodox 'everything which isn't neoclassical', it is necessary to bear in mind that heterodox theories represent something more than a reaction to orthodox theories. These 'heterodoxical' authors and schools of thought recall and elaborate on crucial themes, such as the scope and method of economics; the figure of man as a social individual, not exclusively and completely rational, in opposition to that of the *homo oeconomicus*; the complexity of the ever-evolving economic systems and the consequential skepticism towards a single determination of the market balance; the necessary interaction between microeconomic and macroeconomic perspectives; the interconnection between facts and values and the fallibility of theories (Salanti and Screpanti, 1997; Knoedler and Underwood, 2003; Roncaglia, 2006).

Above all, the heterodox approach explores the need for a paradigm shift and even the search for a new and different economic theory, more satisfactory and able to explain the anomalies of the previous one. This is, in fact, the essential step for a scientific revolution to take place.[2]

It is within this singular perspective that we can fully insert Pasinetti's reflections on social concerns, starting from his dissent on scientific and ethical grounds, to his critique of the dominant economic theory that claims to be positive and ends up being normative.

The aim of this chapter is to look at Pasinetti's work, as a distinctive member of the Cambridge Keynesian School, and consider if and how social concerns constitute a pillar of his scientific research. Primary

[2] As underlined by Mauro Baranzini and Amalia Mirante, in 'the volume *Keynes and the Cambridge Keynesians: A "Revolution in Economics" to Be Accomplished*, Pasinetti reassesses the content of the "Keynesian Revolution" after 70 years and considers the issue of 'Scientific Revolutions and Alternative Paradigms'. He quotes the epistemologist Thomas Kuhn (1970) for whom 'revolutions' in science are connected to 'discoveries' that are not compatible and cannot be accommodated within the preceding theories or scheme of analysis. In other words, such discoveries cannot be 'absorbed', or taken in, by existing paradigms' (Baranzini and Mirante, 2018, p. 11).

literature is therefore the main source of this chapter, because it allows to retrace this theme in the scientific production of the author. After having traced Pasinetti's link to the Keynesian school (Section 9.2), we will look at his critique of mainstream economics (Section 9.3) and how the discontinuity caused by the Industrial Revolution makes the adoption of a paradigm of pure production essential, thus showing how this paradigm is linked to the analysis of specific, crucial issues due to their inevitable influence on society, for example: the centrality of labour, the social function of capital and the role of the institutions (Section 9.4). We shall then suggest some thoughts on the connection between Pasinetti and the Italian tradition of economic thought, looking also at the ethical foundations of his thought process (Section 9.5).

9.2 From Keynes and beyond Keynes

Consider Keynes's 1925 essay 'Am I a Liberal?' In that interesting and provocative essay, Keynes says:

> We have to invent new wisdom for a new age. And in the meantime, we must, if we are to do any good, appear unorthodox, troublesome, dangerous, disobedient to them that begat us. In the economic field this means, first of all, that we must find new policies and new instruments to adapt and control the working of economic forces, so that they do not intolerably interfere with contemporary ideas as to what is fit and proper in the interests of social stability and social justice. (Keynes, 1925, p. 338)

This position is reinforced in *The End of Laissez-Faire* (Keynes, 1926), which Pasinetti quotes when he mentions social concerns as an important Keynesian heritage (Pasinetti, 2007, p. 234). In the volume, published before the Great Depression, Keynes senses that a major revolution is necessary in economics, but not in order to destroy market economies but to modify inappropriate market institutions.

Pasinetti is therefore right to consider this legacy as fundamental. Moreover, Pasinetti spent a significant portion of his scientific career in Cambridge, immersed in the Keynesian mood, and during those years he founded his research programme on the 'dynamics of the wealth of nations'.

This experience makes him the 'senior heir' of the post-Keynesian school of economic thought (see Harcourt, 2006; see also Baranzini and Mirante, 2018), not only because of his direct acquaintance with some members of the Cambridge School – his stay allowed him to get in close contact with Richard Kahn, Nicholas Kaldor, Joan Violet Robinson, Piero Sraffa – but especially for the scientific results he achieved. Some of his relevant contributions have since placed him amongst the most acute critics of the marginalist economic tradition.[3]

The fact that Pasinetti has carried out in-depth research on the fundamental dynamics of industrial societies is of great importance for the theme addressed here. Along the lines adopted after Keynes by Roy Harrod, Evsey Domar, Kahn, Robinson and Kaldor, he has investigated those movements of the economic system over time that are characterised by non-proportional growth and structural change due to non-uniformity in productivity changes and in the hierarchical structure of consumer needs between sectors (the so-called Engel's law).

This work has led him to research new analytical tools and also to suggest changes in the economic methodology itself, especially with reference to the separation of the basic relationships typical of industrial companies from the specific relationships of particular institutions. Thanks to his analysis, many empirical regularities and theoretical contributions seem to find a more natural and satisfactory theoretical explanation, difficult to understand in the field of marginalist theory, such as the distribution of technical progress, the non-linear variations in the composition of demand, the presence of a large number of asymmetrical behaviours and, above all, the complex role of the institutions (Blaug, 1985; see also Baranzini and Harcourt, 1993; Quadrio Curzio and Rotondi, 2004; Bortis, 2007, 2012; Quadrio Curzio and Baranzini, 2012).

The need for a theory that starts from Keynes and goes beyond Keynes is to be found in many of Pasinetti's writings distributed over sixty years of scientific production and often emerges as a reaction to

[3] Pasinetti was the protagonist of two important economic debates of the 1960s: the post-Keynesian assumption that the profit rate and income distribution depend on the capitalists' propensity to save and are independent of the workers' propensity to save (the so-called Pasinetti's theorem) and the debate on the theory of capital that originates from Paul Samuelson and David Levhari's challenge to Sraffa's analysis of reswitching techniques, as Pasinetti was the first to refute Samuelson and Levhari's non-switching theorem (See Quadrio Curzio and Rotondi, 2004; see also Quadrio Curzio and Baranzini, 2012).

the 'domestication' of the neoclassical synthesis that deprives Keynesian thought of any revolutionary impetus (Pasinetti, 1983, 2007): 'It is much better, in my opinion, to take Keynes for what he is without domestication and see how far he is useful to us, and to abandon him, where he is no longer useful (Pasinetti, 1979, p. 3, author's translation).

It is clear that in order to move the Keynesian revolution from the theoretical level to the practical stage, it is necessary to also consider what has remained outside the horizon of its theory – first of all, long-term problems – and thus extend the analytical framework. At the same time, it is necessary to take into account the many cues that were abandoned, or not completed, by the supporters of the theory.[4]

As Baranzini and Mirante, quoting Pasinetti, underline:

> the 'Keynesian Revolution', led by Keynes himself, Kahn and Robinson, had been able to 'create a break with the past' and to convert most of the leading economists and fellow politicians of the 1930s, 1940s and 1950s; but when the time was ripe for a continuation of the 'Keynesian Programme' to issues concerning the long run, the majority of economists did not follow. The 'Keynesian Programme' suffered a halt and its leading members found themselves besieged mainly in Cambridge, England. (Baranzini and Mirante, 2018, p. 5)

The difficulty, of having to go beyond the concerns and modes of intervention suggested by Keynes, emerges here. A contribution by Keynes and post-Keynesian theorists that can remain a valid point of reference is the methodological one that concerns the definition and clarification of the relationships that bind the whole of an economic system regardless of the behaviour of individuals. It is, for example, within this framework that the centrality of the principle of effective demand is highlighted:

> The basic point is that over-all effective demand links together the whole economic system, making of it a whole economic unit. All its parts are thereby revealed to be interdependent, quite separately from, and on the top of, any interdependence arising on the side of inter-industry relations. It is important to realize the source of this interdependence: namely

[4] Pasinetti himself believes that Keynesian theorists today do not oppose the traditional paradigm as much as they should, perhaps considering it too risky or even useless to undertake the Keynesian revolution (Pasinetti, 2007, p. 43). For the causticity of the arguments on this issue, see also King (2017).

specialization in production, on the one side, and extreme wideness of the range of consumption habits and possibilities, on the other side. And it is important to realize that this feature would make the whole economic system interdependent (demand-interdependent!) even if there were no interdependence – in the sense of inter-industry relations à la Wassily Leontief – on the side of technology. (Pasinetti, 1992, pp. 187–188)

From these considerations comes what, in Pasinetti's opinion, may be considered the ideal task of Keynesian economics, 'pertaining to the very nature of the basic task that Keynes and the whole Keynesian School were ideally supposed to carry out' (Pasinetti, 2007, p. 270).

The Marginalists, according to Pasinetti, have in a certain way brought to fruition, by giving it theoretical substance, the Mercantilist conception of wealth as a stock. In fact, Keynes and the Keynesians 'have ideally been called upon to erect a theoretical construction based on the (post–industrial revolution) concept of wealth conceived as a continuous *flow* of net input' (Pasinetti, 2007, p. 271).

Attention must therefore be focused on the nature and causes of the production process, on the laws underlying the distribution of the national output and on the factors that govern its evolution through time. A great effort in size and in scale has to be done to carry on the conception of a 'production paradigm', undoubtedly more complex than the conception of an 'exchange paradigm' (See Pasinetti, 2007, p. 271 ff.).

The production paradigm actually requires a dynamic framework and Pasinetti underlines that the production activity, while relying on individual initiative, is also a social process that cannot be abstracted from historical specificity with changes of the institutions that are wider than those typical of the era of trade.

From this perspective, 'the mere reference to the free market becomes insufficient, and even called into question' (Pasinetti, 2007, p. 272).

Pasinetti therefore seeks his own path so as not to betray the revolutionary perspective inherent in Keynesian thought and, as he himself reminds us, he does so very soon:

I realised, right from the 'model' that I presented to the *Pontificia Academia Scientiarum* in 1963 and then elaborated in my later works, that our world in motion, in its fundamental dimensions, is likely to be represented in a rather simple way by a logical scheme that expresses a 'natural', normatively founded evolution, that is – with a language that is not strictly scientific but significant – ethically correct. (Pasinetti, 2019, p. 160, author's translation)

Each of his subsequent approaches to economic analysis is an attempt to go in this direction.

9.3 The Needed Criticism of the Mainstream Models

Pasinetti repeatedly stresses in his writings the paradox of a theory completely separated from reality. He reconstructs the transition from classical to marginalist economics, characterising it as 'a quantum leap – not in conceptual terms but in analytical terms' (Pasinetti, 2019, p. 216, author's translation). Economics wanted to approach the physical sciences but 'at what price did this come about? That of crouching in a framework that conceptually belongs to the previous era and is therefore anachronistic; that is, in a limiting logical model, what in the following decades – through further elaborations, increasingly attractive analytically, but increasingly (sometimes frighteningly) restrictive in terms of interpretations of reality – has become the general economic equilibrium model' (Pasinetti, 2019, pp. 166–167).

The problem connected with the neoclassical paradigm is that it has removed a number of crucial issues from economic models – including effective demand, the centrality of work and the distribution of resources and incomes – thereby creating a gap between theory and its ability to explain real phenomena. This has become all the more critical given that the model has not been proposed as an idealised one but as an elegant mathematical model similar to those of the physical sciences, with the exception of the impossibility of submitting it to empirical tests (Pasinetti 1983, 1988, 2007, 2012 among others).

Pasinetti highlights what he sees as the greatest limitation of this approach, that of not being able

> to make any distinction between an ethically founded economic system and the construction of the social institutions that bring it into being. No distinction can be made because the two problems are intrinsically considered as being one; i.e. simultaneously a set of optimal relations (no matter the point of departure, to be accepted as given and not to be questioned) and the rational behaviour of agents, who are the only ones to be considered, encouraged and protected; this then translates into a single institution *par excellence* – the competitive free market – which is self-regulating and self-controlling and therefore (if the conditions of universal knowledge of the model, of independence of agents, of atomism of their conditions of competition, can be taken as an expression of reality) it is self-actualising, albeit

with ups and downs, and more boom and bust cycles, all considered as temporary, without any mention of those who suffer because of them. (Pasinetti, 2019, p. 165, author's translation)

Therefore, the soundness of the model is important for academic and normative purposes, which determine the adoption of the institutional structure connected to it: market capitalism (Pasinetti, 2012, p. 106, author's translation).

The paradox, which Pasinetti recently goes so far as to define as the 'foolishness' (Pasinetti, 2019, p. 164) of the logical scheme, emerges in his opinion with incredible clarity in connection with the current crisis, which is first financial and then real – while the ineffectiveness of this theoretical approach has been abundantly demonstrated, its full and complete reaffirmation is still considered desirable. Moreover, this theoretical scheme had already been able to survive the economic crisis of the Great Depression.

With respect to this situation, Pasinetti emphatically stresses what many economists are thinking: it is not the only conceivable theoretical paradigm. The pure exchange model remains a theory, and 'a theory must not be confused with reality' (Pasinetti, 1992, p. 181).

In particular, it makes no sense to reduce economic problems to the matter of an efficient allocation of the given resources, because this does not, in any way, allow us to grasp the peculiarities of post-industrial societies.

9.4 The Industrial Revolution and Globalisation: Technical Progress as a 'Prime Mover'

In Pasinetti's interesting work (Pasinetti, 1965), he had the opportunity to stress the dynamic nature of the concept of industry, underlying that in this context:

> The economist is faced ... no longer with a problem of rationality, but with a process of learning .... The process of learning associated with industry ... means a persistent movement, not a once-for-all change, but a rate of change in time – a movement which is cumulative and irreversible. In this sense, industry comes to realise most properly the concept of progress which is inherent in modern society. (Pasinetti, 1965, p. 575)

The 'production paradigm', which became relevant with the Industrial Revolution, plays a crucial role in Pasinetti's theoretical framework; it is one of the most important relations upon which to rethink economic theory, that is, from the perspective of pure production.

Capital affirms itself as a productive factor whose accumulation marks, together with technical progress and population growth, the transition to a different type of society. After the attention dedicated to the growth of the population and to capital accumulation, economists 'began to pay serious attention to technical progress' that 'owing to its cumulative effects … is emerging more and more as a real crucial "prime mover" of industrial societies' (Pasinetti, 1992, pp. 175–176).

Technical progress requires a change of scenario, as it makes the efficient positions of the economic system change continuously.

To these considerations, Pasinetti binds the need to move from a pure exchange model of general equilibrium model that 'presupposes a society of individuals who are endowed with externally given resources and have well defined fields of preferences' (Pasinetti, 1992, p. 179), to a pure production model 'which has a series of properties that are by far more suitable to grasp the basic features, to interpret the implications, and to lead us to analyse the characteristics of the economic systems that have emerged from the industrial revolution' (Pasinetti, 1992, p. 182).

The main novelty of the pure production model is that while not excluding the idea that perfectly competitive markets might be appropriate, it considers them just as one possibility among many others. At the same time, it leads to the possibility of conceiving the most appropriate institutions for the efficiency of the economic system (Pasinetti, 1992).

If there are negative consequences, for example, in an industrial society, due to its evolution,

> the community as a whole cannot escape the responsibility of taking charge of these negative consequences …. It is quite clear that some institutional mechanism will have to be devised to try to avoid them in the first place, and to alleviate their most painful effects when it has become impossible to avoid them. The same may be said also with reference to technological unemployment. The relevant point that emerges from all this, is that these logical implications concerning social responsibility of the community taken as a whole do not follow from any humanitarian reasons. They follow from the more fundamental requirement of preserving efficiency, of which full employment is one of the most important aspects in the economic system as a whole. (Pasinetti, 1992, p. 189)

The most relevant aspect of Pasinetti's revolutionary approach is that a shift in economic methodology seems to be necessary. The model of pure production, in his conception, 'is indeed open to contributions from outside, and actually requires such contributions, with reference to the fields of economic analysis and economic policy that concern the actual construction of our institutions' (Pasinetti, 1992, p. 192).

It is evident that reducing the economic problem merely to the efficient allocation of the given resources is not enough to fully understand the specific nature of post–Industrial Revolution societies, in which many concrete events have prompted the rethinking of issues such as the precarious conditions of workers, periodic crises, unemployment, inequalities and poverty (Pasinetti, 1988, 2010, 2012).

Among the themes that emerge in connection to the post–Industrial Revolution structure and that elicit social concerns, Pasinetti pays particular attention to labour and employment; physical capital and institutions.

9.4.1 The Centrality of Labour and Employment

The centrality of work and employment is a theme that Pasinetti firmly links to the Smithian conception of the organisation of an industrial society as expressed in the *Inquiry into the Nature and Causes of the Wealth of Nations* (1776). In classical economy, labour remains a key category, from Adam Smith to David Ricardo – who do not stress the rebalancing virtues of the *invisible hand* but emphasise the support given to work by the active bourgeoisie over passive landowners – to the Ricardian socialists who highlight the rights of salaried workers. However, it loses its central role with the assertion of individual behaviour, relating it to the efficiency of the economic system as a whole. It is Keynes who brings the themes of classical economy back to the core of economic analysis and proposes full employment as an explicit economic policy objective in relation to the 1929 economic crisis. The full employment of the productive factor labour, as is well known, is pursued with active government intervention through public expenditure or, in exceptional cases, with budget deficits.

Reference to technical progress as a key variable in the post–Industrial Revolution economic system brings a new dimension to the theme of unemployment. In this new scenario, alongside unemployment, due to the lack of physical capital, new forms emerge: the so called classical unemployment (pre-capitalistic to a certain degree), involuntary unemployment and technological unemployment.[5]

If the first – so-called Keynesian unemployment – is associated with the deep economic depression of the 1930s, that lasted until the beginning of WWII, technological unemployment – Pasinetti prefers the term 'structural unemployment' – is the result of the dynamics intrinsic to industrial societies.

In Pasinetti's words: 'Technological unemployment arises because of the dynamic interaction between technical change and the structural evolution of demand. Both phenomena have been neglected by mainstream economic theory, which has remained intrinsically unable to incorporate them' (Pasinetti, 1992, p. 187).

Within the pure production model, on the other hand, the theme of labour and employment finds a place as

> labour is not a commodity but the basic factor of production, and the wage rate is not only the price of labour but also the personal income of workers. A fall in wages causes a decrease in costs in the production branches (and thus stimulates production), but it also causes a fall in effective demand in the economic system as a whole (and thus depresses production). There is no certainty that the second (negative) effect will be compensated by the first (positive) effect. This is in fact the well-known criticism that Keynes moved to 'classical' theory. Keynes' arguments simply emerge here as moving within the pure production model. (Pasinetti, 1992, p. 186)[6]

However, Pasinetti goes beyond Keynes by arguing that '[a]n economic system, at a given point of time, is said to be in a 'satisfactory' situation when the existing labour force is fully employed and the existing capital goods are neither too abundant to remain idle nor too scarce to be insufficient to provide jobs for all the existing labour force' (Pasinetti, 1987, p. 994).

[5] 'The unceasing pace of technical progress makes the efficient positions of the economic system change as time goes on. In particular, what is an efficient structure of employment at a specific point of time will in general no longer be an efficient structure of employment in the following period of time' (Pasinetti, 1992, p. 188).

[6] According to Pasinetti, an economic system 'is said to be moving "satisfactorily" through time when its dynamic movements maintain through time the full employment of the labour force and the full utilization of the productive capacity' (Pasinetti, 1987, p. 994).

We may link this proposition even with the peculiar social awareness and empathy which derives from his cultural (and family) background. In various works (Pasinetti, 1992, 2010, 2012, 2019), he quotes the Encyclical Letter *Rerum Novarum* (1891), where Pope Leo XIII deals with the 'workers' question', then called the 'social question'. In this document, it is clearly stated that all members of society have the duty to take part in the reflection on social problems brought about by industrialisation and contribute to their solution with a keen sense of responsibility and act on the basis of the principle of solidarity. We will return to this topic in Section 9.4.2.

9.4.2 *The Social Role of Physical Capital*

With regard to the theme of social concerns, it seems appropriate, and very interesting, to mention Pasinetti's reflection on physical capital as a productive factor with a social function. It is a 'courageous' feature that distinguishes his analysis from that of many other economists and it is, in my opinion, an approach that projects him beyond Classical and Keynesian economics. As he himself maintains, economic science had all the elements to recognise that the new factor of production – Capital – had a social function to perform and that the rate of profit associated with it could have the task of providing for economic growth.

> But it did not. Perhaps it had not yet succeeded in developing sufficiently robust analytical tools to address and develop the theoretical paradigm appropriate to the new (industrial) world that was emerging. And it was afraid (in the face of Karl Marx's attacks). Perhaps here lies much of the explanation of the conflicts that have arisen from it, and that we are experiencing. (Pasinetti, 2019, p. 166, author's translation)

In his 2007 volume, Pasinetti highlights the social function of physical capital: 'The capital goods *must* be kept in existence, they *must* be used for the whole period of production, otherwise the whole production process halts! … the existence and then the accumulation of physical capital is an absolute necessity in the production process of the industrialised economies' (Pasinetti, 2007, p. 343). For this reason, 'physical capital goods, unlike consumption goods, perform a function which is *relevant for society as a whole*. They procure jobs for the labourers. We may well say that they fulfill a *social* function' (Pasinetti, 2007, p. 343).

These statements are, of course, connected to the theme of the ownership of the means of production, which is radicalised in the debates between Ricardian, Socialists and Marxists, on one side, and anti-statists, on the other.

Once again, for Pasinetti, it is useless to look for a Third way. The only exit strategy is to change the point of view which considers that, the special social status of capital goods ... raise[s] the problem of how to exercise the rights of property on a factor of production, which is revealed to have a *social function* to fulfill' (Pasinetti, 2007, p. 344).

9.4.3 Institutions in a Framework of Continuous Change

Perhaps the most important question that arises after the discontinuity produced by the Industrial Revolution concerns the role of the institutions and more precisely their necessary continuous evolution.

In this area, more than in any other, it is necessary to go beyond Keynes in view of the fact that the institutional framework has changed a great deal and it has also shown characteristics in contrast with those of the years in which Keynes wrote (Pasinetti, 1983, p. 38). It is therefore necessary to consider a continuous setting-up, as well as a continuous adaptation of economic, juridical and social institutions.

More than that, the responsible construction of this set of institutions 'is the really great challenge that the industrial revolution has brought to modern societies' (Pasinetti, 2007, p. 308).[7]

How can political economy respond to this challenge?

When Pasinetti speaks of separate institutions, he points out that there is a need to separate those relations that are fundamental to what he has called the framework of the Natural Economic System and those relations that refer to temporary events or circumstances in history. The former relations are permanent, the latter may change with time.[8] Pasinetti's natural economic system is definitely *not* aimed

[7] It is hardly worth remembering that the institutional set-up is fundamental for the working of the markets in order to preserve property rights, to promote human dignity and to ensure the provision of public goods and services (Baranzini and Quadrio Curzio, 2012).

[8] As Roberto Scazzieri states: 'The concept of "natural economic system" has clear classical roots, which Pasinetti himself identifies with long-period analysis and the possibility to detect, by means of it, a set of fundamental (relatively persistent) features of the economic systems (what classical economists such as Smith and Ricardo used to call "natural" features). In spite of this classical influence (which

at endogenising institutions, even if 'it has the power to give indications for institutional blueprints. It has the power to clarify the aims pursued by the institutions and in so doing to set the priorities in institutions building' (Pasinetti, 2007, p. 325).

This distinction allows to separate

> those economic problems that have to be solved on the ground of logic alone – for which economic theory is entirely autonomous – and those economic issues that 'arise in connection with particular institutions, or with particular groups' or individuals' behaviour – for which economic theory is no longer autonomous and needs to be integrated with further hypotheses, which may well come from other social sciences. (Pasinetti, 1981, p. xiii)

In this way, we have two different levels of investigation: 'natural' and 'historical'.

Pasinetti introduces a 'Separation Theorem', showing how certain fundamental properties of the economic system may be taken as given across a range of different institutional set-ups (Scazzieri, 2011, p. 228). This tool precisely useful to separate the investigation of the characteristics at the foundation of the production economies – his Natural Economic System – from the investigation of the necessary institutions needed to deal with the specific problems raised by the 'challenge of history' (Pasinetti, 2007, pp. 322–323).[9]

Unlike 'natural' configurations, independent from historical time, those of the institutions are constantly changing. 'Any society must face its "institutional problem". It must face the social responsibility of constructing its institutions, adapting and modifying them as times goes on, perfecting them and (now and when it becomes necessary)

is explicitly acknowledged), Pasinetti considerably extends and modifies the original classical conceptions. In particular, Pasinetti's view of dynamic analysis derives from an original blending of the methods of dynamic analysis followed by François Quesnay and Smith and is remarkably distant from the method adopted by Ricardo. Above all, Pasinetti's analysis in *Structural Change and Economic Growth* concentrates upon properties that are independent of any particular institutional set-up. In his view, such properties have the remarkable characteristic of being of a fundamental nature (they are considered to be common to all economic systems that have moved beyond the early stages of division of labour and productive specialization) and of remaining disguised when the economist focuses upon existing institutions and behavioural principles' (Scazzieri, 2011, pp. 221–222).

[9] Income distribution is a field in which the distinction between natural properties and institutional constraints is most clear (see Scazzieri, 1983).

even discarding some of them, while inventing new ones' (Pasinetti, 2007, p. 306). And in suggesting ways to solve institutional problems, economic analysis can no longer claim exclusiveness. History, culture, legal system, religion, politics, geography ... contribute to shaping through time 'the social framework and thus the social institutions of the economic system' (Pasinetti, 2007, p. 308).

Within this framework, Pasinetti considers even 'the necessity of protecting the whole natural environment in which we live, entailing a global protection from the excesses and distortions imposed by population, technology and irrationality, on a worldwide scale' (Pasinetti, 2007, p. 312).

9.5 A Specific Sensitivity for Social Concerns

If it is fundamental, as I did at the beginning of this chapter, to highlight the ties between Pasinetti and the Cambridge Keynesians, we must not, however, overlook what links him to the Italian tradition of economic thought, to his alma mater, where he began his studies and later spent most of his academic life, and to his cultural roots. In this concluding section, we will focus precisely on the connection between these elements and the attention given by Pasinetti to social concerns.

9.5.1 His Italian Background

Pasinetti's dynamic theory, with its inclusion of historical-analytical components, appears to be perfectly consistent with some features of the Italian economic tradition, in particular with the importance given to the nexus between theory and strategies, the interest in economic dynamics, the emphasis on the institutional side of a theory and the link between economics and ethics (Bellanca, 2000; Quadrio Curzio and Rotondi, 2004; Faucci, 2014; Porta, 2015).

It is well known that Classical economic analysis provides the foundation of Pasinetti's theoretical framework and that his reasoning always takes into account the necessary integration of analysis and history. In his view, history of economic thought and economic history do not serve the mere purpose of providing retrospective vision; on the contrary, they enhance the constructive theoretical work of frontier analysis. As Pierluigi Porta well underlined, 'a notion of what the frontier of current analysis actually is, in Pasinetti's conception, can only be acquired through the awareness and fully-fledged openness to the historical-analytical background' (Porta, 2015, p. 310).

It has been said that the approach adopted by Pasinetti, 'embodies the essence of what has been called "civil economy" in the Italian tradition' (Porta 2015, p. 310).[10]

Paying attention to social concerns, which is clearly linked to this vision, seems to have been on Pasinetti's mind since the very beginning of his academic career. In recalling his contacts with Siro Lombardini,[11] he states: 'I was taking my first steps in my university studies and I was devoting my efforts on the one side to mathematics (I remember Professor Masotti's lectures, which had fascinated me), and on the other side, to lectures on topics of social relevance' (Pasinetti, 2014, p. 97, author's translation). In May 1959, he wrote a letter to Francesco Vito[12] – his mentor at the Catholic University – in which he said that the theoretical scheme he was working on 'places man at the beginning and at the end of all productive activity, which emerges clearly and simply as a tool for achieving human ends. It is not an easy task to express these relationships analytically and rigorously, but I already hope for satisfactory results even in purely analytical

[10] On this subject, see also Quadrio Curzio (2007); Quadrio Curzio, Rotondi and Talamona (2007).

[11] Siro Lombardini (1924–2013) studied economics at the Catholic University of Milan where he graduated in 1946. He later spent one academic year at the London School of Economics. From 1947, he was personal assistant to Professor Francesco Vito, and then, after two years abroad, in 1951 he was appointed Lecturer in political economy at the Faculty of Economics and Commerce of the Catholic University of Milan. In 1956, he was appointed full professor at the University of Bari, in Southern Italy; and one year later, in 1957, he was back at his alma mater in Milan. In 1963, he moved to the University of Turin but was back again at the Catholic University in 1983. During his last years of teaching, he moved back to the University of Turin. Pasinetti can be found on YouTube honouring his master, Lombardini, at the Academy of Sciences of Turin on 24 March 2014, edited by Elena Borgi. See also Pasinetti (2014).

[12] Francesco Vito (1902–1968), obtained three degrees from the University of Naples, in Law (1925), Economic, Political and Social Sciences (1926) and Philosophy (1928). He then continued his economic studies in Germany (University of Munich and Berlin, 1929–1930) and in the United States at Columbia University, New York and University of Chicago. In 1935, he was appointed to a chair in political economics at the Catholic University of Milan, where he headed the Economic Sciences Institute during the years of the Reconstruction and until his death.

terms'.[13] So, while it is true that 'through Kahn [Pasinetti came] in contact with that unique mixture of radicalism, wisdom and social concern that was the distinct mark of Keynes's environment' (Pasinetti, 1981, p. xiv), we may dare not say that his awareness of social issues was already rooted in him before he arrived to Cambridge.

From the founding of the Catholic University – ever since its conception by Giuseppe Toniolo – economic studies focused on economic and *social* inequalities, on the relationship between economics and ethics, on market failures, on the problems of unemployment and a strong critique of a form of capitalism that disregarded the needs of society (Rotondi, 1998).

Thus, when looking at Pasinetti's research programme from his Cambridge years, the peculiar combination of first-rate analytical rigour with a strong historical sense and his deep interest in social concerns, it is crucial to take his Italian background into account.

9.5.2 The Importance of Goals in Economic Activity

A further and significant step in understanding Pasinetti's strong commitment to social concerns is the importance attributed to the aims of economic research.

I think that we should recall here the fundamental essay by John Neville Keynes (1891) where he discusses the scope and method of political economy.[14] We may find the heart of his reasoning encapsulated in this quotation:

> It may be pointed out how enormous is the influence exerted upon the well-being of mankind by the modes in which wealth is produced and distributed; and stress may be laid upon the fact that those human activities, which constitute the subject-matter of the economist's investigations, have an ethical significance, which is at least as worthy of consideration as their economic significance. (Keynes, 1891, p. 46)

[13] Archivio Storico UCSC, Carte personali Francesco Vito, 9.1, Pasinetti's Letter to Francesco Vito, Oxford, 22 May 1959.

[14] 'Neville Keynes split the scope of political economy into three major methodological categories, namely: (1) a positive body of deductive knowledge about the general laws of economic action, or what *is*; (2) a normative or regulative science, dealing with the criteria of ideal conditions or what *ought* to be and (3) economics as an art, or the assessment of specific means to achieve pre-established ends' (Arthmar and McLure, 2017, p. 59).

Neville Keynes's views had an undoubted influence first of all on Arthur Cecil Pigou but more generally on the Cambridge environment which lead to considering economic theory as more valuable for the fruit that it generates than the light it sheds (Pigou, 1932, p. 3).[15] Within this conception, political, social and ethical concerns play an important role, together with economic principles, to evaluate the effectiveness of strategies.

John Maynard Keynes's work, in this perspective, appears to be remarkable when considering its application to public policy:

> Keynes's nexus between public expenditure, the multiplier, effective demand, and the full employment level of output had direct short-period relevance to welfare-enhancing policy in terms of Pigou's first criterion (increase in the national dividend) and third criterion (decrease in the variability of the national dividend) for economic welfare enhancement. But Keynes's work had relevance for Pigou's second (reduction in income inequality) criterion too, as, in the last chapter of *The General Theory*, Keynes referred to the unfair distribution of wealth and income as one of the outstanding faults of modern societies. (Arthmar and McLure, 2017, pp. 64–65)

It is not difficult to highlight the link between Pasinetti's theories and this second criterion. But that is not the reason why the quote is interesting. Rather, it is worth pointing out that on this author and on the tradition of English thought, which sees in economics a science that must give light but also fruit, Francesco Vito has dwelt on them several times. Vito accepts and adopts the fundamental analytical tools of the dominant economic theory, in particular in its Marshallian version. Nevertheless, he opposes the general view that underpinned it, both from an analytical point of view and from an epistemological one. Fundamental to his works is his criticism of the notion that economic theory is neutral and its consequent reconsideration of the goals of economic activity. He advocates state intervention for reasons of both efficiency and social justice, and it is this principle that he applied in his assessment of Keynes's theories (Parisi and Rotondi, 1999). In 1936, Vito is one of the first Italian economists to review the *General Theory* (Vito, 1936), but far from finding in this book a real novelty, he seems concerned to highlight only those aspects that he considers most significant and valuable in Keynes's personality and

[15] Neville Keynes in his essay refers to Francis Bacon's dichotomy between fruit and light (Keynes, 1891, p. 51).

work. In 1946, while commemorating Keynes's death, he writes: 'Those currents of study that from economic science want to derive not only light but also results in welfare ... were carried forward by Keynes in his teaching at Cambridge. It is a trend that must be defended, cultivated and developed, since man can only progress if economics pursues ethical goals in social life' (Vito, 1946, p. 136).

We cannot but consider this point as relevant to the group of economists of the Catholic University of Milan, headed by Francesco Vito, to whom Pasinetti was affiliated through his thesis supervisor and mentor Lombardini.

After all, it is Pasinetti himself who helps us trace this bond. In his 2003 essay, he suggests looking at his own theoretical elaborations 'in light of the objectives that Vito was so fond of' (Pasinetti, 2003, p. 230, author's translation). In order to go beyond the critique of the political economists of his time, developed by Vito, and also to explore its constructive contribution, Pasinetti wonders 'whether – and within what limits – it is possible to establish an interweaving between those ends and the foundations of the theoretical investigations that I have had occasion to develop on several occasions, and which in their latest version I have called *structural economic dynamics*' (Pasinetti, 2003, p. 230, author's translation).

In this attempt, Pasinetti recognises that while the proposal for a fully defined and structured theoretical model cannot be identified in Vito's vision, the elements of 'a pre-analytical proposal, in which the principles and aims on which to base the study of economics are stated, and the implications for economic policy are outlined are, from a constructive point of view, clearly identifiable' (Pasinetti 2003, p. 235, author's translation).[16]

Re-examining some of his theoretical positions, such as those on unemployment in the structural dynamics model, Pasinetti provides a fine-tuning of Vito's results – although not in the initial approach – in particular with reference to the unnecessary opposition between the principle of solidarity and the principle of efficiency. By re-proposing

[16] 'Vito proposes precise goals for economic science. However, given the interdependence between means and ends, this also requires an adaptation of the methodological principles that underpin economic science. The problem that remains unresolved in Vito's work, as he himself acknowledges, is how to fully translate these aims and methodological principles into a coherent economic theory' (Pasinetti, 2003, p. 237, author's translation).

some terms, typical of Vito's phraseology, Pasinetti states that 'by placing at the centre of economic theory, the learning and transformation capacity of the human person, the theory of structural dynamics seems better equipped, than other theories, to accept suggestions for building "an economy at man's service"' (Pasinetti 2003, p. 247, author's translation; Quadrio Curzio and Rotondi, 2004).

9.5.3 *Facing the Distorted Phenomenon of Globalisation*

In this framework that explores the link between Pasinetti and social concerns, it is useful to add another element that his scientific production helps us identify. From 1963 to 2019, his bibliography reveals subtended and at times explicit references to the Social Doctrine of the Catholic Church with which he is confronted and of which he poses the following question: 'if the Church, in her claim to be "expert of humanity", gives advices on the moral principles to be put behind the criteria for a responsible construction of our institutions, can economists object? The main point of this paper is that they would be not merely very unwise; they would be entirely unjustified, if they did' (Pasinetti, 1992, p. 192).

Economists should ask many questions in relation to the distorted phenomena that globalisation has created and exacerbated, such as the unequal distribution of wealth and income and the related inequalities between and within countries, poverty, illiteracy and environmental deterioration (Pasinetti, 2019). The globalised economy shows contradictions that capitalism, in its various forms, cannot alleviate.

The Magisterium of the Church intervenes precisely because conditions are created which are harmful to the dignity of the human person. Although the Social Doctrine does not explicitly mention what separates it from the economic mainstream, Pasinetti makes an interesting analysis and enucleates ten

> concepts and principles of the social doctrine of the Church that are not shared or are in contrast with the dominant economic theory: 1. universal destination of goods; 2. preferential option for the poor; 3. scandal of sensational inequalities; 4. priority of labour over capital; 5. social function of capital; 6. means of production: never against labour; 7. principle of solidarity; 8. principle of subsidiarity; 9. principle of the common good; 10. essentiality of free gift (without coercion and without humiliation). (Pasinetti, 2012, p. 123, author's translation)

On this last principle, Pasinetti develops a reflection that conciliates well with others he expounded in his scientific production. This principle, in fact, is in contrast with the principle, so central in economics, of individual profit (Pasinetti, 2012).

Faced with such an evident contrast, the only way to recompose it is to entrust it to dialogue, a dialogue that is not only essential but also dutiful in order to fill a gap which, in Pasinetti's words 'could even become a scandal, if it does not show signs of convergence towards recompositing, but on the contrary, continues to deepen, as is now happening' (Pasinetti, 2012, p. 113, author's translation).

Pasinetti identifies the major limit of the dominant economic theory in this lack of willingness to dialogue: 'in practice a rigid cage has been built within which all economic relations are ideally forced (no matter how far they may be from reality). In addition – and this is the really serious aspect – penalizing all the researches, which do not foresee this analytical adjustment, as "non-scientific" and therefore not to be considered' (Pasinetti, 2012, p. 119).

Since 1891 – the same year in which Neville Keynes's essay was published – and constantly since then, the Social Doctrine of the Church has called for more attention to be paid to the transformations taking place in society, to the needs connected with globalisation and to the principle of the universal destination of goods, which is still so far from being achieved.[17]

9.6 A Common Ground

Many urgent questions emerge from the consideration of the ethical element connected to economic science that somehow imposes its inclusion of social concerns. Some of these regard the legitimacy of considering certain principles as an integral part of the heritage of a theoretical economist.[18]

[17] 'The universal destination of goods' – Pasinetti points out – 'is sadly emerging as the most conspicuous, failure to achieve globalised economic activity' (Pasinetti, 2019, p. 167, our translation).

[18] Pasinetti takes the case of the 'principle of solidarity': can it be regarded 'as something that legitimately integrates or completes economic theory elaborations or does it appear as a sort of unjustified " interference" or "intrusion" of alien principles into the autonomous realm of economic analysis?' (Pasinetti, 1992, p. 179).

The fear of relativism often leads economists to avoid considering value judgements and induces them to exclude from their research programmes topics such as social concerns (Ramazzotti, 2013).

Yet, the awareness that there are questions that are required to widen the breadth of economic science (den Haan et al., 2017), which clearly emerges from the blend of stimuli with which the Italian and Cambridge backgrounds endowed Pasinetti, allow him to avoid this trap.

Consider Keynes in his own words: 'the outstanding faults of the economic society in which we live are its failure to provide for full employment and its arbitrary and inequitable distribution of income and wealth' (Keynes, 1936 [1973], p. 373).

Compare this with Pasinetti in his own words: 'But isn't one of the most recent scientific discoveries the confirmation of the singularity of the human genome? And therefore, the confirmation of the lack of any justification to the numerous, and always enlarged, discriminations and inequalities?' (Pasinetti, 2019, p. 158, author's translation). 'What else can one do if not invoking, and very strongly searching for, an "alternative economic paradigm"?' (Pasinetti, 2007, p. 236).

Keynes, atheist and anticlerical, and Pasinetti, a believer and progressive, seem to find, in this conviction, common ground for building an economic theory. After all, Pasinetti has been labelled a 'Tool-Maker' rather than a 'Tool-User'.

References

Arthmar R. and McLure M. (2017) 'Cambridge Theories of Welfare Economics', in Cord R. A. (ed.) *The Palgrave Companion to Cambridge Economics*, London and New York, Palgrave Macmillan, pp. 51–71.

Baranzini M. and Harcourt G. C. (eds.) (1993) *The Dynamics of the Wealth of Nations: Growth, Distribution and Structural Change: Essays in Honour of Luigi Pasinetti*, Basingstoke, Macmillan and New York, St. Martin's Press.

Baranzini M. and Harcourt G. C. (1993) 'Introduction' in Baranzini M. and Harcourt G. C. (eds.) *The Dynamics of the Wealth of Nations: Growth, Distribution and Structural Change: Essays in Honour of Luigi Pasinetti*, Basingstoke, Macmillan and New York, St. Martin's Press, pp. 1–42.

Baranzini M. and Mirante A. (2016) *A Compendium of Italian Economists at Oxbridge: Contributions to the Evolution of Economic Thinking*, London and New York, Palgrave Macmillan

(2018) *Luigi L. Pasinetti: An Intellectual Biography*, Palgrave Studies in the History of Economic Thought, London and New York, Palgrave Macmillan.

Baranzini M. and Quadrio Curzio A. (2012) 'From Adam Smith to Structural Dynamics: Luigi Pasinetti's Life-Long Contribution', paper presented at the Conference in honour of Luigi L. Pasinetti 'The Economics of Structural Change: Theory, Institutions and Policies', Cambridge, Gonville and Caius College.

Baranzini M. Rotondi C. and Scazzieri R. (eds.) (2015) *Resources, Production and Structural Dynamics*, Cambridge, Cambridge University Press.

Bellanca N. (2000) *Dinamica economica e istituzioni. Aspetti dell'economia politica italiana tra Ottocento e Novecento*, Milano, Franco Angeli.

Blaug M. (1985) *Great Economists since Keynes: An Introduction to the Lives and Works of One Hundred Modern Economists*, Brighton, Wheatsheaf.

Bortis H. (1997) *Institutions, Behaviour and Economic Theory: A Contribution to Classical-Keynesian Political Economy*, Cambridge, Cambridge University Press.

(2012) 'Toward a Synthesis in Post-Keynesian Economics in Luigi Pasinetti's Contribution', in Arena R. and Porta P. L. (eds.) *Structural Dynamics and Economic Growth*, Cambridge, Cambridge University Press, pp. 145–180.

den Haan W. Ellison M. Ilzetzki E. McMahon M. and Reis R. (2017) 'Happiness and Wellbeing as Objectives of Macroeconomic Policy: Views of Economists', in *The CAGE Background Briefing Series*, 73, pp. 1–10.

Faucci R. (2014) *A History of Italian Economic Thought*, London and New York, Routledge.

Harcourt G. C. (2006) *The Structure of the Post-Keynesian Economics: The Core Contributions of the Pioneers*, Cambridge, Cambridge University Press.

Harcourt G. C. and Kriesler P. (2013) (eds.) *Oxford Handbook of Post-Keynesian Economics*, vol. II, Oxford, Oxford University Press.

Hodgson G. M. (2001) *How Economics Forgot History: The Problem of Specificity in Social Science*, London, Routledge.

Keynes J. M. (1891 [1897]) *The Scope and Method of Political Economy*, 2nd ed., London, Macmillan.

(1925 [1963]) 'Am I a Liberal?', in *Essays in Persuasion*, New York, W. W. Norton, pp. 312–322.

Keynes J. M. (1936) [1973]) 'The General Theory of Employment, Interest and Money', in Moggridge D. (ed.) *The Collected Writings of John Maynard Keynes*, vol. VII, London, Macmillan, pp. xiv–653.

Kerr P. and Scazzieri R. (2013) 'Structural Economics Dynamics and the Cambridge Tradition', in Harcourt G. C. and Kriesler P. (eds.) *The Oxford Handbook of Post-Keynesian Economics*, vol. I: *Theory and Origins, Oxford*, Oxford, Oxford University Press, pp. 257–287.

King J. E. (2017) 'Post Keynesian Economics in Cambridge', in Cord R. A. (ed.) *The Palgrave Companion to Cambridge Economics*, London and New York, Palgrave Macmillan, pp. 135–155.

Knoedler J. and Underwood D. (2003) 'Teaching the Principles of Economics: A Proposal for a Multiparadigmatic Approach', in *Journal of Economic Issues*, 37(3), pp. 697–725.

Myrdal K. G. (1958 [1998]) *Value in Social Theory*, London, Routledge.

Parisi D. and Rotondi C. (1999) 'Keynesian Elements in a Long-term Analysis: The Views of Two Influential Pre-and Postwar Economists', in Pasinetti L. L. and Schefold B. (eds.) *The Impact of Keynes on Economics in the 20th Century*, Cheltenham, E. Elgar, pp. 153–159.

Pasinetti L. L. (1965) 'A New Theoretical Approach to the Problems of Economic Growth', Proceedings of the Semaine d'etude sur le role de l'analyse econometrique dans la formulation de plan de developpement (7–13 October 1963), Vatican City, Pontificia Accademia Scientiarum Scripta Varia, 28, Part II, pp. 1–126.

(1974) *Growth and Income Distribution: Essays in Economic Theory*, Cambridge, Cambridge University Press.

(1979) 'La teoria di Keynes ed i problemi del nostro tempo', in *Annali della Facoltà di Economia e commercio*, A.Y. 1977–1978, Università degli studi di Perugia, 5, Tip. Porziuncola, Assisi, pp. 87–114.

(1981) *Structural Change and Economic Growth: A Theoretical Essay on the Dynamics of the Wealth of Nations*, Cambridge, Cambridge University Press.

(1983) 'Il principio della domanda effettiva di J. M. Keynes', in *Piemonte vivo, Rivista della Cassa di risparmio di Torino*, pp. 31–38.

(1987) '"Satisfactory" versus Optimal Economic Growth', in *Rivista Internazionale di Scienze Economiche e Commerciali*, 34, pp. 989–1000.

(1988) 'La centralità del lavoro nei sistemi economici industriali', in *Una repubblica fondata sul lavoro, Convegno di studio dell'Associazione Città dell'uomo: L'Italia repubblica democratica fondata sul Lavoro (Milan, 12–13 December 1986)*, Rome, Editrice AVE, pp. 79–95.

(1992) 'Unemployment and the "Principle of Solidarity"', in Quadrio Curzio A. (ed.) *Issues on International Development and Solidarity*,

Proceedings of the study week Science for Development in a Solidarity Framework, Vatican City, Pontificia Accademia Scientiarum, Scripta Varia, 82, pp. 175–193.

(1993) *Structural Economic Dynamics: A Theory of the Economic Consequences of Human Learning*, Cambridge, Cambridge University Press.

(2001) 'The Principle of Effective Demand and Its Relevance in the Long Run', in *Journal of Post Keynesian Economics*, 23, pp. 383–390.

(2003), 'Una teoria per un'economia a servizio dell'uomo', in Parisi D. and Rotondi C. (eds.), *Francesco Vito. Attualità di un economista politico*, Milan, Vita e Pensiero, pp. 229–252.

(2007) *Keynes and the Cambridge Keynesians: A 'Revolution in Economics' to Be Accomplished*, Cambridge, Cambridge University Press.

(2012) *Dottrina sociale della Chiesa e teoria economica*, Milan, Vita e Pensiero.

(2014) 'Ricordo di Siro Lombardini (1924–2013)', in *Annali della Fondazione Luigi Einaudi*, 48, pp. 97–101.

(2019) 'Una rivoluzione in economia da portare a compimento', in Totaro F. (ed.) *Filosofia ed Economia*, Gallarate, Brescia and Morcelliana, Fondazione Centro studi filosofici di, pp. 157–167.

Pigou, A. C. (1932) *The Economics of Welfare*, 4th ed., London, Macmillan.

Porta P. L. (1998) '"Structural Analysis in Retrospect", in A Note on Luigi Pasinetti's Structural Economic Dynamics', in *Storia del pensiero economico*, 35, pp. 43–60.

(2015) 'Conquering Scarcity: Institutions, Learning and Creativity in the History of Economic Ideas', in Baranzini M. Rotondi C. and Scazzieri R. (eds.) *Resources, Production and Structural Dynamics*, Cambridge, Cambridge University Press, pp. 299–319.

Porta P. L. and Scazzieri R. (2008) 'A Revolution to Be Accomplished: Keynes and the Cambridge Keynesians', in *Economia politica. Journal of Analytical and Institutional Economics*, 3, pp. 455–480.

Quadrio-Curzio A. (1993) 'On Economic Science, Its Tools and Economic Reality', in Baranzini M. and Harcourt G. C. (eds.) *The Dynamics of the Wealth of Nations: Essays in Honour of Luigi L. Pasinetti*, Basingstoke, Macmillan and New York, St. Martin's Press, pp. 246–271.

Quadrio Curzio A. and Rotondi C. (2004) 'Sulle ricerche di economia politica in Cattolica' in Garofalo G. and Graziani A. (eds.) *La formazione degli economisti in Italia*, Bologna, Il Mulino, pp. 361–422.

Quadrio Curzio A. Rotondi C. and Talamona M. (2007) 'L'identità e l'eredità economico-civile di una Accademia plurisecolare', in Quadrio Curzio A. (ed.) *Economisti ed economia. Per un'Italia europea: paradigmi tra il XVIII e il XX secolo*, Bologna, Il Mulino, pp. 117–152.

Ramazzotti P. (2014) 'Shared Economic Thought and the Neglect of Social Costs: Why Progressive Economists Often Stick to Conventional Wisdom', in *Journal of Economic Issues*, 48(4), pp. 1113–1132.

Roncaglia A. (2006) *The Wealth of Ideas*, Cambridge, Cambridge University Press.

Rotondi C. (1998) 'Cultura economica e azione sociale: l'insegnamento dell'economia nel Seminario di Milano,' in Porta P. L. (ed.) *Milano e la cultura economica nel XX secolo. I – Gli anni 1890–1920*, Collana Ciriec and Milan, Franco Angeli, pp. 193–237.

Salanti A. and Screpanti E. (eds.) (1997) *Pluralism in Economics*, Cheltenham, E. Elgar.

Scazzieri R. (2012) '"The Concept of 'Natural Economic System": A Tool for Structural Analysis and an Instrument for Policy Design', in Arena R. and Porta P. L. (eds.) *Structural Dynamics and Economic Growth*, Cambridge, Cambridge University Press, pp. 218–240.

Vito F. (1936) 'Review of: Keynes J. M., The General Theory of Employment, Interest and Money, London, Macmillan, 1936', in *Rivista Internazionale di Scienze Sociali*, November, pp. 654–656.

(1946) 'L'opera scientifica di J. M. Keynes', in *Rivista Internazionale di Scienze Sociali*, April–June, pp. 132–138.

10 *Why the Classic-Keynesian Trend May Be of Interest to a Young Scholar Today*

NADIA GARBELLINI

When I was about to finish my undergraduate studies, I was extremely disappointed with economics. After the illuminating course by Giorgio Lunghini the very first year – which made me think I was in the right place – I had to study mathematical models based on unrealistic assumptions and dealing with uninteresting topics. I was therefore more than happy to get my degree and look for a job. Everything changed when Gianni Vaggi, my supervisor, suggested that do my thesis on the work of Luigi Pasinetti. He gave me a list of books and papers to read. The first one was Pasinetti's *Structural Change and Economic Dynamics* (1981).

It was an enlightenment but also a challenge: it was something totally different than anything I had ever come across before. Immediately afterwards, I started working with him on the proofreading of the book *Keynes and the Cambridge Keynesians*. It was by reading those pages that I definitively understood that the university had given me a partial and ideological vision of the subject, without providing me with the tools for a critical study.

> The time came, inevitably, when Keynes's pupils of the first hour reached retirement age. They had not cared to appoint genuine successors. The event happened to coincide with a really bad time for Keynesian economics, an anti-Keynesian counter-revolution being under way and spreading from the other side of the Atlantic. In the Cambridge Economics faculty, for the 'neoclassical' group the process of taking over all key positions was child's play. (Pasinetti, 2007, p. 217)

Unfortunately, *mutatis mutandis*, I may have written these words myself. Many of the great masters – confining myself to the Italian case, I am thinking above all of Lunghini, Pierangelo Garegnani, Augusto Graziani, but the list is long – are no longer with us. Those belonging to the following generation have been marginalised and reduced to irrelevance, at least in the academic arena. The 'neoclassical group', on the other hand, has closed its ranks and built a powerful machine of cultural hegemony. It is very difficult for those who pursue non-'mainstream' lines of research to build an academic career – and thus continue to do research.

And still, if paradigm shifts are most likely to happen in the wake of epochal transformations, the world is changing rapidly enough to advocate for one. The building-blocks of this 'new' paradigm are all there. All we have to do is to circumscribe its perimeter and close our ranks to join forces and knowledge and provide a complete, coherent and alternative interpretative framework to the dominant one.

10.1 Fighting for Independence

> The list of building blocks reviewed above is a rough but appealing starting point . . .. Yet it must be recognised that a coherent theoretical framework cannot simply grow out of a list, no matter how rich, of building blocks *if these remain unconnected with one another.*
>
> (Pasinetti, 2007, p. 236)

In what follows, I will make the bold attempt to connect these blocks, giving a (non-comprehensive) list of readings, authors or research lines which could fruitfully cooperate in creating the school of thought Pasinetti is advocating for.

10.1.1 A Strong, Deeply Felt Social Concern

The last item in Pasinetti's list will be our starting point. In my opinion, the real strength of the 'production paradigm' is that it is a theorising process based on observable, measurable, concrete categories, closely connected to national accounting, constantly aiming at explaining reality. But, most of all, deeply concerned with social matters. Not economic science, but Political Economy. And in fact, being an economist implies an ideological choice of position. Far from being a drawback, such a choice provides the interpretative key to understand the dynamics underlying the evolution of capitalism.

Neoclassicals do exactly the same – they put forward an ideological stance. They assume a peaceful society, in which the interests of labour and capital coincide and therefore class conflict is eliminated. This is the point of view of the elites, as Pasinetti pointed out when illustrating the origin of marginalism, born as a reaction of the elites themselves to the social disorder prompted by Karl Marx's reflections. In Classical – and of course in Marxian – theory, capital is first of all a property and a social relation: monopoly ownership of the means of production enables the capitalists to appropriate the surplus value generated by labour in the production process. Distributive variables are not determined by technical relations of production – and in this respect, Piero Sraffa was also very clear – but by *class struggle*. Classical/Sraffian theory – including Pasinetti – take them as exogenous, which does not mean denying they are the result of social dynamics but simply circumscribe the scope of the analysis to a different field.

Societies are not the mere sum of individuals with their own personal interests but the field where groups of individuals with conflicting interests collide: the owners of the means of production, on the one hand, and those who have to sell their workforce, on the other. This means that the generic 'social concern' needs to be substantiated in a specific choice of sides.

For an excellent review of Pasinetti's contributions in the light of his philosophical approach to economics, see Halevi (2016): 'Chronologically, after Marx, Pasinetti is the thinker that has most strongly put labor at the very center of economic activity. He has done it in a different philosophical framework which, in its own right, has vastly enriched our understanding of both theory and society' (Halevi, 2016, p. 17).

10.1.2 *Reality (and Not Simply Abstract Rationality) as the Starting Point of Economic Theory*

> [A]ny theory needs to be based on factual evidence, to be evaluated right from the start and not only to be empirically tested at the end. This feature becomes crucial when the reality under investigation is that of industrial societies, with their tendency towards change and an evolving structure, as against the more static conditions of pre-industrial societies.
>
> (Pasinetti, 2007, p. 220)

Again, the strength of Pasinetti's framework is that it builds on objective, measurable variables, with a close relation to national accounts. This is probably Pasinetti's greatest intellectual debt to Wassily Leontief – who was one of the pioneers of national accounting.

National accounts are a powerful tool for collecting, organising and interpreting empirical data for economic analysis. The necessity of tracking all the flows and stocks of an economic system shaped the way in which these are recorded within the System of National Accounts (SNA), making it crystal clear that the economy is a circular process and that the creation of new income and wealth derives from the activity of production which takes place as a circular flow of goods and commodities. The production, generation and distribution of income complies first of all with physical requirements for reproduction and only in a second stage with institutional principles determining the entities legally entitled to accruance of such an income.

From a theoretical point of view, the origin of national accounting can be traced back to François Quesnay (1759). Both Leontief and Richard Stone explicitly acknowledge Quesnay as having inspired their work and paving the way for the subsequent development of national accounts:

> Apart from statistical estimates, two conceptual innovations which are relevant to my theme should be mentioned at this point. In 1758 François Quesnay, Louis XV's physician, conceived his ingenious *Tableau Économique* which is now regarded as the beginning of the analysis of intersectoral flows. And about a century later Marx carried out his analysis of simple and extended reproduction which appeared in 1885, shortly after his death, in volume II of Das Kapital. (Stone, 1986, p. 121)

Quesnay's *Tableau Économique* was the first attempt at studying the conditions for social reproduction of the system, showing that (simple) reproduction is the result of production activity and a set of transactions that makes it possible to carry on such a production activity period after period on a constant scale. More specifically, Quesnay introduces an embryonic system of accounts including both starting and final balance sheets and a set of transactions leading from the former to the latter.

Three main concepts characterising Quesnay's approach proved to be fundamental for the development of a theory of the circular flow (for details, see Gilibert, 1977):

(i) Production and consumption as a circular flow. For the system to be viable, production must at least replace those commodities worn out during the production process.
(ii) Analysis in terms of social classes, according to the role in production activity.

(iii) Advanced means of production. Production takes time, and hence subsistencies and instrumental goods must be available already at the beginning of the production process itself for it to be carried out.

Marx's reproduction schemes can be seen as an attempt at updating Quesnay's *Tableau Économique* to make it suitable for the analysis of a capitalist economy (Gilibert, 1977, 1991). Two main modifications are needed. First, eliminating Quesnay's exclusive productivity of agriculture, which implies describing manufacture too in terms of capitalistic organisation of production, and hence singling out profits, instead of rents, as the main form of net income. Second, and following, substituting the distinction between productive and sterile sector for that between industries producing subsistencies, on the one side, and raw materials and instrumental goods, on the other side. As Giorgio Gilibert (1977, pp. 55–56) stresses, this distinction reflects that between variable and constant capital which is a key feature of Marx's explanation of exploitation.

Hence, in Marx's reproduction schemes as well as in Quesnay's *Tableau Économique*, individuals are grouped into classes according to their economic function. Finally, the industry producing constant capital provides replacement for worn out capacity to both industries.

Surplus value entirely goes to capitalists who use it for buying subsistencies and so on. The simple scheme presented here is Marx's very first attempt at drafting his schemes; he will then add a third industry – producing luxuries – and analyse the case of extended reproduction too. However, the logic is the same: identifying the physical requirements for the reproducibility of the system, which is guaranteed by the fact that, for each sector, revenues equal expenditures.

The same logic can be identify in Leontief's framework. This clearly emerges from his PhD thesis:

Economic phenomena are characterized by a multiplicity of causal relations. For example, there is a variety of inputs which may be used in the production of a particular good, and each good in turn may be used in a variety of ways .... This leads to a system of economic interrelationships between economic processes. However, it does not mean that the economic sphere is isolated from other spheres; precisely because of the many-sidedness of economic relationships the interaction with the non-economic sphere will be particularly close .... At this point the notion of a circular flow comes into play as a tool which enables us to identify *those causal relations that are specific to the economic sphere*. Circular flow analysis only takes into account those relationships which allow us to return to the initial starting point. . . . For example, in the case of cost items such as used-up coal or worn-out machinery, the principle of the circular flow allows us to follow step by step the entire process of their 'reproduction'. (Leontief, 1928, p. 182, emphasis added)

To conclude, Quesnay's *Tableau Économique* was a source of inspiration for both Marx and Leontief – and also for Stone, as stated above. The analysis of production as a circular flow, and the identification of the conditions for it to take place again period after period, is a key feature of Leontief's Input-Output scheme, which is an integral part of the System of National Accounts. Whereas neoclassical theory sees production as a linear process, from inputs to outputs, Classical economists set their analysis in terms of circularity.

The ideas of Quesnay and Marx inspired a 'school' of economic thought which was especially active in Germany and Russia at the very beginning of the twentieth century, which applied algebraic tools to the analysis of the circular flow in order to make it computable and hence apt to be used as a tool for empirical analysis. These ideas influenced many economists who did actually work to implement systems of national accounts with the aim of directing economic policies. Leontief himself was part of this school in the years spent first in the Soviet Union first and later in Germany. As Stone mentions in his Nobel Lecture:

After the first world war the statistical pace accelerated. In the early 1920's the Central Statistical Administration of the Soviet Union compiled a large body of data on material outputs and their uses, cast in the form of an input-output table for 1923–24, as a basis for planning production. This was published in 1926 and the names associated with it are those of Vladimir Gustavovic Groman and Pavel Ilich Popov. Similar work continued until 1932. By this time national income estimation was flourishing. (Stone, 1986, p. 121)

A thorough knowledge of the SNA is therefore extremely important, especially for a young scholar, if reality is to be kept at the roots of economic theory and analyses. This is especially important at a time when – as was already the case in the 1980s[1] – major organisational

[1] In Italy in the 1980s, the debate about tertiarisation was intense. In fact, at that time, big industrial companies started to externalise services to external suppliers. The profession interpreted this fact as an epochal structural change that was reducing the importance of manufacturing and increasing that of the tertiary sector. The debate was quite intense in the Italian academy; and a group of

changes are also affecting the structure of flows and stocks and thus the determination of added value, investment and income distribution.

10.1.3 Economic Logic with Internal Consistency (and Not Only Formal Rigour)

Economic theory does not only need to respect facts from the very start. It also needs to maintain close contact with economic reality, while the analysis is carried on. This is because any economy is a typically complex and evolving system, in which it is important to single out – and not lose sight of – *the underlying emerging patterns*. A good economic analysis cannot be built exclusively on abstract deductive logic.

(Pasinetti, 2007, p. 221, emphasis added)

Maintaining close contact with economic reality is a crucial point, quite too often forgotten by economists, focused as they are on pure theory. The world is changing rapidly and underlying patterns need to be investigated making use of different tools, most of them coming from outside economics strictly speaking.

First of all, we need a sociological analysis of social relations and how they shape technological trajectories. Secondly, we need to study elements of organisational science, to understand how new business models work. Thirdly, it is necessary to bring the new technology frontier into the picture – which nowadays go under the name *Industry 4.0*. What organisational needs do they meet? How do they interact with new business models in supporting their operation? What consequences do they have on production processes and working conditions?

10.1.4 Necessity of Finding an Appropriate Analytical Framework for Dealing with Technical Change and Economic Growth

Whereas a thorough knowledge of sociological, organisational and technological aspect is fundamental in order to understand what dynamics

scholars, taking advantage of Pasinetti's own scheme, showed that once subsystems, and not individual industries, were taken as the unit of analysis, the picture changed considerably, since it was clear that most of the 'new' services were actually triggered by traditional manufacturing, see, for example, Siniscalco and Momigliano (1982); Momigliano and Siniscalco (1986); Rampa (1986).

drive productivity change – and which sectors are at risk of developing high unemployment rates, together with a significant deterioration in working conditions – such information must be complemented by a genuine macroeconomic analysis of patterns of national and international specialisation through inter-industry analysis. International trade is closely connected with technological trajectories, specialisation patterns and distributional issues – as well as with geopolitical matters.

Pasinetti's scheme offers exactly an analytical framework for dealing with technical progress in its interaction with structural dynamics, especially when one extends it to the study of the structure – and its evolution – of the so-called Global Value Chains (GVCs).

What we need to do is to extend such a framework – following the path already paved by chapter XI of Pasinetti (1981). In fact, studying the dynamics characterising a single country or region is not enough in a world characterised by international division of labour.

In this respect, an interesting research line is the one put forward by Andrew Trigg and Ricardo Araujo (see, for example, Trigg and Araujo, 2015, 2018; Trigg, 2020). The authors provide a multisectoral, disaggregated version of Kaldor-Verdoorn laws, Thirlwall's law and Harrod's foreign trade multipliers, by means of a vertically integrated Input-Output framework. Whereas the aim of Trigg and Araujo (2015) is that of explicitly taking into account the role of demand in the generation of technical progress, Trigg and Araujo (2018) stress the link between Balance of Payments and internal output, employment and productivity. Finally, Trigg (2020) introduces a multisectoral approach to Balance of Payment constraints and hence a disaggregated, macroeconomic explanation of uneven development – a relevant topic for Pasinetti, who addresses the main theoretical issues in chapter XI of his 1981 book.

10.1.5 Disequilibrium and Instability (Not Equilibrium) as the Normal State of the Industrial Economies

> This characteristic, which has been prominent in Kahn, Joan Robinson and Kaldor, expresses the conviction that a modern production economy can never be in a position of perfect equilibrium.
>
> (Pasinetti, 2017, p. 229)

Among the many contributions that Professor Pasinetti gave to economic theory, I think the most important is the attention he pays to the interplay between technological progress and structural dynamics – and their social consequences.

In the aftermath of WWII – and in the following decades – economists had to face one, stringent, problem: growth. How to achieve it? Where and how to invest? In other words, how to ensure strong and stable growth to war-torn countries?

At that time, technological progress seemed essential to meet the ever-increasing world demand – and the Cold War had triggered a real race for growth.

And in fact, growth rates were actually high, and unemployment at an all-time low, for at least twenty-five years after the world conflict. Countries such as Italy experienced an economic boom, with the working classes seeing their material well-being bettering for the first time, also thanks to their struggles. Planning was a priority for governments at the time, not only in centrally planned systems, but also in market economies.

Today, technology could make it possible to produce more than enough for everyone, and problems such as income distribution are returning to the fore. International competition, in turn, crucially depends on and determines distribution issues.

In fact, the very nature of technical progress – taking place at an unpredictable pace and affecting different industries in an asymmetric way – continuously changes the structure of economic systems, even if everything else (population, structure of final demand, etc.) is stationary.

Pasinetti's conclusion is straightforward: if full employment is to be achieved and maintained, institutions must *actively* take care of these disequilibria. Whereas slumps can be fought with 'Keynesian theories and Keynesian anti-cyclical remedies', putting the economic system on a growth path requires more than that: it requires productive investments and the identification of target industries to be expanded in order to keep up with structural change (Pasinetti, 1981, p. 238).

In other words, it requires *planning*. Always keeping in mind that full employment is the ultimate objective. Planning is an extremely topical issue. To provide an example, direct control of strategic sectors and their supply chains would have been and would still be the optimal tool to manage the COVID-19 emergency in a timely and efficient manner. We have seen how the absence of a central decision maker has resulted in a shortage of basic necessities, even very simple goods such as surgical masks.

We must therefore strongly reject the argument that planning involves bureaucratic sclerotisation and misallocation of resources: these are rather characteristics of capitalist systems, which are endemic to what neoclassics call ‘market failures’.

10.1.6 Non-ergodic (in Place of Stationary, Timeless) Economic Systems

Joan Robinson perhaps more than anybody else emphasised this characteristic by making a sharp distinction between historical time and logical time: while the former is crucial to the understanding of economics because it allows the flow of events to be organised from an irreversible past to an unknown future, the latter may become a misleading concept precisely because human history is not like a hydraulic system that can be turned back or forth indifferently (Pasinetti, 2007, p. 226).

Not only is the past incorporated into the present, but it also determines its possible trajectories of evolution, limiting the range of alternatives available to deal with possible shocks or react to certain situations. The installed production capacity at a given time is determined by decisions taken in the past.

Labour is not an abstract and monolithic entity but a varied group of human beings all different in physical, demographic and social characteristics, with different training, tasks, etc. These individuals interact with each other and organise themselves into groups to defend acquired rights and make new claims. The same applies to capital and its representations, which in turn will try to take advantage of power relations to increase the exploitation rate of the workforce.

Moreover, technology – more precisely, the technical conditions of production – also changes continuously as a result of choices made in the past on the basis of certain objectives. The technological trajectories are therefore in their turn determined by class conflict and by the interests of the ruling class.

It is therefore clear that framing our analyses in the historical time, trying to understand social dynamics laying beyond the surface, is vital to avoid ‘misleading concepts’ and interpretations.

10.1.7 Causality vs. Interdependence

> The notion of historical time opens up the question of causality. This notion is mentioned here to underline the conviction that economic relations should not necessarily all be forced into systems of simultaneous equations.
>
> (Pasinetti, 2007, p. 226)

It is important not to limit ourselves, in interpreting the real world, to the analysis of technical production relations and sectoral interdependencies. Understanding the structural dynamics of a complex system is fundamental in order to identify the global trends within which social relations unfold – not only at the national but also at the supranational level.

Understanding how GVCs are structured, and how this structure has changed over time, is crucial. However, this analysis alone is incomplete. It does not allow us to understand what happens at a more granular level.

What happened in the past? What capitalist relations contributed to produce such structural changes? How do these relationships continue to produce their effects, and how can we use this knowledge to give substance to our social concern? Again, we need to put together economic history, a sociological account of the evolution of social and political relations and the knowledge of the strategies of big multinational groups. In this respect, see, for example, Simonazzi and Fiorani (2018); Russo (2019); Gaddi (2020); Pardi et al. (2020).

Simonazzi and Fiorani (2018) study the evolution of labour market reforms and industrial relations in Italy, illustrating how it has aggravated inequality and poverty and highlighting how industrial policy can address the crisis and the emerging techno-economic system in a globalised, competitive world. Russo (2019) aims to study the impact of digital transformation on the relocation and reorganisation of the different stages of automotive supply chains, focusing on the effects of the adoption, at different paces, of digital technologies, taking into account the size of companies. The impact of such heterogeneity in relation to European industrial and innovation policy is discussed at length. Pardi et al. (2020) analyses the effects of the evolution of technologies and organisations on employment and work, focusing on changes at the shop-floor level resulting in work intensification. The authors advocate for an alternative, human-centred vision of the future of work. Finally, Gaddi (2020) frames the theme of company strategies in terms of industrial plans and geographical location of factories via the study of the transformation in technologies, production processes and business and labour (re-)organisation.

10.1.8 Macroeconomics before Microeconomics

The behaviour of the economic system as a whole is not reducible to, in the sense that it does not emerge as the exclusive result of, the sum of its single individual parts, except under very restrictive conditions. So many times, what emerges is that the sum of the single parts has to adapt to independently determined macroeconomic outcomes or constraints.

(Pasinetti, 2007, p. 227)

We come to one of the most relevant conceptual differences between the neoclassical/marginalist approach and the classical/Keynesian one.

The first adopts methodological individualism and a reductionist approach: society is the 'algebraic sum' of the individuals that compose it; the system is broken down to the minimum terms, extending the properties of the lower levels to the higher ones.

The second, on the contrary, is characterised by methodological holism and a systemic approach: individual behavior is constrained by the characteristics of the aggregate system, and social phenomena are determined by collective entities – such as social classes.[2]

And in fact, microfoundation of macroeconomics has been the goal of the neoclassical school at least since the 1970s, and not even heterodoxy has remained immune. It is the very distinction between micro- and macroeconomics, however, that makes no sense in the context of the classical Keynesian approach, at least in Pasinetti's vision. Many confuse the inter-industry approach with microeconomics, but this is a mistake – and it is Pasinetti himself who points out that his scheme is genuinely macroeconomic.

Is it possible, therefore, to study phenomena occurring at a more granular level without falling into microfoundationalism? Once again, (labour and industrial) sociology provides us with the tool to do so.

[2] Attention to the composition of social classes and its evolution is a characteristic feature of the Italian school of economics. See, for example, Sylos Labini (1975, 1986).

Of course, there are different sociological 'schools' as well, based on different theoretical, methodological and ideological approaches. It is therefore necessary to make a choice and to make sure it is consistent with the criteria included in our list. In Section 10.2, I will explore the personal choice I made, based on my research interests and political convictions. Without claiming to identify the only way forward, the objective will be to emphasise the reasons why I believe it is a fruitful way, in line with the methodological principles identified by Pasinetti and briefly recalled here.

10.1.9 Malthus and the Classics (Not Walras and the Marginalists) as the Major Inspiring Source in the History of Economic Thought

> I am frightfully afraid of the tendency, of which I see some signs in you, to appear to accept my constructive part and to find some accommodation between this and deeply cherished views which would in fact only be possible if my constructive part has been partially misunderstood.
>
> (Pasinetti, 2007, p. 233, quoting Keynesrebuking Harrod)

According to Pasinetti, revamping classical economics in a modern guise means 'not only the immediate recovery of different theoretical principles but also the resumption of very different theoretical roots' (Pasinetti, 2007, p. 223). Too conciliatory attitudes towards the prevailing views, therefore, must be avoided.

A battle to vindicate Keynes's original ideas, Pasinetti maintains, was legitimate and perfectly justified to break away from orthodoxy. In particular, Keynes regards as 'the most extraordinary thing ... the complete disappearance of the theory of supply and demand for output as a whole' (Pasinetti, 2007, p. 224).

This is what we must at all costs avoid: incorporating Keynes's ideas into a Walrasian simultaneous equations scheme, which is in radical contrast to the idea of Keynes's *General Theory* – and with Pasinetti's own approach.

10.2 A Choice of Sides: Raniero Panzieri and the 'Quaderni Rossi' Group

In the early 1960s, a group of students, researchers and intellectuals of Marxian inspiration, under the guidance of Raniero Panzieri, founded the journal *Quaderni Rossi*.[3] Engaged in the workers' struggle and mobilisation, the group developed the instrument of 'workers' inquiry' ('*inchiesta operaia*') in order to study the transformations of Italian capitalism starting from those of the factory and its organisation. In calling for a socialist use of the inquiry, the group tried to find new ways to channel the action of the workers' movement.

Vittorio Rieser, one of the leading figures of that season, clarified the meaning of *inchiesta operaia*: 'I have some objections to the use of the term "worker inquiry" which is either restrictive (if taken literally) or ideological (if it hypostatizes the "universal role of the working class" or – worse – one of its components such as the massified worker).'[4]

For the 'Quaderni Rossi group', workers are not the mere object of research but active subjects whose needs and orientations we need to know in order to build, together with them, a path of struggle, of political and trade union demands. Workers, therefore, are not objects to be studied from outside but active subjects of the investigation – so much so that some define the workers' inquiry as '*con-ricerca*': a research conducted jointly by researchers and workers.

Although it never became a school in the strict sense of the word, this group of intellectuals made an important and unique contribution to sociology. First of all, they were the first to reconstruct the production cycle *in the field* – following Marx's exhortation to enter the 'hidden abode of production'. Secondly, they managed to grasp transformations in the 'highest stages of capitalism', that is, in the then most advanced, innovative factories – Fiat, above all, but also Olivetti. Finally, they broke with the Italian tradition which saw technical progress as something positive in itself, without questioning its social nature.

10.2.1 No Admittance Except on Business: The Importance of Field Inquiries

The consumption of labour-power is completed, as in the case of every other commodity, outside the market or the sphere of circulation. Let us

[3] Literally, '*Red Notebooks*'.

[4] 'Ho qualche obiezione sull'uso del termine 'inchiesta operaia' che è restrittivo (se assunto letteralmente) o ideologico (se ipostatizza il 'ruolo universale della classe operaia' o – peggio – di una sua componente tipo l'operaio massa).' My translation. See Pugliese (2009).

therefore, in company with the owner of money and the owner of labour-power, leave this noisy sphere, where everything takes place on the surface and in full view of everyone, and follow them into the hidden abode of production, on whose threshold there hangs the notice 'No admittance except on business'. Here we shall see, not only how capital produces, but how capital is itself produced.

(Marx, 1992, pp. 279–280)

Marx's hidden abodes – and the social relations that are being determined there – are part of what Pasinetti generically calls 'institutions'. Recall that Pasinetti investigates *technical* relations of production (the 'pre-institutional' stage, in his terminology) – 'this noisy sphere, where everything takes place on the surface'. However, he does not deny, and on the contrary he continually stresses, the importance of understanding what happens in the institutional sphere as well – and, in a way, above all. Pasinetti's pre-institutional analysis concerns the 'sphere of the circulation' of goods – the realm of interdependence.

The sphere of circulation or commodity exchange, within whose boundaries-the sale and purchase of labour-power goes on, is in fact a very Eden of the innate rights of man. It is the exclusive realm of Freedom, Equality, Property and Bentham. Freedom, because both buyer and seller of a commodity, let us say of labour-power, are determined only by their own free will. They contract as free persons, who are equal before the law. Their contract is the final result in which their joint will finds a common legal expression. Equality, because each enters into relation with the other, as with a simple owner of commodities, and they exchange equivalent for equivalent. Property, because each disposes only of what is his own. And Bentham, because each looks only to his own advantage. The only force bringing them together, and putting them into relation with each other, is the selfishness, the gain and the private interest of each. Each pays heed to himself only, and no one worries about the others. And precisely for that reason, either in accordance with the pre-established harm only of things, or under the auspices of an omniscient providence, they all work together to their mutual advantage, for the common weal, and in the common interest. (Marx, 1992, p. 280)

This is actually the story we are normally told by the 'Free-trader Vulgaris' – we would call them the marginalists/neoclassicalists. The system is the sum of the actions of individuals, that each of them acts exclusively on the basis of their own personal interest, which in turn depends on their 'initial endowments', whose total amount is given: 'Scarse means which have alternative uses' (Robbins, 1935, p. 16) whose optimal allocation is the very subject matter of economics.

But Marx continues:

> When we leave this sphere of simple circulation or the exchange of commodities, which provides the 'free-trader vulgaris' with his views, his concepts and the standard by which he judges the society of capital and wage-labour, a certain change takes place, or so it appears, in the physiognomy of our dramatis personae. He who was previously the money-owner now strides out in front as a capitalist; the possessor of labour-power follows as his worker. The one smirks self-importantly and is intent on business; the other is timid and holds back, like someone who has brought his own hide to market and now has nothing else to expect but – a tanning. (Marx, 1992, p. 280)

This is what workers' inquiry is for: to 'pierce the veil' between the world as it appears and as it really is, laying bare its contradictions and looking for a way to take advantage of them.

10.2.2 Technological Progress and Capitalistic Control

> The development of technology takes entirely place within capitalistic process .... Capitalistic development of technology implies, through the various stages of rationalisation and more and more refined forms of integration, an increasing capitalistic control.[5]
>
> (Panzieri, 1961, p. 54)

Capitalistic development of technology entails a growing capitalist control, whose power is based on newer and newer 'technical bases'. For this reason, in the vision of the Quaderni Rossi group, the neutral character of the technologies must be demystified: 'The attention rightly paid to the modifications that accompany the current technological and economic phase is distorted in a representation of them in a "pure", idealized form, stripped of the concrete connections with the general and determining elements (of power) of the capitalist

[5] 'Lo sviluppo della tecnologia avviene interamente all'interno [del] processo capitalistico .... Lo sviluppo capitalistico della tecnologia comporta, attraverso le diverse fasi della razionalizzazione e di forme sempre più raffinate di integrazione, un aumento crescente del controllo capitalistico.' My translation.

organization' (Panzieri, 1961, p. 57) and hence '[c]haracteristic new aspects assumed by the capitalist organization are exchanged as stages of development of an objective "rationality"' (Panzieri, 1961, p. 58) or a process dominated by technological fatality.

Capital has always looked for ways to rationalise production processes as much as possible, closely coordinating the various phases, constantly monitoring production indicators in order to extract cognitive and predictive information. An in-depth, granular knowledge of production data allows to identify all operations that can be shrinked or eliminated, reducing costs and increasing profit margins. In addition, it allows to codify procedures to be followed, to minimise the possibility of error and time 'lost' thinking or performing activities that, in business logic, are not directly functional to the production of value added.

Angelo Dina,[6] already in 1982, used the expression 'technological phase' ('*fase tecnologica*') to indicate the use of technology not only to increase profits and modify the balance of power but to replace human activity in the elaboration of a growing amount of information. Describing the process of introducing ICT between late 1970s and early 1980s, Dina notes a significant difference compared to Detroit-type automation. At that time, numerically controlled machines were equipped with an unalterable mechanical memory, which integrated the information defined in the design phase. No real time reprogramming was possible, so there was no room for so-called informal organisation.

In the 1970s, on the other hand, the so-called flexible automation was introduced: machinery capable of processing more than one type of product, changing the production mix, introducing new models, etc., without having to replace production lines but simply reprogramming them. This also increased the degree of adaptability to the target markets and the ability of the production system to withstand disturbing elements. Real-time information processing were designed to introduce flexibility, automation and increased productivity – or better, profitability.

[6] Dina was not part of the editorial staff of *Quaderni Rossi*, but he was strongly influenced by that experience, so much so that most of his writings are in the interpretative vein of Panzieri. We can therefore consider him, in this sense, a member of the 'Quaderni Rossi group'.

The investments in ICT in the 1980s therefore concerned the flow of information on production processes. The aim was to achieve the greatest possible degree of flexibility while maintaining real-time control over the production process.

The technological phase of the 1980s served capitalists to increase flexibility and regain control over labour, which is exactly what's happening today – the significant difference being that today there are the technologies that Capital never dreamed of in the 1980s. And they exist precisely because, in these decades, Capital has worked hard to develop them.

In reality, they have gone far beyond what Capital was hoping for at the time of Dina's writings: while the aim of the investments of the 1980s was an ever-increasing integration of ICT systems within the production process, beyond the individual machines, the aim of Industry 4.0 is to push beyond this integration, to the entire production chain.

Moreover, developments in technology from the 1980s to the present day have been accompanied by developments in organisational science, which has, at the same time, developed, implemented and refined new business models suitable for large multinational companies committed to maximum rationalisation of resources.

10.2.3 Pasinetti and Panzieri: The Odd Couple?

At this point, we are in a position to state that the sociological approach proposed by what we have called the 'Quaderni Rossi group' is perfectly in line with the building-blocks listed by Luigi Pasinetti.

Let us start from social concern. As stated above, Panzieri and the other members of the group were young Marxians involved in class struggle in favour of workers.

Pasinetti is certainly not a Marxist, nor has he ever explicitly expressed his thoughts on the events of workers' struggles. However, observing the characteristics of what he calls the 'natural system', it is not difficult to draw a conclusion: the rate of growth capable of guaranteeing the full employment of the labour force and productive capacity can only be achieved if, in fact, the capitalist class is eliminated from the picture.

Pasinetti's natural profits, in fact, are nothing more than investment rates. Everything that is not invested, in his scheme, is distributed to the workers in the form of wages.

In a socialist society, all the members of the community belong to the category of workers. There is no place for capitalists; the responsibility for carrying on the production process and the direct ownership of all means of production are taken over by the State. However, the State, as such, cannot consume: consumption can be carried out only by individuals. Therefore, if any amount of the national product is not distributed to the members of the community, either as wages or as interest on their loans to the State, that amount is *ipso facto* saved .... The amount of investments that must be undertaken in order to maintain full employment – once this has been reached – is indeed that which is required by technical progress and population growth .... In the case of a capitalist system, the additional problem arises of whether the capitalists will or will not *spontaneously undertake* the amount of investments necessary to cope with the natural possibilities of growth. (Pasinetti, 1962, pp. 278–279, emphasis added)

Concern for workers is present throughout all Pasinetti's contributions. Full employment, for him, is and must always be the ultimate goal of any institutional system, which must actively pursue it with all the means at its disposal: 'Even if the absolute amount of consumption had a limit, the alternative would always be open to devoting the continually increasing productivity to reducing labour time (and increasing leisure time), instead of increasing production. The point is that this process is not one to be expected automatically' (Pasinetti, 1981, p. 242).

Even when talking about international trade and the circulation of goods and services, Pasinetti is very clear about the conflict of interests between capitalists and workers and immediately takes a stand:

The importation of any commodity which, by having a lower price than that possible at home, prevents an increase of local employment ... entails a net loss for the country. For, although *some particular people* ... might well gain by paying the lower international price, *the workers* who would otherwise produce that commodity *remain unemployed* and produce nothing .... *In such a situation, it would clearly be advantageous to the country not to import that commodity* at all and to produce it at home, in spite of the internal higher cost (and price). (Pasinetti, 1981, p. 255, emphases added)

Also with regard to adherence to reality, rejection of abstract rationality and keeping close contact with economic reality, the approach of the Quaderni Rossi group is fully consistent with what Pasinetti advocates. Let us think about the analysis of technical progress by Panzieri and, above all, of Dina – which links organisational models, power relations, capitalist control and technological trajectories. And indeed, as we will see later, Dina predicted in the 1980s exactly what is happening today, and his analysis is still extremely topical.

Of course, no Marxian would argue that the 'normal' state of an economic system is equilibrium. On the contrary, as noted above, Panzieri and his fellows set themselves the goal of laying bare, and taking advantage of, the *contradictions* of capitalism. For example, Dina places the intrinsic *asymmetry of capitalist control over labour* at the centre of his reflection, identifying a *causal chain* which, starting from this asymmetry, explains the direction taken by progress – not only technological in the strict sense but also organisational.

We are in Joan Robinson's historical time, where social relations and the power relations they generate and feed back contribute decisively to determine the transition 'from the irrevocable past into the unknown future'. After all, they were Marxian and therefore historical materialists.

Finally, the Quaderni Rossi group entirely rejected stereotyping work and capital as if they were monolithic categories –just as we reject the concepts of individual and representative enterprise.

We have now come to the last point on our list – 'Macroeconomics before Microeconomics'. Pasinetti does not deny the 'role of microeconomics as a genuine field of economic investigation'. However, asserting the microfoundation of macroeconomics is normally a process of trying to explain macroeconomic dynamics through individual behaviour. As stated above, even the heterodox economists are not immune to the temptation to approach the issue in this way.

The approach adopted by the Quaderni Rossi group is radically different, and it is my contention that it is the only way of looking at what happens at the level of specific groups of individuals without falling into contradiction with Pasinetti's list of methodological standpoints.

10.3 Global Value Chains, Industry 4.0 and Lean Production

In the world of today, the effects of technological change couple with another phenomenon – the GVCs. In a nutshell, GVCs are nothing else than what Pasinetti would probably call 'international vertically integrated sectors'. While the head of these chains lies in the country producing the final good or service, the other links normally cross *industry and country borders*, making the whole process much harder to define, trace and measure.

As an obvious corollary, it is also much harder to make such chains subject to the control of institutions in charge of designing industrial policies, since they are beyond their jurisdiction. Moreover, technological progress is advancing at an increasingly rapid pace, so much so that the term Industry 4.0 has been coined to stress that we stand in the way of the fourth industrial revolution.

Let us take the example of the EU, a large free trade area within which the movement of goods and capital is free, in the face of huge disparities in regulations, social and environmental standards, wages, tax systems, etc.

This generates enormous arbitrage possibilities for large companies, which may decide to locate tax headquarters, parent company, production facilities and administrative offices in different countries, depending on convenience. Therefore, we are told, the optimal strategy for each country is to specialise in a specific function, offering to Capital all optimal conditions for an efficient – from the point of view of Capital itself – geographical allocation of production phases. Of course, managing these long production chains is very complex, as it involves coordinating a long series of different phases, located in different geographical areas – and subject to different regulations. Research activity has been fully organic to this strategy and has been directed towards the development of new technologies able to facilitate a process of 'centralization without concentration' (Bellofiore and Halevi, 2012; Bellofiore et al., 2014). As stated above, however, developments in technology always couple with developments in organisational science.

It is precisely the case of Lean Production, which pursues the objective of eliminating, or at least reducing, a series of 'wastes' and 'losses': overproduction; waiting times; transport operations between stations, departments and warehouses; processes involving the use of expensive resources and/or additional functions; stocks of raw materials or semi-finished products in stock; unnecessary handling; defective parts, etc.

Industry 4.0 technologies do exactly that. Digital technologies are crucial in compressing work performance times and thus reducing waiting times – which results in a heavy intensification of the pace of work.

In the same way, when applied to machinery and plants, 4.0 technologies make it possible to reduce reset times and hence increase 'productivity' – at the cost, again, of a heavy intensification of the pace of work.

This has a first, relevant, consequence on labour productivity.[7] We are used to think that one working hour corresponds to one hour of actual working time. However, this is not correct: actual working time is only a fraction of the time spent at the workplace, the ratio between the former and the latter being the so called saturation of working time.

To compute actual working time, one must first of all subtract breaks (mainly for lunch and physiological needs) from the time spent at work. Secondly, one must apply corrective factors, such as the fatigue factor.

From the time thus obtained, however, one should also subtract the time devoted to a series of activities such as moving from one point to another of the workplace to pick something up, the time needed to reset the machines, the waiting time between one production phase and another, the time devoted to checks, etc. – in other words, all the non-value-added tasks that Lean Production wants to eliminate.

These times, however, are a 'waste' from the point of view of the company – but not of the worker, who takes advantage of them to ease the physical and psychological tension.

The productivity increases achieved in this way are quite different from those resulting from simple automation, or in general from the introduction of increasingly efficient technologies. Here technological innovation simply prevents workers from any unnecessary movement, thus increasing the saturation of her working time.

Simply looking at data, therefore, we cannot say whether observed productivity gains are the result of the use of more efficient tools or simply of an increased rate of extraction of relative surplus value.

To be sure, Italian metalworkers complain about a strong intensification of the pace of work (Gaddi et al., 2018).[8] This intensification is also due to the fact that production flows are subject to huge fluctuations connected to fluctuations in demand, and workers have to adapt. One of the pillars of Lean Production, in fact, is just-in-time:

7 Recall that, in Pasinetti's framework, labour productivity is computed at the level of each vertical (hyper-)integrated sector, as the reciprocal of vertically (hyper-) integrated labour coefficients.

8 His cited study is a workers' inquiry carried out in collaboration with FIOM CGIL, involving workers from forty companies in the metalworking sectors.

thanks to the availability of data and the speed with which they can be used anywhere along the entire value chain, there is no reason to produce upstream what is not required downstream.

To achieve this, rigid synchronisation of the different links of the chain and continuous visibility of the entire process is needed – even remotely, via connected devices. It is the Internet of Things, which connects devices, machines and human beings, within a single network that collects, processes, interprets data and issues directives.

This has further implications on working conditions, as emerged from the interviews with workers. First of all, data on production processes are collected via connected devices which are often univocally associated to each single worker. This means a real-time monitoring of what they do during the whole working day. Secondly, the production to order system involves very tight deadlines, which must necessarily be respected. According to workers, working times and conditions are not negotiated but unilaterally imposed by companies.

Of course, control must be extended to suppliers as well, who in turn must respect delivery times to the exact second. If large multinationals have an easy game in exploiting power relationships to impose their own times on the majority of direct suppliers – mostly located in the territory, at least in the case of Italy – 4.0 technologies allow the branching of production orders and the control of adherence to programming on a daily basis.

This is why many companies that are introducing 4.0 technologies already implement Lean Production: technological innovations go hand in hand with organisational innovations.

Obviously, this makes it possible to push relocations as never before and to restructure production chains according to criteria, including *geographical* criteria, more functional to just-in-time production. This is how, for example, to produce a German car today, a certain number of modules are produced and assembled in countries other than Germany, where the final assembly of the car takes place. The more sophisticated ones, such as instrument panels, come from countries such as Italy – from companies such as Magneti Marelli, with decades of know-how.

Other modules, less technologically advanced, are produced in Eastern Europe – in Hungary, Romania, Poland, etc. However, even the countries included in the EU eastward enlargement have a periphery, from which they import less specialised components. This is the case of Turkey, which produces such components using raw materials purchased in Asia and India, for example.

Thus, value chains are organised in concentric circles, taking advantage of the central-periphery relationship between each of them and the one immediately outside. It is clear that, given this configuration, two additional elements become fundamental: logistics and physical networks (think of 5G) and the material transmission belts of these gears, which are a counterbalance to the 'immaterial' one represented by 4.0 technologies.

Again, interviews with workers provide us with very interesting hints on how supply chain integration works and its consequences on labour conditions. The relation with OEMs is particularly apparent in the automotive sector, within which Italian companies are strongly connected mainly to German manufacturers such as Mercedes, BMW, Porsche – but also Chrysler, now part of FCA Group.

For example, Magneti Marelli produces high-tech systems and modules – mainly control units – for big German OEMS. During interviews, workers mentioned the case of Porsche, which allows customers to fully customise their cars and then synchronises the various actors in the supply chain via EDI (Electronic Data Interchange), a centralised informatic system periodically delivering production plans to suppliers.

Magneti Marelli receives the order to *start producing* the specific sequence of board tools required by Porsche five days before final assembly of the car takes place in Germany.

But which specific IT tools are used, and how do they work?

As stressed above, Industry 4.0 relies on Cyber Physical Systems (CPS) – that is, online networks of machines interacting as in a social network – and the Internet of Things (IoT) – that is, on the virtualisation of production chains.

Software tools such as MES (Manufacturing Execution Systems), ERP (Enterprise Resource Planning), APS (Advanced Planning and Scheduling) and MRP (Material Resources Planning) are used for M2M (Machine-to-Machine) connection, with the whole system connected to a central server. This triggers both 'vertical integration' (the connection of different departments within the same plant) and 'horizontal integration' (the connection between different plants belonging to the same group or to its suppliers, both located domestically and abroad).

These software tools allow production planning; operations scheduling; the delivery of production orders to suppliers, departments, lines and workstations; real-time rescheduling of production plans and collection of the corresponding data.

It should be clear how much this impacts and feedbacks with GVCs: the further we move away from the head of the chain, the more the specificity of submodules produced decreases. Since automation is more closely related to labour-intensive processing phases, this also means that its effects will be asymmetric according to the positioning in the value chain.

Moreover, whereas employment is likely going to decrease in countries devoted to these stages of production, it is going to increase in those which are producing Industry 4.0 technologies – software, next generation robots, etc. – deepening asymmetries between centre and periphery.

Hence, studying the connections between the topology of GVCs – and the positioning within them of different countries – new business models, and the spread of Industry 4.0 technologies is of utmost importance in order to understand the potential impact of the transformation of global production structures and the consequences on the main macroeconomic imbalances between countries.

10.3.1 Everything as a Service: The Myth of 'Dematerialisation'

As mentioned at the end of Section 10.1.2, all these organisational changes are bound to have effects on the very nature of stock and flows. Not only, as happened in the 1980s (see note 1), in-house services are externalised to third-party suppliers; physical capital is also 'externalised'.

For example, 5G will push the diffusion of managed private cloud and public cloud further. This is basically a way of moving physical ICT infrastructures to the premises of a supplier, which then manages the flow of services. This is already spreading the so-called EaaS (Everything as a Service) model. In other words, companies do not buy software to be used by their own employees, running on on-premise servers: they buy services from specialised companies which run those software for them in exchange for a subscription.

This very fact has important consequences in terms of accounting. From the point of view of the 'externalising' company, fixed capital turns into circulating capital: whereas software (or a server) is registered as an item of the stock of installed capital, services are intermediate costs. On the one side, this means a decrease of ICT investments and a parallel increase in intermediate costs – which means a reduction in value added.

In turn, this means a smaller cake to be distributed to taxes, profits and wages – and depreciation. If the former slice is normally almost proportional to value added, wages are harder to compress, which in turn implies, *ceteris paribus*, less profits. However, less investments in fixed capital also reduces depreciation.

However, we have to take the point of view of the provider into account as well. These companies of course also generate value added which then distribute to profits and wages. This is something we have to take into account when interpreting figures about functional income distribution: profits *might* appear artificially lower or higher than what they actually are, and the overall effect on income distribution is unpredictable. This also makes it difficult to make comparisons through time, if we do not take into account structural differences in business organisation.

Also, the dynamics of investments needs to be interpreted in the light of these phenomena, especially (but not only) ICT investments, since this organisational transformation represents a genuine structural break with respect to the past.

Another issue to take into account is that companies make more and more use of temporary employment agencies. When the hiring of workers is outsourced, the consequence is not only the reduction of the HR department. Something else also happens: if workers used to be employees of the company, which paid them a salary, now they are employees of the agency, to which the company pays remuneration for the service rendered.

This means shifting an expenditure item from wages to intermediate costs for goods and services. Where the former reduces the share of value added distributed as profits, the latter reduce value added itself. Profits, in absolute value, do not decrease – indeed they increase, because outsourcing only takes place when it suits the company. Moreover, there will be additional profits in the temporary employment agencies themselves.

Finally, the Lean model minimises, and tends to eliminate, warehouse stocks, whether unsold production or components. This also has an effect in accounting terms, since the change in stocks is a component of gross capital formation (but not of gross *fixed* capital formation). Hence, when making long-term considerations about the distribution of value added, structural changes in the background must be taken into account.

10.4 Back to the Future of 'Keynesian' Revolution

In conclusion, why should a young researcher choose to abandon the neoclassical paradigm and devote herself to the study of alternative approaches?

We know that, from the point of view of academic career, this is not an easy choice to make. In Cambridge as elsewhere, 'for the "neoclassical" group the process of taking over all key positions was child's play', and this tendency is still ongoing.

The reason is already known. The neoclassical paradigm is perfectly useless for studying the dynamics of the real world. It is a formally perfect analytical complex, capable of finding within itself an explanation for everything, forcing all economic relations into a system of simultaneous equations. It completely disregards social and power relations, denying the inherently conflictual character of capitalism. It describes a harmonious world in which everyone, pursuing their own individual interests, contributes to the general well-being. Initial endowments are given, and they determine the path towards equilibrium and its speed and pace. Its prescriptions, however, would hold true only in a hypothetical world in which its initial assumptions were true – a world which is definitely not the one in which we live.

That this theoretical corpus is inadequate should be clear by now, after the failure to predict the imminent arrival of the great economic crisis in 2007. A failure that was stressed with astonishment by Queen Elizabeth II when, in November 2008, she asked why no one saw the financial crisis coming. Or by Olivier Blanchard, chief economist of the IMF, when he candidly admitted that the IMF was wrong in its Spring 2010 World Economic Outlook (IMF, 2010). Blanchard and Leigh's (2013, p. 4) findings, in fact, revealed 'that multipliers implicit in the forecasts were, on average, too low by about 1'. More specifically, the implicit multipliers used in forecasts were around 0.5, while ex post evidence suggested that they were around 1.5. IMF, European Commission and World Bank forecasts were systematically wrong during the crisis.

This, obviously, calls for a theoretical rethinking.

Fortunately, we already have the tools we need to conduct an analysis based on a radically different standpoint, with the objective of piercing the veil that hides the real functioning of capitalism. The literature is so extensive that the list I provided in the previous pages is absolutely partial – not only because of space limitations but also because of my inevitable ignorance.

For example, in the previous pages, I have not mentioned a crucial topic: money. This is a subject that I have never explored in depth in my studies but which is of key importance in understanding a monetary production economy:[9]

> The great achievement of Marx was to try to present a *monetary theory of value* .... In the first three chapters ... Marx deals with commodities that have already been produced. Starting from chapter five, instead, he deals with the (capitalistic) process of production of commodities: we must then move towards a *monetary theory of production* of (plus)value, based on the capitalistically determined *form* of labour, which is historically specific, and whose specificity is that of being abstract work, work that produces (plus) value .... When the analysis turns to consider the commodities to be produced, in a truly monetary economy this implies that production must be monetarily financed in advance. (Bellofiore, 2019, p. 26, emphases in the original)

Let me stress that going beyond the boundaries of individual disciplines – often the result of mere convention – is the fundamental step to take to return to the tradition of the Classicists and Marx, who today would probably entirely reject them. No knowledge is possible if one

[9] '[I]l grande risultato conseguito da Marx è stato quello di provare a presentare una teoria monetaria del valore .... Nei primi tre capitoli ... Marx tratta di merci che sono già state prodotte. A partire dal capitolo quinto, invece, egli affronta il processo (capitalistico) di produzione delle merci: dobbiamo a quel punto muoverci verso una teoria monetaria della produzione di (plus)valore, basata sulla forma capitalisticamente determinata del lavoro, che è storicamente specifica, e la cui specificità è quella di essere lavoro astratto, lavoro che produce (plus)valore .... Quando l'indagine si volge a considerare le merci che devono essere prodotte, in un'economia veramente monetaria ciò implica che la produzione deve essere finanziata monetariamente in anticipo.' My translation. The reader interested in a deeper view of the Marxian/Post-Keynesian tradition may also refer, in English, to Graziani (2003) and Godley and Lavoie (2007) – to mention only two of the most famous contributions.

remains inside watertight compartments that do not communicate with each other.

> It would certainly be out of place to develop a theory of technical progress here. If such a theory should ever be developed, it would pertain to a *much wider field than economics*, because it could not avoid *some definite conceptions about the aims and ends of human societies*. (Pasinetti, 1981, p. 67, emphases added)

I believe that this is ultimately the lesson we must learn from Pasinetti's Postlude: a 'school' is not made up of researchers dealing with the same problem, all using the same tool. On the contrary, it must necessarily be composed of people who deal with the different aspects of capitalism, using heterogeneous instruments – and coming from different disciplines. Each of them will obviously specialise in the field for which they feel more inclined or which they find most interesting but always in a continuous dialectic with the others. There is no hierarchical scale between research themes: they are all equally important to arrive at a *collective understanding* of capitalism and its evolution.

What is really important is to identify the methodological and ideological standpoints, just as Pasinetti tried to do by identifying the building-blocks of that radical school that we have unfortunately not yet managed to build.

References

Bellofiore R. (2019) 'C'è vita su Marx? Il Capitale nel bicentenario', in Bellofiore R. and Fabiani C. (eds.) *Marx Inattuale*, Roma, Edizioni Efesto, pp. 9–68.

Bellofiore R. Garibaldo F. and Mortagua M. (2015) 'A Credit-Money and Structural Perspective on the European Crisis: Why Exiting the Euro Is the Answer to the Wrong Question', in *Review of Keynesian Economics*, 3(4), pp. 471–490.

Bellofiore R. and Halevi J. (2012) 'Deconstructing Labour: A Marxian-Kaleckian Perspective of What Is "New" in Contemporary Capitalism', in Gnos C. Rochon L. and Tropeano D. (eds.) *Employment, Growth and Development: A Post-Keynesian Approach*, Cheltenham, Elgar, pp. 11–27.

Blanchard O. and Leigh D. (2013) 'Growth Forecast Errors and Fiscal Multipliers', IMF Working Paper WP/13/1.

Dina A. (1982) 'Tecnologia e lavoro. Richiami storici e problemi attuali', in *Classe*, 22, pp. 5–37.

Gaddi M. (2020). 'Technological and Organisational Innovation under Industry 4.0 – Impact on Working Conditions in the Italian Automotive Supply Sector', in Drahokoupil J. (ed.) *The Challenge of Digital Transformation in the Automotive Industry: Jobs, Upgrading and the Prospects for Development*, Brussels, ETUI, pp. 127–152.

Gaddi M. Garbellini N. Garibaldo F. (2018) (eds.) *Industry 4.0 and Its Consequences for Work and Labour*, Bologna and Milan, Fondazione Sabbattini.

Gilibert G. (1977) *Quesnay – La costruzione della 'macchina della prosperità'*. Milan, Etas Libri.

(1991) 'La scuola russo-tedesca di economia matematica e la dottrina del flusso circolare' in Becattini G. (ed.) *Il pensiero economico: Temi, problemi e scuole*, Torino, UTET, pp. 387–403.

Godley W. Lavoie M. (2007) *Monetary Economics: An Integrated Approach to Credit, Money, Income, Production and Wealth*, London and New York Palgrgave Macmillan.

Graziani A. (2003) *The Monetary Theory of Production*, Cambridge, Cambridge University Press.

Halevi J. (2016) 'Luigi Pasinetti and the Political Economy of Growth and Distribution', INET Working paper 40.

IMF (2010) *World Economic Outlook: Rebalancing Growth*. Washington, DC, IMF.

Leontief W. (1928 [1991]) 'The Economy as a Circular Flow', in *Structural Change and Economic Dynamics*, 2(1), pp. 181–212.

Leontief W. Duchin F. (1986) *The Future Impact of Automation on Workers*, Oxford, Oxford University Press.

Marx K. (1880) *A Workers' Inquiry, La Revue socialiste*. www.marxists.org/archive/marx/works/1880/04/20.htm.

(1992) *Capital: Vol. I*, London, Penguin Books.

Momigliano F. Siniscalco D. (1986) 'Mutamenti nella struttura del sistema produttivo e integrazione fra industria e settore terziario', in Pasinetti L. L. (ed.) *Mutamenti strutturali del sistema produttivo. Integrazione tra industria e settore terziario*, Bologna, Il Mulino.

Panzieri R. (1961) 'Sull'uso capitalistico delle macchine nel neocapitalismo', in *Quaderni Rossi*, 1, pp. 486–495.

Pardi T. Krzywdzinski M. and Luethje B. (2020) 'Digital Manufacturing Revolutions as Political Projects and Hypes: Evidences From the Auto Sector', Geneva, ILO Working Paper 3.

Pasinetti L. (1962) 'Rate of Profit and Income Distribution in Relation to the Rate of Economic Growth', in *The Review of Economic Studies*, 29(4), pp. 267–279.

Pasinetti L. L. (1981) *Structural Change and Economic Dynamics*, Cambridge, Cambridge University Press.
(1988) 'Growing Subsystems, Vertically Hyper-integrated Sectors and the Labour Theory of Value', in *Cambridge Journal of Economics* 12(1), pp. 125–134.
(2007) *Keynes and the Cambridge Keynesians: A 'Revolution in Economics' to Be Accomplished*, Cambridge, Cambridge University Press.
Pugliese E. (2009) *L'inchiesta sociale in Italia* Rome, Carocci.
Quesnay F. (1759 [1972]) 'Tableau Économique', in Kuczynski M. Meek R. (eds.), *Quesnay's Tableau Économique*, London, Macmillan.
Rampa G. (1986) 'Misure alternative dell'integrazione fra industria e terziario', in Pasinetti L. L. (ed.) *Mutamenti strutturali del sistema produttivo. Integrazione tra industria e settore terziario*, Bologna, Il Mulino.
Robbins L. (1935) *An Essay on the Nature and Significance of Economic Science*, London, Macmillan.
Russo M. (2019) 'Digital Transformation in the Automotive Supply Chain: China, Germany, Italy and Japan in a Comparative Perspective', DEMB Working Paper Series, Università di Modena e ReggioEmilia, 151. http://merlino.unimo.it/campusone/web_dep/ wpdemb/0151.pdf.
Simonazzi A. and Fiorani G. (2018) 'Industrial Relations and Social Dialogue in Italy', in *Economia & Lavoro*, 1, pp. 71–86.
Siniscalco D. and Momigliano F. (1982) 'Note in tema di terziarizzazione e deindustrializzazione', in *Moneta e Credito*, 35(138), pp. 143–182
Stone R. (1986) 'Nobel memorial lecture 1984 – the Accounts of Society', in *Journal of Applied Econometrics*, 1(1), pp. 5–28.
Sylos Labini P. (1975) *Saggio sulle classi sociali*, Bari, Laterza.
Sylos Labini (1986) *Le classi sociali negli anni'80*, Bari, Laterza.
Trigg A. (2020) Thirlwall's Law and Uneven Development under Global Value Chains: A Multi-country Input–Output Approach, in *Journal of Economic Structures* 9(1), pp. 1–22.
Trigg A. and Araujo R. (2018) 'A Multi-sectoral Approach to the Harrod Foreign Trade Multiplier', in *The European Journal of Economics and Economic Policies, Intervention* 15(1), pp. 91–104.
(2015) A Neo-Kaldorian Approach to Structural Economic Dynamics, in *Structural Change and Economic Dynamics*, 33(C) pp. 25–36.
United Nations (2009) '*System of National Accounts 2008*', New York, UN Statistical Division.

11 *Pasinetti's Separation Theorem*

BERTRAM SCHEFOLD

I have known Luigi Pasinetti for more than 50 years. He gave me the famous paper by Carlo Felice Manara (1968), which questioned the existence of the standard commodity in the case of joint production. To answer that became the subject of my thesis, and Pasinetti was one of my examiners. I told the story recently, when I had to defend my solution.[1] We often met at conferences, during the Summer Schools at Trieste, I was invited to teach at the Catholic University of Milan and we collaborated for the foundation of the European Society for the History of Economic Thought, of which he became the first and I the third president. So, I would read his books and papers and could observe how his thinking converged towards his masterpiece *Keynes and the Cambridge Keynesians* (Pasinetti, 2007), which he presented to me at my sixty-fifth birthday, a little more than a decade ago. The editors of this Festschrift have asked me to provide a concluding essay at the end, based on the readings of the other contributions.

11.1 Protoeconomics

Pasinetti's book is his monument for the Cambridge economists, followers of John Maynard Keynes and Piero Sraffa, among whom he once represented the younger generation. The book bears the subtitle *A Revolution in Economics to Be Accomplished*. By this he means that the approaches of the Cambridge economists form a body of thought that should be developed into a coherent theory, in order to complete the Keynesian revolution, which has been accepted by the economic profession only in a mutilated form. The book expounds this diagnosis; it seems to be truer than ever. On the one hand, important aspects of the Keynesian theory have become mainstream economics and dominate economic policies. Everybody believes that stimulating

[1] In response to Yoann Verger in the book edited by Ajit Sinha (Sinha, 2021).

demand will increase employment or at least help to avoid a slump. Interest rates are at a historical low (at the time of writing in September 2020). One may recall Keynes's euthanasia of the rentier (Keynes, 1973, p. 376), for the yields of bonds are negative. On the other hand, the mainstream is far from having adopted Cambridge theory. Neoclassical theoretical tools are what is being taught in most universities, and the rentier is quite alive, investing in shares and funds but not in bonds as in the old days. Asset prices are high, there are deflationary tendencies in some countries that experience growth, and these ambiguities are also reflected in attitudes towards deficit spending, which is desired in the short run and feared in the long. Criticisms of economic theories abound, but on which can we rely? It is easier to tear down than to build.

The main ideas in Pasinetti's book are presented as results of a lifelong endeavour towards a foundation of an economic theory that isolates the stable elements and provides a framework for thinking about economic questions by complementing the basic scheme with a broad analysis of institutions in constant change and evolution. He speaks of a 'separation theorem' (Pasinetti, 2007, p. 274) to distinguish these stages of investigation. He is aware that similar distinctions have been made by others. He mentions Sraffa's scheme of *Production of Commodities by Means of Commodities*. Sraffa's equations show how long-run prices result as equal to cost of production, with a uniform wage rate and uniform rate of profits, if the structure of commodity production is given, but demand and distribution are determined by other forces. I have described Sraffa's model as open, in that it leaves room for changing historical influences on the composition of output, on the evolution of real wages and profitability and, in particular, on the effects of different forms of technical progress. Pierangelo Garegnani (1981) speaks of a 'core' of economic theory, described by the Sraffa equations, and of a 'periphery', where historical, social and political forces are at play. Pasinetti himself recalls Joan Violet Robinson's distinction between logical and historical time. From here we could go back to older methodological distinctions of a similar nature between pure theory and the consideration of institutions or between 'rational' and 'visual' or 'intuitive' theory, as Edgar Salin and Arthur Spiethoff would call it, or between abstract laws and individual events or even between Kantian philosophy and phenomenology (Schefold, 2011). Finally, there is also an ethical dimension to the idea of a separation theorem, to which we shall come at the end of this chapter.

Pasinetti is cautious in approaching the broader horizon. His main effort is to go beyond Sraffa by capturing structural change, which consists, with given techniques, in the adaptation of the levels of output in different industries to demand that increases for each commodity according to Engel laws, while at the same time there are returns to scale, reducing or increasing unit costs, and there is not only a gradual technological change, but also the possibility of technological revolutions, which upset the structure of production, when individual industries undergo a more profound transformation. Growth is based on cumulative causation. As in Adam Smith, increasing division of labour allows to produce more cheaply but also to conquer larger markets, and the great question is: what coordinates these manifold activities?

Pasinetti does not turn to the supply and demand mechanism in order to explain this coordination. He associates that with neoclassical theory, and neoclassical theory is flawed; he here takes the result of the Cambridge controversies on capital as something given. He does not seek an alternative causal theory. His reference to institutions can only mean that he does not believe in the existence of one alternative theory, because the institutions, on which the day-to-day development of the economy depends, are various and changing. He does not say, perhaps he even does not realise that, in so doing, he accepts the scepticism of the Historical School with regard to a theory which would at the same time claim a general explanatory power and be capable of prediction. He surprisingly turns to a normative idea, singles out full employment as an important goal and postulates that the political economist should attempt to realise it both by using existing institutions and by transforming them. Although only a few economists have taken such a turn, there are predecessors and parallels. I here only want to recall that Adolph Lowe completed his theory of growth with an analysis of the policy instruments that might allow to stabilise growth to avoid the cycle and to attain permanent full employment.

Pasinetti speaks of the 'production paradigm', and he confronts it with the neoclassical 'exchange paradigm'. Where is the difference? One, to be sure, concerns the subjective theory of value, but Pasinetti uses Engel curves, and these may nicely be derived from stable preferences, without using the word 'utility', by letting incomes increase and seeing how households allocate and reallocate their means between different consumption goods. Modern neoclassical theory uses activity analysis to describe technology, and the formalism used is not so different from that employed by either Sraffa or Pasinetti. So, the real difference concerns distribution. Classical theory does not assume that factors are supplied by balancing consumption and effort or sacrifice. What is the heart of the matter?

I think it can be elucidated by going back to the controversies Eugen von Böhm-Bawerk had with the Ricardian economists of his time in Germany. The corresponding essays have never been translated into English, as they seem to be only of local interest, because it was a peculiarity of German academic economics that Ricardianism had survived the neoclassical revolution in some universities, where professors had been impressed by Karl Marx but did not want to accept his system with all its implications as the alternative to the incipient neoclassicism. So Böhm-Bawerk would try to convince these Ricardians by conceding that the theory of natural prices in David Ricardo was alright (see Schefold, 2019a). He understood it quite well, including the complications deriving from the different times it takes to bring a commodity to market (the time structure of production) and the invariable standard of value (which would later become the standard commodity in Sraffa's hand and for which Pasinetti [1981] would propose an intertemporal extension). Böhm-Bawerk concentrated on one single criticism of Ricardo.

Surprisingly, Böhm–Bawerk would accept that Ricardo treated profits as a residual, depending on the level of the necessary wage, if there was only one technique, that is, if the method of production in each industry was given without an alternative so that there was a given level of the physical surplus, to be appropriated by the capitalists and possibly landowners. But capitalists would not be content with profits as a haphazard residual; capital would be forthcoming only if capitalists could expect an adequate return, and the return in the form of the given residual, derived from the given technique and the given necessary wage, could be too much or too little. Hence, to make it possible for capitalists to get the adequate return which would guarantee an equilibrium (and equilibrium really meant full employment), techniques would have to be variable. This is explained in *Kapital und Kapitalzins*, vol. I, using a Ricardian corn model (Böhm-Bawerk, 1884 [1921], p. 82). Böhm-Bawerk had to work out a theory of the supply of capital, based in his case on time preference, and of the demand for it, based on the choice of techniques, in his case analysed by means of the average period of production. Production functions and saving functions are only variants of this idea and so is the marginal efficiency of capital in Keynes in the absence of uncertainty.

Keynes, having introduced the marginal efficiency of capital as that amount of investment to be undertaken which would make the investment equal to the discounted expected returns from the investment, withdrew the idea immediately, as it were, by evoking the animal spirits, which could in principle lead to any level of investment. To the extent that he maintained the investment function, it was dependent on the rate of interest; the rate of interest was a monetary phenomenon. Now speculative forces could prevent the economy from reaching the equilibrium (with full employment) that Böhm-Bawerk had postulated on the basis of his specific vision of the process of investment or of the demand for capital goods.

So, the core of the production paradigm, as opposed to the exchange paradigm, seems to be that the economist is agnostic as to the level of investment and of desired capital equipment, unless expectations of future returns can firmly be taken as given – and even if they are given, they can be wrong so that equilibrium is not reached. Capital investment then is a historical process in historical time, as Robinson would put it. In fact, there is no investment function in classical economics; Marx explicitly denied a significant influence of the rate of interest on investment. It is true and everybody knows and agrees that existing investment plans must be curtailed, if the interest rate rises suddenly because of a speculative event or because the central bank intervenes, for the existing funds are then not adequate to carry out the plans that have been made, but that does not mean that new investment plans are formed, if the interest rate is – also surprisingly – lowered.

The capital controversy has been concerned with the influence of the rate of profit or of the rate of interest on capital since the times of Böhm-Bawerk and Irving Fisher. Keynes had criticised the neoclassical theory of the demand for capital, which we have sketched following Böhm-Bawerk, by analysing it in the short run, looking at the process of investment based on expectations that were uncertain, possibly wrong, and the investment demand was dependent on a rate of interest that was influenced by monetary (speculative) forces unrelated with the full-employment equilibrium position. The capital critique that we associate with Sraffa states that a demand function for capital goods, leading to a stable equilibrium, may not exist, even if one abstracts from uncertainty, because the profit-maximising amount of capital, valued in long-run prices, may increase with the rate of interest, so that a high rate of interest and a low wage rate may paradoxically be associated with a high capital intensity. It means that low wages in a situation of unemployment will not necessarily lead to the introduction of labour-using techniques that might absorb the unemployed.

The later Pasinetti does not speak much about the capital theory debate, in which he had been a pioneer when younger (Pasinetti, 1975, pp. 200–213). The Cambridge theory of distribution also remains in the background (but we shall return to it later). My name for his scheme of structural evolution as a dynamic extension of Sraffa's theory is 'protoeconomics', because the analysis of real change is subsequent to it, and to me, protoeconomic seems also to be a good designation for Sraffa's pure theory as an 'open' model. Pasinetti goes beyond protoeconomics by analysing the conditions under which full employment can be maintained. For instance, if a country strives to raise employment in an international context, it must, in order to sell more, raise productivity, but this reduces the labour required per unit of output. Pasinetti emphasises learning as the essential condition for realising growth with cumulative effects. He also mentions intertemporal and, indeed, intergenerational transfers, as in Böhm-Bawerk, without, however, postulating a general trend for time preference in the sense of Irving Fisher's impatience.

As an aside, I should like to observe that there is more institutional content to Sraffa's and Pasinetti's protoeconomics than is apparent, and they are not quite invariant to different theories of distribution. For instance, the standards which define the homogeneity of commodities have different historical origins. They may be based on the convention of guilds of artisans and merchants; they reflect national characteristics, or they are supervised by institutions created by governments (Schefold, 1999). More complex is the question of what defines the standards of needs and efforts in the case of labour. Here distributional problems enter. However, there is no room to discuss why we may abstract from these institutional givens in the construction of the protoeconomic scheme and why we treat other institutions as separate. It is now my task, by assignment of the editors, to attempt a conclusion on the bases of the contributions written by the other authors of this volume. There is not much room for this; I must speak in adumbrations. The editors have explained in their Introduction that Pasinetti provides nine essential characteristics of Cambridge and, indeed, his own theory, and the contributors to this volume have taken up the characteristics one by one. How do they fit together?

11.2 Effective Demand and Methodology

We thus come to Pasinetti's characteristics of Cambridge economics, expounded in his book on pp. 219–236; they are discussed, one by one, by the authors of this volume. The first theme is possibly the most difficult. It is treated by Cristina Marcuzzo. Pasinetti argues that 'reality (and not simply abstract rationality)' should be the 'starting point of economic theory' (Pasinetti, 2007, p. 219). Realism comes first. But is this not the basic principle of any economist? Many years ago, I was introduced to a colleague. His subject was theology. I responded by confessing to be an economist. 'Ah', he replied, 'the opposite!' Economists are the 'worldly philosophers' in Robert Heilbroner's (1980) words. As is well known, Karl Polanyi distinguished between economics as the science of the material reproduction of man on earth and the alternative definition as the science of the rational use of scarce means of production for the alternative ends of utility maximisation on the part of the consumer and profit maximisation on the part of the entrepreneur. The neoclassical economist would concede that the former definition is realist, but does not lead to theory, while, he would claim, the latter concern also is realist, insofar as it starts from fundamental characteristics of economic action. Both ways to understand the worldly pursuits of man are different from other sciences, which try to capture other realities of nature, of human creation or indeed of metaphysical entities, that the religious person believes to have been revealed. Curious role changes can thus be observed if one pursues the methodological question of what realism means in economics. This happens in economic history. Often mainstream economists of these days are attracted by cliometrics, that is, by the attempt to explain past economic development on the basis of quantitative measurement of economic data, in order to prove, for instance, that the work of slaves on plantations could be as efficient as that of wage labourers. Weberians insist that economic history cannot be understood without tracing the slow change of economic rationalities. Relatively abstract cliometric work shall lead to realism, a sociological approach explains history in terms of changing modes of thought.

An example: Realism as opposed to abstract rationality does not simply mean that one should start from the description of the lives and actions of the specific historic individuals. Not even the Historical School would have been content with that. Werner Sombart pointed out that Marx had explained the origin of the proletariat but had failed to explain both the origin and the characteristics of entrepreneurship. Hence, Sombart developed a historical typology of entrepreneurs, distinguishing, for instance, between attitudes typical for mercantilism and those that emerged with the Industrial Revolution. Max Weber thought that entrepreneurship and capitalist forms of acquisition were as old as antiquity but that modern entrepreneurship came about only through a contingent religious movement, represented by certain Calvinist sects. Weber's use of ideal types to characterise historical transformations of the economy was not realist in the direct sense, in that the ideal types were not realistic images of historical formations but constructs, which could be counterfactual, for it was necessary to show why old formations such as the Roman economy were modern in one sense and not in another. There was mercantile entrepreneurship, but it was linked to political interests, there was free labour, but slavery predominated at the time, when Rome was strongest, etc.

Socio-economics was built on a synthesis, in which the formation of economic types replaces 'abstract' rationality. It seems to me that Marcuzzo arrives at a similar conclusion, though she restricts her argument to the domain of Cambridge economics. She begins by distinguishing the latter from the positivist approach, represented by Milton Friedman, who thought that models could be useful for capturing reality, if they were successful in prediction, without being realistic in their assumptions. She uses Keynesian analyses of speculative behaviour, in particular, formulations by Richard Kahn, to illustrate that investment decisions are not optimising choices on the basis of the identification of a certain behavioural function but constrained choices of individuals subject to uncertainty and forced to make guesses. Keynes, when discussing the stock exchange, used the metaphors of 'bulls' and 'bears', hence a very specific typology. Marcuzzo presents Nicholas Kaldor's formation of stylised facts as an expression of a similar symbolism. It also leads to typologies, I should say, and Marcuzzo investigates the history of this way of thinking about the economy, starting from Alfred Marshall. She also admits objections. Animal spirits do not suffice to explain investment; they are one of those important negative characteristics which we need in order to avoid an imaginary faulty realism in the form of an ahistorical investment function based on a stable relationship between the rate of interest and entrepreneurial activity.

Typologies can be a starting point for an economic theorising that is not mere abstraction but built on concepts with a real counterpart. We find typologies in Pasinetti, for instance, in his distinction between different savers: there is the inherited distinction between saving out of profits and saving out of wages, to which he added the saving out of the profits of workers, who own capital (Pasinetti, 1974). This was a new animal in the zoo of the agents in the capitalistic markets. The neoclassicals hoped that the workers, with their savings coming from two sources, would outperform the capitalists and end up owning the total capital in the economy in the long run, but Pasinetti's prediction was more realistic, in that he showed that a stable distribution of wealth was possible in a steady state; at present, it seems that the distribution of wealth is growing more unequal. Whatever the outcome, we may observe that it was the underlying typology which provided intuition, realism and relevance for what otherwise might have remained a discussion of a very abstract model.

Neri Salvadori and Rodolfo Signorino are concerned with Pasinetti's second proposition. Cambridge economists pursue an economic logic, which shall be internally consistent, and this is more than the formal rigour of a model. Again, a tricky proposition! Models can be formally rigorous without being concerned with economics at all. What then does internal consistency add to formally consistent models that are concerned with economic issues? To explain it, Salvadori and Signorino start from the IS-LM model, which was meant by John Hicks to capture the essence of the Keynesian revolution, but which was not accepted by Keynes as an adequate representation of his ideas. Why did the Hicksian approach come to dominate the textbooks all the same and why were Keynes and the Cambridge Keynesians not able to present a victorious alternative? There are contingent historical reasons: Keynes's early death, his followers were not cooperative, etc., but enough time has elapsed since, I should say, to develop a valid substitute. If one says that the revolution is unaccomplished, one suggests that a real revolution is possible, but then one ought to be able to say what it is, almost a century after the revolution itself!

Salvadori and Signorino emphasise the importance of the choice of the assumptions, not the results we derive from those assumptions. 'The explanatory value of a given theory depends on its ability to provide a logically consistent description of the *true* (their emphasis) causal mechanisms working in the world out there' (see Section 2.2).

They illustrate the significance of this methodological position by reproducing Sraffa's argumentation, starting with his critique of Marshallian economics in 1925 and culminating in the Symposium of 1930, when Sraffa said: 'I am trying to find the assumptions implicit in Marshall's theory.' (see Section 2.2). Data can usually be explained by several theories. They probably here think of a rather restricted data set. But if this the case, it is important to check whether the causal mechanisms postulated in the theory operate also in the reality. How is this to be tested? Is this causal mechanism correctly identified, if it allows correct predictions? Do we go back to Karl Popper? Or is it not rather a matter of 'understanding' ('*verstehen*')? Sraffa, in his discussion of Marshallian economics in 1925, distinguished a number of representative cases (increasing returns, diminishing returns, partial equilibrium, general equilibrium, etc.), and he would analyse the internal logic. This is Salvadori and Signorino's way of opposing a Friedmanite to a Sraffian methodology. They continue, speaking of the very traditional method of successive approximations. I also believe that this principle remains important, but I should add again that Sraffa's method involved a historical specific *Verstehen*. One example: Sraffa criticised Ann Robert Jacques Turgot in 1925 for thinking that output per head and the marginal product are low at first, if a given large piece of land is to be cultivated by a few workers, that both rise, as more labourers are added, until an optimum is reached, when marginal product and average product are equal; diminishing returns to additional quantities of labour set in thereafter, and output per head rises more slowly. Sraffa points out that, if land is divisible, the optimal technique can be used from the start, so that marginal product and average product remain equal up to what had been the optimum, and both are falling thereafter. In the light of the present discussion and in the spirit of Pasinetti, we might say that Turgot had an abstract rationality in mind which led him to overlook the possibility that only part of the land could be cultivated, if land was divisible, so as to get a maximum return. We can call Turgot's rationality abstract, but we can also see that it is simply faulty, and it is moreover ahistorical. For ordinary texts on agriculture in the eighteenth century would advise farmers not to cultivate their entire land, if they did not have enough workers to do it well, and the Book of Changes in China said thousands of years ago that weeds would grow abundantly if one tries to cultivate too much land. Realism involves a holistic understanding that incorporates social conditions.

If political economy in the nineteenth century had taken its start from Thomas Robert Malthus and not from David Ricardo, the world would be 'a much wiser and richer place' today, Keynes once famously exclaimed (Keynes, 1933 [1972], p. 101). Keynes did not say that we should have better theory but a better understanding, and he made the very strong statement that this imagined change in the world of ideas would have changed the actual world. Pasinetti does not take up this amazing challenge to any materialist theory of history. He cautiously reduces Keynes's claim to the suggestion that, starting from Malthus, there could have been an enrichment of classical economics by somehow incorporating the principle of effective demand. He thus projects our modern problem of reconciling classical and Keynesian theory on the beginning of the debate about true classical analysis in the exchanges of Ricardo with his friends and correspondents like Jean Baptiste Say and Jean Charles Léonard Simonde de Sismondi, of whom Malthus was the most important. Heinz Kurz, in his contribution, stays in the same ditch and digs deeper. He musters the analytical apparatus of Malthusian economics and shows convincingly that they are deficient. The view that there can be a general glut cannot be transformed into a theory of an economy in a state of underemployment. He shows that Malthus sticks to the classical view of accumulation undertaken by capitalists who both save and invest so that the two appear as identical. As Pasinetti (1974, p. 30) states, Ricardo referred to Say: Every producer wants to consume the product or to sell it. In the latter case, the producer obtains a quantity of money equivalent to the value of the product, which will be spent, so that new purchases equivalent to the value of the product will take place. But why should someone, who has sold, be compelled to buy, Marx would later ask? If one can find a systematic reason why sellers do not necessarily become buyers, one has found an explanation for a slump, and if one has reason to believe that the cause will persist, so will the effect of underemployment. Kurz says very rightly that Malthus fails to find an explanation of why money can become a bottomless sink, and he later describes how Keynes explained the phenomenon. The consumption function has to come in; it provides a stable grounding for expenditure of current income but also for a flow of savings. This must match investment; investment, in given circumstances, depends on the rate of interest, but this is subject to speculative movements. Say's argument seems ludicrously superficial in a Keynesian perspective, but Say gave a reason why the money would be spent, and it has briefly been noted by Pasinetti (1974, p. 30): Say observes that the value of money is perishable, so the income-receiver spends his money 'lest its value should vanish in his hands'. Say therefore speaks of a situation in which there is, contrary to the situation which Malthus has in mind, a systematic reason to spend, namely, inflation. He lived and published during the Napoleonic Wars, when inflation was a recurring phenomenon, and hence his theory was historical in that it referred to an economic constellation in which Keynesians also expect full employment normally to obtain.

Kurz shows very nicely how Malthus tries to construct a scenario in which landlords save. For Malthus, this was kind of a counterfactual by which he wanted to demonstrate that their high propensity to consume in reality helped to keep employment up. For if they did not consume, they would employ fewer productive labourers, these labourers would be employed in industry and become productive, but who would buy their products? Ricardo answered that then these products would not be produced in the first place, and the scenario really did not show more than that, if consumption is reduced, employment will fall; but it is not shown why this should happen systematically and affect the economy as a whole.

Kurz and Pasinetti therefore are of one opinion: Malthus lacked the analytical apparatus to prove his case. Pasinetti praises Malthus for having tried, Kurz scolds him for not having succeeded.

How then could Keynes be so enthusiastic about Malthus? Perhaps because, when he wrote that phrase in 1933 or earlier, he did not have the desired analytical apparatus himself but hoped to find it. And Keynes felt that the Malthusian attempt was of historical significance because it took the historical context seriously. Of course, it is true that, if the rich landlords in England, much richer at the time than even the rich bourgeois, according to Eric Hobsbawm (1969, pp. 31 and

80), had saved more, without investing the savings themselves, employment would have fallen, for industrial production was, even with faster growth, unable to absorb most of the labour force for a long time, and I doubt that a possibly lower rate of interest could have induced the entrepreneurs to accumulate much faster (see above). In this, Malthus was a realist, and if one wants to speculate like Keynes – perhaps I should not do that because I am not Keynes, but if I try nonetheless – one can point out that – to the extent that intellectual currents among economists played a role in this – the historical economists and the institutionalists in the nineteenth century were more successful in the nineteenth century on the basis of simple theory and pragmatism than the analytically more sophisticated Ricardian and later neoclassical economists, for the United States and Germany, both starting from a lower level of per capita production, would overtake the United Kingdom as regarded the strength of industrial production.

11.3 Logical and Historical Time

Pasinetti mentions a fourth characteristic of Cambridge economics: 'Non-ergodic (in place of stationary timeless) economic systems'. He notes that Paul Davidson introduced the term ergodicity as a concept taken from statistical physics, first used in thermodynamics by Ludwig Boltzmann. It originally meant that the particles of a perfect gas would move in a random manner such that, in a given volume, all possible states would be reached approximately in the long run, and hence it would, once disturbed, return to its former state approximately, whereas, in the non-ergodic case, interactions between the particles could lead to a qualitative transformation similar, for instance, to the formation of a magnet. Initially, the molecules have magnetic moments that point in all directions and cancel on average. After a phase transition, induced by a change of temperature, they line up so that they form a macroscopic magnet, and the system does not spontaneously return to its former state. This path-dependence is called hysteresis. Non-ergodicity is therefore nothing but a fancy expression for the irreversibility of processes and hence for a simple form of historicity which is not due to conscious action but to physical laws. I suppose it has become a catchword for economists, because their theories treat economic agents like automata with unchanging reaction patterns such as profit maximisation, and even satisficing behaviour as a generalisation is of this sort, while human history has to deal with individuality. Non-ergodicity is not really a good metaphor for Keynesians, for animal spirits stand for human inclinations that change with historical contingencies, not for the physical properties of molecules that are inanimate. Ariel Dvoskin and Paolo Trabucchi start from Robinson's opposition between history and equilibrium, a stable equilibrium being a state to which one returns, while we wander off into an uncertain future in real history.

The question now is: how can theory and history be compatible at all? Mathematics, physics, even Darwinian evolution describe abstract phenomena and processes that may help to explain history out there, but the natural sciences are not themselves historical in the sense of the humanities, even if they describe irreversible transitions like magnetisation or events in the struggle of survival of species or geological 'history'.

Uncertainty and expectations were the decisive argument for Robinson, who questions the usefulness of equilibrium analysis: 'As soon as the uncertainty of the expectations that guide economic behaviour is admitted, equilibrium drops out of the argument and history takes its place' (quoted in Section 4.2).

This statement provokes questions. First, is the equilibrium not stable after all, if there is little uncertainty and expectations are formed on the basis of unchanging data? Such situations are conceivable, of course: classical political economy would regard the technique and the real wage as given. Normal prices would then be defined under competitive conditions which led to a uniform rate of profits. The same holds for traditional neoclassical theory, according to which the choice of technique depended on profit maximisation and distribution on preferences, in particular, time preference and the disutility of labour, on condition that the alternative methods available were given and known by the entrepreneurs in the respective sectors and that the preferences of households also were given and stable (I here leave aside objections derived from capital theory; they will be discussed later). Dvoskin and Trabucchi correctly point out that the prices so defined are a theoretical concept; they predict actual prices only if a whole set of conditions is fulfilled, starting with the homogeneity of products, the uniformity of prices and factor prices, and special conditions must be added, specific for the theory. In the classical case, the composition of output must correspond to effectual demand, which is determined in another part of the theory. It is historically given, we may say here, and the coincidence of the expected and of realised returns of the investors is assumed. What this means for the theory as an element to predict the future will have to be considered later. Neoclassical theory is not open in this same sense. Quantities are endogenous, except for the endowments, and traditional neoclassical theory took the value of total capital as given, with the sectorial amounts of capital needed for reproduction as endogenous magnitudes, so that a uniform rate of profit could be assumed, contrary to the modern neo-Walrasian approach, where endowments are inherited from the past and expectations are formed, looking to the future without any lessons being taken from experiences in the past.

The question then asked, common, I believe, both to the classical and the old neoclassical approach, is whether this equilibrium, based on stable givens, results in stable states, if the equilibrium is disturbed. It should be stressed once more, as far as the classical equilibrium is concerned, that Pasinetti is less interested in this technical question than in the normative perspective: under what conditions, regarding distribution and employment, such an equilibrium is socially acceptable, and if it has deficiencies, how they can be mended, in particular, how full employment can be reached. In a more theoretical perspective, both types of equilibria have in common that the theory must treat the question of stability as an *axiom* of the theory, for the possibilities of disturbances and of the ways the system can adapt to them are endless. When Smith talks about market prices gravitating to his natural prices, he talks, for instance, of a beleaguered city in which there is a market price even for the meat of rats. Prices return to normal when the war ends. There is a so-called Walrasian approach describing how prices react if one starts from false market prices, a Marshallian approach, if quantities adapt, there are cross-dual-dynamics, there are disturbances due to imperfections in competition, there are competitive processes leading to the homogenisation of products, while others lead to diversification. Classical and neoclassical economists have discussed such matters *con amore*, singling out a few stability problems that seem to be of special theoretical interest. The most important in our context is connected with the debate about capital theory. It does not concern the micro behaviour of prices but a macroeconomic relationship. If, in neoclassical theory, the possibilities for the choice of techniques are such that the profit maximising technique tends to be associated with a higher capital labour ratio, if the rate of profit is increased, the neoclassical mechanism for stabilising the labour market cannot work. For if the rate of profit increases and the wage rate has fallen, for instance, in consequence of an immigration, any increase of the intensity of capital will, with a given endowment of a capital, lead to a further reduction of employment so that unemployment gets worse. The outcome is the simplest consequence of reswitching and of non-neoclassical Knut Wicksell effects. The latter are frequent; the former effect, however, is rare, both empirically and for theoretical reasons so that the critique must be modified (Schefold, 2020).

This, with perhaps little differences of emphasis in details, is common ground between Dvoskin and Trabucchi and myself. They go on to consider neo-Walrasian equilibria, with dated commodities, which are therefore intertemporal with a finite or infinite time horizon, and with given endowments not only of labour and land but also of produced capital goods, to be used in subsequent periods, so that, because of their contingent composition, the rate of profit cannot be uniform from the start. They say that the difference between theoretical and actual prices here disappears. Perhaps this is an exaggeration. The theoretical postulate of a uniform rate of profit has, so it seems in the beginning, disappeared, but other theoretical postulates remain, like the homogeneity of prices for homogeneous products, which one does not encounter in markets where sellers try to get special prices and buyers try to obtain special conditions and where, on average, homogeneity perhaps results but cannot be assumed. I should rather say that the *neo-Walrasian equilibrium is a special kind of equilibrium of market prices*, to use the classical terminology, and – again in special conditions – it converges towards a system with a uniform rate of profit, that is, if there is a regular supply of the factors, stationarity of preferences and an infinite horizon. The system then tends to a neoclassical equilibrium that may also be called classical. As such, it is of a special kind: distribution is determined by supply and demand and full employment obtains. It is also special as a market price model, in that prices from homogeneous goods in the same location and at the same time are assumed to be homogeneous. Dvoskin and Trabucchi cite interesting examples of neoclassical economists who, in the endeavour to render their market price model more realistic, invent new assumptions and, in particular, shorten the time period ever more. A classic example was the agricultural year, which appears in the beginning of Sraffa's book. Here we find the Hicksian week, we find day trading, one may refer even to machine trading, and as the time periods get shorter, the number of commodities to be distinguished according to date multiplies.

What has become of historical time? The hope to achieve realism by means of successive approximations is often illusory, in that what is gained by this additional sophistication to represent a specific phenomenon is lost through the introduction of another abstraction. However, we cannot do better. As regards the classical approach, the chapter nicely describes how Sraffa dealt with uncertainty by providing his protoeconomic scheme after assuming that the system is capable of self-replacement, but virtual self-replacement does not mean that an actual system continues to reproduce undisturbed. There may be an upswing, a crisis or there may be exogenous events. What the protoeconomic scheme teaches is how to order reality with coexisting techniques, with joint production, with commodities that are not really homogeneous. The task of finding the dominating technique, therefore to discover what industries really produce and what is only a by-product or even waste turns out to involve sophisticated mathematics. Confronted with real data and actual industries, the task of identifying the underlying Sraffa system is not trivial. The man from the moon, which young Sraffa wanted to interview to solve this task would probably be quite at a loss and taking snapshots (the metaphor of the photographer) is also somewhat ingenuous; the fundamental forces governing the economy are not so easily discovered. The man from the moon would not know whether CO_2 or NO_x in the exhausts of cars were free wastes or commodities to be paid for; he would have to read law books and newspapers and it would not do to register material flows. The dominating technique cannot be identified by means of a snapshot. What is the dominant technique in electricity production? Wind, solar panels, nuclear power or still coal? The metaphors of the snapshot and man from the moon may serve to attract students and may help them to comprehend simplifying assumptions, but they should not be used to create the illusion that the gulf that separates the model from its application in concrete circumstances, involving institutions, can easily be bridged. Sraffa was wise to refrain from publishing the metaphors. Protoeconomics is an expression formed after protophysics (Poser, 2012, p. 96), a name for constructivism. We have to make our concepts by synthesising elementary intuitions, and we understand the conceptual tools we have made. Then we enter history and a different kind of understanding becomes necessary. We have to understand the rationale for the genesis of the institutions we observe and to fathom the motives of the agents we encounter. What we experience is a historical process, which we try to understand, and we use protoeconomics as a framework only to order our thoughts.

11.4 Interdependence

Pasinetti certainly is right in asserting that all Cambridge economists share the desire to identify the causes of different economic developments and are not easily satisfied with the assertion that there is general interdependence, although, in a sense, this is true and some problems cannot be treated adequately without representing the relationships of interdependence. The question then is: Which are the relevant ones? A simple example usually convinces my students. Having explained Sraffa's equations for single product systems, I define a numéraire, so that only one degree of freedom remains. I identify it with a monetary commodity, gold, and I observe that, from a formal point of view, the system could be closed by fixing one of the relative prices – the state prescribes that a kilogram of apples shall cost as much as a kilogram of cauliflower. Does anybody believe that the rate of profit and real wages would adapt? Of course, nobody, although the conclusion is mathematically stringent. So, we have to work out how the deeper forces operate, which we feel must be there, and the task is to configurate the analytical apparatus to express them. Pasinetti then goes on to mention cumulative causation, which we may describe as different causal forces, sequentially reinforcing each other.

Enrico Bellino and Sebastiano Nerozzi report that the young Pasinetti was interested in transforming interdependent systems of equations so that they could be solved sequentially – this means, in the linear case, to transform the matrix describing the constraints into a triangular shape. Then came the study of the classical economists, who would visualise the successive determination of interdependent magnitudes such as values and prices and the distributional variables. The discourse here returns to core and periphery, to causality in Ricardo, starting from the corn model, and to Marx in the early formulations of the transformation problem. On the one hand, it is clear that Marx approached the problem sequentially, on the other, the solution was not satisfactory in his case, precisely because he could not explain the interdependence of the system of prices of production, starting from values. But if one starts from an interdependent system of prices of production, the system of values appears to be redundant from the point of view of price determination.[2]

Bellino and Nerozzi then show that the standard commodity can be used to give distribution prior to the formation of prices, insofar as the standard commodity allows to say what the real wage, expressed in terms of the standard, will be, if the rate of profit is given exogenously, and it can be shown in a transparent way how relative prices and wages change with changes of this rate of profit. In the present perspective, the chief merit of the derivation of the standard commodity therefore consists in the possibility it offers to go from distribution to prices and from one distributional variable to the other sequentially.

The authors then turn to Keynes. There is a general interdependence of the variables in the *General Theory*, but we may distinguish more direct and stronger causal relationships from weaker ones, considering sequentially the multiplier, the dependence of investment on the rate of interest and other forces and considering finally the money market. A crucial variable is effective demand.

Something similar can be observed in post-Keynesian theory, where it is concerned with the long run, and here we encounter Pasinetti's own contribution, which the authors could have discussed more extensively, but, perhaps, being younger, they do not realise how much the general public of economists was struck by Pasinetti's derivation of the Cambridge theory of distribution, showing that total profits in the steady state really only depended on capitalists decision to invest and to save, even if workers also saved (Pasinetti, 1974); we mentioned this worker who saves and owns capital as a new type above. The savings propensity of the workers would be less than that of the capitalists, but if they saved, they owned part of the capital stock. A steady state then was possible, as long as what they saved less from their capital incomes was compensated by their savings from wages, so that the rate of their total savings was equal to that of the capitalists. The income

[2] Nonetheless, there are more possibilities than has been thought to relate the value system and the price system in such a way that profit appears as a redistribution of surplus value. Marx wrote that this relationship held 'on average' and this can be confirmed, if one assumes that the technology is random (Schefold, 2019b).

distribution between capital and labour could remain the same through time. Pasinetti introduced this behaviour as if it were a norm, thus anticipating his later methodology. The neoclassicals speculated that the workers might save more and might therefore in the long run accumulate more capital than the capitalists so that they would end up owning all the capital in the economy. It was a wonderful outlook at the time of the luckily peaceful coexistence of Soviet communism and capitalism. At present, it seems that the wealth distribution is getting ever more unequal so that a norm, and corresponding political action, are called for to prevent a relative immiseration of the workers. Cambridge economics continue to be particularly relevant in this domain. History matters.

Pasinetti moves from here to the thesis that macroeconomics comes before microeconomics. He illustrates it quite extensively with the works of the Cambridge economists. Murray Milgate and John Eatwell continue the discourse with a very learned chapter about the history of macroeconomics after Keynes, without forgetting that, under different names, the subject had been discussed a great deal in the earlier history of political economy. More recently, Robert Lucas created a watershed with his introduction of rational expectations in the debate about the Phillips-curve. It is difficult to understand in retrospect, they observe, why this critique was not advanced earlier. If expectations played a role in the Keynesian models, why did government decisions and anticipations of such decisions not affect the formation of the outlook of the agents in the play? The fashions in macroeconomics now began to change rapidly, but, at the same time, there were also the researches about general equilibrium theory, which resulted in the Mantel-Sonnenschein-Debreu Theorem. It was not assured any more that market excess functions would be falling, hence equilibria, though they existed, could be violently unstable. Milgate and Eatwell use this possibility to question the DSG-models as a foundation for macroeconomics, and they opt for a return to Keynes.

There is no room here to comment on the manifold details of this exposition; I prefer to look at the principle, which is here enunciated: macro before micro. It really means, in a more traditional formulation, that the whole is more than the parts. Where is it really used in Keynes? There is the multiplier; investment determines saving in the closed economy. This is based on the consumption function, which has a microeconomic basis, for it results from the aggregation of the consumption functions of the individual households. The average household may be replaced by a representative household, without affecting the principle that the individual decisions determine the outcome. Similarly, the investment function seems to be derived from the aggregation of the investment decisions of individual entrepreneurs, who calculate the expected return on investment, given the rate of interest and expectations of future proceeds. But Keynes here opens his theory for another determinant, the famous animal spirits, and these are a collective phenomenon. Even if they affect each entrepreneur in a specific manner, depending on individual psychology, the cause is a swing of general opinion, due to some exogenous event, which is perceived by the business community as a whole. He explains the process in more detail in the context of the stock exchange, where people speculate, anticipating how the news of an event are taken in by others. The theorists summarise Keynes's analysis of mass psychology by speaking of the 'beauty contest' and 'herding'. Post-Keynesians generalise the approach, when they discuss growth and cycles. Investment influences not only the current level of activity but the rate of growth determines distribution, and national characteristics may well influence the growth rate.

I don't see why one should not interpret this turn of the theorists as a partial acceptance of historicism. Traditions and systems of education result in dispositions in economic matters, which are shaped by national institutions and are of relevance for development. It must be remarked here that Weber, one of the founders of sociology, vehemently opposed the facile use of collective notions of the Historical School; he adopted the methodological individualism of Austrian economics. I am inclined to take sides in this debate with the Historical School, but one should be aware that such a stance involves a change of method. If one intends to make use of collective notions, one has to make plausible that they exist and this means that one must reconstruct a social reality in a convincing manner. We are here not talking about the usual aggregation from given and behaviourally stable microeconomic elements. Rather, the approach should consist in a comprehensive representation of a complex phenomenon, based on *description*, which is plausible because it reflects an understanding of a complex of motives. It therefore resembles more a work of art than an analysis, even if it was possible to summarise the characteristics in the end in a number of indices, as in the comparison of different economic systems, of models of regulation or economic styles – all concepts that stand for somewhat different, but in principle similar, approaches to the problem of characterising collective phenomena that cannot completely be reduced to microanalysis. We can observe such endeavours in several subdisciplines of economics and in several currents of the economic schools. Pasinetti refers to Kaldor and his stylised facts and he certainly is right that the principle to let macroeconomics precede microeconomics is a Keynesian heritage in the Cambridge School that reflects a broader principle.

11.5 Stabilising Growth and Employment: How and Why?

Pasinetti can easily cite evidence that Cambridge economists would regard disequilibrium and instability 'as the normal state of the industrial economies' (Pasinetti, 2007, p. 229). The statement is deliberately vague, for there are different equilibrium concepts in economics. The most striking disequilibrium is unemployment (however that is defined), but Keynes wanted to show that unemployment could be persistent, so that he would speak of underemployment equilibria. Ariel Wirkierman leads step by step from Pasinetti's methodology and his formulation of the theory of effective demand to the discussion of the equilibrium concepts, growth and structural dynamics.

If prices can adapt to clear markets, what is the obstacle? One answer is to say that markets for future goods are largely absent. Hence producers do not know, indeed, cannot know how much capacity is needed to satisfy future demand, so that, in the absence of markets for the future, the present market for investment goods may clear but the quantities are not adequate for future demand and the incomes generated are not adequate for a demand for current output, which would lead to full employment.

Pasinetti, however, has something else in mind: he is no doubt right that most economists regard unemployment as a short-term phenomenon, and he refers to Robert Solow who felt that he could be a Keynesian for the short run and a neoclassical in the long. Pasinetti counters: 'This statement, it seems to me, has a sense only in the context of dynamics of the *proportional* (Pasinetti's emphasis) type, which is never the case in industrial systems' (Pasinetti, 2007, p. 231). Why do structural dynamics afford a reason for long-term unemployment, which would not be captured by the Keynesian analysis of the short run?

Pasinetti gives an answer in the subsequent section on 'Necessity of finding an appropriate analytical framework for dealing with technical change and economic growth.' He refers to Keynes's famous essay of 1930, on *Economic Possibilities for Our Grandchildren* (Keynes, 1931 [1972], pp. 321–334), in which he points to the growth of productivity and output that he expected to result in the coming generations (and in this, he surely was right), but also to technological unemployment. The growth of productivity would be faster than the discovery of new uses for labour. Wirkierman's essay traces the way by which Pasinetti, starting from classical economics and post-Keynesian growth theory, arrived at a detailed description of technological unemployment within the framework of his structural dynamics.

Harald Hagemann shows that Pasinetti always emphasised structural change; steady states are only stationary systems at a higher level. Pasinetti thus analyses the conditions under which full employment can be kept, if there is technical progress and demand changes moreover in its composition because of Engel curves. Sectors are vertically integrated in order to avoid a too detailed discussion of the composition in the demand for intermediate goods. A problem is the representation of the different growth rates of different integrated sectors. It becomes easier, if one abstracts from circulating and fixed capital so that production takes place by means of direct labour as in Pasinetti (1993).

Hagemann's comparison of Pasinetti and Adolf Lowe is of special interest. Pasinetti stresses the need to discuss institutions, once the system of structural growth has been described and understood. The transition from planned economies to the market affords a splendid example of Lowe's analysis of policy instruments; the choices made by the several Eastern European countries were quite different, and the choices of instruments they made had consequences which can still be felt today.

In the end, Pasinetti insists on the social concern, which the Cambridge economists had and have in common. He is here not concerned with political positions, which ranged from moderately conservative to Marxist, but he mentions instead a neoclassical economist in Cambridge, James Meade, felt to be on the left. Pasinetti here means an ethical orientation. This could take different forms and have different origins. The editors of this volume had the good idea of asking a social scientist of the same university as Pasinetti's for a depiction of his social views and his engagement. The Catholic

University of the Sacred Heart of Milan is not ideologically neutral and demands an ethical commitment from the students and even more from the professors. It turns out that Pasinetti himself has not so much worked on the institutions that should complement his theoretical scheme but on the moral principles to be observed. It is, it seems to me, an essential part of his contribution to bridging the two sides of the separation theorem. Capital has a social role not only in the supply of goods but to procure jobs for the labourers. Capital must be accumulated. Pasinetti does not argue in favour of a nationalisation of industry, he is sceptical with regard to a Third Way; he relies on a reformist control of what he calls the 'natural' system. He says that the term is taken from the classical economists. Others found nothing 'natural' in the economic concept of a normal price, as discussed by Smith; the 'natural system of liberty' came into being as a historical creation. The term may have appealed to Pasinetti nonetheless because of the scholastic and Aristotelian tradition; an institution is natural, if it is appropriate.

Claudia Rotondi speaks of Pasinetti's 'cultural roots' (see Section 9.5). She regards as Italian the nexus between theory and strategies, the interest in economic dynamics, the emphasis on the institutional side of a theory and the link between economics and ethics. She then traces the intellectual origins of the social concern and points to the specific tradition of the Catholic University, founded by Giuseppe Toniolo, at the time when the Catholic Church under the influence of the Encyclica *Rerum Novarum* took up the social question of the ninetheenth century. Pasinetti himself enunciated a number of Catholic principles that are in contrast with dominant economic theory, of which the last is the one most obviously opposed to the standard economic utilitarianism: the 'essentiality of free gift (without coercion and without humiliation)' (see Section 9.5.3).

I once was invited to the Cattolica with the task of explaining Weber's theory of the origin of modern capitalism (Schefold, 2014) at a conference dedicated to Amintore Fanfani – formerly a professor of economic history at the Cattolica, later a famous Italian politician, prime minister and president of the General Assembly of the United Nations – who sought the origin of capitalism in the late Medieval Italian city republics and contrasted the spirit of capitalism with the Catholic doctrine. We need not go into the usury debate. He would emphasise the changed, indeed perverted motivations, which came along with the rise of the capitalist spirit. It seemed useful if sons in the family became priests, if that secured incomes, and if the daughters became nuns because one then could save the dowry. Catholic dedication to work and working for gaining wages are not the same, fear of loss and forgetting solidarity are incompatible with the Catholic vision. Catholicism educates to be honest but not for utilitarian reasons. Life without capitalism seems not to be possible in the present world, however. Hence, compromises are inevitable, and Fanfani prepared for such a compromise and helped to shape it within the Christian Democratic Party. A similar conception existed in Germany in the form of the social market economy, which also had taken inspiration from Catholic social thought. Fanfani had coined the famous phrase in the Italian Constitution: 'L'Italia è una Repubblica democratica fondata sul lavoro' ('Italy is a democratic republic based on labour'–my translation).

In a paper at a conference entitled by this same phrase, Pasinetti discussed the role of labour in the industrial economic systems (1986). The exposition runs from labour in Smith to Marginalism and the present. A crucial step is the consideration of the Catholic doctrine in *Rerum Novarum* (1891), the encyclical by Pope Leo XIII, already mentioned, in which he states that the teaching of the Church does not declare which economic theory is appropriate. It notes the abstract character of all economic theory is itself pragmatic in its judgement of economic institutions, but 'Le argomentazioni si riducono ad affermare che ci deve essere qualche cosa di sbagliato nelle argomentazioni teoriche (o nelle istituzioni della nuova società industriale), se esse danno luogo a conclusioni ... che sono moralmente inaccettabili'.[3] Pasinetti thus identifies with the moral criticism of the Church, on the one hand. On the other, he criticises the abuse of social institutions, where they are obstacles to the free movement of labour and thus contribute to unemployment.

These short hints must suffice to indicate where Pasinetti's social commitments are anchored. In the end, they overlap with those of the other Cambridge economists of his generation and the generation before, although their cultural roots and political aims were different

[3] 'The arguments can be reduced to the claim that there must be something erroneous in theoretical arguments (or in the institutions of the new industrial society) if they result in conclusions ... which are morally inacceptable' (my translation).

and more diverse than the variations of their theory. To appreciate the group of Cambridge economists, to whom Pasinetti dedicated his book, one must see both, as Pasinetti does, one of the last witnesses. We are grateful for what he has added but also simply for his testimony.

References

Böhm-Bawerk E. von (1921 [1884]) *Kapital und Kapitalzins. Erste Abteilung. Geschichte und Kritik der Kapitalzins-Theorien*, 4th ed., Jena, G. Fischer.

Garegnani P. (1981) 'Valore e distribuzione in Marx e negli economisti calssici', in Garegnani P. (ed.) *Marx e gli economisti classici*, Torino, Giulio Einaudi, pp. 5–52.

Heilbroner R. L. (1980) *The Worldly Philosophers*, 5th ed., New York, Simon and Shuster.

Hobsbawm E. J. (1969) *Industry and Empire*, Harmondsworth, Penguin.

Keynes J. M. (1931 [1972]) '*Essays in Persuasion*', in Moggridge D. (ed.) *The Collected Writings of John Maynard Keynes*, vol. XVIII, London, Macmillan.

(1933 [1973]) 'Thomas Robert Malthus', in Moggridge D. (ed.) *The Collected Writings of John Maynard Keynes*, vol. X: *Essays in Biography*, London, Macmillan, pp. 71–108.

(1936 [1973]) '*The General Theory of Employment, Interest and Money*', in Moggridge D. (ed.) *The Collected Writings of John Maynard Keynes*, vol. VII, London, Macmillan.

Manara C. F. (1968) 'Il modello di Piero Sraffa per la produzione congiunta di merci a mezzo di merci', in *Collettanea Mathematica*, vol. 1, Milan, Editrice L'industria, pp. 3–18.

Pasinetti L. L. (1974) *Growth and Income Distribution: Essays in Economic Theory*, Cambridge, Cambridge University Press.

(1975) *Lezioni di teoria della produzione*, Bologna, Il Mulino.

(1981) *Structural Change and Economic Growth: A Theoretical Essay on the Dynamics of the Wealth of Nations*, Cambridge, Cambridge University Press.

(1988) 'La centralità del lavoro nei sistemi economici industriali', in Angelini G. Barucci P. et al. (eds.) *Una repubblica fondata sul lavoro*, Rome, Editrice Ave, pp. 79–95.

(2007) *Keynes and the Cambridge Keynesians: A 'Revolution in Economics' to Be Accomplished*, Cambridge, Cambridge University Press.

Poser H. (2012) *Wissenschaftstheorie. Eine philosophische Einführung*, Stuttgart, Reclam.

Schefold B. (1999) 'Use Value and the "Commercial Knowledge of Commodities": Reflections on Aristotle, Savary and the Classics', in Mongiovi G. and Petri F. (eds.) *Value, Distribution and Capital: Essays in Honour of Pierangelo Garegnani*, London, Routledge, pp. 122–144.

(2011) 'Political Economy as "Geisteswissenschaft", Edgar Salin and Other Economists around George', in Lane M. S. and Ruehl M. A. (eds.) *A Poet's Reich: Politics and Culture in the George Circle*, Rochester and New York, Camden House, pp. 164–204.

(2014) 'Amintore Fanfani e le tesi di Max Weber', in Cova A. and Besana C. (eds.) *Amintore Fanfani: Formazione culturale, identità e responsabilità politica*, Milan, Vita e Pensiero, pp. 115–128.

(2019a) 'Continuity and Change in the Transition: From the Classical to the Neoclassical Theory of Normal Prices', in Rosselli A. Naldi N. and Sanfilippo E (eds.) *Money, Finance and Crises in Economic History: The Long-Term Impact of Economic Ideas*, London and New York, Routledge, pp. 11–26.

(2019b) 'The Transformation of Values into Prices on the Basis of Random Systems Revisited', in *Evolutionary and Institutional Economics Review, Japanese Association for Evolutionary Economics*, 16(2), pp. 261–302.

(2020) 'What Remains of the Cambridge Critique of Capital Theory, If Reswitching and Reverse Capital Deepening Are Empirically Rare and Theoretically Unlikely?', in *European Journal of Economics and Economic Policies*, 17(2), pp. 220–240.

Sinha A. (ed.) (2021) *A Reflection on Sraffa's Revolution in Economic Theory*, London, Palgrave/Macmillan.

Author Index

Afriat S., 179, 183
Akerlof G.A., 26, 28
Åkerman J., 161
Angelini G., 315
Araujo R., 266, 289
Arena R., 81, 109, 229–232, 255, 258
Arestis P., 109
Arnon A., 29
Arrow K.J., 103, 106, 109, 162, 168, 173, 183
Arthmar R., 249–250, 254

Bacon F., 250
Baranzini M., 214, 224, 229, 234–236, 238, 245, 254, 257
Barro R., 166, 169
Barucci P., 315
Baumol W., 55, 76
Becattini G., 16, 28
Becker G.S., 179, 183
Bellanca N., 247, 255
Bellino E., 13, 91, 109, 115, 119, 152, 187, 227, 230, 307
Bellofiore R., 276, 284, 287
Benassy J.P., 166
Bentham, 273
Bentham J., 273
Bernanke B., 30, 46
Besana C., 316
Bharadwaj K., 80, 89, 109, 136, 148, 152
Blanchard O., 176, 183, 285, 287
Blankenburg S., 81, 109
Blaug M., 45–47, 49, 236, 255
Bliss C., 171, 183
Boehm, S., 110
Böhm-Bawerk E., 293–295, 315
Boltzmann L., 302
Borgi E., 248
Bortis H., 236, 255
Bortkiewicz von L., 122, 126, 152
Boulding K.E., 159, 183
Boumans M., 49
Box G., 38
Bradley I., 109
Bronfenbrenner M., 158, 183
Brown M., 109
Buiter W., 166, 186

Caffè F., 12
Campbell R.H., 77, 111, 155
Card D., 172, 183
Cardinale I., xviii, xx, xxii
Chakravarty S., 229
Chenery H.B., 215, 232
Chipman J.S., 168, 175, 183
Ciccone R., 84, 106, 109, 126, 132, 152
Claar V.V., 30, 46
Clapham J.H., 36, 44, 46
Clower R., 55, 76, 166, 168–169
Cobb C., 178
Coniglione F., 33, 46
Cord R., 152–153, 254, 256
Courvisanos J., 145, 152
Cova A., 316
Cozzi T., 200, 205, 210
Crawford I., 179, 183

Dal Pont Legrand M., 223, 230
Damon M., 176
Dardi M., 13, 22, 25, 28
Davidson P., 133, 141, 149, 152, 154, 302
Davis J.B., 48
De Rock B., 179, 183
Debreu G., 162, 170–172, 179, 183, 185, 309
Deleplace G., 13
Dimand R.W., 230
Dina A., 275–276, 278, 287
Dobb M., 77, 110, 147, 158, 183, 231

Domar E.D., 65, 187, 197–198, 202–203, 211, 221, 236
Dornbusch R., 196, 211
Douglas P.H., 178
Dow S., 144, 152
Drahokoupil J., 288
Duchin F., 288
Dvoskin A., 79, 303, 305

Eatwell J., 36, 47, 49, 77, 80, 92–93, 96, 104, 106, 108–109, 131–132, 152, 157, 183, 213, 309
Einstein A., 170
Elizabeth II, 285
Ellison M., 255
Engel E., 217, 219, 226, 236, 292, 312

Fabiani C., 287
Fanfani A., 313, 316
Faucci R., 247, 255
Feiwel G.R., 110–111, 149, 152
Fiorani G., 269, 289
Fischer S., 196, 211
Fisher I., 67, 161, 181, 294–295
Fleming J.M., 164
Forstater M., 29
Forster G., 30, 46
Fratini S., 30, 39, 47
Freni G., 36, 47
Friedman M., 30, 45, 47, 160, 163, 166, 168, 171, 174–175, 184–185, 297
Frisch R., 158, 187–188, 211
Frobenius F.G., 127

Gaddi M., 269, 280, 288
Galileo G., 42
Garbellini N., 189, 203, 208, 211, 259, 288
Garegnani P., 39, 45, 47, 59, 74–76, 80, 90–91, 104, 106, 109, 111, 115, 126, 132, 149, 152, 159, 184, 259, 291, 315
Garibaldo F., 287
Garofalo G., 257
Gehrke C., 61, 76, 108, 110
Gilibert G., 262–263, 288
Gnos C., 287
Godley W., 286
Good P., 1–2
Goodley W., 288
Goodwin R., 140, 222
Gordon R.J., 184
Grandmont J.M., 166
Graziani A., 257, 259, 286, 288
Green J., 103, 110, 185
Grierson P., xviii, xx
Groman V.G., 264
Grossman H., 166, 169
Guillebaud C.W., 154

Haan den W., 254, 277
Haberler G., 158, 184
Habermas J., 24, 28
Hafner M., 172, 184
Hagemann H., 50, 76, 214–215, 218, 223, 226, 230, 312
Hague D.C., 34, 48
Hahn F., 105–106, 109–110, 166, 187, 211
Halevi J., 153–154, 261, 279, 287–288
Hammarskjold D., 161
Hands D.W., 48
Hansen A., 163
Harcourt G.C., 33, 47, 109, 138, 140, 144, 153–154, 211–212, 214, 235–236, 254–255, 257
Harrod R., 65, 140, 144, 146, 153–154, 163, 184, 197, 199–200, 202, 211, 216, 221, 230, 236, 271
Hawtrey R., 160
Hayek von F., 34, 37–38, 43, 49, 67, 77–78, 179
Heertje A., xix
Heilbroner R., 296, 315
Henry J.F., 138, 152
Hicks J., 110, 137, 153, 163, 165, 184, 224, 230, 298
Hirschman A., 215
Hobsbawm E.J., 301, 315
Hodgson G.C., 233, 255
Hood W.C., 155
Hoover K.D., 38, 47
Horn G., 76
Howards M., 109
Hume D., 114

Ilzetzki E., 255

Jaffé W., 156
Jahnsson Y., 165
Jevons W.S., 136, 157, 161, 184
Johnson E., 28
Juglar C., 161

Kahn R.K., 15–16, 18, 21–22, 25–28, 32, 140, 147, 236–237, 249, 297
Kaldor N., 16, 140, 145–146, 148, 153, 214, 236, 266, 297, 311
Kalecki M., 73, 140, 143–145, 152–154, 158, 184
Kalmbach P., 50, 64, 76
Kerr P., 256
Keynes J.M., 14–15, 18, 21, 23–31, 39, 46, 48, 51–52, 54, 57, 59–69, 73, 75–77, 109–111, 115, 132–133, 135, 138–139, 141, 144, 147, 152–154, 157–158, 160–162, 164, 166, 170, 173, 181–185, 188, 191–192, 211–212, 214, 216–218, 221–222, 230–231, 233–238, 242–243, 245, 249–250, 254–256, 258–259, 271, 290–291, 294, 297–298, 300–302, 308–309, 311–312, 315
Keynes J.N., 249–250, 253, 256
Kincaid H., 29
King J.E., 47, 146, 152–155, 237, 256
Kirman A.K., 171, 175, 184
Kitchin J., 161, 184
Klaes M., 49
Klein L., 159, 184
Knoedler J., 234, 256
Koopmans T.C., 155
Kregel J., 139, 148, 153
Kriesler P., 138, 140–141, 143–144, 153–154, 255
Krueger A., 172, 183
Krugman P., 185
Krupp H.J., 76
Krzywdzinski M., 288
Kuczynski M., 289
Kuhn T., 31, 234
Kurz H.D., 30, 33, 36, 39, 45–48, 50–51, 61, 64, 67–68, 70–72, 75–77, 110–111, 126, 154, 191, 211, 300–301
Kuznets S., 215, 232
Kydland F., 168–169

Landesmann M., 215, 224, 230
Lane M.S., 316
Lange O., 163
Laroque G., 166
Lavington F., 160
Lavoie M., 32, 47, 140, 146, 153, 226, 230, 286, 288
Lawson T., 14, 28, 146
Layton W., 160
Leigh D., 285, 287
Leijonhufvud A., 55, 76, 166, 185, 216, 230
Leontief W., 174, 185, 188, 190, 206, 212, 215, 224–225, 238, 261, 263–264, 288
Levhari D., 236
Levrero S., 47
Lindahl E., 158, 161
List F., xiii
Lombardini S., 112, 248, 251, 257
Lowe A., 224, 228, 231, 292, 312
Lucas R., 30, 46, 167–168, 175, 185, 309
Ludwell Moore H., 161
Luethje B., 288
Lundberg E., 161
Lunghini G., 259
Lutz F.A., 34, 48

Machlup F.A., 25, 29
Mäki U., 14, 29, 34, 38, 41–42, 47–48
Malinvaud E., 181, 219, 231
Malthus R.T., 31, 50–53, 55–58, 60–62, 64–65, 67–68, 73, 75–77, 119, 131, 159, 185, 271, 300–301, 315
Manara C.F., 290, 315
Mankiw G., 169, 185
Mantel R., 170–172, 179, 185, 309
Marcuzzo M.C., 13–14, 16, 18, 23, 29–30, 34, 48, 111, 149, 154, 296–297
Marget A., 159, 185
Marschak J., 159, 185
Marshall A., 14, 16, 20–21, 25, 29, 34–36, 38–39, 48, 71, 74, 77, 84, 89, 96, 109, 124, 136, 139, 150, 154, 157, 160, 162, 173, 177, 298–299
Martins N.O., 46, 48

Marx K., 50, 52, 57, 63, 69, 74, 77, 102, 110, 115, 120–123, 126, 131–132, 151–152, 159, 217–218, 221, 223–224, 228, 244, 261–264, 272–273, 288, 293–294, 297, 300, 307, 315
Mas-Colell A., 103, 110, 185
McCulloch J.R., 54
McIntyre L., 47
McKenzie L.W., 105, 110
McLure M., 249–250, 254
McMahon M., 255
Meade J.E., 137, 163, 312
Meek R., 289
Metcalfe S., 111
Milgate M., 46, 93, 109, 157, 183, 185, 213, 309
Mill J.S., 57, 63, 76, 84, 89, 223
Mirante A., 214, 229, 234, 236–237, 254
Mises von L., 74
Mishkin F.S., 30, 48
Mitchell W.C., 161
Modigliani F., 163
Moggridge D.E., 28, 76, 156, 184, 230, 256, 315
Momigliano F., 264, 288–289
Mongiovi G., 29, 36, 48, 109, 316
Mortagua M., 287
Munchausen von K.F.H., 66
Mundell R., 164
Musgrave A., 38, 48
Myrdal K.G., 140, 144, 161, 233, 256

Naldi N., 111, 316
Nataraj S., 184
Nerozzi S., 13, 112, 115, 152, 227, 230, 307
Nevile J., 141, 153–154
Newman von P., 47, 109, 184, 213
Nicola P.C., xx
Nisticò S., 212
Nowak L., 33, 48

Palma G., 109
Palumbo A., 47
Panico C., 36, 46
Panizza R., 152
Pankowska P., 184
Panzieri R., 271, 275–277, 288
Parchure R., 50, 59
Pardi T., 269, 288
Pareto V., 124, 136
Parisi D., 250, 256–257
Parrinello S., 123, 154
Pasinetti L.L., 49, 75, 200, 229–230, 247
Patinkin D., 166, 168–169
Pecchi L., 218, 231
Pellizzari F., xiii, xxi
Perron O., 127
Petri F., 109–110, 316
Petty W., 74
Phelps E., 166
Phillips W., 30, 164, 166–167, 185, 309
Piccioni M., 102, 110
Piga G., 218, 231
Pigou A.C., 48, 65, 77, 109, 124, 160, 174, 186, 250, 257
Pivetti M., 110
Polanyi K., 296
Pope Leo XIII, 244, 314
Popov P.I., 264
Popper K., 38, 48, 299
Porta P.L., 229–232, 247, 255, 257–258
Poser H., 306, 316
Prescott E., 168–169
Pressman S., 29
Pugliese E., 272, 289
Pullen J., 77

Quadrio Curzio A., 236, 245, 247, 252, 255–257
Quesnay F., 224, 246, 262–264, 289

Ramazzotti P., 254, 258
Rampa G., 265, 289
Ramsey F., 174
Ravagnani F., 100–101, 110
Rawls J., 24, 28–29
Reis R., 185, 255
Riach P.A., 154, 212
Ricardo D., 39, 50–51, 53, 55–57, 59–60, 64–65, 69–71, 73, 75–78, 83, 89, 92–94, 96, 110–111, 115–117, 119, 126, 129, 131–132, 140, 151, 156, 159, 185, 216, 218,

223–224, 227, 231, 242, 245, 293, 300–301, 307
Rieser V., 272
Rima I.H., 29, 109, 152–153, 155
Rizvi Abu Turab S., 185
Robbiati Bianchi A., xx
Robbins L., 30, 176, 274, 289
Robertson D., 14–15, 29, 32, 37–38, 79–82, 85–93, 96, 104–105, 108–110, 136, 138–141, 147–148, 152–155, 160, 164, 186, 236–237, 268, 278, 291, 294, 303
Robinson H., 158
Rochon L., 287
Roncaglia A., 13, 19, 29, 36, 48–49, 77, 81, 101, 107, 111, 234, 258
Rose W., 183
Rosenberg A., 47
Ross D., 29
Rosselli A., 13, 18, 29, 34, 48, 91, 111, 316
Rostow W.W., 215
Rotondi C., 228, 233, 236, 247, 249–250, 252, 254, 256–258, 313
Ruehl M.A., 316
Russo M., 269, 289

Salanti A., 30, 39, 49, 234, 258
Salin E., 291, 316
Salvadori N., 30, 33, 36, 39, 45–48, 51, 70–72, 76–77, 111, 126, 191, 211, 298–299
Samuelson P., 111, 152, 159, 163–164, 174, 186, 223, 231, 236
Sanfilippo E., 18, 29, 111, 316
Sargent T., 30, 168, 185
Sato K., 109
Sawyer M., 109
Say J.B., 50, 52, 55, 59–61, 65, 70, 75–76, 93, 135, 141, 182, 300–301
Scazzieri R., 211, 213, 215, 224, 227, 229–231, 245–246, 255–258
Schefold B., 70, 75, 77, 91, 96, 111, 226, 232, 256, 291, 293, 295, 305, 308, 313, 316
Schumpeter J.A., 50, 217, 222–223, 230, 232
Screpanti E., 234, 258
Sen A., 180, 186
Seton F., 126, 155
Setterfield M., 139, 153
Shaikh A., 178, 186
Shiller R.J., 26, 28
Shionoya Y., 29
Sills D., 109
Simon H., 113, 155, 315
Simonazzi A., 269, 289
Sinha A., 20, 29, 48, 290, 316
Siniscalco D., 265, 288–289
Sismondi J.C.L.S., 300
Skidelsky R., 158, 161
Skinner A.S., 77, 111, 155
Smith A., 50, 52, 55–57, 68, 76–77, 82–84, 89, 96, 102, 111, 115, 117–118, 126, 138, 155, 158–159, 163, 170, 178, 242, 245, 255, 292, 304, 313–314
Snowdon B., 30, 49
Solow R., 186, 229, 232, 311
Sombart W., 297
Sonnenschein H., 170–172, 179, 185–186, 309
Spiethoff A., 291
Sraffa P., 14, 18–21, 27, 29–30, 32–34, 36, 39, 42, 44–49, 51, 53, 67–77, 79, 81, 87, 89, 91, 97, 107, 109–111, 115, 120, 123–127, 130–132, 147, 149, 151–152, 156, 174, 185, 191, 211, 213, 215–217, 219–220, 223–225, 230–231, 236, 261, 290–295, 299, 306–307, 315–316
Srinivasan T.N., 232
Stathakis G., 77
Steedman I., 75
Stepanek M., 184
Steuart J., xii
Stewart, 176
Stigler G., 73, 78
Stiglitz J., 177, 186
Stirati A., 47
Stolk van C., 184
Stone R., 190, 212–213, 259, 262, 289
Streeten P., 215
Sturn R., 110
Svennilson I., 161

Sylos Labini P., 270, 289
Syrquin M., 215, 232

Talamona M., 248, 257
Taylor J., 184
Tobin J., 166, 186
Toniolo G., 249, 313
Torrens R., 74
Tosato D., 212
Totaro F., 257
Trabucchi P., 30, 79, 91, 111, 303, 305
Trigg A., 187, 195, 213, 266, 289
Tropeano D., 287
Turgot A.R., 299

Underwood D., 234, 256

Vaggi G., 77, 259
Vane H.R., 30, 49
Varian A., 179–180, 186
Varri P.P., 1
Veblen T., 140
Verdoorn P.J., 266
Verger Y., 290
Vianello F., 84, 111
Vicarelli S., 155
Vint J., 111
Vito F., 112, 248–251, 257–258
De Vroey M., 30, 46

Walras L., 31–33, 50, 64, 84, 103, 105, 109, 111, 126, 136, 156–157, 162, 170, 223, 271
Weber M., 297, 310, 313, 316
Webster E., 143, 156
Weinblatt J., 29
Whinston M., 103, 110, 185
Wicksell K., 53, 72, 96, 103, 111, 161, 223, 305
Wilkinson F., 81, 109
Wirkierman A., 187, 189, 211, 311–312
Woodford M., 176, 186
Woods J.E., 1–2

Xiaoping D., 34

Young W., 29, 138, 144, 156, 174, 186

Zanella A., xx
Zarembka P., 109

Printed in the United States
by Baker & Taylor Publisher Services